goodbye to catholic ireland

Mary Kenny is a leading journalist, writer and broadcaster, publishing on both sides of the Irish sea. She is a senior contributor to the *Daily Express* in London; in Ireland she is the anchor columnist for the *Irish Independent* magazine. She also writes for the *Irish Catholic*, contributes to *The Spectator*, *The Tablet*, the *Catholic Herald* and the *Sunday* and *Daily Telegraph*s. She was born in Dublin in 1944. She has previously written books on the subjects of feminism, religion, abortion and drug abuse. Her most recent book, *Death by Heroin: Recovery by Hope*, was published by New Island in 1999. Mary is married with two sons and lives in both Ireland and England.

goodbye to catholic ireland

Revised and Updated Edition

Mary Kenny

**NEW
ISLAND**

Goodbye to Catholic Ireland
First published September 2000 by
New Island Books, 2 Brookside
Dundrum Road, Dublin 14, Ireland

1 3 5 4 2

ISBN 1 902602 26 9

British Library Cataloguing in Publication Data
A catalogue record for this book is available from the
British Library.

The Arts Council
An Chomhairle Ealaíon

New Island Books receives financial assistance from The Arts
Council (An Chomhairle Ealaíon), Dublin, Ireland.

Cover design: Slick Fish Design
Typesetting: New Island Books
Printed by ßetaprint, Dublin

Contents

To the memory of my brother,
James Kenny (1932-84),
for whom Faith and Fatherland
were fiercely yet merrily intertwined.

"In Ireland, the people is the Church, and the Church is the people."

> – George Bernard Shaw
> *John Bull's Other Island*

"I love God.
I love the faith.
I love Ireland.
I hate pride.
I hate ignorance.
I hate dissension.
I will not boast.
I will not quarrel.
I will not be intoxicated."

> – An t-Athair Peader O Laoghaire
> (Father Peter O'Leary)
> *A card of dedication which he carried*

"If Ireland is not a Catholic country, then what is Ireland for?"

> – Bruce Anderson of *The Spectator*

Preface

"The people [of Ireland] are thus inclined: religious, frank, amorous, sufferable of infinite paines, verie glorious, manie sorcerers, excellent horsemen, delighted with wars, great alms-givers, passing in hospitalitie."

Holinshed's Chronicles, 1578

One of the most successful movies to open in Ireland — and around the world — in the year 2000 was *Angela's Ashes*, Alan Parker's film of Frank McCourt's phenomenally successful memoir of the same name.

Alan Parker might as well have made a film called *How All Irish People Are Absolutely Horrible*. For there is scarcely anyone in the whole story of provincial Ireland in the 1930s and 1940s with an ounce of humanity. The McCourt family are all vile: the father is an aimless drunk, and the mother a weak slut. The grandmother is a bigoted old bitch and the aunt is an embittered, scolding spinster. They are, as a clan, entirely devoid of family feeling or kindness for one another, at least when the children are young. Indeed, everyone in the Limerick of *Angela's Ashes* is especially beastly to children.

If the family is awful, the neighbours are ugly and mean-spirited, the representatives of the Irish state are cruel and hard-hearted, and teachers, with one exception, are sadistic, twisted tyrants who deliberately mock poor children for their poverty.

It goes without saying that the Catholic Church is sneering, cruel and exploitative, and the charity the St Vincent de Paul is represented by the most odious characters who taunt poor women before they patronise them. You cannot libel a group of more than eight people, but if you could, the St Vincent de Paul certainly would have a case on its hands. Anyone who did not know them would receive the impression that they were scarcely above the level of Stalin's bullies.

Who else is thoroughly nasty in the Catholic Ireland of *Angela's Ashes*? The middle classes, who live remote lives away from the poor of the lanes, are decadent: if a bourgeois young girl is afflicted with tuberculosis, then it only serves to rouse her lust, and she is hungry for sex without any formalities — before expiring. Voyeurism, too, thrives as a hunchback boy derives revenue from giving other lads a Peeping Tom's view of his naked sisters. There are squalid "wanking competitions" among the youth and unfunny confessional scenes which dwell on bestiality that do nothing to raise your esteem for any of the characters.

There is a repellent moneylender who exploits the poor of Limerick, and although historically moneylenders in Ireland were traditionally Jewish, there are now regulations in Ireland that you are only allowed to be nasty about Catholics; so the moneylender in the story has to be made into a spiteful Catholic vixen, complete with statues of the Blessed Virgin scattered around her extortionate book-keeping.

There is, as mentioned, one individual teacher and one passing Franciscan priest who show a rare glint of decency in *Angela's Ashes*. They are underlined as the exceptions, for Irish people in general are surly, unpleasant, have no sense of humour and are also devoid of imagination. Neither music, nor hospitality, nor good conversation plays any part in their lives. The dark rain that falls ceaselessly on Limerick is a metaphor of the most miserable kind of childhood that anyone can endure — an Irish Catholic childhood. This view of Catholic Ireland and of the Irish, portrayed as a hateful people, was shown all around the world.

This was not the way the Irish saw themselves in that era when they identified their country as "Catholic Ireland". The Irish saw themselves as a religious but merry people, full of good humour and neighbourliness, sharing their poverty and bearing it with cheerfulness, courage and wit. The brave and valiant mothers in the Dublin slums, so faithfully portrayed by Sean O'Casey, represented the sweetness and holiness of the people's faith, as did the working men marching underneath the banners of their guilds and sodalities. Alan Montgomery, an Ulster Protestant who wrote under the jokey pen-name of Lynn C. Doyle (Linseed Oil), observed that spirit of Catholic Ireland in 1934, when he noticed a stationary bread-van parked on a Dublin street. Glimpsing inside, he saw the bread delivery man snatching a moment of prayer. It touched him. That, he thought, was so charmingly Irish.

A Jewish observer of the 1920s, Harold Speakman, thought that the courtesy and kindness he found in Ireland sprang directly from its Catholic culture.

When Pope John Paul II visited Ireland in 1979 — among the first overseas trips of his extraordinary papacy — it was seen as a tribute to "Catholic Ireland", a country he designated as *semper fidelis*, forever faithful to the Catholic faith. As indeed it had been, for so long.

In my generation, we were taught that, alone among the English-speaking lands, Ireland was primarily a Catholic country, with wayside shrines to Our Lady, a special devotion to the Sacred Heart, and an almost Latin warmth of intensity in the practice of the faith.

Moreover, the Republic of Ireland was an independent nation *because* she was Catholic, for Ireland's Catholicity had been the main distinguishing characteristic which set her apart in the British Isles, to which she clearly belonged geographically. Ireland was not British because she was Catholic, and she would not have asserted her difference from Great Britain if she had not been Catholic. It was not the Irish language, spoken by a minority, which made Ireland different from Britain — the Welsh had retained their language much more successfully and still remained within the United Kingdom. It was not different laws or different education which distinguished Ireland — Scotland had those without seceding. It was her religion, which linked her with much of continental

Europe, and a wider world we once called "Ireland's Spiritual Empire".

When I went to Beijing in 1995 for the United Nations women's conference, I attended a Mass for Catholic women from everywhere in the globe. Nearly all the women from the Third World present had at one time or another been taught by an Irish sister or priest. That was "Ireland's Spiritual Empire."

The Pope's 1979 visit was thus a kind of crowning glory to Ireland's historical star status as a Catholic nation. It was a happy occasion and was remembered by many with joy and a remarkable sense of inclusiveness and celebration. But it was also, as it turned out, the beginning of the end of that entity known as Catholic Ireland. For, from the start of the 1980s, the faith was faltering among the younger Irish, and the notion of Ireland as a quintessentially Catholic country was fast receding. Perhaps the Troubles in the North prompted the thought that a Catholic national identity was a form of sectarianism (though the Irish Constitution did separate Church from State, legally and politically, even if the power of the Church seeped into the political process).

By the end of the 1990s, for most younger Irish people, Catholic Ireland, as such, was gone: it was Goodbye to Catholic Ireland, to which many added "good riddance". They might, or might not, be privately religious, or "spiritual" — which could be called the new form of "religion lite" — but Catholicism was no longer seen as part of their national identity. Indeed, the very phrase "Catholic Ireland" makes many younger Irish people shudder (and quite a few middle-aged people, too). It sounds to some like a theocracy, which is not at all a modern concept.

Yet Catholic Ireland was, and is, part of the deposit of our culture and our heritage. It is there from the monastic chants of early Christian Ireland to the decade of the rosary for so long recited over the grave of the founder of Irish Republicanism, Wolfe Tone (an atheist). It is forged in the collective unconscious of the race, as it was indelibly marked in James Joyce himself, though he ceased being a believer. Those who fail to acknowledge the presence of something called Catholic

Ireland in the inheritance of what we are, are in denial of the facts of cultural history.

This heritage does not exclude other Irish Christians — Anglicans or non-conformist Protestants — Jews, other religions, or unbelievers. (Protestant Ireland, in any case, dominates the literary heritage of Ireland.)* But the Catholic Ireland inheritance does carry something essential to the heart and soul of the nation. A scientific interpretation of Catholic-Irish identity was suggested by the journal *Nature* in March 2000: the people of Connaught are it claimed, the most indigenously "Irish", in terms of their genes. They are also the most consistently Catholic.

And despite accusations of patriarchy, no one has forged, sustained, or upheld the faith of Catholic Ireland more purposefully than the women of Ireland; that also is a historical fact. There is a famous Irish hymn of old called "Faith of Our Fathers", but it is even more the faith of our mothers, and our grandmothers, and that emerges whenever people in Ireland tell the story of their childhood, even to this day. It was the mothers and the grandmothers who transmitted the faith. In remembering and recalling the essence of Catholic Ireland, perhaps I, in my turn, feel that it is part of my historical duty as an Irish mother to transmit and recall what we inherited from this faith of our mothers and grandmothers, which they regarded as our Irish soul and a pearl beyond price.

---

* I have sometimes used "Eire" to convey the 26 counties of the Irish Republic, which was formerly the Irish Free State. "Ireland" signifies the nation, but Eire, the Free State or the Republic signify the state.

Part One

The Way We Were

One

Catholic Ireland in the Celtic Dawn

"It would be hardly too much to say that for an Irish Catholic his nationality is inseparable from his religion — so much so that an Irish Protestant never quite knows to what country he belongs. But for their religion ... Irishmen would probably have forgotten political separatism as the Scots have forgotten Jacobitism."

Arland Ussher, *The Face and Mind of Ireland* (1949)

From time immemorial, Ireland has been unfailingly described, occasionally admired and frequently denigrated as a deeply Catholic country. Those who loved Ireland called it ever loyal to the faith of its fathers; those who disliked Ireland called it "priest-ridden". The priests, who emerged as the natural leaders of the people when clan chieftains were exiled and politicians floundered or fell, were objects of criticism by the British Left and Right equally — George Orwell and J.B. Priestley disliked the priests as much as Lord Salisbury — but historically their leadership was accepted and endorsed by the majority of the Irish people, who saw the clergy as "their own".

Yet, surprisingly perhaps, the invention of modern Irish nationalism was not the creation of the priests, or of Catholic Ireland, but was very largely the product of Protestant Ireland in leadership and concept. The Catholic Church has always been ambivalent about nationalism in any form, and sometimes went so far as to describe it as a Lutheran heresy.

Catholicism has been jealous of its reputation for universality and saw nationalism as a threat to its purchase on internationalism. My own father's life was an illustration of this internationalism. Born in 1877 (he was 65 when I was born), he went to a Jesuit school in Co Limerick, and thence to a Jesuit seminary in Beirut. He decided against the priesthood, but the order encouraged him to complete his university degree in Madrid. For many years, he taught in Santiago, Chile. Although he died when I was a young child, I always had this idea that although we should be proud of our Irish national heritage, we were also part of an international Catholic culture.

It is significant that many of the traditional heroes of Irish nationalism were not Irish Catholics, but Irish Protestants. Robert Emmet, Wolfe Tone, Lord Edward Fitzgerald, Isaac Butt, Henry Grattan and Charles Stewart Parnell were all born into the tradition of Protestant (and mainly upper-class) Ireland. Jonathan Swift, who was actually an Englishman but is often counted among Irish nationalist icons for his savage satires against English rule in Ireland, especially despised Irish Catholicism, as did Wolfe Tone, a point carefully edited out of most Irish school history books for reasons of tact. Swift believed that the decline of Popery, which he felt was imminent in the 18th century, was the only hopeful aspect of the future for Ireland. Wolfe Tone, who described Catholic prayers as "the blathering of idiots", died confident in the hope that the French Revolution would finish off the Catholic Church. Like others inspired by the Enlightenment, he believed Catholicism could never survive democracy — or, indeed, the rise of 19th-century nationalism.

The growth of nationalism in Europe was indeed generally accompanied by a decline in religion: the historian D. George Boyce calls nationalism "a modern substitute for religion". In countries like Italy, a nationalist such as Garibaldi was by definition an anti-cleric — and Garibaldi was welcomed in England *because* he was seen as an opponent of Catholic power, which he was. Small wonder the Catholic Church did not endorse nationalism: it was a rival and a potential substitute.

But there are nuances of nationalism, all the same. Catholic Ireland had traditions of patriotism and a deeply engrained hostility to English rule. That hostility derived from England's suppression of "the Popish faith" in Ireland and the confiscation of land following English and Scottish Protestant domination. The bitter conflicts in Northern Ireland are a race memory of such events. When a relation of mine married an Englishman in the 1970s, her aunt, living in the border county of Cavan, enquired as to whether he was a Protestant. Well, in a kind of a way, yes (those baptised in the Church of England do not necessarily affirm themselves as whole-hearted Protestants.) "Aye, the Protestants got the best land," was the aunt's only disparaging comment. This had dwelt in the race memory since the 17th century.

When Yeats wrote his famous lament for Irish patriotism 'September', including the lines: "Was it for this the Wild Geese spread/The grey wing upon every tide?", he did not underline the point that the Wild Geese — the Catholic Irish clan leaders who fled to France and Spain in 1607 after a crucial military defeat — were under English prohibition for being Catholics, not for being "nationalists" in the modern sense.

It was the faith that the Irish people had most cared about during the years of their persecution. The faith came first. Then came land. In the 19th century Catholic Ireland was aroused politically by Daniel O'Connell, but O'Connell's greatest, and most successful, campaign was not for "nationalism" but for Catholic Emancipation — to lift the many disabilities under which Catholics suffered — which was achieved in 1829. O'Connell went on to campaign for the repeal of the Union between England and Ireland. He prepared the ground for what was to become the political drive towards Home Rule. Yet he also believed in the British Empire; he was not a nationalist in the Wolfe Tone mould, seeking to "break the connection" with England in every particle.

O'Connell sought fair play for Catholic Ireland: he was first a Catholic and second an Irishman (though his Catholicism was of the more relaxed 18th-century brand). For example, although he spoke the Irish language beautifully, he professed no great ardour for its revival. He had been educated in France — because of the British Penal Laws against Irish Catholics, many gentrified Irishmen went to the Continent for their education —

and had witnessed horrific events associated with the French Revolution of 1789. These imprinted on his young mind and gave him a lifelong revulsion for violence or any acts of terrorism. He also saw the French Revolution as anti-Catholic, which it was; they guillotined as many priests as aristocrats.

Nationalism would spread throughout the 19th century, and the patriotism of the Irish people, which was a mixture of feeling for land, country (even region) and faith, would gradually become more recognisably nationalistic in harmony with the spirit of the age. The key decade for nationalism in Europe was the 1840s. The most popularly recognised mid-century Irish nationalist was Thomas Davis, a young Protestant poet who died in 1845, at the age of 31. Davis was leader of the Young Ireland movement, similar in ideals to the Young Italy movement led by Mazzini and Garibaldi — which the Catholic Church naturally deplored as a seedbed of revolution and rebellion against authority.

And yet ideas and movements imported into Ireland are always distilled into Irish culture, and Irish culture was imprinted by Catholicism. After Davis died, priests and bishops also became devotees of his patriotic ballads and poems, such as 'The West's Awake' and 'A Nation Once Again'. Ireland has always had a reverence for the dead, and the dead Young Irelander Thomas Davis took on a mantle of beauty and respect. In life, Davis would have been a thorn for Catholicism, since he believed in the secularisation of education, one of the causes to which the Catholic Church was most vehemently opposed.

Nineteenth-century nationalism saw the state replacing the Church as the focus of the individual's loyalty and emotional attachment. In Ireland, the Catholic Church would eventually accommodate European nationalism, then absorb it, and for thirty years — roughly from the 1930s to the 1960s — dominate it.

Modern Ireland can be said to date from the fall, and then death, of the great Irish parliamentary leader Charles Stewart Parnell. Parnell, a Protestant landlord from Wicklow, was the son of an American mother. It is said that his anti-English feelings came more from his American side than his Anglo-Irish side. As a Protestant, he did not favour the established Anglican churches, with their intertwining of throne and altar, but rather the small nonconformist sects, such as the Plymouth Brethren, for whom he built a meeting-house on his Wicklow estate. Personally, he was not religious but he was superstitious and would always avoid the colour green, which he thought to be unlucky.

Parnell was the leader of the Irish Parliamentary Party at Westminster, a realm he virtually dominated for over a decade. He was a magnificent parliamentarian who put the issue of Home Rule for Ireland on the parliamentary map. Opponents of Irish Home Rule were gradually being made to face the fact that nothing would pacify Ireland except the granting of self-rule of some kind. Home Rule did not suggest a complete break with the Crown but a devolved government in Dublin retaining some association with Westminster. There remained a substantial body of British (and Ulster) parliamentarians opposed to Home Rule, but nevertheless it was an argument which Parnell, with Gladstone's support, was gradually winning.

But Parnell fell from power in 1890 and died in 1891, aged 45. Gladstone's Second Home Rule Bill, which was to give Ireland self-government within a British framework, was defeated in 1893, and after that Irish politics seemed to go into abeyance.

The end of the Parnell era is often described as a period of disappointment and disillusionment. There was a split in Parnell's party after a divorce scandal concerning his private life. The Home Rule policy of the British Liberal Prime Minister William Gladstone — a man of religious conscience and integrity — was finally defeated by the House of Lords, in defence of landed interests. It is generally held that culture, not politics, now became the agent of change in Irish life.

Bitter differences had arisen in Ireland over the scandal of Parnell's involvement with Katharine O'Shea's divorce, when it became public knowledge. Charles Stewart Parnell, "the uncrowned king of Ireland", was living with another man's wife and had fathered children with her. This relationship was a love-match. Katharine's husband, Captain O'Shea, was complaisant, and would never have sued for divorce if he could have been bribed — his asking price was £20,000, which was a great deal of money at the time. Mrs O'Shea's aunt would leave her a considerable fortune, but the aunt in question lived to be 97, and the inheritance was not forthcoming in time to pay off the Captain. Thus he proceeded with the divorce petition, and the scandal erupted.

Parnell died soon afterwards, in a manner that seemed almost careless of his life: it might be said that he got his death of cold. (After speaking in the pouring rain in the West of Ireland, he failed to change out of his wet clothes, fell ill and never recovered.)

It became common to blame the Catholic Church for Parnell's downfall, as illustrated by a famous passage in James Joyce's *Portrait of the Artist as a Young Man*. This unforgettable episode describes a disastrous Christmas dinner when the pious women taunt the political menfolk over the scandalous fall of the "lost King". There is evidence that women turned against Parnell after the divorce scandal: seldom does a mistress attract the sympathy of wives. And the churches were certainly critical, beginning with the English and Welsh nonconformist clergy. The Revd Hugh Price Hughes led an energetic campaign in the *Methodist Recorder* against the lax morals of Mr Parnell, to which W.T. Stead, the noted radical and crusader against child prostitution, gave his support.

At first, the Irish Catholic Church held back from attacking Parnell. The English cardinal, Manning, urged them to assert themselves, especially since Parnell had been against the influence of the priests. Some of the Irish hierarchy, such as the legendary Archbishop Croke, advised Parnell to take a back seat for a while, to follow Gladstone's tip and disappear off to France for a long rest. (Disappearing to France was a common Victorian remedy for a public sexual scandal. The same course was urged upon Oscar Wilde.) Yet the Catholic Church could hardly be outdone, in moral indignation over the sanctity of marriage, by the *Methodist Recorder,* and moved gradually towards condemning Parnell's offence.

Moreover, Parnell, described even by his admirers as "high and mighty", was too proud to take wiser counsel, and insisted that he remained master of his party even in the eye of the storm. He had lied to Michael Davitt, the founder of the Irish National Land League (and a former Fenian), about the affair, and was unmoved when Davitt then turned against his leadership.

There was consequently a swell of animosity against Parnell in rural Ireland, which meant Catholic Ireland. Some priests spoke openly against him, and nuns had never been counted among his followers. But some Irish Catholics remained unswervingly loyal to "the Chief", particularly in Dublin, for Parnellism was a great Dublin cause. My paternal grandfather, Michael Kenny, a Dublin printer, remained both a Parnellite and an active Catholic throughout the period. There were always some Parnellite priests too, including one who kept a parrot trained to repeat to any visiting bishop: "Say a little prayer for the soul of Parnell. Ah, don't forget poor Charlie's soul."

Where Parnell left off the stewardship of Ireland, the poet William Butler Yeats seemed to take it up. "The modern literature of Ireland ... began when Parnell fell from power in 1891," he wrote in his book of memories, *Autobiographies.* "A disillusioned and embittered Ireland turned from parliamentary politics." Yeats may have been shaping the narrative to suit his own purpose, but the decline of the politician's power and the rise of the poet's influence fell into a pattern of remarkable symmetry. When Parnell died, his body was transported back to Ireland and as the ship carrying his coffin made its way into the port of Dublin, the poet Yeats was waiting on the quayside.

Willie Yeats had not been aware that Parnell's remains were on that ship. He was awaiting the return to Ireland of his friend, muse, and unrequited love, Maud Gonne, who, by sheer chance, was on the same vessel. Yeats was the Dauphin by the dockside, the man who would do so much to revive Ireland's spirit; Maud Gonne was a tall and striking beauty who would play Cathleen Ní Houlihan, the personification of Ireland, in the drama that he wrote for her, and play a continuing role, too, in the drama of the Irish resurrection.

Parnell's funeral took place in a drenching Dublin downpour; one hundred thousand people attended it. His grave was suffused with flowers. The Belfast committee of the Irish Parliamentary Party sent a floral wreath in which the word "Revenge" was spelled out. Many of the Belfast Parliamentarians were also members of the Irish Republican Brotherhood, the Fenian society founded in 1858 and the true ancestor of the IRA. They meant to avenge the death of the Chief.

But now was not the moment for politics. Now was the moment for art. The fashionable movement of the 1890s and 1900s was the Celtic Renaissance, or Celtic Dawn, which was to produce such a rich spring of writers and poets and make Dublin a city celebrated in literature and the arts.

W.B. Yeats and James Joyce are the twin geniuses of the Celtic Dawn era, one a Protestant nationalist, the other a Catholic cosmopolitan. Neither was actually a believing Christian, though Joyce could never shake off his obsession with the Catholic Church (whose rituals and emotional power nourished his work), and Yeats was a kind of mystic pagan, believing in occult forces and in fairies — illustrating G.K. Chesterton's theory that those who stop believing in God do not believe in nothing, they believe in anything.

The Celtic Dawn movement would also include J.M. Synge, Sean O'Casey, George Moore, Lady Gregory, George Russell (AE) and to some extent George Bernard Shaw, whose work and imagination were animated by Ireland and Irish events, even though these were not central to his concerns of socialism, rationalism, vegetarianism and feminism. In his book *Celtic Dawn: A Portrait of the Irish Literary Renaissance,* Ulick O'Connor also brings Oscar Wilde into the movement peripherally, because of Wilde's early encouragement of Yeats and because his parents were Irish nationalists (his mother, Speranza, was a renowned folklorist). But though Ireland gave Oscar the gift of the gab, and though his colourful effigy now adorns a corner of Merrion Square, in Dublin, where his family lived (where it is fondly known to Dubliners as "the quare on the square"), Wilde does not truly qualify as an Irish writer. He showed no interest in Ireland in his work, and even when he considered the afflictions of urban poverty in his remarkable essay *The Soul of Man Under Socialism*, the problems of Ireland never featured.

All the principal writers of the Irish Literary Renaissance, with the single exception of Joyce, were Protestants. Historically, there were always more Irish Protestant than Irish Catholic writers partly because Protestants were more educated; and partly (it has been persuasively argued) because reading the King James Bible, with its wonderful language and striking drama, is the best possible schooling for any budding writer. Sean O'Casey's mother was a Bible teacher who had come down in the world somewhat, but her early recounting of Bible stories to him nourished the dramatist in the boy.

Thus Irish nationalism was to be re-energised by a literary, rather than a political, renaissance. And the Irish Literary Renaissance which was to fuel a new nationalism was predominantly from Protestant rather than Catholic Ireland. The contribution from Catholic Ireland to the rebirth of 20th-century nationalist Ireland lay more substantially in sport: the Gaelic Athletic Association had been founded in 1884 to promote Irish sports and was almost exclusively composed of rural Catholics. Its emphasis on physical training was based on Czech gymnastic clubs, and it was enthusiastically embraced by the Christian Brothers. The GAA was split between a clerical and a Fenian wing — those who accepted the leadership of the local priest and those who did not. By the same token, the Catholic Church itself was in two minds as to whether the GAA was a good thing or not: good where it meant healthy sports activities for rural and working-class youths, not so good when it was under Fenian influence. Echoes of these differences were to continue right until the end of the 20th century.

Catholic Ireland was slow to embrace the literary renaissance of the Celtic Dawn, particularly since so many of those leading it came from Anglo-Irish, and Protestant, culture. Catholic Ireland was not philistine: priests were encouraged to read and be cultivated. In 1896, for example, a list of required books for young priests appeared in the *Irish Ecclesiastical Record*. These included works by Shakespeare, Milton, Pope, Byron, Wordsworth, Burns, Tennyson (much favoured), Dickens, Thackeray, Scott, Macaulay and Carlyle, as well as the Irish writers Maria Edgeworth, Charles Kickham, D'Arcy M'Gee and Aubrey de Vere. History was represented by Sir Charles Gavan Duffy, A.M. Sullivan, Canon O'Rourke and Father Denis Murphy. But it took Catholic Ireland quite some time to appreciate William Butler Yeats, whom they initially considered subversive.

Yeats was at the centre of the literary and cultural renaissance: a lofty, middle-class Protestant who identified with the Ascendency class, loved peasants for their magical ideas (that is, superstitions) and detested the commercial middle classes. His political mentor had been John O'Leary, a veteran, stoical Fenian of the 1850s generation and a stubborn anti-cleric. Yeats founded the Irish National Literary Society, and subsequently the Irish Literary Theatre, which was to become the Abbey Theatre, with Lady Gregory, Edward Martyn and Frank and Willy Fay. This was to be a theatre of events in Ireland in many senses of the word; almost all the leaders of the 1916 Easter Rising were deeply influenced by the theatrical and literary activity centred around the Abbey.

The first of these highly significant events was a lecture delivered by a modern language professor and parson's son, Douglas Hyde, at the Abbey in 1892, in the year following Parnell's death. The lecture was called 'The Necessity for De-Anglicizing Ireland' and its impact was sensational. Michael Collins considered it to be the most formative event of his young life, and it led to the foundation, in 1893, of the Gaelic League. Collins saw that lecture — in which Douglas Hyde urged the Irish people to turn to their own ideas, to assert their own cultural identity, and to reject what he saw as the philistinism and vulgarity which marked so much of English mass communication — as the foundation for everything that happened in Ireland subsequently. This was the conceptual act which would eventually give birth to the Free State.

The central purpose of the Gaelic League, co-founded by Hyde and Eoin MacNeill, was to revive the Irish language and everything which they saw as beautiful and Gaelic and pure, in contradistinction to the vulgarity of the new mass culture coming into existence at that time. Douglas Hyde, another Protestant of course (and later the first President of the Irish Free State), had devotedly collected the love songs and religious songs of Connaught just as they were about to disappear, rescuing yellowing manuscripts which were on the point of disintegration, annotating stories from old peasants who remembered being punished at school every time they spoke the Irish language, in the period of Anglicisation. Douglas Hyde was an altruistic man, a true scholar who cared deeply for the culture of Gaelic Ireland and saw it receding everywhere before the onslaught of the penny-dreadful press. He also urged families to give their children Irish names, and the strength of his influence was evident: the birth columns showed a new trend of Kevins and Seamuses, of Eileens and Brigids, of Colms and Eoins, replacing the Arthurs and Roses and the Violets and Alberts of yesteryear.

Dr Hyde's co-founder, Eoin O'Neill — a young historian from an Ulster Catholic background — had himself been christened John, but duly de-Anglicised his name. (Douglas Hyde also Gaelicised his name to Dubhglas de hÍde — but "Douglas" does not translate quite as felicitously as "John".)

Although emphatically a youth movement, the Gaelic League was a very inclusive movement in the early years. It attracted a colourful mixture of language students, bicycling enthusiasts, radicals, romantics, temperance reformers, spirited young women, revolutionaries and lower-middle-class self-improvers who had not had the educational opportunities they desired, or deserved. Irish society was riven with petty snobberies which erected barriers of class; shop assistants, for example, being in the lower end of "trade" found themselves socially barred from various clubs and sports. In 1904 the Cork Drapers Association, composed of shop assistants of modest social standing, had their cheque returned by the Irish Rugby

Football Union with the remark that they only accepted "Varsity men". The Cork drapers' shop assistants immediately joined the GAA — and in many cases the Gaelic League.

And the Gaelic League became, rapidly, an astonishingly successful movement. Within ten years of the Hyde speech, it was calculated that the League had about 50,000 members. By 1906 Douglas Hyde was a celebrity who could tour America and collect generous donations for the League's support. By 1912 it had branches all over the country — and 13 in Belfast alone. More than half a million people were voluntarily learning Irish.

It is piquant that in the 1990s the Protestants of Northern Ireland objected to the use of Irish language, in education and culture, as being foreign to their traditions. In the 1900s, by contrast, Protestants were to the forefront in promulgating the Irish language. An Irish-speaking Belfast clergyman, R.R. Kane — who had Gaelicised himself to "O'Cathain" — had an Orange lodge called after him, which is still in existence. It has been suggested that in the cult of the Irish language the young Protestants of the 1900s had found a way of being Irish without necessarily being Catholic. This is only half true, since Protestant and Anglo-Irish scholars had shown an interest in the Irish language from at least 1845, when the Celtic Society was first formed, with patrons including Prince Albert — Queen Victoria's German consort — the Duke of Leinster, the Marquess of Kildare and the Earl of Dunraven. When Yeats discovered the myths and legends of the Gaelic past, which he used extensively in his early poetry, he was inspired to do so by a fine Protestant scholar, Standish O'Grady, who had been ably assisted by Eleanor Hull, a woman from Alexandra College, Dublin, who has almost been effaced from the picture.

At the beginning of the 20th century, it is possible that a quarter of the Gaelic League membership were young Protestants, enthused by the ideals of Douglas Hyde and drawn naturally into a lively youth movement which included both sexes. By 1908 Protestants were writing letters to the *Church of Ireland Gazette,* the weekly Protestant paper (*The Irish Times* being the daily Protestant paper), beginning *A Chara,* the vocative "O Friend" which is the formula opening for a letter in

Irish, and signing *Mise le meas* (Yours respectfully). The *Gazette* itself gave a qualified welcome to the Irish-language craze, but expressed some anxiety — later to be wholly justified — that this could well lead to that which they feared most: a break with the Crown and a forsaking of the Union.

Catholic Ireland sometimes — though not always — automatically did the opposite of what Protestant Ireland was engaged in. (If the Protestants had a good idea which seemed to be working, such as temperance, sometimes the Catholics copied it. Orphanages were another Protestant innovation eventually copied by Catholics, as were Magdalen Homes for "fallen women" — a Scottish Calvinist concept imported into Irish Catholicism.)

Catholic Ireland was wary, at the beginning, of the Gaelic League and this fashion among the young for everything Irish and Celtic. Firstly, the Catholic Church was lukewarm about the Irish language. There were some individual priests and bishops who were Irish-language scholars: Archbishop MacHale of Tuam was a great 19th-century scholar who translated Homer's *Iliad* from the Greek into Irish, and Father Peter O'Leary, whose autobiography *Mo Scéal Féin* every schoolchild was to read over a period of 50 years, was a celebrated *Gaeilgorí*. Father Peter's story underlined just how solidly educationalists of his period had worked — he was born in 1839 — to stop children speaking Irish, regarded by progressives as a backward language akin to a patois.

This view became ingrained. When the Dominican nuns in Galway offered to teach schoolchildren Irish in 1896, they found that "most of the day pupils are unwilling to learn it". A "bright little girl", when asked why she did not care to learn Irish, said: "It is a vulgar language, the language of the poor Cladach people, and there is nothing refined or nice about it." Claddagh was a part of Galway associated with poverty at this time. My mother, who was born in Galway county in 1902, had some of these innate prejudices against the Irish language. In a throwaway aside I once heard her say lightly: "It was spoken by the island people, riddled with whiskey and incest." English was for those who wanted to get on in the world.

And this was the "progressive" view during the 19th century — that small, minority languages were, in the words of Karl Marx, for "rural idiots". Marx, Engels and other progressives such as John Stuart Mill thought that peasant peoples should abandon their insularity and speak the great tongues — French, German, English (rather than Breton, Flemish, Czech, Welsh). The Catholic Church, as an institution, shared that Marxist-progressive view, as part of its universalism and its ambitions for world evangelisation. After all, you would not convert China using the Irish language. The Welsh Nonconformist churches had helped to keep Welsh alive by using Welsh in their religious services, but when did Welsh Nonconformism conquer the world? How many Welsh Nonconformists were there in Africa?

There were other reasons not to endorse wholeheartedly the Gaelic League at the start. Many Irish Catholics at this time were just beginning to do well within the British Empire. Obstacles to Catholics joining British institutions such as the civil service or the higher echelons of university life were beginning, at last, to fade away (though Catholics, even in Dublin, remained at a disadvantage in business because of closed networks within Freemasonry). But things were beginning to change for Catholic Ireland and for the better.

And then there was the sex issue. The Gaelic League believed in boys and girls healthily going on hikes and attending mixed classes of the Irish language together. Some priests thought this could lead to moral temptations. There was a famous case in Portarlington, Co Laois, in 1905 when the parish priest denounced the Gaelic League's mixed classes from the pulpit, describing them as "not conducive to the good morals of his flock". Little did he know; the flavour of the Gaelic League was deliberately and, to some participants, exasperatingly, wholesome. In his autobiography, *Vive Moi!,* Sean O'Faolain recalls the League's egalitarian and comradely ambiance with rueful humour. In a satirical novel of the period, *The Plough and the Cross,* the writer W.P. Ryan describes the Gaelic League (and Sinn Féin) as thoroughly "sexless": far too much "comradeship" and not enough flirtation.

There were also priests who, like the socialist James Connolly, thought there were more important issues than the revival of language and culture. Connolly deplored the fact that people were putting their energies into the revival of the Irish language at a time when Dublin's slums had some of the worst housing conditions, and among the highest infant mortality, in Europe. Dublin priests were still trying to halt the practice of working men being paid by their employers in the pub at the end of the week, which caused indebtedness to the publican and promoted a drink habit. Devotional magazines such as the *Irish Messenger of the Sacred Heart* considered domestic improvement and the fight against tuberculosis more important than Gaelic League enthusiasms. And, again, the church itself would always be wary of anything which might lead to Fenianism, for Fenianism meant revolution, and revolution was anathema. Revolution was descended from Lutheranism: it was "I will not serve".

Yet certain sympathetic and patriotic priests got involved in promoting the Irish language and Irish culture. Father Patrick Dineen produced a well-respected Irish-English dictionary in 1904, and Father Eugene O'Growney virtually provided the Gaelic movement with a dead hero: a delicate, scholarly, idealistic young man, he died of consumption at the age of 31. Father O'Growney's book *Simple Lessons in Irish* sold 32,000 copies in its first printing, and after he died in California, his body was brought back to Ireland in 1903, acclaimed as though he had been a martyr to a cause, always a compelling thing in Irish culture.

There remained divisions over the place of the Irish language and the Gaelic revival. Catholic Ireland was in some ways quite British, or some aspects of it were. Many Catholic parents in the 1900s wanted their children to succeed in the world of the 20th century, which they correctly foresaw as an American century, not the world of the 17th century. The Catholic Church in Ireland was opposed to Irish being made compulsory for university students — a leading Jesuit educationalist, Revd Dr Delaney, said he didn't see why "the language of uneducated peasants" should be made a test for college fellows — and an ugly row broke out in 1908. This ended in a humiliation for an Irish-speaking scholar at Maynooth College, Dr Michael O'Hickey: he was relieved of his post for speaking ill of his bishops, who championed English.

There was one aspect of Douglas Hyde's vision, however, which especially attracted Catholic Ireland, and that was Hyde's puritanical view of the world outside the Celtic realm. As noted above, Douglas Hyde disliked the vulgarity, the sauciness, the cheapness and the increasing explicitness of the mass culture which was quickly spreading via a popular press. The tabloid newspapers of the 1890s were full of crime and (only slightly veiled) sex stories. Dr Hyde deplored the fascination with low life; Yeats called it "this filthy modern tide". Maud Gonne more than once blamed this tendency of crass, and sometimes sexualised, commercialism on the Jews, a habit of mind she probably picked up from her time in France, where anti-Semitism was extremely active.

When Dr Hyde addressed Catholic groups, he took care to underline the purity and chastity of Gaelic tradition — as exemplified by devotion to the Blessed Virgin — in contrast to the coarseness of the English-speaking world, then becoming globalised. It was this vision of a pure, chaste, Gaelic — and then Catholic — country which was to lay the foundation for a draconian censorship that would prevail in an independent Ireland from the 1930s to the 1960s, when the worst excesses of Anglo-American "filth" were to be so carefully held at bay.

By the 1900s, Britain's rule in Ireland was modifying and becoming generally more conciliatory. The old coercive approaches were dying off; Lord Salisbury's notions of the Irish as a barbarous people no more fit for self-rule than the Hottentots, or Disraeli's pronouncements that the Irish were a people moved by "coarse idolatry", were growing distinctly old-fashioned. In the new century England's policy was to "kill Home Rule by kindness". The establishment of local democracy through the elections of county councils, in 1898, had done more to "pacify" Ireland than centuries of repression. The introduction, by Lloyd George, of the old age pension in 1909 made a huge difference to the condition of the old in Ireland. The Wyndham Land Act of 1903, which gave peasant-farmers the chance of owning their own small plots had a truly radical impact on Irish life and culture.

The Wyndham Act turned land-hungry anarchists and rebels into property-holding conservatives; nothing promulgates conservatism like private property. It turned his wife into a most enthusiastic student of domestic economy and domestic improvement generally. Engels' spiteful characterisation of the Irish housewife as a slut who did not know the difference between straw and bedding was outdated by opportunities for improvement in living standards. Catholicism endorsed home life enthusiastically, for a good home helped to avoid the temptations of the tavern or worse.

Along with home life, Catholic Ireland was much concerned with education, which had again become universal and compulsory in the 1890s (up to the age of 14). But education was another area where the Catholic Church in Ireland had reason to be relatively pro-British.

By the 1890s the Catholic Church in Ireland was beginning to win its long battle with the British authorities over education. The British had originally hoped for integrated education in Ireland "free from religious or political controversy". But the Catholic Church wanted control over Catholic schools, which would turn out to be the schools of the majority. Broadly, a kind of deal emerged with the British authorities: if the British agreed to denominational education — Catholic and Protestant schools operating freely along parallel lines — the Catholic Church in Ireland would continue to oppose the excesses of nationalism.

The more indulgent attitude of the British government towards Catholic schools contrasted with what was occuring on the Continent at this time. In Bismarck's Germany, there was a policy of *Kulturkampf* — cultural war — against the Catholic Church. In France, the situation was extremely alarming. During the 1890s, more than a century after the seminal revolution of 1789 so deplored by the Church, the Third Republic in France was entering its most radical and anti-clerical phase. The French Left and French republicans were determined to oppose the power of the Catholic Church wherever they saw it: their slogan being Gambetta's — *"Le clericalisme – voilà l'ennemi!"* Jules Ferry, the French education minister, embarked on an all-out onslaught against Catholic education which culminated in a draconian secularisation law of 1904. Church property was seized and confiscated, and in many cases compensation was not properly paid. Sometimes there was political corruption involved – for example, the Grande Chartreuse monastery, and its profitable liqueur production, was forcibly sold off to Cuisinier, the chocolate manufacturer, for a pittance, because the State's valuers had been bribed. In Brittany, there were distressing scenes when Catholic villagers gathered to defend their church schools and convents against the coercive decrees of the republican state. Rigid laws were introduced which forbade any Christian symbol – not so much as a cross – appearing in any school or institution sanctioned by the State.

With the rising tide of nationalism, politicians were determined to wrest power away from a powerful international body like the Catholic Church – and, of course, to take it for themselves, which is what politicians like to do.

Against this European background of nationalism and republicanism, small wonder that the Irish Catholic Church was prudently defending itself against the spread of these contagious ideas. And small wonder that it considered London more acceptable than Paris or Berlin in the matter of Catholic education. London, by the 1900s, was a lot less anti-Catholic than Paris or Berlin.

Catholic Ireland and Nationalist Ireland were not always different to one another; but they were not always the same either. Catholic Ireland was internationalist, less inclusive of Protestants (or any non-Catholics) but willing to deal with the British once the British stopped persecuting the faith. Nationalist Ireland, or Irish-Ireland, was more inclusive of Protestants, or others who accepted the nationalist agenda, but could be insular, was anti-British and sometimes, among the men (more rarely among the women), anti-clerical.

Catholic Ireland and Nationalist Ireland diverged very sharply over the Boer War of 1899-1901, for example. Nationalist Ireland cheered on the "gallant little Boers" because they were challenging the British Empire. Catholic Ireland was more concerned to pray for "the Irish Tommies" fighting with the Crown, and was opposed to the Boers for their anti-Catholic Dutch Calvinism. Articles in the *Irish Catholic* newspaper also pointed out that the Boers were domineering and exacting towards "the kaffirs", whom the Irish missionaries were seeking to convert.

The year 1907 was the high point of the Celtic Dawn renaissance. It was a very optimistic time, despite the poverty and such afflictions as tuberculosis which still existed in Ireland. But life was getting better — the key ingredient for optimism. The literary revival had picked up Ireland's spirit after the fall of Parnell. Sinn Féin, founded in 1905, in the slipstream of the Gaelic League, was an honourable movement with the goal of encouraging national self-belief and high-minded culture. Home Rule was on the way. Standards of living were gradually rising, reflected in the fact that parents were spending more on their children, an indication of disposable income.

In 1907 a row famously erupted over the staging of John Millington Synge's play *The Playboy of the Western World*, which caused riots in the Abbey Theatre. The play, which has since attained the status of a classic, concerns the story of a young man who claims to have killed his father, and in telling the tale, becomes a hero, particularly to a group of admiring village women. It is written with an intense feeling for language: it is poetic and rich in character and texture.

But it offended. It offended nationalist Ireland because it revived, on stage, something which nationalist Ireland abhorred — the stage Irishman, drunken and foolish. It offended Catholic Ireland because it seemed indecent — there was open talk of women's underwear — and because its moral was essentially sinful: it endorsed patricide as a heroic gesture. It also implied (whether this be true or not) that women actually prefer violent men who are exciting to law-abiding, conscientious men who are boring.

But Yeats defended it passionately on the grounds that it was art, and the riots were not damped down by Unionist students from Trinity College Dublin drunkenly waving Union Jacks and singing 'God Save the King'. The *Playboy* riot is seen as indicating the rising nationalist temperature and presaging the violent times to come. It also remains a significant example of politics and religion versus art. There was an element, too, of the sheer enjoyment of street democracy.

The Playboy was a front-page story in the general press in Dublin at the time, but not in the Catholic press. Far more important things were happening elsewhere, for Catholic Ireland. The Cork County Council, the Cork Chamber of Commerce, the Bantry Urban Council, the Urban Councils of Macroom, Mallow, Cashel and Newry, and the Corporations of Waterford and Sligo had all passed solemn resolutions condemning Clemenceau and the Godless state of France, and this was being transmitted to the Vatican. Resolutions condemning the French Government's attack on the Catholic Church followed from the municipal authorities of Carlow, Enniscorthy, Wexford, Carlingford, Gornahoe, Limerick, Rathkeale, Glin and Ballyshannon.

It is sometimes a matter of merriment that the Kerry newspaper the *Skibbereen Eagle* once proclaimed it was keeping its eye on the Czar. The municipal guardians of Ballyshannon certainly had their eye on Georges Clemenceau, the Prime Minister of France, who was waging a cultural war on the faith. The rural denizens of Catholic Ireland were watchful and energetic in defending the faith, a task with an international dimension, not merely a national one.

Two

The Power of the Priests
and the Faith of the Mothers

"God's life is revealed to us in the hearts and lives of
our mothers — aye — of our sisters too."

Bishop Shanahan of Nigeria

Women are seldom anti-clerical. Anti-clericalism — a very
distinct dislike and distrust of clergy and Church sometimes
amounting to an obsessive hatred — has historically been
almost exclusively a male preserve. There might be a Freudian,
competitive element of men challenging the power of other
men; in Catholic countries, the priests certainly did have
psychological power, and they were morally controlling. Males
between the ages of 15 and 35 are at their most macho, their
most radical and their most atheistic; in these years of virile
manhood they most resent the power of priests to interfere with
their lives. In Catholic countries, anti-clericalism among young
males has been endemic, not least because the priests seemed to
be in alliance with the power of the mothers.

At least until the 1960s and the Pill revolution, young
women — and all women — generally behaved favourably
towards priests, respecting and indulging priestly power where
it arose, and indeed, when they were the mothers of clergy,
encouraging it. In his Left-wing critique of the Catholic Church
in modern Irish history, Tom Inglis described this as a sinister
alliance between Church and mother, an alliance forged in
hearth and home. "It was within the home that a new power

alliance between priest and mother began to emerge, an alliance that was founded on her dependence on the Church for moral power." I am not sure if I go along with Prof Inglis's view that mothers must depend upon a church for moral power: anyone with experience of raising a small child from birth must know that nature, not any institution, gives a mother huge moral, and actual, power over the formation of the child. Anthropologists have observed this quite widely, and most tellingly in Ireland itself.

In 1938 two American anthropologists from Harvard, Arensberg and Kimball, lived in a village in Co Clare for two years, noting the habits of the Irish natives. They were particularly observant about the way women on farms kept their children near until the age of seven, carefully training them in small tasks from about the age of three. The rural mother was parent and teacher to her young children; Irish autobiography is particularly insistent on the power and presence of the mother, often characterised as a strong personality in the home. The poet Padraic Colum, in his lovely book about a year spent in Connaught, *My Irish Year*, published in 1912, noted that the woman with the strong personality was a feature of Irish community life, which was almost an extension of the home. Women who could talk articulately were admired: a common phrase of esteem at the time was "a well-discoursed woman".

This strong Irish mother — and grandmother — was almost invariably a most ardent defender of the faith. When I hear the Irish hymn 'Faith of Our Fathers'— now seldom sung, though it had a brief revival on CD in recent times — I think how faith was held, upheld and transmitted so much more emphatically by our mothers. Despite the feminist critique of patriarchy, Catholicism was a very feminine faith. Indeed, that was very particularly the charge made against it at the beginning of the modern period — the cusp of the 19th-20th centuries.

Catholicism was seen as soft, feminine, dependent, yielding, over-indulgent: Protestantism was masculine, self-reliant, robust, energetic and productive of the work ethic. "Catholicism commonly softens, while Protestantism strengthens the character," the Irish Protestant historian Lecky had written in the 19th century. "But the softness of the first often degenerates into weakness, and the strength of the second into hardness."

When Oscar Wilde converted to Catholicism, shortly before he died in 1900, the Catholic Church was considered a more suitable repository for homosexuals, with its perfumed sanctity, its operatic rituals, its robing ceremonies and sweet incense. In the 1900s, there was a tinge of decadence about the softness of Catholicism: it was the religion of Huysmans and Beardsley, as well as the faith of womenfolk. Its femininity — or effeminacy — was what its critics despised about it: "Rome," wrote Lord Salisbury, the British Prime Minister in 1900, contemptuously, "is content to base her power upon the credulity of women and of peasants."

The beginning of the 20th century was not, as it is sometimes portrayed in costume TV dramas, a stately era of *belle-époque* ladies and cap-doffing lower orders. It was a time brimming with promise, tumultuous with change, disturbance, invention, speed and globalisation. This period so wrongly portrayed as dainty Edwardianism witnessed the expansion of nationalism, socialism, feminism, sexual radicalism, global capitalism, anti-Semitism and all the modern genres in literature and art. It is from this time that the phrase "avant-garde" comes: coined around 1905, it is still being used to describe the experimental or ultra-progressive in the 21st century as if it were newly minted. The art revolution — modern art, conceptual art — can be dated to this age of Picasso and Marcel Duchamps, as can psychoanalysis and perhaps the whole field of psychology, for it was at this time that Freud and Adler flourished. The motor car, the aeroplane, jazz music, rhythm and blues — which would lead to rock — and broadcasting all date from this same modernist period, too. Virginia Woolf believed that the world changed absolutely crucially in 1909; she was proud indeed, that "gay pride" began with the Bloomsbury group. "The word 'bugger' is never far from our lips!" she exclaimed, and though it was in common usage as an insult, she meant it as a compliment.

At this time conventional religion was in decline among "modern-minded" people. On the Continent, political radicalism and nationalism were ranged against church and clergy. In Britain, and to a lesser degree the United States, science and evolution had dealt what seemed a mortal blow to the biblical version of truth. Charles Darwin's theories of evolution, first published in 1859, were gradually whittling away the concept of humanity as God-created, and gradually proposing a view of man that was animal-centered. In Europe and the United States, eugenics — the idea that human beings should be bred for good genes and restrained from breeding when they had bad genes, which was known as "dysgenic" — was seen as the science of the future, as in a most horrible way it turned out to be so.

And in the 1900s women were beginning to emerge into public life in an exhilarating way. This decade marks the true beginning of modern feminism.

The "women's question" — that is, the emancipation of women — had been developing throughout the 19th century, not just in terms of the vote but of access to higher education and property rights. The Married Women's Property Act of 1882 was an important milestone: until then, the property of a married woman automatically belonged to her husband. (Single women have generally had more legal entitlements than married women, who traditionally ceded much to their husbands in the act of becoming "one flesh". This was in law. In practice it may often have been otherwise; it was Dr Johnson who claimed that because nature had given women so much power, "the law had wisely given them little".)

The entry of women to universities, from the 1880s onwards, was very significant and was to lay a foundation for the militant suffrage struggle in the 1900s. Educated women were less and less tolerant of being forcibly consigned to the role of wifely consort, less tolerant of the idea that proletarian men could now vote while upper-middle-class women could not.

The franchise for men had been progressively enlarging throughout the century — full male franchise was achieved in the United Kingdom in 1884 — but women were excluded from voting in general elections. Women's emancipation was a hotly debated topic, and the last 30 years of Queen Victoria's reign — the Queen herself was horrified at women being degraded by politics — saw a proliferation of organisations clamouring for votes for women, of which the most sensational and dramatic was to be that led by the Pankhursts.

Emmeline Pankhurst was, interestingly, politicised as a very young child in 1867 when she witnessed the public hanging of three Fenians, later called the Manchester Martyrs, which was considered to be a miscarriage of justice. (Allen, Gould and Larkin were involved in the death of a policeman during an affray, but there was no proof of intent to murder.) From the age of nine, she vowed that she would advance all causes of justice.

But it was the cause of women that was to claim her energies. And as a widow, supported by her three daughters, Mrs Pankhurst's militancy became a *cause célèbre*. Dramatic street demonstrations, brilliant street posters and public art work, controversy, arrest and imprisonment — Emmeline Pankhurst was imprisoned 13 times in all — brought an exciting focus to the cause of votes for women.

There had been various leagues supporting votes for women, but the Pankhursts' Women's Political and Social Union (WSPU), founded in 1903, launched the sensational years of the suffragettes. Using street theatre and acts of defiance, the suffragette movement was thoroughly modern, thoroughly media-oriented. The movement knew how to sensationalise, and how to get headlines.

Its cause was deserving and worthy, but nearly all political parties, from Left to Right, were split on the issue of votes for women. The Left feared that votes for women would disadvantage working-class men. In France, the Left also feared that votes for women would give the Church more influence, because women would, they believed, vote as the priests directed them. The Right disliked the notion of women becoming manly and aggressive.

Yet women's emancipation was an exciting cause, and, as elsewhere, women in Ireland were drawn to it. My maternal grandmother, Mary Conroy, was born in 1870 in Connemara, Co Galway. A dedicated schoolteacher all her life, she was a supporter of votes for women: she also thought women's education very important. Distinguished Irishwomen such as Countess Markievicz, born Constance Gore-Booth, cut their political teeth on the cause of women's suffrage. An Irish Women's Suffrage Society had been founded as early as 1872 by Isabella Tod in Belfast, and a Dublin parallel started in 1876.

But women's emancipation in Ireland was always in competition with the cause of Home Rule or the wider issue of "the national question". Sinn Féin, founded in 1905 on the crest of the Celtic renaissance, practised equality between men and women, and women speakers were encouraged on Sinn Féin platforms. The very name Sinn Féin — Ourselves Alone — had been coined by a woman, Maire de Bhuitlear. But Sinn Féin would always take the view that the national question came first: women's emancipation would naturally follow in its slipstream. And thus it was that many of the lively, radical, active and political young women, who in Britain or America would have been in feminist organisations at this period, in Ireland were drawn to nationalism. Countess Markievicz herself, though always a feminist and as a matter of a fact the first woman ever to be elected to Westminster (though she did not take her seat), made nationalism her priority.

A group of spirited and highly motivated young women joined Maud Gonne in forming Inghinidhe na h-Éireann (the Daughters of Ireland), whose priority was Irish self-rule and national self-esteem. This has been claimed as a feminist organisation of the suffragette generation — it was formed in 1900 — but its main purpose was "to encourage the study of Gaelic, of Irish literature, History, Music and Art ... And to discourage the reading and circulation of low English literature, the singing of English songs, the attending of vulgar English entertainments at the theatres and music hall, and to combat in every way English influence, which is doing so much injury to the artistic taste and refinement of the Irish people." One of the first undertakings of the Inghinidhe na h-Éireann was to start Irish-language classes for slum children; a socialist would have concentrated on social reform, a feminist on votes for women, but for the Daughters of Ireland the cause of Ireland came first. As it happened, the classes, which told stories and legends of

Ireland, were hugely popular, and taking the form of dramatic tableaux, were probably also hugely enjoyable. The Irish love for theatre always emerges.

Similarly, with my own grandmother, the cause of Sinn Féin took priority over the cause of women's emancipation. She became more drawn to Sinn Féin than to the suffragettes. Some women activists, such as Jenny Wyse Power who was later to become a nationalist Senator in the Free State, actually ascribed the problems of sex division in Irish society to British culture. The "false sex and class divisions ... were the result of English influence," she said. Nationalism, rather than feminism, would reorganise society justly and equally.

Thus the suffragettes, admirable though they might be, carried with them the cultural baggage of being a British organisation and were sometimes seen as being composed of upper-class British women. In Ireland, the suffrage societies were launched by, and continued to be upheld by, Unionist women; indeed, until 1912, when they too were pulled back by political and tribal loyalties, there was a growing number of suffragette Orangewomen. Dublin newspapers frequently featured pictures of women's emancipation leagues in this period before the First World War, and it is very noticeable that the names and appearance have a strong Unionist flavour. These were evidently ladies from prominent Unionist and Anglo-Irish families who were also active in the Royal Society for the Prevention of Cruelty to Animals, or various Ulster Unionist causes — the Misses Birch, Irwin, Browning, Montgomery, Carson. In Ireland, causes are often defined not just by reason, but also by kinship. Suffragism was not a nationalist — and seldom a Catholic — cause.

Moreover, the needs of women in Ireland were different from those in England. Because of the growth of convent schooling throughout the latter part of the 19th century, girls in Ireland had increasing access to education. Convents such as the Mercy Sisters were particularly dedicated to educating "the daughters of the poor". Among farming people, the girls in a family might be better educated than the boys, because farmers wanted their sons at home attending to the farm, while their daughters acquired the necessary polish at a convent school, which would help them make a good match, or a future life as a nun, perhaps. As for property rights, in rural cultures property is much more a question of family acquisition, rather than ownership and control by an individual. Irish property was dynastic.

Yet feminism can be more widely defined than simply the acquisition of individual rights by women. Sometimes it can just mean women feel that their lives — including their family lives — and their opportunities are improving. For many Irishwomen in the early years of the 20th century, a prime goal of women's empowerment was the improvement of home life. A better home life was probably what most women wanted. This was not in contradiction to enhancing women's education, a goal most ardently aspired to within Catholic Ireland: requests for prayers published in the devotional magazines show mothers hoping for good exam results for their daughters, for example. Nor was it in conflict, necessarily, with women's vocational ambitions, and the desire of clever women to enter the professions. But to be "Queen of the Home" was, at this time, a genuinely feminist aspiration. This is partly explained by the conditions of previous times.

During the 19th century Ireland had repeatedly been described as having the worst home dwellings in the United Kingdom, and among some of the worst in Europe. The home, for many ordinary people, was a hovel. A British researcher described, in 1884, the conditions of a typical Irish rural home. "Floors of mud; roofs of rotten thatch; one wretched chamber often doing duty as a kitchen by day, and as a bedroom, pigstye and stable by night; one bed, or a truss of straw having often to accommodate the whole family of all ages and both sexes." Descriptions of the dire housing conditions which prevailed in Ireland have appeared repeatedly since Tudor times, but this was within my own father's lifetime.

Nevertheless, as the outstanding social historian Joanna Bourke has demonstrated in her work on women and economic change in Ireland from 1890 to 1914 *(Husbandry to Housewifery)*, these conditions were changing fast by the end of the 19th century. As the peasant farmer acquired the right to buy his own land, so his wife began to assert more control over her own home. During the period when so many Irish homes were hovels, women went out to work elsewhere, either in domestic service — in the 1880s, 30 per cent of Irishwomen were working as domestic servants — or as agricultural labourers. But from the later 1890s, the numbers and percentages of women in paid employment began to drop: standards of living were rising, and more Irishwomen were able to afford to live in, furnish and adorn their own homes.

From the beginning of the 20th cenury Irish people could invest more capital in their homes. Such banal, yet significant items as floor coverings experienced a boom: between 1904 and 1911 the purchase of carpets and mattings expanded, as the displeasing dirt floors associated with the old hovels began to disappear. The invention of linoleum made a big difference; some women described it as very heaven, and lino brought with it a new pride in the home. In cottages and cabins with dirt floors and resident animals, the process of cleaning was irrelevant.

English critics (and Ulster housewives) thought the Catholic Irish dirty: in the poverty of their dirt-floor cabins, how could they be otherwise? But now, in the 1900s, animals were being removed to outhouses, and the subsequent sealing of floors created a new form of household labour in the cleaning and maintenance of carpets, rugs and linoleum. My generation of feminists — born in the 1940s — thought housework a tedious business, but it is clear from the research that women in the 1900s were delighted with their home improvements.

Standards were improving all around. People were eating more meat, again an indication of better diet at the time. The purchase of toys for children greatly increased — between 1904 and 1911 this rose by 54 per cent. This indicates more disposable income, more leisure and a greater enjoyment of children by their parents.

The rising status of the woman in the home was hugely encouraged by two crusading agencies: first, the self-improvement movements headed and inspired by Sir Horace Plunkett, the agricultural reformer, who founded the influential magazine, the *Irish Homestead*. Second, the Catholic Church, which had always endorsed the sanctity of motherhood, and had also come to believe that a better home life would decrease drunkenness and intemperance.

Sir Horace (1854-1932) was the son of Lord Dunsany, of Dunshaughlin in Co Meath; he was educated at Eton and Oxford. After an illness as a young man he spent ten years ranching in Wyoming, and returned to Ireland fired up with ideas for agricultural change and pioneering cooperation. He believed (with reason) that too much time had been spent talking about politics in Ireland, and too little on practical measures to help people to improve themselves. Economic development was the true engine for change and development, he thought, and he wrote a book outlining his ideas, *Ireland in the New Century*, published in 1904. His magazine the *Irish Homestead* was designed to help home improvements and further agricultural development.

Sir Horace, who was, of course, a Protestant, believed that the Catholic Church held people back from economic development, an idea that was current at the time and advanced in Germany by Max Weber in his influential study *The Protestant Ethic and the Spirit of Capitalism*. This suggested that Protestantism was mercantile and that its work ethic encouraged progress and prosperity, while Catholicism was passive, fatalistic and too easy-going. "Roman Catholicism strikes an outsider as being in some of its tendencies non-economic if not actually anti-economic," wrote Sir Horace, though he was quite careful not to offend the clergy by adding, "I have come to the conclusion that the immense power of the Roman Catholic clergy has been singularly little abused." He also understood the historical background of the penal times "when the hunted *soggarth* (priest) had to celebrate the Mass in cabins and caves on the mountain side".

He further added that as a Protestant he had met no personal prejudice or bigotry in Ireland: his point was, simply, that Catholicism failed to develop the rugged individualism needed for self-improvement schemes. The faith in Ireland fed the people "on fancies and fictions" instead of equipping them with sound Calvinist virtue of the type that made Protestant countries successful. Sir Horace, a lifelong bachelor (he carried a torch for the pretty and witty Daisy, Countess of Fingall), was saying, as Lecky had said, that Catholicism was too feminine. It was suffused with mothers' prayers and stories of female saints — St Brigid, who refused all suitors and founded women's wells all over Ireland, St Dympna, daughter of an Irish king who became the patron saint of the mentally disturbed, the perfumed St Therese of Lisieux, the "Little Flower", and St Bernadette of Lourdes, to whom the people built grottoes all over Ireland. Better if they were building cowsheds! Under Sir Horace's tutelage, though, they *were* building cowsheds as well.

Sir Horace was by no means alone in his views at this time: books poured off the printing-presses denouncing the backwardness of Catholicism, and the way in which it caused the people to be priest-ridden, yet Plunkett's endeavours were actually quite well supported by priests. A Jesuit priest, Father Thomas Finlay, helped him launch his cooperative agricultural movement, and in the devotional magazine the *Messenger of the Sacred Heart* (whose circulation went from 7,000 to 300,000 in a little over 30 years, from the end of the 19th century to the 1920s) the cult of home and hearth flourished. There were many inspiring and useful articles on home improvements ("How to whitewash a kitchen wall"), on childcare ("chide not the rapture of the lark", parents were advised: children should not be scolded unreasonably) and what was coming to be known as domestic science, that is, cooking and home management.

Articles on cuisine and needlework as taught in the culinary schools of Vienna had to be reprinted again and again. Given the opportunities, women loved the idea of improving their homes, of learning how to make charlotte russe and accomplishing modest do-it-yourself repair tasks. And this was also considered to be a form of feminism, in that it was helping to develop women, helping to give them self-esteem and power in the home, and in many cases equipping them with a profession — to become a domestic science teacher was a flourishing new career.

As Joanna Bourke has noted, far from wanting men to share half the chores of the home, girls at this time voted to exclude boys from learning domestic science. Let the males keep to their own business, they were told. In rural life, let the men see to the outside jobs: the home was the woman's realm, and she alone would rule and reign within it.

As the century wore on — and particularly after the First World War, when men came back from the terrible experiences of the trenches — all European countries began to encourage, and some to coerce, women back into the home: Hitler coined the phrase *Kinder, Kuche, Kirche* (children, cooking, church) to define women's realm. But before the Great War of 1914-18 ordinary women themselves had exercised choice in wanting to be in their improved homes, ruling and reigning over their families.

Thus it was that from the early days of the 20th century the power of the home was growing, because the homes were improving and more mothers could afford to be at home. In Victorian times, for a married woman to go out to work was a sign of poverty: to be able to stay at home, a sign of family prosperity.

And within the crucible of the home, the mothers taught and transmitted the faith. As the home became more important, even more prosperous, so did the mother's ability to control home life. Over and over again, mothers proved themselves to be the allies of the church and the defenders of the faith.

It is a theme which appears repeatedly in Irish autobiography, not always positively. Sometimes a man would become anti-clerical and atheistic in a bid to rebel against the power of the mother: rejecting the faith became an Oedipal struggle of cutting the umbilical cord. This is a theme in James Joyce. Sean O'Faolain, the novelist and short-story author, wrote of his childhood faith: "I despise and hate many of its effeminate ways." He recalled how his mother would bring him to the church in Cork, where as a small boy he would be made to gaze upon the statue of "the pendant body of Christ, with the Magdalene, St John the Divine and the Virgin". He forever associated this intensely Catholic scene with the faith of his mother, and it is clear that mothers and Mother Church were symbolically intertwined in his imagination.

Similarly with the poet Austin Clarke, who was profoundly formed by his mother's faith. He describes the sensuousness of the statues and holy pictures which were such a central part of the imaginative life. While Catholicism insisted on the ascetic, it nevertheless underlined the flesh — "incarnation" not coincidentally means "made flesh" — in its images of suckling Madonnas, the afflicted naked Jesus Christ or the masculine beauty of a Michelangelo sculpture. And then there were "the exclamatory prayers, perfumed as incense, sharp as the red hot charcoals ... *O most adorable, precious and infinitely tender Heart pierced for the love of me, pierce my heart with the love of Thee ... Sacred Heart, I put my trust in Thee, Inflame my heart with Thy love, O wisdom of the Sacred Heart ... consume me in Thy fire."* This was indeed the "feminine faith" which Lecky feared would make men soft, and Sir Horace believed would make people unfocused on economics.

The church, at this stage, did not have to enforce censorship of literary material. The mothers did it first. Austin Clarke gives a vivid description of his mother determinedly burning books in the kitchen range, when she judged them to be a danger to faith and morals. Matthew Arnold's *Literature and Dogma* went up in flames, as did Renan's *Life of Jesus* and the evolutionist *Descent of Man* — Mrs Clarke had quite highbrow taste in book-burning.

Nationalist mothers were the most zealous in pursuit of censorship since they wished to defend both the faith and the purity of Gaelic culture. Progressing from her organisation Daughters of Ireland, Maud Gonne went on to found an organisation with the English suffragette Charlotte Despard called "The Mothers", in which they most particularly targeted "English filth" which was growing all too popular in Ireland. In 1911, Ladies Vigilance Committees began to appear in the Catholic press, actively suppressing and controlling "bad literature". These Catholic mothers were, in their own way, an outpost of suffragism, since the activities of the suffragettes gave other women confidence to affirm their values; and sometimes, as with Charlotte Despard, there were shared values between feminism and Catholicism. Mrs Despard, like her friend Maud Gonne, became a Catholic, as, incidentally, did Constance Markievicz.

If in the memoirs of writers and poets the faith of the mother is seen as prohibitive and controlling, in the memoirs of priests it is more often portrayed as a source of strength, inspiration and intellectual ambition (as in D.H. Lawrence's *Sons and Lovers* where the drive, the ambition and the refinement come from the mother). "I love to think of my mother," wrote Dr Walter McDonald in *Reminiscences of a Maynooth Professor,* written in 1919 when he was dying, "who was quite unlike — superior to — any other woman whom I have met, of her class ... She was always at work, heavy work very often, about the house — cleaning, washing, ironing, sewing, cooking; about the dairy — milking cows, setting milk, making butter and cleaning vessels, and even about the pigs and cattle — helping to prepare their food and to feed them.

"On Sundays, nevertheless ... she turned out quite genteel, though her dress was such as, till then, was worn by the married women of our place: frilled cap and hood cloak, which my mother wore fairly rich and which became her admirably. I remember, above everything else, the reverent care with which she undressed us and put us to bed, reminding us of our guardian angels, and telling us how shocked they would be if they saw us do anything unseemly. She had been to school to the nuns at Mooncoin, who certainly trained her well."

When he thought of his mother, he wrote, the one word which summed up his memory of her was this concept of "refinement". Refinement mattered to people a lot more when life was rugged and raw; the Victorian drive for refinement and respectability was a struggle against the rough facts of their everyday lives.

Many Irish autobiographies underline the role of the rosary (which had been a much-loved devotion in Ireland since the early 16th century) as the mother's prayer. It was the family prayer whereby the mother, and the grandmother, exercised moral authority in the home. John Healy, the Co Mayo writer and *Irish Times* political commentator, wrote a vivid memoir about his early life in the west of Ireland. "The clock would strike ten. Grandma would put her sewing aside. From a nail on the wall she'd take the big Rosary beads, and without any more than her ritual 'Let ye get down on yer knees, and we'll say the Rosary in the name of God', we got up from our seats, knelt down with our backs to the fire and one another, leaned our elbows on the seat or the form, and made the responses."

There was also "the trimmings on the rosary", extra prayers, litanies and devotions given out by the mother or grandmother, according to the matriarch's inclinations or preoccupations. These also taught the child something else: "It was from the trimmings that I learned there was another world and another family bigger than that gathered in this place," recalled John Healy. The trimmings would mention the diaspora family overseas and all the special requests and perhaps problems that existed at home and abroad.

Sometimes, faith and motherland were conjoined, and the evening rosary would take on a nationalist dimension. In families where the Fenian tradition or sympathy was strong, the trimmings on the rosary might carry the extra nationalist message. Kathleen Clarke, the Republican activist — she married the 1916 signatory Tom Clarke — recalled her grandmother's nationalist values being interwoven with the recital of the family rosary.

> My grandmother ... was a devout Catholic and took great pleasure in teaching us our prayers. At bedtime, we knelt around her and repeated the prayers after her. The first was always for Ireland's freedom, and when Uncle John was imprisoned (for Fenian activities), the second was for his release. Then we prayed for all the relatives alive and dead, ending up with 'God make a good child of me'. She was the kindest and most generous-hearted woman I ever met, with a fine broad outlook on life; she could see good in everyone and everything but England.

There is a limit to Christian charity, after all!

Kathleen Clarke's grandmother would have been proud that when Mrs Clarke became Lord Mayor of Dublin in 1939, her first action in office was to have the portrait of Queen Victoria removed from the walls of the Mansion House, the Mayor's official and historic residence, where it had reposed for half a century.

For many political women like Kathleen Clarke, Maud Gonne, Constance Markievicz and Charlotte Despard, there was no apparent conflict between the Fenian tradition and Catholicism, despite the fact that the Catholic Church had rained denunciations on Fenianism, for its resort to violence and its challenge of authority.

But women do not compartmentalise mental attitudes in the same way as men: women tolerate ambivalence and paradox more serenely, thus apparently holding contradictory views, but actually achieving what computer buffs nowadays admire as "fuzzy logic". A passionate male Irish nationalist of old who identified with the Fenians would turn his back on the church: indeed, the first signs of a young man having become a Fenian was that he stopped going to the sacraments. Moreover, the Church would sometimes refuse the sacraments to those known to have Fenian inclinations: in 1909, a group of "Fianna" scouts, who formed a Nationalist version of the Boy Scout movement, were actually refused Holy Communion on the grounds that their movement supported the tradition of violent uprising.

But the women were different. Irish nationalist women found it perfectly comfortable to reconcile, in their own consciences, their Catholicism and violent nationalism. Charlotte Despard, who was Lord French's sister, was a Republican, a socialist, a feminist and a financial backer of a Bolshevik-inspired group called *Saor Eire*; she actually approved of the assassination attempt on her brother, who, in 1920, was Lord Lieutenant of Ireland.

And yet, Charlotte Despard was also an extremely devout Catholic — a convert from Anglicanism. Constance Markievicz, also a Catholic convert, wrote pious, even mawkishly religious, poetry, and was yet an ardent supporters of the Bolsheviks, who the Church had denounced in their every manifestation. Not only was there a distinct group of Catholic Irish women nationalists who supported violent rebellion, but women who became attracted to Irish nationalism almost invariably became ardent Catholics as well, if they had not been brought up as such. Maud Gonne and Constance Markievicz fell into this category, as did Dorothy Macardle, the noted author of *The Irish Republic*, which was to become the definitive text of the events after 1916. Miss Macardle, employing a masculine logic at one point, quarrelled with the Catholic Church over its disapproval of the Republicans, but was reconciled before her death in the care of the Medical Missionaries of Mary. Another most influential and altogether typical convert to Irish nationalism and Catholicism was the best-selling author Annie M.P. Smithson, whose novels sometimes went into more than 70 print-runs. Brought up as an Irish Protestant and Unionist, she became a passionate convert to Irish nationalism and Catholicism, and all her books carry the values of her conversion (like Maud Gonne, she retained one pointed criticism of Irish Catholicism and nationalism: it was not kind enough to animals).

Catholicism in Ireland was so marked by the traditions of the mother and of femininity that women seemed to feel at ease with it, whether they were political or not. While priests and priestly power — priestcraft, as it was sometimes called — were regarded with the greatest suspicion by Anglicans and other Protestants, women usually wrote sympathetically about the priests. Joyce Collis, born towards the end of the 19th century into a distinguished Irish Protestant medical family, wrote a charming autobiography, *The Sparrow Hath Found Herself a Nest*, in which she describes, with a sense of surprise, the reticence of the Irish priest. Her family and friends had warned her that the priests would get at her in some occult way; they were, she had been told, trained in crafty psychological tricks which could seize the unwary.

Yet far from being the object of the priests' manipulations, she had the greatest difficulty making the acquaintance of a Catholic priest at all. People of her milieu seldom mixed with

Catholics, and the few Catholics she knew never spoke about their religion at all, out of a kind of a delicacy.

Then a woman she knew slightly became a housekeeper to a priest. "I used to go often to the presbytery to see her, and noticed a shy-looking priest going about, but contrary to what I had always heard in regard to priests, he did not try to press his company upon me in any way. In fact, he seemed positively to wish to avoid me at all costs." She observed him, nonetheless, with his bashful ways, and in the end it was not anything he said to her but how he behaved that impressed her. "During my short acquaintence with this priest I had been impressed by something in his aspect which I had never noticed before in clergymen … which I can best define as a kind of cheerful holiness, a quality I have since remarked in nearly all priests." Joyce Collis saw in Catholic priests both supernatural grace and a winning refinement. "The refining influence of Catholic teaching is such that even the roughest and most uncouth of men are usually gentlemen at the end of their seminary training … In my experience the refining effect of the Church works through the whole Catholic body and is particularly noticeable in the bearing of some of our people from the South and West of Ireland. The religious fervour and easy courtesy of such people was in fact one of the things that attracted me towards the Church."

Women born within the reign of Queen Victoria (and perhaps many women to this day) liked this idea of refinement. And as Lecky had observed, Catholicism seemed to have a refining and a softening effect on those who had embraced it. A cultivating effect too. The writer Katharine Tynan, a cradle Catholic and a good friend to Yeats, described the Irish priesthood in terms of kindness, culture, gentleness and the hospitality of country priests in the early years of the century. She describes the parish houses she visited as "full of books and … of spiritual and intellectual brightness, whatever the weather", recalling most particularly the priests she had known who were scholars of classical learning. For the critics of Catholicism, such as Michael MacCarthy in his excoriating *Priests and People in Ireland,* these womanly indulgences were precisely what made the Irish priests lazy, idle, lax in enforcing morals — unlike the energetic Protestant Evangelicals — and far too prone to the Sunday amusements of hurling, football, coursing, rabbit-hunting and cycling.

"There is no doubt that religion was very important in the lives of women," writes Maureen Langan-Egan in an absorbing study of women in Co Mayo in the 19th century. "Belief in God sustained them in the difficult lives they led. Devotion to Our Lady and the locally revered Saints made religion a very personal experience for them. Women (in the Mayo records) are anxious about religious observance such as attendance at Mass and reception of the Sacraments of Baptisms, Marriage and the Last Rites." This is also true among Protestant and Quaker women in Mayo: women were active in evangelising and in temperance movements (the temperance movements attracted women at all levels; in the United States, Prohibition was virtually a "woman's movement").

Religious ceremonial also provided merriment and entertainment. While the primary devotion was the rosary, notes Mrs Langan-Egan, there were other traditional Irish devotions too "such as patterns, pilgrimages, holy wells". (Patterns were devotions to a patron saint.) Occasionally, bishops would warn that some of these religious traditions bordered on the pagan, but if the women wanted to practise them, they tended to do so whether the bishop liked it or not. Pilgrimages, as we know from the *Canterbury Tales*, have always had a charabanc element, besides a devotional purpose. Irish pilgrimages traditionally had a strong social side: occasionally, too, a fight would break out.

The practice of stations, described so well in Alice Taylor's charming text *To School Through the Fields*, was extremely important to women in Mayo in times gone by. The home had become an important location of religious practice in Penal times because Catholicism was prohibited in the public realm and whatever becomes practised in the home becomes feminised. After Catholic Emancipation in 1829, Catholic churches in public grew in number and confidence of architecture, yet rural women were sometimes so poor that they would not have a respectable set of clothes in which to go to the church: this was an important dimension of self-respect for women. And thus the "stations" evolved, as Mass and devotions, on a rota basis, were held in the homes of the people.

Poor as they were, these women sewed and embroidered beautiful devotional samplers (some of which can be seen at the Knock Folk Museum in Co Mayo), generally on a theme of Marian devotion. One piece of needlework from the Famine year of 1846, worked by Mary Lucas of Curlody, is particularly lovely. The stitching reads:

> At morning's dawn, at evening's shade —
>   Mary, to thee we call for aid
> At every breath while swift it flies —
>   Mary, to thee our souls arise.
> Yes, yes, thy dear and sacred name —
>   Till life's last breath shall be our theme.
> Mary! our guide from childhood's day —
>   Mary! to thee, to thee, we pray.

This tradition of Marian devotion in Ireland was proudly and passionately invoked by Irishwomen as a kind of feminist spirituality. In her widely read and well-loved book of 1938, *The Queen of Ireland*, Helena Concannon claims that this special Irish devotion to Our Lady goes back to the era of St Patrick, who spoke of the Mother of God. She cites a mediaeval Irish litany to the Blessed Virgin which gives the flavour of this passionate, poetic and feminine tradition of devotion: "O Gate of Heaven: O Golden Casket: O Couch of Love and Mercy: O Temple of Divinity: O Beauty of Virgins: O Mistress of the Tribes: O Fountain of the Gardens: O Cleansing of the Senses: O Washing of the Souls: O Mother of the Orphans: O Breast of the Infants: O Solace of the Wretched: O Regeneration of Life: O Beauty of Women: O Enclosed Garden: O Mother of God."

It is considered linguistically significant that the Irish language had a special proper name for the Blessed Virgin Mary, distinct from the everyday name of Mary itself: *Mhuire*, which means the one and only Mary. The usual form of greeting in Irish — *Dia 's Mhuire dhuit* (God and Mary be with you) — again underlines how deep the roots of Marian devotion were in Irish. Ernest Blythe, a Presbyterian nationalist in the early de Valera administration, allegedly tried to introduce an Irish-language form of greeting acceptable to his Ulster co-religionists: *Dia 's John Knox dhuit* (God and John Knox be with you), as an alternative for the non-Marian Protestants.

The ardour of feminine devotion was not, of course, restricted to rural women in Ireland, though it was more marked in rural life — and still evident in wayside Marian shrines and grottoes. But it was also characteristic of life in the Dublin slums, as was quite faithfully reflected by Sean O'Casey, with his strong, devotional tenement mothers. "Even the most barren tenement rooms always had the ubiquitous oil lamp with red shade burning in front of a statue of the Sacred Heart which kept flickering hope just barely alive," writes Kevin Kearns in his study of Dublin slum life in the early 20th century. "It has been said, with much truth, that men had their local pub while women had the parish church." It was suggested in many of the critical books written about Catholic Ireland in the early years of the century, that Catholicism increased women's passivity, especially in the face of such afflictions as high infant mortality and consumption: this was not exact, in that Catholic organisations took up the fight against consumption quite actively, especially emphasising women's role in learning how to introduce hygiene into the home.

But the faith certainly provided a solace against those ills for which there were few remedies. Kevin Kearns also writes that the women's faith in these Dublin's slums had a moralising effect on the Dublin poor. Because of their religion, the Dublin poor had a "high moral character". Crime was neither widespread nor vicious. "Robberies, vandalism, muggings and sexual crimes were virtually unknown ... People walked the streets at all hours without fear of violation. Most robberies ... were those of the desperately poor breaking into their own penny gas meters to extract money for food."

Through home, prayers, feminine traditions and familial ties, the mothers transmitted the faith which they saw as upholding and expressing their values and their beliefs. Sometimes mothers and grandmothers used the faith as a form of moral control in the home and even within the wider community. Almost without exception, they upheld, supported and endorsed the power of the priests.

Mother Ireland and Mother Church would coexist in the system of matriarchal values. Until it came to the revolutionary period of 1916, when Mother Ireland would challenge Mother Church for possession of the soul of the nation.

Three

1916 and the Spirit of Sacrifice

"The founding act of the modern Irish State — the 1916 Rising — is a religious as much as a political act, and conceived by its leader, Patrick Pearse, as such."

Fintan O'Toole, *Black Hole, Green Card:*
The Disappearance of Ireland (1994)

"The Irish are the most religious soldiers in the British Army; and it is because they are religious that they rank so high among the most brave."

Michael MacDonagh, *The Irish at the Front* (1916)

The Easter Rising of 1916 came to be widely regarded as the founding act of the modern Irish State: what 1776 was to the United States, what 1789 was to the Republic of France, or what the October Revolution of 1917 was to Bolshevik Russia. This is the sacramental act which brought into being the new state — Eire, or Ireland, at Easter 1916.

Originally, Catholic Ireland was profoundly against this act. Home Rule for Ireland had been agreed (in the teeth of opposition from Ulster Unionists) before the First World War of 1914. Home Rule would have been what we describe today as devolution. There would not have been a full break with the Crown, but self-rule within the British family of nations. But Home Rule was deferred for the course of the Great War, as it was called (as were votes for women: Mrs Pankhurst withdrew her demonstrations and threw herself behind the war effort).

Catholic Ireland backed the British Empire to the hilt, certainly at the start. The Catholic Leader of the Irish Parliamentary Party, John Redmond, the bishops, the clergy, and the Catholic popular press all saw the need to support Great Britain — not to mention France, and "Catholic Belgium" — against the German onslaught. My uncle Kevin Kenny, a brilliant advertising man and a militant Dublin Catholic, obtained the British Army account for recruitment of soldiers in Ireland. His winning slogan was: "Fight for Catholic Belgium." This was most effective.

From 1914 onwards, the devotional press was full of prayers for "our brave Irish Tommies". Contempt for pacifists of any kind was not unusual in the Catholic press, as elsewhere. A special hero of the *Irish Catholic* newspaper was Father Bernard Vaughan (he also makes an appearance in James Joyce's *Ulysses*), a London preacher and brother of Cardinal Vaughan who was an especial pulpit scourge of those opposed to, or shirking from, the war. The first two years of the First World War, from 1914 to 1916, were treated in triumphalist manner generally. It was very little understood, in everyday life, just how disastrous an enterprise the generals on both sides had embarked upon.

Then in Dublin, at Easter 1916, a group of rebels led by the mystical nationalist Patrick Pearse, and the socialist nationalist James Connolly, mounted a surprise rising against British rule. The Rising lasted merely a week, when Pearse, whose conscience was disturbed by the loss of human life, agreed to a surrender. The Irish bishops did not issue a collective statement but there was widespread condemnation of the event from Church sources. The *Irish Catholic* called the Easter Rising "partially socialistic and partially alien": this "alien" element was a covert reference to Pearse's gratitude to "gallant allies in Europe" in the Proclamation of the Republic. The "gallant allies" meant Germany, which the Irish Catholic Church regarded with great hostility, not only because it was at war with the Crown, but because Bismarck had placed severe restrictions on the Catholic Church in his *kulturkampf*, and had made an enemy of the Church. Germany was frequently described in the Catholic Irish press as a Lutheran power. The

Church did not esteem Sinn Féin for "acting under German inspiration", and Dublin Castle — the seat of British rule in Ireland — was criticised for being lax in not preventing this insurrection.

Many individual bishops condemned the Easter Rising in their sermons, and the Vatican expressed its wishes that order be restored as soon as possible in Dublin. The Catholic Church at this time was inordinately careful never to support rebellion, following St Paul's doctrine that a legitimate authority should be accepted. The idea of overthrowing authority was almost heretical. It was pointed out that the saintly Pope Pius IX had pronounced anathema on those who replaced constitutional means by armed rebellion.

Public opinion was not, initially, supportive of the Easter Rising. John Horgan, a prominent Cork lawyer and Gaelic League supporter, writing in his memoirs in 1947, recalled that the Rising had been "universally and explosively unpopular." His own father wrote of the leaders of the Rising: "May God save Ireland from such devils."

My mother heard the news, as a young girl home from school on holiday, while visiting a local shop in the village of Kilconnell, Co Galway. "Blast it anyway," said the shopkeeper. "A rising in Dublin! That'll interfere with all my supplies." The war economy was actually boosting everyday commercial life in Ireland, and trade was brisk. Mother regarded news of the rebellion as an exciting distraction from the *longueurs* of village life, but my grandmother, a cultural supporter of Sinn Féin, reacted with anxiety.

Yet when the 15 rebel leaders were executed by firing squad (the 16th, Roger Casement, was to be hanged as a traitor later, in August that year), the mood was to change, first gradually, and then inexorably. Yeats recognised this when he wrote that celebrated line: "A terrible beauty is born."

The leaders were tried and executed quickly, within three weeks of the insurrection. They died with valour and, almost without exception, with an inspiring sense of religious martyrdom. James Connolly, too wounded to stand for the rifle volley of the execution squad, had to be strapped to his chair. And, though a Communist, he received the last rites of the Holy Catholic Church.

The priests who attended the condemned men were mostly, though not exclusively, Capuchin monks, who were less controlled by, or deferential to, the hierarchy of bishops. They spoke for many years afterwards of the piety, fortitude and sweet acceptance shown by the men of 1916 in the face of death. Of Joseph Mary Plunkett, a signatory of the Proclamation and a son of Count Plunkett, the Capuchin Father Augustine wrote: "His face reminded me of St Francis, and 'Welcome, Sister Death'."

John MacBride, the estranged husband of Maud Gonne, whom Yeats called "a drunken, vainglorious lout" in his celebrated poem of 1916, was seemingly transformed by the 1916 experience. "On reaching the prison I was immediately shown to a cell and on its being opened I gripped the hand of Major MacBride," wrote Father Augustine. Major MacBride was "quiet and natural" with the Capuchin priest. He expressed "sorrow for the surrender" and then, "placing his Rosary tenderly in my hand, he uttered a little sentence that thrilled me: 'And give that to my Mother.'" ("Thrill", at this time, meant "startle" or "amaze".) "Then, having given me a message for another that convinced me he was a man of very deep faith, he began his Confession with the simplicity and humility of a child. After a few minutes I gave him Holy Communion and we spent some while together in prayer."

The priest promised to be with MacBride until the end and duly accompanied him to the execution yard. The prisoner asked not to be blindfolded, but the British soldier replied, "Sorry, sir, but these are our orders." Just before the firing squad began, the priest felt moved to whisper in MacBride's ear: "We are all sinners. Offer up your life for any faults or sins of the past." Then, "this brave man, fearless of death, responds like a child, yet firmly: 'I'm glad you told me that, Father. I will.'" The volleys rang out and MacBride fell down dead.

Each and every 1916 execution took similar patterns of holiness, humility and courage from the rebels — all recorded by Piaras MacLochlainn in his book *Last Words* — and, in several cases, courtesy and respect from the British firing squads. Sean MacDermot (MacDiarmada), the Co Leitrim tram worker, lame from childhood polio, wrote tenderly to his brothers and sisters: "By the time this reaches you, I will, with God's mercy, have joined in heaven, my poor father and mother as well as my dear friends who have been shot during the week ... I have priests with me almost constantly for the past twenty-four hours." The condemned man felt a happiness "the like of which I have never experienced in my life before". The priest who was with him until the end — a doctor of divinity from Maynooth rather than a friar of the people — wrote a not very good, yet deeply felt poem to MacDiarmada's simple heroism. But then virtually everyone involved with Easter 1916 wrote poetry, often with a religious flavour, including Connolly, the trade unionist and Countess Markievicz, the feminist sympathiser with the Bolsheviks.

The deaths of the 1916 men were told and retold, around the country, as perfect Christian parables. Thomas MacDonagh, whose last lecture as an academic had been about the pleasures of Jane Austen's prose ("There's no one like Jane," were his parting words to his students), died "with the Crucifix clasped in his hands ... with no rancour in his heart, with his courage high and unshaken and with a firm faith in the Saviour by whose Precious Blood we are redeemed."

Sean Heuston, aged 25, and one of Countess Markievicz's "Fianna" scouts — a scouting movement with an Irish-Ireland flavour which she had launched at the height of Gaelic League enthusiasm — knelt for many hours with Father Albert, the Capuchin, while they prayed to "St Patrick, St Brigid, St Colmcille and all the saints of Ireland: we said many times the beautiful ejaculatory prayer 'Jesus, Mary and Joseph, I give you my heart and my soul' which appealed very much to him." The last quarter of an hour of his life was passed in a kind of religious ecstasy. Dublin's finest railway station, built by the British at the height of Victorian rococo, is named after this deeply religious 1916 signatory.

As for Con Colbert, Pearse's most special lieutenant who had, according to the historian Edward Norman, once been a circus acrobat and went on to be a gym instructor, his death was so brave and so glorious that one of the British soldiers who witnessed it wept and said: "If only we could die such deaths." Soldiers admire heroic deaths, and think better of a man who dies willingly for his country.

According to Father Augustine, the veteran Capuchin who witnessed the scene, the British soldier, before binding the arms of Con Colbert for the firing squad, first shook his hands. And so, "his lips moving in prayer, the brave lad went forth to die." In Irish republican mythology, to die before a firing squad was much more honourable than to be sent to the gallows. "Shoot me like a soldier — do not hang me like a dog," went a celebrated line from a traditional ballad.

And thus it was with all of them. Even the hardened old Fenian Tom Clarke — who had a long-standing quarrel with the Church, which had so repeatedly condemned the secret Fenian brotherhood — like James Connolly, apparently died a Catholic death. Roger Casement, a homosexual whose diaries revealed him to be a paedophile with erotic fantasies of pubescent boys (though these are still regarded by some Irish people as maliciously forged by the British), also died an intensely Catholic death in the arms of Mother Church.

Patrick Pearse, the acknowledged leader, was a man of intense, even perhaps mawkish, religious faith. Some Catholics even in his own time regarded his metaphors of Ireland as a crucified Christ, and a reawakened Ireland redeemed through a risen Christ, as wrong-headed, even verging on the blasphemous. Jesus Christ is not supposed to serve mystical nationalism but redemptive, universal Christianity. Nevertheless, it is the case that religion mattered to him as much as an independent Ireland. The night before Patrick Pearse died, what was most on his mind was the question of James Connolly's reconcilation with the Lord. "Thank God!" Pearse exclaimed, when he heard that Connolly had seen the priest and received Communion. "It is the one thing I was anxious about."

James Connolly's decision to embrace the rites of the Catholic Church on his deathbed, when he had been a Socialist, a Marxist and a Communist — by definition atheistic at this time — has never been really explained. Connolly was not a cynical man — honesty was his ruling passion — and it is unlikely that he would have done this for cynical reasons. The accepted interpretation is that "something came over him", that he was struck by a sense of the sacred during his last moments on earth. Connolly's death can be seen as an example of the way in which Catholic values tend to seep into Irish identity; or indeed that God works in mysterious ways.

Patrick Pearse, whose younger brother Willie was also executed with him (mainly just for being his younger brother), went to his death utterly fulfilled and happy. "I have just received Holy Communion," he wrote to his mother before dying. "I am happy except for the great grief of parting from you. This is the death I should have asked for if God had given me the choice of all deaths — to die a soldier's death for Ireland and for freedom."

Towards the end of the 20th century, some historians and commentators came to regard the events of 1916 as a hysterical evocation of Catholic-nationalist sentimentality, with macabre, unwholesome and sectarian undertones. The revisionist view now is that it did no favours to the cause of a united, or even an agreed, Ireland. It was just too Catholic altogether, in its language, imagery and martyrdom. The blood sacrifice, the crown of thorns, the sorrowing *mater dolorosas*, the rosaries recited solidly by the rebels during Easter Week, came to be seen as something which excluded Protestants, Nonconformists, Non-believers and those of other faiths, thus betraying the Wolfe Tone ideal of replacing the word "Irishman" for Catholic, Protestant or dissenter.

Indeed, it not only excluded Protestants — its mystical imagery was actually repellent to them. In his most prescient memoir, John Horgan made this point, which other historians would take up a generation later. "[1916] made Partition inevitable, it furnished the necessary excuse for the civil war of 1922 and it still plagues the rulers of a divided Ireland." Horgan thought Pearse "blasphemous" for turning nationalism into a religion.

In a highly influential essay published in 1971 (suppressed in 1966, the 50th anniversary of the Rising) Father Francis Shaw, SJ, dismembered Patrick Pearse as a national icon. Pearse was, said Father Shaw, "aggressively unorthodox" in his sanctimoniousness: the men of 1916 were way out of line when comparing Jesus carrying a Cross for human redemption to themselves carrying a cross for Ireland. The "blood sacrifice" element of 1916 was highly unpleasant: Pearse had said that "bloodshed is a cleansing and a sanctifying thing, and the nation which regards it as the final horror has lost its manhood." He had prefaced this with the oration: "We must accustom ourselves to the thought of arms, to the sight of arms, to the use of arms. We may make mistakes in the beginning and shoot the wrong people ..." This offhand reference to the unfortunate error of shooting the wrong people as a kind of preamble to cleansing and sanctifying bloodshed was deplorable, Father Shaw pointed out. It provided an excuse for appalling and unjustified bloodshed in Northern Ireland in the 1970s.

The paradox about the Catholic character of the 1916 Rising was this: the Irish Church itself did not advance this blood-sacrifice Catholicism at the time. The bishops deplored the whole thing. But it appealed to the mysticism and sacrificial element within the people, once it became known. Because the people responded to the sacrifice of the dead leaders, the Church was subsequently carried along on this tide of enthusiasm, for the Catholic Church in Ireland is seldom out of step, for too long, with the people.

For it was the word-of-mouth excitement about the holiness of the 1916 rebels which seems to have appealed to the people. Stories spread quickly throughout the country of the religious and sacrificial nature of the Rising itself: this was not a mere rebellion against the proper authority — it was a beautiful and voluntary martyrdom. The British Prime Minister, Lloyd George, was most alarmed not just by the news that there was a rebellion in Dublin, but by reports that little Irish girls were already praying to "St Pearse", and that Con Colbert, Pearse's pure-thinking young adjutant, had already shown proof that he was in heaven by granting a spiritual favour.

And yet, though the Rising of 1916 was so intensely Catholic, and so profoundly Irish (not least, as Terry Eagleton has pointed out, in its impassioned theatricality), it was not disconnected to the spirit of the age elsewhere. The values which animated it were quite similar to those prevailing among young radicals in Germany, France, England, Russia and Serbia. Easter 1916 was but the mystical Irish-Catholic version of the *Zeitgeist*, that spirit-of-the-age fever for sacrifice and patriotism, for poetry and drama (including self-drama), and for combat as art, which marked that generation of 1914.

The generation of 1914 was a special phenomenon. This was the generation born in the 1880s, which was the beginning of what we would call modernity. The 1880s were an optimistic time. Ordinary life was measurably beginning to improve. Infant mortality was starting to drop quite appreciably. And infant mortality, the death of new-born babies, is not just a medical statistic. It affects the entire notion of individuality, and alters perspectives about attachment and ambition. As parents develop confidence that their children will survive, so they become, paradoxically, more child-centred, more focused on the education of the child and more ambitious for its future.

This generation was indeed one that was pulsating with ideas, and feverishly excited by the artistic and creative activity swirling around in its aura. The late 19th century had produced radicalism and secularism; but following that, and perhaps in reaction against it, came a romanticism and an idealism which came to be added to revolutionary theories in art, politics and life.

The intellectual movements which were so much astir in Dublin in the 1900-14 period, which led up to all the drama of 1916, were most definitely a "youth culture" of the time. What Mary Colum, a young American student, most observed about Dublin in 1907 was that "everything seemed to be run by the young". The city was all a maelstrom of poetry, art, drama, conversation, mysticism, high talk, political ideas and general animation. "The intellectual excitement brought into our lives by the theatre, its dramatists and the literary movement generally roused our minds to more of a pitch than all the [formal] learning we were imbibing ..."

Mrs Colum notes, with a feminine eye, a detail that other observers might have overlooked: the way in which costume was changing so swiftly. There were so many costume eccentrics, and a great vogue for Celtic dressing in kilts, capes and flowing gowns.

"The city was not too large and it was not difficult to take part in every intellectual proceeding in the whole town: we [young people] were visible at every artistic and intellectual function — exhibitions of pictures, private views, meetings ... We were young and eager, and this was our way of having a grand time. We were not satisfied to go to one performance of each of the plays [at the Abbey Theatre in Dublin], but went to every performance until we knew the plays by heart. Our excitement was so great that we would stay awake most of the night discussing the play."

Their elders disapproved of all this excitement and staying up late, which of course greatly enhanced the pleasure.

But similar feelings were being experienced by the same generation elsewhere. In England, Virgina Woolf said that this generation was simply different from all others that had gone before: human nature, she proclaimed, changed "on or about December 1910". In Germany, Carl Zuckmeyer, who was to become the leading playwright of his time, came up with the same thought, though quite separately; he dated this striking change in human nature as being "somewhere between 1911 and 1913". It was, he said, during these two years that the works of Kafka and Werfel (an expressionist poet and dramatist described as "an ecstatic sensitive") began appearing in the windows of Zuckmeyer's local Rhineland bookstore.

Suddenly, it seemed, his generation spoke of nothing but expressionism: this was to them what the Rolling Stones and The Who were to the youth of the 1960s — "talkin' about my generation". The generation gap was born, not in the 1960s, but around 1910-12. Stefan Zweig, the Austrian Jewish writer who so captured the Vienna of the 1900s in his memoirs, emphasised how this generation gap seemed to flow across all frontiers at the time, so that youth pulsated with a heightened collective self-consciousness. And youth yearned for the new, discarding the old. "We found the new ... because we hungered for something that belonged to us alone and not to the world of our fathers." Poetry, art and drama were instantly transmitted from one culture to another, even before electronic media. "We scented the wind before it crossed the frontier, because we constantly lived with quivering nostrils."

"It was *our* time, *our* world, *our* sense of life that came rushing upon me, falling upon me, and suddenly I awakened to the consciousness of a new generation, a consciousness that even the most intelligent, most aware and unbiased parents could not share," wrote Carl Zuckmeyer. The whole idea of a generation as a peer group, had started. Zuckmeyer in his small German town and Mary Colum in Dublin were gripped by the same spirit of the age.

Filippo Marinetti, an Italian futurist, was hugely influential over that generation, perhaps rather as Herbert Marcuse was with the generation of 1968. Marinetti believed people should live out drama, not merely watch it. Young people should make artistic expression part of their political lives — an uncannily true description of the way in which artistic and political events were developing in Ireland, where a rebellion was to be led by poets, and where the event itself was perceived as a culmination of an artistic movement. "A work of art," as the French critic Maurice Golding has called Easter 1916: thus the perfect Marinetti act.

And yet, what also marked the generation of 1914, was a self-sacrificing idealism and a willingness to throw themselves on the altar of national purification. The themes in poetry written by the Irish poets of 1916, with their allegories of blood and wine, their attachment to Christian imagery, were present similarly in the work of English poets. As Paul Fussell has written in his memorable study *The Great War and Modern Memory*, the "religio-erotic" (and sometimes the "homoerotic", though of the chaste love genre) was a common and prominent theme in the artistic imagination of the 1914 generation. Patrick Pearse was captivated by the idea of the beauty of young men facing death or dying: such images are similarly present in the war poetry of Wilfred Owen and Siegfried Sassoon. As Pearse sees Christ in the road to the Easter Rising, so Sassoon sees Christ in the trenches as 'The Prince of Wounds'. Wilfred Owen, the young English poet (almost certainly, too, a homosexual in temperament, as Patrick Pearse very likely was), frequently sees God on the battlefield.

Owen, who died just as the armistice was declared, had many parallels with Pearse. He too had a brother who died on the battlefield. He too had a mother, Susan Owen, who, like Margaret Pearse, afterwards devoted her life to serving her son's memory.

In Germany, also, the generation of 1914 was animated by sentiments of purity and sacrifice. Ernest Wurche was the idealized German soldier portrayed in a book which became a sensational best-seller in Germany, *Wanderer Between Two Worlds*; published in 1917, it went through 39 editions and sold 250,000 copies in under two years. Wurche had been a paragon of the *Wandervogel* organisation, a hiking and boy-scout movement, rather like the Fianna.

He had been a Lutheran theology student and always took with him into battle a copy of the New Testament, the lyrical poetry of Goethe, and Nietzsche's *Thus Spake Zarathustra*, another of the cult texts of the time. Ernest Wurche's motto was "Remain pure and become mature" (Rein bliben und reif werden.") This was something very like the motto of the Fianna, in Ireland, Constance Markievicz's Republican boy scouts, which was "Strength in our arms, truth on our lips and purity in our hearts".

The German religious idealist Ernest Wurche would have approved of Pearse's speeches about the honour of taking up arms and the cleansing element of bloodshed: his ideals were the same. He also believed that in offering themselves up in war, men came close to the mystery of life. War was a moral test, and by the sacrifice of death, life was eternally regenerated. This is the very kernel of 1916. Life springs from death, Pearse said in his famous oration at the grave of O'Donovan Rossa in 1915, "and from the graves of patriot men and women spring living nations".

This spirit of sacrifice was the spirit of the age, as Robert Wohl describes it in his study *The Generation of 1914*. One young German 1914 volunteer wrote in a letter home: "We fight for our *Volk* and spill our blood and hope that the survivors are worthy of our sacrifice. For me, it is the struggle for an idea, the *Fata Morgana* of a pure, true, noble Germany, free from wickedness and deceit. And even if we go down to defeat with this hope in our hearts, it is probably better than to have been victorious and to see that it was only an outer victory without improving men within." The triumph of failure. Indeed, the triumph of failure is the theme of another key German work of the period — Fritz von Unruh's expressionist novel *Way of Sacrifice (Opfergang)*, written at Verdun in 1916. It was banned by the German general staff precisely because it affirmed the idea that winning or losing the war was of no consequence: what mattered was the beauty of sacrifice, and the way in which this would pass on a legacy to future generations. What mattered was to uphold "the creative function of death and the existence of a 'holy communion' with the fallen."

The slaughter of the First World War is often blamed on the blood-thirsty generals in command. But the generals, too, were part of the same spirit of the age, which worshipped soldierly sacrifice.

The events of 1916 were seen at the time in contradiction of the First World War: Britain regarded the Rising as not merely a vexation but a stab in the back while she was engaged in war on the Western Front. Yet 1916 could almost be seen as part of the First World War, and the sacrifices in Flanders Field very similar to those of Dublin at Easter.

Willie Redmond, the younger brother of John Redmond — leader of the Irish Parliamentary Party — was one of the few senior Catholic officers in the British Army in Ireland. He had a picture of the Blessed Virgin over his bed, and he took pride in marching his battalion, stationed at Fermoy, off to Mass. Willie, also an Irish M.P. at Westminster, made his last appearance in the House of Commons in March 1917, home briefly from the trenches. "Standing there, grey-haired and tired in his war-stained uniform," John Horgan wrote, "he expressed with simple dignity the thoughts uppermost in the minds of his comrades at the front, many of whom were to sacrifice their lives for Ireland." The Irishmen fighting with the Crown, in the trenches, also thought of themselves as "sacrificing their lives for Ireland" — since Home Rule was due to follow the conclusion of the Great War.

And it was an Ireland based on North-South cooperation which Willie Redmond had in mind. In his last letters to John Horgan, he wrote about the comradeship that he had forged with Ulster Loyalists, whom he had fought alongside. "I wish I had time to write you all I have seen out here. My men are splendid and we are pulling famously with the Ulster men. Would to God we could bring this spirit back with us to Ireland. I shall never regret I have been out here." When Willie Redmond was killed, his body was carried to burial by those Ulster Loyalist comrades who had themselves lost so many men in the slaughter of the Somme.

Contrary to the impression given by Frank McGuinness in his celebrated play *Observe the Sons of Ulster Marching Towards the Somme* — in which the Orangemen fight for King Billy and in contempt of all Papist culture — there was much cooperation between Irishmen North and South, Catholic and Protestant, in this terrible theatre of war. According to Michael MacDonagh, writing in 1917, Irish Catholics and Protestants even said prayers together, and Irish Protestants accepted Catholic medals as amulets of good luck. "Yesterday we were reciting the Litany of the Sacred Heart while the shells were annoying us," wrote a Catholic Irishman. "I was reading the beautiful praises and titles of the Litany, and both my Protestant and Catholic mates were answering me with great fervour." Every night the Irish would say the rosary in the trenches, and the prayers would be joined in by all. Other witnesses, too, attested to the ecumenical endeavours of Irishmen fighting together at the front. As MacDonagh remarks, at times of battle, secular images seem cold and comfortless next to the religious symbols which seem to have more power to touch the human heart.

The sacrifices made in the Great War were immense, and for so much of the 20th century were ignored or occluded by official Ireland, which iconised 1916 as a unique event. In 1966 C.S. Andrews — an old IRA man who became a powerful political figure in the Free State — suggested to the then Taoiseach Sean Lemass that the Easter 1916 celebrations should be widened to honour the Irishmen who died in the Great War.

Andrews always remembered the friends and neighbours he knew who had gone off to the Western Front so willingly. Mr Lemass turned down the suggestion, saying it was now "too late". Yet it was not too late in 1994: a more generous-minded attitude began to prevail in Dublin, not least, I would suggest, due to the campaigning work of *The Irish Times* journalist Kevin Myers, who insistently reminded his readers of the Irish participation in the 1914 war. In a memorable essay he wrote for the Abbey theatre he recalled some of the Irishmen who had died in that conflict: forty different Irishmen called Patrick Byrne; five brothers, the Furies, from Castlerea, Co Galway, who all died within the first ten months of the outbreak of war; and John Condon, the drummer boy from Waterford, who died at Ypres aged 14, the youngest soldier to fall. These too deserved to be honoured in death.

Catholic Ireland's involvement in the 1914-18 war can be measured by the poignant requests for prayers for men at the Front sent in to the *Messenger of the Sacred Heart*. "An Irish officer thanks the Sacred Heart for escape during a recent bombardment." "A mother thanks the Sacred Heart for the recovery of her son from severe wounds received at Beaumont." "Infantryman thanks the Sacred Heart for protection during twenty-two months in France." "A Mother's Prayer for her Soldier Son at the Front: Soothe in Thy Mercy all my fears/To me my darling spare ..." Obituaries and prayers for those who fell were also copiously reported, and the stories of grief seem assuaged by the comforts of the faith. (After the Great War, there was a surge of conversions to Catholicism because of its care for the dead, to which other Christian faiths took a more austere approach.)

In wartime service in France, "Irish Tommies" were urged to benefit from the spiritual opportunities there. Lourdes and Notre Dame were to be visited, and holy places such as Lisieux too. The Catholic papers were sometimes anxious that there might not be enough chaplains to serve at sea. On land, priests were regarded as a great comfort and often a heroic example to the men: 12,000 French priests served in the ranks, a fact which subsequently modified the former anti-clericalism of the French state.

In the *Irish Catholic,* a weekly feature appeared under the headline "Our Brave Priests": these faced the hazards of the battlefield to minister to the men, often at the risk of their own lives, and we should be proud of them. Father Willie Doyle, SJ became a noted example of a priest who showed reckless courage in bringing dying men the Last Rites, under the fire of battle, and was killed doing so: he too was somewhat in the mould of Patrick Pearse, open to self-sacrifice.

Father Gleason of the Munster Fusiliers, described by Robert Graves in *Goodbye to All That* as "jovial Father Gleason", became something of a legend. "When all the officers were killed or wounded at Ypres, [he] had stripped off black badges [of the clergy] and taking command of the survivors, held the line." Michael MacDonagh quotes a soldier's view of Francis Gleason: "There's no man at the Front more brave or cooler. Why, it is in the hottest place up in the firing line, he do be there to give comfort to the boys that are dying." There were many other Irish priests like this: Father John Gwynn of Youghal, who went on administering the sacraments even when he was dying himself; Father James Stack, mentioned for courage and leadership in Field Marshal Lord French's valedictory despatch; Father Fahey of Tipperary, who served with great distinction at Gallipoli; Father Donal O'Sullivan from Killarney, Co Kerry, "a fine character, cheerful and energetic", and just a year ordained when killed by a shell.

If a priest survived the battlefield, he would try, afterwards, to visit the family of the fallen: this was of great comfort to the family, to know that a priest had been with a young man at the last, and they would talk about this together.

The Irish Catholic priests were, at the time of the Great War, quite evidently with the Allies. When Roger Casement tried to win over some Irish prisoners of war in a German camp to the cause of Rebellion, the chaplain in charge regarded his endeavours as treason. An Irish Dominican, Father Crotty, told the Irishmen that even though "the German Emperor" wanted them to fight on his side, it was their duty as "good Catholics to keep the oath you have taken to be loyal to your King". The men preferred to do as their priest advised them and rebuffed Casement's pleas.

The Great War of 1914-18 underwent a crucial change, itself, in 1916. Until this halfway point, it had been pursued in a spirit of soldierly courage and manly idealism — on all sides. But the year 1916 proved to be a climax and a turning-point. The terrible losses at Verdun (French losses — 315,000 men, German losses — 281,000 men) and the nightmare of the Somme (60,000 casualties on the opening morning, July 1) signalled the end of the triumphalist phase of the war and the onset of disillusion and war-weariness. In all, British casualties at the Somme numbered 420,000; the French lost nearly 200,000; the Germans 450,000. The British comedian Rowan Atkinson cracked a dark joke in a popular television series of 1990, *Blackadder,* to the effect that "we might as well have stayed at home and shot 50,000 men a week", which emphasised to an end-of-century generation just how unspeakable the conditions had been.

(Between 1915 and 1917 the Pope, Benedict XV, tried to mediate for peace, though he got scant thanks for it, and each side suspected he was siding with the other.)

"By the winter of 1916-17," writes the historian Paul Johnson, "the war-lust was spent." In Ireland, the enthusiasm for a new age of patriotism was just beginning, and in the year of 1917 feelings of nationalism began to grow quite passionately.

The Crown handled the Rising of 1916 maladroitly. With the perspective of time, we can see that the execution of 16 rebellious Irishman was as nothing against the backdrop of the Western Front; or indeed the backdrop of execution for mutiny or desertion which the British and French commanders pursued quite ruthlessly. The British court-martialled and executed over 300 of their men at the front for alleged cowardice and sabotage, though many of these soldiers were actually suffering from shell-shock. The French military authorities executed over five thousand on similar grounds, including mutiny. War had cheapened human life most horribly.

But in Ireland, the executions of the 1916 men, seen then in isolation, had a profound impact. In addition, the British most ill-advisedly tried to enforce conscription all over Ireland, after the early rush of volunteering had begun to dry up. This roused the ire of the Church, which did not agree with pressing a man

into war: a soldier served voluntarily. Prayers and novenas —
notably to Our Lady of Lourdes — started up all over the
country to "save Ireland from conscription" and this too fanned
the flames of nationalism. There was an Irish Convention of
1917, a forum designed to discuss some of the differences
between Dublin, London and Belfast, as a prelude to Home
Rule, but its waffling tone and rigmaroles of procedure
contrasted limply with the dramatic self-sacrifice of the men of
the 1916 Rising.

Thus, as time went on, the events of Easter 1916 gradually
flowered. Within 18 months of the Rising, a significant item was
to appear in the *Messenger of the Sacred Heart*. Eamon de Valera,
as a Sinn Féin candidate, had won Willie Redmond's
parliamentary seat in East Clare, signalling the end of the
moderate Home Rule party, and the beginning of a more
uncompromising nationalist Republicanism. The Catholic
Church did not initially approve of de Valera because he
appeared as a revolutionary overthrowing "the proper
authority", but they did warm to the devotional piety of his
wife, Sinead. The *Messenger* highlighted this in a special feature
about an English reporter who had visited Mrs de Valera at
home. "As I rose to leave," the Englishman wrote in the London
Evening Standard, "I noticed fastened upon the very centre of
the drawing-room door the figure of Christ, with these words:
'I will bless the Houses in which the image of My Heart shall be
exposed and honoured.' As we both paused before this
Presence [Mrs de Valera's] demeanour became one of devotion,
and wishful as I am to get at the inner meaning of the Sinn Féin
movement, I was emboldened to take the liberty of inquiring
about it."

The reporter asks Sinead de Valera if the Sacred Heart was
her husband's Leader. She replies quietly: "I placed it there out
of devotion to the Sacred Heart, and I believe my husband has
been spared as the result of our prayers for him."

This was underlined as a meaningful insight, and it marked
a change in the devotional literature towards Sinn Féin and the
events following 1916. Soon the prayers for "Our Brave Irish
Tommies" would be replaced by prayers and novenas for "Our
Brave Sinn Féin Prisoners". Catholic Ireland was, perhaps even

unconsciously, beginning to transfer its loyalties to the state about to be born from the "terrible beauty" of 1916.

Four

Goodbye to Protestant Ireland

"There was a widespread belief among Northern Protestants that the whole Sinn Féin rebellion and the demand for independence was being backed by the Catholic Church for its own ends ... The *News-Letter* (in November 1919) laid the blame for the violence squarely at the feet of the Church."

Dennis Kennedy, *The Widening Gulf*

"In the last few years, the Protestants have had to swallow many bitter pills. They have seen virtually a clean break with the traditions which they held very dear, which helped to make them what they are. But this country is still our country. We have thrown in our lot definitely and irrevocably with our country and we must stand by it now ..."

The Church of Ireland Gazette, 6 February, 1925

The ideologies of nationalism — ideologies which were growing throughout the 19th century all over Europe — often began with high ideals and lofty notions of brotherhood and equality. They often ended with civil wars, exclusion of minorities, expulsions, ethnic cleansing and a narrowly tribal definition of who belongs and who does not.

After 1918 — notes the historian Paul Johnson — and when the Treaty of Versailles awarded national status to smaller countries which had been incorporated in larger empires, each of these states began to oppress their own minorities. "All the various Diets and Parliaments, in Budapest, Prague, Graz and Innsbruck were arenas of merciless racial discord. In Galicia, the minority Ruthenians fought the majority Poles. In Dalmatia, the minority Italians fought the majority South Slavs."

Ireland too began to move inexorably towards separate status, from 1917 onwards. Contrary to the opinions of Ulster Unionist newspapers, the Catholic Church never backed rebellion, and it remained loyal to the rightful authority of Westminster until at least the end of the war in 1918. The Catholic press in Ireland was still running articles entitled "What Ireland is Doing for the Empire" in 1918. But gradually the Church itself would be drawn along by the undercurrent of popular feeling towards a separate Ireland. The Church joined in the protests against British conscription, and the ill-fated Conscription Bill of 1918 was to be a key landmark in Irish parliamentary politics. The Irish Parliamentary Party withdrew from the House of Commons in protest against this bill (which would have forced Irishmen to go to the war front) and returned temporarily to Ireland. They never went back to Westminster.

The stand against conscription was to unite what was in fact Catholic Ireland: the Irish Parliamentary Party, the trade unions, Sinn Féin, the Labour Party, the Catholic hierarchy and the Irish Volunteers. Ulster stood apart and considered the anti-conscription protest as a confounded display of disloyalty. The fissures which were to make partition inevitable were well under way.

By 1917, to support Sinn Féin was becoming the fashionable thing amongst the young; it was the equivalent of wearing an Aids ribbon at a Hollywood Oscars ceremony in our time. It was cool. Sinn Féin was, wrote P.S. O'Hegarty, an experienced Fenian who later became disillusioned, at that stage "a moral movement, ascetic and clean". A secret report by British military intelligence underlined this high moral tone and noted that no one associated with the movement was ever seen drunk. This was to change, later, when war and blood-letting made men coarse, and there is evidence that sectarian killings occurred under the influence of alcohol.

But the atmosphere in Ireland in 1917-18 was high on hope. "Although the trouble had not begun acutely in Ireland, "wrote Katharine Tynan in a vivid memoir, "no one had forgotten Easter Week 1916, and the youth of Ireland was wearing the Republican colours even when it was in the service of [British] Government officials. To have his chauffeur wearing the Republican colours was something to which the Resident Magistrate had to turn a blind eye." Resident Magistrates were the legal representatives of the Crown, and very seldom were they Catholic.

There were stories of beaters at pheasant shoots for the gentry sporting the Sinn Féin tricolour, an emblem that some of the Anglo-Irish upper classes knew was significant and regarded as threatening. Others thought it just a phase, and a few found it amusing. One or two actually commended the Sinn Feiners for helping to direct the horse-traffic so efficiently.

Then came the election in December 1918. This turned out to be a landslide victory for Sinn Féin – 73 seats won as against only 6 for the old Redmondite Parliamentary Party advocating a gradualist Home Rule policy. All through the rest of the 20th century, Sinn Féin has regarded this 1918 election as their historical purchase on democratic endorsement.

The actual percentage of votes was not as impressive – Sinn Féin gained 47 per cent of the votes on a 60 per cent turnout. That is to say, less than 29 per cent of the electorate voted Sinn Féin. And there was an element of ballot-rigging: voting early and often. Nevertheless, the triumph of Sinn Féin, coming from nothing, represented the mood of the country at the time. As Dan Breen, the notorious gunman, recounted merrily, "The people went Sinn Féin mad." He and his cronies campaigned energetically, and "we didn't leave a dead wall or a cross-roads in the country that we did not decorate with appeals to 'Rally to Sinn Féin', 'Vote for the Republic', 'Stand by the men of 1916' … We knocked plenty of fun out of the election."

But the pattern of voting was to foreshadow the partition of Ireland. While Sinn Féin captured its 73 seats, the Unionists won 26: in what was to become Eire, the Unionists took no seats; in what was to become Northern Ireland, in four of the counties the Nationalists took no seats. Only two counties in the whole island were mixed, or, as we would now say, "pluralist". This course of events would pave the way for an Anglo-Irish war, a scorching civil war, and a partition which was to deepen the political, and religious, divide.

The period from Easter 1916 until the first Dáil of 1919 is often described as wonderful by those who lived through it. "Most people [today] find it hard to realize the spirit, at once enthusiastic and indomitable, which then permeated almost our entire population," recalled Edward MacLysaght in 1978.

These feelings were also registered by younger priests, who had been brought up with all the traditional prohibitions against Fenians. A Father M'Dermott, a chaplain with the American Forces, noted in his travels through Ireland in May 1919 that he had never before seen such optimism: from Dublin to Donegal, "a look full of hope and confidence" had been on Irish faces. Speaking to the Sinn Féin club in his native town of Ballybofey, Co Donegal, he said he was proud to see the self-sacrificing spirit of the young men of Ireland. He asked them never to disgrace their sacred cause and noble struggle by any act of violence.

This hope and optimism was also reflected in the Church itself, where seminary lists were closed because theology colleges were over-subscribed. It was evident as well in the flurry of prayers and good works: religious activity often rises when people feel faith in the future, and the "Treasury of the Sacred Heart" (in the *Irish Messenger of the Sacred Heart*) in which people "banked" their prayers and good works increased its deposits remarkably. From the 1918 election until the early 1920s "Visits to the Poor", "Acts of Victory over Temper" and other acts of self-denial zoomed upwards. Before the Great War, the monthly figure for "Visits to the Poor" was registered at an apathetic 910. By February 1920, the spiritual Treasury was logging 2,263 Visits to the Poor. Plus 8,622 Acts of Unselfishness, 27,634 Acts of Victory over Uncharitableness, 34,849 Acts of Victory over Temper, 42,728 Acts of Resignation, 15,000 Acts of Study (a new feature, reflecting increasing ambition in education) and a remarkable 21,000 Acts of

Examinations of Consciences, besides numerous Masses, Rosaries, Novenas, Holy Hours and Spiritual Readings.

But the sense of uplift remarked upon by the clergy such as Father M'Dermott was evidently accompanied by an anxiety that there should not be a descent into violence, which they must have sensed behind all the high spirits. At a Sinn Féin meeting in Baillieborough, Co Cavan — attended, incidentally, by a staggering 10,000 people — the local parish priest, Revd Gaffney, read a letter exhorting Sinn Feiners to shun secret societies and any incitement to rebellion. This was soon after the 1918 election. "The eyes of the world are upon you; show that you are Constitutional." In Wexford, Father David Bolger, perceiving that the Dan Breen wing of the Republican movement was growing at the expense of the constitutionalist wing, warned: "Be Sinn Feiners if you like. Cherish your country, your love of liberty, your politicial opinions as much as you like. But be no party to any cause which must end as this rebellion — preached and developed and contemplated — must end."

Catholic Ireland had largely voted for independence in December 1918, and was looking forward to securing that independence. It was now two generations since the first Home Rule bill of 1885. Yet at the end of 1918 Britain still needed time to settle Irish Home Rule. Not only was the problem of the Unionists unresolved, but the world had been turned upside down by the 1914-18 War. It was a period of shattering international upheaval in which British interests were substantially involved.

Europe was in pieces. The Ottoman Empire was in ruins — a matter of some importance to the British Government, with its interests in the Near East. The dismemberment of the Habsburg Empire had unleashed a flood of conflicting demands which were eventually to facilitate the rise of the European dictators.

And there was something else abroad: a bitterness, a cynicism, and a collective feeling of tragedy not yet acknowledged. (It was not until 1929 that any public criticism of the slaughter of the Great War emerged.) "There came to every combatant nation a moral coarseness, hardness, callousness," wrote P.S. O'Hegarty, though he added that at first, because of the post-1916 euphoria, Ireland seemed to have escaped all that. The change in the German people was dramatic: an exceptionally law-abiding society before 1914, after the war ended in 1918 Germany was overrun by disorder. Then there was the effect of the Great Flu epidemic of 1919, remembered afterwards with fear and loathing, though it was instrumental in releasing Irish political prisoners from English jails. Yet, world-wide, it killed over 40 million people. That, too, somehow added to the moral coarsening and callousness that O'Hegarty recalled.

In all this turmoil London was now in no hurry to resolve the Irish Question by handing over Parliamentary reins. This was a mistake: once the vote had been registered, the business of an Irish parliament should have been immediately engaged.

Because, duly elected, the Sinn Féin members congregated for the first Irish Parliament — Dáil Éireann — on 21 January 1919. It opened proceedings in Irish, French and English, and issued a message to the Free Nations of the World. It selected delegates to attend the Versailles Peace Conference in Paris.

The first agenda of this new Irish Parliament would sometimes be described as Utopian: some of the resonances of Pearse and Connolly — such as the virtual abolition of private property — alarmed the Bishops of Catholic Ireland, who most certainly did not favour any form of Bolshevism.

This Dáil meeting was not recognised by the London Government on the grounds that so many other political parties had stayed away, such as the rump of the Irish Parliamentary Party at Westminster, the Ulster Unionists and the Labour Party, for more quixotic reasons. Moreover, several of the leading players of the new Dáil were still imprisoned, following the disturbances of 1916.

The new Dáil was not recognised, either, by the body of Irish bishops with two individual exceptions: Bishop William Walsh of Dublin, a known nationalist whom the British had tried to block in his appointment to the Dublin see, and the Bishop of Killaloe, Michael Fogarty, a veteran of the struggle against landlordism who was to have the longest episcopate in Irish history (from 1904 until his death in 1955). But even the two supportive Bishops were careful in their language, using the phrase "Dáil Éireann, our Irish Parliament" in balanced counterpoint to "our present Government", this being the properly recognised British authority. Irish bishops never, ever advocated open defiance against the proper authority: it was laid down by St Paul himself that "the proper authority" had to be respected.

But on the very day that this new Dáil convened, Dan Breen, Sean Treacy, Seamus Robinson and five others effectively opened proceedings in the War of Independence by leading an ambush against a party of policemen at Soloheadbeg, Co Tipperary. This was an important turning-point in events. Once again it seemed that as the constitutional process dragged its feet, the men of the gun took the initiative.

Dan Breen, a roistering character who attained semi-mythic status, something like an old frontier cowboy, for 50 years after these events, was a gun-totin' — but probably rather likeable — scoundrel. He swanks away heartily in his celebrated autobiography *My Fight for Irish Freedom*, about how he liked to "plug" policemen, or any other individual associated with the uniform of the Crown. While some hoped that Dáil Éireann in 1919 would develop into an ordered constitutional parliament, Breen openly boasted that his aim was to make the country ungovernable. Breen was also what we would now call a sectarian, as was another epic gunman, Tom Barry, who wrote the classic *Guerrilla Days in Ireland*. They wanted to get the Protestants out of the country for they represented to them the old order which must go.

Breen and his cronies killed two policeman at that ambush. The Catholic authorities rained denunciations against Breen and his policemen-killing cronies; and yet the ground was constantly shifting beneath their feet. A guerrilla war had now begun, and what Breen had started, Michael Collins was to take up: to make Ireland ungovernable, and to fight the British, not to wait upon London's deliberations for Irish Home Rule.

Yet a guerrilla war, by definition, is one that is not formally declared. And it was some time before the people knew that there was a war on. The political organisation of Sinn Féin was — as it still is — most effective in being constructive at local level and spreading its political network throughout the country. It was setting up Sinn Féin Courts, which were forums of arbitration, notably involving agrarian disputes (which are always a feature of rural Irish life); these worked remarkably well. They would often be presided over by the local priest, being recognised as the *de facto* leader of the community.

But if the political wing of Sinn Féin was conducting itself most usefully, a growing terrorist wing of the whole movement was also developing. Throughout 1919, policemen, magistrates and representatives of the Crown began to be eliminated by gunmen. One of the first dramatic assassinations which was to shock the country was the murder of Jack Milling, the resident magistrate at Westport, Co Mayo, in May 1919. Katharine Tynan describes the episode in her memoir *The Wandering Years* as being the first event of the Troubles which really horrified — perhaps because it went one step beyond killing a policeman wearing a uniform and on duty. Attacking a man at home was something new, and breached an Irish sensibility about the hearth and family.

The writer Katharine Tynan was perhaps a typical educated Catholic bourgeois of the time. Her sons had served in the British Army in the Great War of 1914-18 (and she was painfully aware how fortunate she had been that they had both survived). She was of that background and generation which saw no conflict between working for the Crown and being an Irish patriot — her husband had been a resident magistrate himself. She could be critical of some of the landed gentry in Mayo, who were all Protestants: it irked her that they kept their own social circles so closed, and that they would never show hospitality to a Catholic priest, however educated and cultivated they might be (and the ones she knew often were). But of course she was thoroughly horrified by the murder of Jack Milling, who was shot by a gunman in his home, just as he was about to wind the clock on to British Summer Time. An open blind at his window gave the gunman helpful vision.

Milling had been unpopular locally because he had sent Volunteers — the Irish Volunteers were founded in 1913 and had attracted Sinn Feiners, Gaelic Leaguers and GAA men — to prison for unlawful assembly and he had just despatched another pair off to jail for cattle-driving (that is, driving cattle off their owners' lands, a common practice in agrarian agitation). Yet Jack Milling himself was not a member of the Anglo-Irish gentry, the Protestant aristocratic class who were now being characterised as the occupying enemy: he was a middle-class Ulsterman and a member of the Plymouth Brethren sect — a Protestant cult not unlike the Quakers and once numbering among their members Charles Stewart Parnell. He had carried out his actions as a magistrate because he believed in simple values of law and order, which were now about to break down.

Protestant Ireland was, of course, outraged at this killing, and the Belfast press described the south of Ireland as a primitive and lawless place. Catholic Ireland was also outraged. "An appalling deed," the *Irish Catholic* called it "... calculated to make one's blood run cold to find that such an appalling deed is possible in a Christian land. Such crimes are a violence of God's law and of human law ... The criminals [who perpetrate such deeds] are not fit to live, and it is the duty of any member of the community who is in a position to do so to tender assistance to the authorities in their efforts to secure that justice shall be vindicated."

In other words, it would not be right for Catholics to shield the perpetuators of assassination. The Archbishop of Tuam proclaimed that it was the duty of all citizens to "do all in their power to bring to justice one who is an enemy of God, an enemy of society and an enemy of Ireland".

All through 1919 and 1920, as the activity of the Volunteers — who were now the IRA — increased, as more attacks were mounted on symbols of British authority and Protestant power, the Catholic Church struggled to keep abreast with, and in control of, the changes. Irish Protestants, understandably, watched in dismay, as one after another the representatives of law and order, mostly belonging to their own community, were picked off. While some Southern Protestants had been sympathetic towards Irish nationalism, and the younger ones had shown enthusiasm for the revival of the Irish language and culture, they had not intended it to lead to shootings and assassinations.

On 7 September 1919, a squad of soldiers of the Crown on church parade outside the Methodist church at Fermoy were fired upon — one shot dead and two wounded. A corporal who went to get help from a doctor had doors slammed in his face twice. (By contrast, a Unionist doctor had tended to James Connolly's wounds in 1916 and, not only that, afterwards started a fund for his widow and children.)

Irish Protestants North and South thought "the Fermoy outrage" a terrible business. The *Church of Ireland Gazette* wrote that "no more terrible or dastardly crime has sullied the fair name of Ireland". .The *Irish Catholic* also denounced the Fermoy attack under the headline of "Crimes Against God and Country". They took particular exception to the fact that it was carried out in the proximity of a church. "A foul and dastardly deed, one incapable of palliation and the mere recital of the details of which is calculated to make Irishmen all over the world hang their heads for shame."

And yet, notes the Protestant *Church of Ireland Gazette*, "public opinion all over Ireland seems apathetic and afraid". The Protestants and Unionists were, in effect, being picked off almost, it seemed, with the silent compliance of the people. A week after the Fermoy incident, the murder of Constable Daniel Hoey took place in the streets of Dublin. This, wrote the *Gazette*, "adds one more to the long list of brutal and sordid crimes which have disgraced Ireland's name in recent months ... The rapid succession of callous murders in Ireland point to a campaign of anarchy which threatens to engulf ordered society." Detective Hoey had identified the 1916 signatory Sean MacDiarmada for the military: he thus counted as a spy, in the eyes of Republicans.

At the end of November 1919, Sergeant John Barton was murdered in the streets of Dublin, the 14th policeman to have met his death in this manner. Nobody was apprehended, and the crowd who had witnessed it gave the impression they had seen nothing. This was what exasperated the voice of Protestant Ireland: the Sicilian-like *omerta* which seemed to afflict witnesses, as well as the disinclination of anyone in a crowd to help a dying man. Sergeant Barton had lain dying in the Dublin street crying out for assistance; nobody answered his cries of agony. This event is chillingly replicated in J.G. Farrell's novel set in this period, *Troubles*. The *Gazette* in early 1920 reports pathetic cases of wounded men being refused a drink of water at farmhouses, a previously unknown breach of the traditions of hospitality.

The country *was* becoming ungovernable. Magistrates were resigning all over Ireland, and juries were refusing to convict, either from sympathy with the IRA or from fear. In such circumstances, there is no law and order.

The Catholic hierarchy were becoming increasingly distressed by the course of events, and were at pains to point out that there was never any justification for murder. Parents were under a special obligation to keep their young people out of "secret societies". Dan Breen would boast in his memoirs that "the priests were with them", but he was an unreliable braggart: the Catholic papers were full of clerical condemnations of these occurrences. There would always be some "rebel" priests, whose nationalist sympathies caused them to look more indulgently on the IRA men. Yet these were exceptions. More often, the priests denounced (from the altar, even) individuals with IRA sympathies. A great-aunt of mine walked out of Clifden cathedral in 1920 after a jeremiad from the canon against the gunmen.

In February 1920, the Dean of Cashel, Monsignor Ryan, denounced the whole state of the country in the strongest terms. There was no crime they used to have such a horror of as murder, he said, but now, alas, it was so frequent … People should remember that not only the actual murderer but everyone who helps, whether by advice, encouragement or cooperation of any sort in a murderous enterprise, is guilty before God of the heinous crime. If people think themselves justified in killing the props of English rule, he said, then England's soldiers in our midst would be justified in shooting us. "Honesty with God, and courage before men are much wanted today," he said.

Like Hamlet's father, the clergy thought it particularly foul for an individual to be sent unprepared before his Maker. Such a case was highlighted by the most Revd Dr Thomas O'Dea, the Bishop of Galway: one of his own flock "had been shot dead at his door. The unfortunate victim had almost reached his threshold, after an honest day's work ... when his face was blown away in the sight of his little boy, who had run to welcome him. Death was instantaneous, so that the unhappy man was sent to his Great Account without notice or preparation ... These wicked murderers [were] guilty of the murder of a human soul."

In December 1920, the Bishop of Cork, Daniel Cohalan, issued a decree of excommunication against those taking up arms in this manner. "Anyone who shall, within the Diocese of Cork, organize, or take part in an ambush or in the kidnapping or otherwise, shall be guilty of murder or attempted murder, and shall incur by the very fact the censure of excommunication." Although the mayhem continued, this excommunication did have some effect. One of Michael Collins's agents, Seamus O'Maoileoin, wrote in a memoir that Collins sent for him to ask about the impact of the excommunication. "If the priests were with us, things would be better," Collins said, irately. "If I had my way, that ------ of a bishop would be shot. There is neither sense nor reason in shooting poor, uneducated idiots and spies and letting people like the Bishop of Cork get away with it."

After some deliberation, Michael Collins decided not to shoot the Bishop of Cork. It might cause complications among "political friends". Some Sinn Feiners (such as de Valera) would be devout Catholics, and would disapprove of the act. Were it not for such considerations, the Bishop of Cork, too, would have been "plugged".

Some historians have regarded the condemnations of violence by the Irish bishops as equivocal and carefully elastic. This is not a fair criticism, it seems to me. The bishops were altogether against the kind of violence that was occurring. But the situation did, of course, begin to change after the arrival of the Black and Tans in August 1920 — the British Army auxiliaries composed of ex-officers, many misfits and offenders, men who really had seen hell on the Western Front and been thoroughly coarsened and demoralised by it. At this point, as the American scholar David Miller puts it, the Catholic Church in Ireland began to withdrawn her sanction from the British State.

The bishops did approach the question of Terence MacSwiney with great theological care. For this, too, proved to be a turning-point in the course of events. MacSwiney was the Sinn Féin Mayor of Cork, a much-liked playwright (and former accountant) who was arrested in August 1920 and charged with the possession of a police cipher or secret code. The assassination rate of policemen was such that the offence was regarded as a grave one by the Crown authorities, but MacSwiney went on hunger-strike, in Brixton jail, to protest his innocence. As with the Bobby Sands case 60 years later, the hunger strike attracted world attention, and Terence MacSwiney, aged 41, died in October on the 74th day of his hunger strike.

During this controversial (and tumultuous) period, the Catholic bishops chose not to regard MacSwiney's chosen action as suicidal, which would have been a grave sin against the Church's teaching. There were no condemnations against self-slaughter, but a prudent silence. Feelings were running so high, and it seems likely that the hierarchy could not bear to think of the adored MacSwiney as a suicide, but rather as a self-sacrificing martyr. A week after MacSwiney died, Kevin Barry, an IRA volunteer aged 18, was executed at Mountjoy jail for the murder of an even younger British soldier during a raid two months previously.

These were indeed troubled times: day after day, week after week, there were reports of murder and mayhem. Towns were sacked by Crown forces; the IRA ambushed and attacked Crown targets. Catholics and their churches were burned out in Belfast; priests were seized by Crown forces in the South; Bloody Sunday occurred, when Michael Collins's squad killed 14 British secret service agents.

In the midst of these troubles of 1920, Catholic Ireland was much exercised by the beatification of Blessed Oliver Plunkett. This was a genuinely pious occasion, but, as with the canonisation of St Joan of Arc in France at around the same time, there was a patriotic subtext. Oliver Plunkett (1625-81), Archbishop of Armagh, had been hung, drawn and quartered by the English during one of their more ferocious persecutions of Irish Popery. He would become a full saint in 1975, but the 1920 beatification brought out a huge procession in Dublin. It was, said the papers, composed of seven different sections and "comprised all classes". Indeed, it most especially attracted the Dublin working class. Irish trade unionists actually organised themselves in working men's religious sodalities, and for the occasion of Blessed Oliver's celebratory procession, the railwaymen, the Labourers' Union (with their own band), and the Amalgamated Society of Tailors and Tailoresses had an especially strong showing.

This was Catholic Ireland affirming faith and fatherland in a *peaceful* manner, as the Catholic papers pointed out, not with gun in hand. Yet it was also a show of people-power just at a time when the political power-base was shifting. Arthur Griffith (the founder of Sinn Féin) and Count Plunkett were among the notables who led the procession, and Dublin Corporation and Dáil Éireann were both represented. There were twenty Dublin confraternities (religious associations, often with romantic feudal names such as The Knights of the Shrine) and sodalities, ranging in number from two hundred to four thousand for each association.

The city streets swelled with the sounds of bands and hymns, as Blessed Oliver's procession wended its way from the Liffeyside to Mount Argus, by Harold's Cross in West Dublin, where two rosaries were recited, and Father Joseph Smith gave an address in which he said that the life of Blessed Oliver "was expressly the same as the life of the Church in Ireland — a life of ardent, fiery faith, but a faith united with a large-hearted charity for even those of his countrymen who were not of his faith." Blessed Oliver should guide the country at this time, "so that by his intercession the ancient glory of the Irish Church and Irish nation may at length return ..."

What Father Smith said did not sound, in a narrow sense, sectarian: but in his manner of linking the Irish Church with the revival of the Irish nation, there was an identification of faith with fatherland. Catholicism *was* associated with Irishness, but now, willy-nilly, it began to be associated with an Irish State. This was partly because of the way the cards had fallen: most

Unionists were Protestants (in the North of Ireland, virtually exclusively so), and the parts of Ireland that had voted Nationalist were Catholic. But the notion of an Irish Catholic state began to occur now in the devotional literature. Until the end of the First World War, the Irish Catholic popular literature generally accommodated the Crown. There were always prayers for "our Irish Tommies" and nationalism was more cherished culturally than politically.

This began to change in 1919-20: in May 1919, for the first time, the requests for prayers in the *Irish Messenger of the Sacred Heart* included prayers in thanksgiving for Republican prisoners released from English jails. "Dear Revd Father" went a mother's letter. "Please publish in the *Messenger* my grateful thanks to the Sacred Heart for the release of the Irish [Sinn Féin] prisoners in February, when we had lost all hope of their release. I promised the Sacred Heart, if they were home by the First Friday in March, I would have it published in the *Messenger*. How wonderful! It was on the First Friday their release was announced."

Little by little thereafter, the prayers for the husbands and sons in the British Army — although they continued to appear up until 1920 — are replaced by devotions to the Sacred Heart for (and sometimes by) Sinn Féin men. "Revd Father," writes a Republican ex-prisoner in August 1920, "I wish through your little *Irish Messenger* to return my heartfelt thanks to the Sacred Heart for a great favour received. Arrested last spring, I was sentenced to death by military court-martial. I started a Novena to the Sacred Heart. The Novena was finished on the day I was to be executed, and on that same day I was reprieved. Now, thank God, I am at home with my people again."

IRA men even gave thanks when a raid was successful. "We wish to return heartfelt thanks to the Sacred Heart of Jesus and His Holy Mother for the safety of all concerned in the recent raid on the barracks. We promised the Sacred Heart during the raid that if all came safe out of it, we would have it published in the *Messenger* for God's greater honour and glory." Some interned republicans also wrote that they had distributed Catholic literature and Sacred Heart badges, to ward off "the unclean literature" which might otherwise be a risk among men.

Throughout this period of 1919-20, the consciousness that Ireland was "a Catholic nation" took hold in the Catholic press. The *Irish Catholic* began to carry a logo by its masthead with the words *Eire Abú!* (Long Live Ireland!) and *Dia Linn!* (God be with us) Articles began appearing showing that Ireland had always been a "Catholic nation". At this time too, the suggestion was made in the Catholic media that the statue of Admiral Nelson, standing in O'Connell Street, should be replaced by something more appropriate. The Sacred Heart was one possible candidate — the Sacred Heart, that is, bearing an Irish flag (somewhat incongruous, since the cult of the Sacred Heart was most specifically French). Our Lady of Lourdes was another idea. St Patrick was also a popular notion. Throughout the 1920s, this was episodically discussed in the Catholic press, and it is perhaps a pity that St Patrick — who is after all a thoroughly ecumenical figure — was not placed atop the fine Pillar in Dublin. If he had been, the IRA would not have blown up the monument in 1966 — because it still carried Lord Nelson — thus ruining Dublin's finest boulevard for the rest of the 20th century.

There was no deliberate drive, within the Catholic press, to exclude Protestants from the burgeoning Irish identity. But there was a sense that the boot was now moving to the other foot: Protestants had been the ruling class in Ireland, and they would now have to accept that things were changing. "Genuine Catholicity is kind and charitable to all," wrote the *Messenger* loftily, "full of consideration for the religious beliefs or prejudices of those outside its fold." Irish Protestants would be in no way deprived in a new state — but they would have to accept majority values.

Attacks on Catholics in the North (besides the atrocious behaviour of the Black and Tans) were a constant source of distress, quite justifiably. Yet in an age before "rights" were acknowledged, Catholics were not encouraged to harbour a sense of grievance. They were encouraged to pray, and to keep a picture of the Sacred Heart in their home at all times. Where

Protestant neighbours behaved "decently" to Derry or Belfast Catholics, this was also commended.

By 1921, however, Protestants in the south of Ireland were leaving in noticeable numbers. The exodus had already begun, indeed, before the First World War: between 1911 and 1926 the Church of Ireland population (the principle Protestant group, being the equivalent of Episcopalians) fell by 34 per cent, from 249,535 to 164,215. Some Irish Protestants left because the "feeling" of the place was no longer congenial to them: memoirs of the period underline how wretched Irish Protestants felt to see so much of what they had loved, associated with the Crown, rebuffed and trampled upon. Some left because they felt unwanted and even hunted out. Those who remained had the lowest fertility rate in Europe — nearly always a sign of little confidence in the future. When people feel hopeful about the future, they get married and start families. (Catholics in the North of Ireland, who also felt excluded and discriminated against after the partition of Ireland in 1920 nevertheless went on getting married and having babies: their alienation was not perhaps so marked.)

In the 26 counties which were to be called Southern Ireland, the burnings-out of the "big houses", long associated with Ascendency and Protestant rule, began around 1920, initially as a tit-for-tat strike against the Black and Tans sackings and "reprisals". There had been raids on big houses since 1918, but these had mostly been for guns and ammunition and had often been accompanied by a kind of quixotic courtesy which softened the hostility by drollery. There was a story of an Anglo-Irish schoolboy returning home for the vacation to find his parents' house robbed of shooting ammunition; and then a gunman dropping by a package containing cartridges with a note — "Wouldn't it be a pity for Master Tom not to have his bit of shooting, and him home for the holidays?"

Even when the burnings-out began in earnest, there were many reports of the IRA first knocking at the main door to announce that the house was to be burned shortly, but giving the residents 15 minutes' grace "to have a cup of tea" and to collect their belongings. There were said to be occasions when the IRA men even helped bring out the furniture and the paintings, or when they allowed a maid to go back upstairs to rescue a canary, or out to the stables to free the horses. But there were times, too, when many beautiful treasures went up in flames. Most lamentable was the burning-out of Castle Bernard, seat of Lord Bandon, in Co Cork. A Titian and a Leonardo da Vinci original were among the many works of art consigned to the fire. (A cousin of Lord Bandon, Albinia Broderick, "went over" to Sinn Féin and acted as nurse to wounded gunmen, rather more flintily turning her back on her own kinsfolk.)

Yet while the IRA had few scruples about burning works of art, and none about shooting policemen or others regarded as spies, they could be strict about not permitting looting. After the burning-out of Oakgrove, one of the two family homes in Co Cork of Captain John Bowen-Colthurst, his sister was summoned to a mysterious address in Cork City. She went along and was shown into a room upstairs, which was a veritable Aladdin's cave of jewellery from various country houses. She was left alone and told to take back whatever belonged to herself and her mother. Looting did, of course, take place, in the end: but it was not approved of by the IRA leadership.

The burnings-out were terrible, and continued during the Civil War which followed the 1921 Treaty — drawn up to bring an end to the Anglo-Irish War — since most of the Protestant Ascendency, the owners of the big houses, sided against the IRA and with the Free State. Over 200 stately homes were destroyed in all, Palladian mansions, mediaeval castles and Georgian piles which we would now regard as part of our Irish heritage and add to the glittering attractions for well-heeled tourists. In 1920 such dwellings were simply seen as symbols of British rule and nothing else: indeed, almost all architectural constructions built at any time over the previous 800 years were seen as despised relics of a colonial regime until well into the 1960s. A quite serious attempt was made to destroy Georgian Dublin in the 1960s, inspired by old IRA men who graduated into nationalist politicians and had cronies in the building trade; fortunately, the means were not available for the wholesale destruction of the capital city and, as the century wore on, the beauties of past architecture were reclaimed by a new generation with a more educated eye and a finer understanding of the visual arts.

The loss of these stately homes was sad and regrettable, but more distressing were the attacks on ordinary Protestants which occurred at this time. This was what we would now call ethnic cleansing: Protestants received threatening letters to the effect that "you will be hunted out of the country and all other Orange dogs with you". Some IRA members routinely described Protestants as "English" and characterised them as spies simply for being law-abiding or for turning to the police for protection.

The Dunmanway massacre in West Cork, in April 1922, when more than a dozen Protestants were picked off was a reprehensible example of this ethnic cleansing procedure. As Peter Hart's study, *The Irish Republican Army and Its Enemies* shows, the West Cork Protestants were undoubtedly killed as part of a planned attack, and in this manner: James Buttimer, a retired draper at Dunmanway, was shot in the face as he opened his front door to a group of anonymous men. John Chinnery, a farmer, was shot in the back after he was ordered to harness a horse, an order with which he was complying. Alexander McKinley, a youth of 16, was shot in bed, three times, in the back of the head. Ralph Harbord, a curate, was badly wounded while standing on the rectory steps. Jim Greenfield, a farm servant, and described as "feeble-minded", was shot in the back of the head while trying to hide his face from his attackers. Robert Nagle, the son of a farmer, was shot in bed while his mother was forced to watch — she later testified that the gunmen appeared to be drunk. John Bradfield, a farmer of Killowen, confined to bed with rheumatism, was shot in the back of the neck.

None of these men were big landowners, or members of a "ruling class" against which the guerrillas were waging some titanic struggle. They were ordinary farming folk. But the effect of these attacks had the result desired by their perpetrators: they frightened Protestants out of the country. The boats to England were suddenly full of Protestants fleeing in terror: as the old Chinese maxim held "Kill one: frighten ten thousand."

It is true that Catholics were being attacked in Belfast by Orangemen at this time, and there was a mirror-image element in these atrocities. In April 1922, for example, an entire streetful of Catholics, in Antigua Street, Belfast, was subjected to "wholesale clearance", and there were horrible incidents of Catholics being picked off by killers. "Murder of a young Catholic wife and mother," ran a Dublin newspaper headline, "who was proceeding on her way to seven o'clock Mass in St Mathews [Belfast] when she was mortally wounded by a bomb flung at her by an unseen sniper. She was conveyed into the church where the Last Rites were administered and in her baptism of blood the poor martyr of the Faith expired. Thus, the boast of the Belfast brutes has come to pass, and perhaps a further persecution is in store for the hapless minority!"

Each side, understandably, saw its own victims rather than its own perpetrators. And there was an element of denial. Mary MacSwiney, the diehard Republican and ever-devoted sister of the late Terence MacSwiney, made a speech claiming that the sectarian horrors which existed in Belfast could *never* occur south of the border: "I say no unoffending Protestant citizen would be murdered as a reprisal for the Orange murders in Belfast. Protestant and Catholic have lived and still live, side by side, in perfect harmony with each other all over Ireland, except in Belfast." Any murders that did take place of "innocent" Protestants (as opposed to "collaborators" and "spies") must have been the work of English agents. To his credit, Eamon de Valera made an anti-sectarian speech at this time saying that no helpless minority should ever be attacked or persecuted. The Catholic clergy, too, went on condemning all murders; the local Catholic priest might sometimes be the only Roman Catholic present at a murdered Protestant's funeral (in some cases, he would be the only member of the community given "immunity" to attend by the IRA).

Yet in the matter of establishing national identity at this time, there was an anguishing internal struggle for Irish Protestants, and it is evident in the pages of their weekly newspaper, the *Church of Ireland Gazette*. Were they Irish or not? Were they to be part of a new, partitioned Ireland, a partition to which they had most vehemently objected? Or should they all depart, *en masse*?

Two new states of Ireland were effectively brought into being by the Government of Ireland Act of 1920 — which set up a British parliament at Stormont in Belfast — and the Anglo-Irish Treaty of 1921. This divided the 32 counties of Ireland into Six Counties, under the Crown, in the North, and 26 Counties, under the Free State, in the South. It was an artificial division, to be sure, and a civil war was fought in response to the 1921 Treaty. Yet the situation came to be accepted, for the time being, as a working compromise.

The two groups most passionately opposed to this partition were the Republicans of Sinn Féin and the IRA, who held out for a united Ireland — and the southern Irish Protestants, who saw this as a decimation of their community, and indeed a wound in the realm of Ireland. Irish Protestants saw themselves as Irish Unionists — which meant the Union of Ireland under the Crown. "Permanent Partition is a thing of evil," editorialised the *Gazette*. "It is repugnant to every Irishman and to every Irishwoman who has the good of the country at heart.

"When the women came to Solomon to seek his judgement as to which of them should have possession of the child, she who owned the child and loved it would rather lose it than see its body cut in two ... The Partition of Ireland means the doom of Ireland."

Wednesday, 10 March, 1920 was "a sad day for Irish Unionists. It witnessed the acceptance by the Ulster Unionist Council of Mr Lloyd George's Home Rule Bill ... the die has been cast and the spectre of Partition has become a thing of flesh and blood. Irish Unionists ... cannot but look to the future with consternation."

The *Gazette* most touchingly lamented the division of Ireland in a way that summed up their dilemma: "We would not be Unionists if we did not deplore the collapse of the Union, and we would not be Irish if we did not protest against Partition to the end." They blamed the intransigence of Ulster as much as the extremism of Sinn Féin. "None of the Ulster Members ... showed the least sign of building from their position."

Tom Barry, the ruthless IRA guerrilla leader who regarded all Protestants as "Britishers", would have been surprised, had he been a reader of the *Church of Ireland Gazette,* by the sweet tone of genuine love for Ireland, and indeed of Christian charity, which often permeated Irish Protestant values at this time.

"There is no one who would not sacrifice virtually everything for the better of our little land," cried the voice of Irish Protestantism, "but what can we do? Before peace comes to Ireland, there must be a change of heart in the vast majority of the people. Hatred must give way to charity and the spirit of human brotherhood must appear in our midst ... The very fabric of society in Ireland seems to be in dissolution ...

"[Yet] we Irish Church folk, whether of North or of South, are Irishmen and Irishwomen and in our hearts is the love of the Motherland that bred us."

Affection for Ireland even surfaces in the gardening notes. In contemplating rhododendrons the gardening contributor adds: "Ireland is a wonderful country. Nature insists upon the beautiful amid the squalor and strife and the sordid squabbles of human beings."

There must have been, in this period of the early 1920s, many an Irish Protestant who had to decide whether to leave Ireland, since the political and cultural landscape was now changing so radically, or to throw in his lot, all the same, with "the Motherland that bred us". Those who went felt either frightened and unwanted or that the new nationalist Irish state would be too alien for them. Some may have gone for purely practical reasons, as many Irish Catholics did, to seek their fortune elsewhere in more prosperous lands. But there must have been communities all around the south of England, in which Irish Protestants tried to recreate the ambiance of their Irish youth, before the Great War of 1914, when everything in Ireland had seemed so hopeful.

For those who made the decision to stay, there had to be a more conscious commitment to the new order. In the pages of the *Church of Ireland Gazette* one can see this gradually taking shape. By 1923 it is noted that things are settling down — the Civil War had ended, with a victory for the Free State.

Protestants should welcome the Free State, it was said, because there was a better chance now of reconciliation with the North.

By 1925, the *Gazette* was urging Irish Protestants to participate fully in the new Irish state, and to use their vote democratically and constructively. There were, naturally, feelings of regret at having to make a break with past traditions. "We admit quite freely that ... in the last few years [the Protestants] have had to swallow many bitter pills. They have seen virtually a clean break with traditions which they held very dear, which helped to make them what they are.

"They have seen the flag under which so many of their sons have served and died banished from the country whose children always did it credit ... But this country is still our country ...

"We have thrown in our lot definitely and irrevocably with our country and we must stand by it now when it is assailed from many quarters. For better or for worse, we and our children have got to live our lives and make our livings in the Irish Free State and nothing could be more cowardly or less worthy of the ideals of the Protestant faith than to adopt an attitude of blank negation towards the vital problems of our National Government."

From now on, the *Church of Ireland Gazette* would refer to the Dáil as "our Parliament" and the elected Irish Government as "our Government", even if, as the author Brian Inglis recalls in a memoir, some members of the Ascendancy could never bring themselves to speak thus, and "Parliament" was always Westminster, and "Government", His Majesty's. But the official voice of Protestant Ireland insisted on this commitment to Ireland, all the more poignant perhaps, because they had had to swallow the bitter pill of the break with their Unionist tradition.

It was not the intention of any party, political or religious, to partition Ireland into two parts: in the North, a Protestant state for a Protestant people, and in the South, a state built on the concept of Catholic Ireland. But it happened like this, just the same, and endured until the last years of the 20th century.

Five

Ireland's Spiritual Empire

"There are eight hundred churches around the world named after Patrick. St Patrick's Day means the tolling of bells for Ireland's saint from Buenos Aires to Shanghai."

Alannah Hopkin, *The Living Legend of St Patrick*, (1989)

"Intention of the month: CONVERT CHINA."

Irish Messenger of the Sacred Heart, August 1920

Those who opposed Home Rule for Ireland pointed out that in leaving the British Empire, the Irish would lose contact with a great, multiracial, multinational organisation with a global outlook. Conor Cruise O'Brien has written that the one advantage of the British Ascendancy in Ireland was that they were accustomed to "thinking in global terms". But they were not the only ones with globalised vision. Sister McCarthy, of Kilmichael in Co Cork, also had such a vision: she started a hospital in Shanghai in the early years of the 20th century.

Father Carbery, SJ, was accustomed to thinking in global terms as well. His mission station was in Dibrugarh Gauhai in Assam and he covered 962 miles on his "parochial rounds", often by bicycle.

Father Michael Toher, a Westmeath priest who left his Dublin parish in 1922 to work among the Mexican poor, had a globalised outlook which drew him to a far-distant land. The Irish Ursulines in Alaska, the Irish Dominicans in South Africa, the Irish Loreto Sisters in India and the Irish Vincentians in China were surely as global in their outlook as the scions of the British Empire.

As for America, why, the Catholic Church in the United States was virtually an outpost of Irish culture — not always, aesthetically, for the best, according to critics. "American Catholicism derives a great part of its character from Irish Catholicism," writes Thomas Day in "Why Catholics Can't Sing", a witty critique of American Catholicism's lack of musical tradition, precisely *because* Americans took their Catholic faith from the Irish, rather than from the Germans or Italians.

Of 464 American bishops between 1789 and 1935, more than half had Irish names. The first American cardinal, John McCloskey of New York, was from Derry in the north of Ireland, and it was normal that when New York's first Catholic Cathedral was opened by Cardinal McCloskey in 1858, it should have been called St Patrick's.

So Irish was the American Catholic Church for most of the 20th century that even priests with Polish or Italian names took on the prevailing attitudes of the Irish; the deep commitment to the faith was characteristically Irish too. The Irish were dominant in the American Church partly because they just got there first. "By the time Tony (the Italian) got here, Pat was already running the Church," wrote Bob Considine in his book *It's the Irish* in 1961. Catholic Ireland established itself in the Americas in the 1800s, although the big increase started in the 1840s, during and after the Great Famine. Ironically, the fact that the Irish Catholics spoke English, which had been imposed on them by the conqueror, gave them an advantage over Polish and Italian immigrants in the United States.

By 1890, almost one in two American Catholics was Irish-born or had Irish-born parents. This pattern continued throughout the first half of the 20th century: even in 1960, two out of five American Catholics claimed Irish ancestry. It is reckoned that American Catholicism did not really have a distinctive non-Irish identity until the 1970s.

Priests and nuns, as pastors and educators, naturally accompanied the diaspora of Irish people emigrating to the New World. That was one aspect of what became known as "Ireland's Spiritual Empire". The other dimension was the missionary one, in which Catholic Ireland saw its role as going forth to evangelise the whole world.

The British Empire, in which the Catholic Irish had been a subject people, had its dominion over a quarter of the earth's peoples in 1900. Yet it was Catholic Ireland's contention that it belonged to a greater, more multiracial and multicultural empire, based on the immutable concept of universality: *unam, sanctam, catholicam, et apostolicam ecclesiam.* And *this* empire had a constituency in the hereafter as well!

Indeed, long before it was "politically correct" to advocate a multiracial or multi-ethnic society, the annals of Catholic Ireland proudly referred to its saints and holy men and women of different races. There was a strong cult, in Ireland, of Blessed (now St) Martin de Porres, a black Dominican lay-brother from Peru who died in 1639. Statuettes of Blessed Martin were a strong feature of my schooldays: you would put a penny in a missionary collecting box "for the black babies", and the figurine of Blessed Martin would nod in appreciation. Blessed Martin, who was eventually canonised in 1962, had been a most interesting historical character: a surgeon-barber before he entered the Dominican order, he nursed the sick, the destitute, ill-treated slaves, and also stray animals, with remarkable healing skills. Many Irishmen born in the mid-20th century were called after Martin de Porres.

It was also frequently alleged, in Irish devotional literature, that St Anthony of Padua was probably a black man (he was said to be Moorish). This, somehow, added to his allure; or it added to the claims of Catholic multi-ethnicity.

Publications such as the *Irish Ecclesiastical Record* were also devoted to a native American holy woman, the Blessed Kateri Tekakwaitha, called the Mohawk Martyr, and "the Fairest Flower that ever bloomed amongst the red man". Blessed Kateri was in fact a half-Iroquois and half-Algonquin Christian

— apparently a pious and selfless young woman, who died in 1680 aged a mere 24.

This "universal church" was quite genuinely multiracial, and it did take a stand against racism of any kind, which was always described as unchristian. (Catholic cultures could be stained by anti-Semitism: but this was seen as a *religious* difference, rather than one based on "race"; that is, Catholicism could be anti-Semitic in the same way that it could be anti-Protestant.) But racism as such was in conflict with Catholicism's remit, which was, ambitiously, for Ireland to spread the faith to the whole world.

When Catholic Ireland spoke about "our people" in an overseas country, it did not mean white people, or people of any particular ethnicity. "Our people in Rhodesia" meant — to the British Empire — the whites; to Catholic Ireland, "our people in Rhodesia" meant those who had been evangelised by our Irish Catholic missionaries.

Consciously, or unconsciously, however, this Irish "spiritual Empire" — that is, the Catholic world — did mirror aspects of the British and, indeed, French empires overseas. It would be said today that some of the attitudes towards "colonialised" peoples would have been patronising or imperialist. But it wasn't seen that way at the time and, to be fair, colonialism regarded itself as helping and advancing underdeveloped peoples, as in some ways it did: in India, the British put a stop to suttee, the tradition of a widow being burned alive on the funeral pyre of her husband; Protestant missionaries in India also halted the practice of child brides (when it was widely believed that a grown man with venereal disease could be cured by sexual intercourse with a girl of nine or ten). And in Kenya, American missionaries tried to intervene in female genital mutilation as early as 1929.

The Irish missionaries did sometimes feel that, having come from a background of subjection to a greater power, they could identify more with ordinary people than their British or French masters. When Bishop Joseph Shanahan — a pioneering Irish missionary who helped to launch the Medical Missionaries of Mary — went to Africa in 1902, he felt that his own background as the son of evicted, poor tenant farmers in Tipperary gave him an understanding of the grievances of the Ibo people, who also had many problems of land and dispossession. Some Irish priests even imparted to their African subjects a kind of transmogrified socialism, arising from their Irish radicalism: both Julius Nyerere of Tanzania and Robert Mugabe of Zimbabwe ascribed their Marxist values to having been taught by Irish missionaries.

The Irish missionaries tended to go to those countries where British rule had been established, since the Irish were English-speaking and would often have the cooperation of the local authorities. Yet the Irish also worked extensively with the French. Many missionary orders with a strong Irish base were actually of French origin, such as the Holy Ghost Fathers (the Compagnie de Saint-Esprit), the Vincentians (called after St Vincent de Paul) and the Sisters of Charity, the Society of African Missions (Société des Missions d'Afrique), and many more. The SMA, with a strong base in Cork, remains an active order helping third world countries to this day.

The French found the Irish useful associates in British Africa, especially when there was a prohibition — as in Mauritius — on French nationals teaching in a particular territory. Thus Irish priests in French orders became the go-betweens. In the annals of Mauritius, there is a long roll-call of Irish priests who have served there over three centuries. In South Africa, Irish priests often worked in conjunction with French priests from Alsace, with whom a special relationship seemed to emerge. From the time of the Boer War, incidentally, Irish missionaries were writing home describing the unfair treatment meted out to "kaffirs" (this was not a pejorative term at the time).

Ireland's missionary endeavours were to hit a high point in the years between 1916 and the late 1930s — scholars have suggested that the political idealism which was driving events in Ireland was also producing religious vocations. But of course there had been a long tradition, going back to the early Irish church, of spreading the faith.

The Irish Church traced its original missionary role back to the sixth, seventh and eighth centuries, when Irish missionaries were said to have civilised Europe. This was an aspect of early

Irish history re-emphasised, and perhaps even rediscovered, in the 1920s during the early and high-minded phase of establishing the Irish state.

"Hard-Won Freedom to be Nobly Used," announced the *Irish Catholic* newspaper after the Treaty was signed in 1921. "Catholic Ideals to be Realized. Justice, not Mammon, the Standard." Justice, decent and comfortable homes for all, sufficiency of food, clothing, security, hope, "opportunities for enjoying the amenities of life; for mental culture; for liberty and life" would be pursued. Ireland would be a classless society, where workers and business people would cooperate in a spirit of conciliation.

With this new idealism, the Catholic literature looked back to the charitable achievements of "Celtic civilisation" in the past, which so often went with missionary endeavour. The origin of the modern hospital was attributed to Irish monks who started Alpine refuges for afflicted travellers in the eighth century. Irish monks were said to have preached and taught in northern Holland since the year 690.

It was pointed out that St Brendan the Navigator, who died around 583, first discovered America (not proved, but not disproved: he did voyage around the islands of Europe). It was claimed that one of the first ever missionaries to China was an Irishman, known only as Brother James, who apparently worked there around 1318 with some Portuguese brothers.

New nations need self-esteem: a small nation, quitting the protection and inclusive identity of a great empire needs to have something unique in its own past. That something unique included the tradition that Ireland had, at one time, civilised Europe.

And it was not a fanciful claim, either. In Lord Clark's celebrated BBC television epic, *Civilisation*, made in 1966, he opens his discourse on the nature of our civilisation with pictures of wild and rugged rocks of Co Kerry around the south-west corner of Ireland. During the dark ages, Irish monks preserved the elements of Christian culture in these last outposts of Europe, which was itself overrun by vandals and marauding tribes, he pointed out. Christian culture was almost extinguished in Continental Europe but Ireland clung on and kept the faith and the Gospels alive through the beautiful illuminated manuscripts made by the monks.

This was an early version of "Ireland's spiritual empire," for from these monkish island cells, the faith was reinvigorated all over Britain and the Continent by Irish holy men and women who went far and wide to preach. Cornwall, Wales, Brittany, the Isle of Man, Scotland, parts of England, Germany, Italy, France, Belgium, Iceland and even Egypt were said to have been evangelised by Irish preachers including women, who played a full part. The list of saints cited in popular works (notably by J.J. O'Kelly, sometimes writing as Sean O Ceallaigh) is prodigious, from Sts Cianan, Columba, Finian, Fiachra, Breaca, Dympna — still the patron saint of Brabant in Belgium — to Colman, Cormac, Malachy, Ronan, Bees (a great abbess of Cumberland who founded a monastery in 646), Chad, Pellegrinus (who gave his name to San Pellegrino in Italy), Gobain, Ultan and John Scotus Erigena. "There is scarcely a country in Europe," wrote a popular Irish missionary magazine in 1919, "that does not owe a large debt to their [Irish missionary] labours. France, Spain, Italy, Switzerland and Germany were in great part converted and civilised by them." Indeed, even in the 1980s, there were archaeological finds in Poland which indicated that Irish missionaries had been there in the seventh century.

The theme of *How the Irish Saved Civilisation* was rediscovered once again in a popular book by Thomas Cahill in 1995, published in New York. The tone was one of great surprise, that little old Ireland could have had such an influence on the great civilisations of Europe. Yet, back in the 1920s, the idea was in the common stream of thinking, and for decades after that was taught to schoolchildren as a matter of pride.

If the modern political era began after the French Revolution of 1789, the modern epoch for Irish Catholicism really began after 1829, which marked Catholic emancipation. Before that period, Irish (and British) Catholics suffered under a variety of legal restrictions, which were receding from about the end of previous century.

But the 1829 Act released a new energy, and Irish missionaries began to go overseas in significant numbers soon afterwards. Between 1840 and 1900, one Dublin seminary alone — All Hallows — sent more than 1,500 priests abroad: a lot of priests for a small country with a diminishing population itself. These included characters who became, in their own way and in their time, legendary: Father James McDonald from Co Kilkenny, in the 1830s, "the Apostle to the Maoris" with his "splendid physique, great big Irish heart, skill as a sportsman"; Father William Dollar, "Apostle to the Red Indians"; and Father Gordon, "Apostle of the Canadian Backwoods".

Irish sisters too were active from the 1830s in missionary education. Germaine Greer, Britain's best-known and Australian-born feminist, has pointed out that many Australian women would not have had an education at all if it had not been for 19th-century Irish nuns tramping across the broiling Australian outback to found schools for girls. (Germaine ascribes her own intellectual development to the encouragement of Irish-Australian nuns.) As in America, the Irish put their indelible mark on Australian Catholicism. Indeed, the very first Mass celebrated in the colony of Australia was said by an Irish priest, Father James Dixon, brought out there as a convict. He celebrated this Mass in 1803 although as soon as it was known that he had done so, Catholic worship was declared illegal. The Governor of Australia, Arthur King, became nervous that if the Irish met together to worship, they might soon meet together to plot sedition against the Crown. (What an idea!) Catholic Mass was not officially permitted again in the colony of Australia until 1820.

The Irish Sisters of Charity arrived in Australia in 1838, and the popular devotions of Ireland soon became part of the Australian Church: the Forty Hours Adoration, the Nine First Fridays, the sodalities, the confraternities, the daily recital of the rosary and the special devotions to the saints which were so much a part of Irish life.

The flow of the faith from Ireland kept up at a robust pace from the 1830s until the 1930s, and it was not really until the Second World War that the Australian Church ceased being the Irish Church in Australia. In 1901, about 87 per cent of Catholic priests in Sydney were Irish-born; by the 1920s, the proportion was still 75 per cent. Only gradually, throughout the century, did it drop. After the Second World War, new immigrants from Germany, Italy and Croatia began to influence the culture of Australian Catholicism, but the Irish roots were strong. The same picture obtained in New Zealand.

Queen Victoria's reign — which began in 1837 — was to be a period of immense energy and high evangelical purpose among both Catholics and Protestants. Irish nuns began to travel widely from just before the commencement of the Victorian era. In 1833, the Irish Presentation Sisters first went to Newfoundland; the Loreto and Presentation Sisters were established in India in 1841. In the 1840s, Irish nuns founded convents in Pittsburgh, Pennsylvania; in Perth, Western Australia; and in Oceania.

The Irish Mercy nuns founded convents in Buenos Aires, Argentina, in 1856, in Brisbane, Australia, in 1860, in Adelaide, Australia, in 1880 and in Belize, Central America, in 1883. They were in South Africa by 1897, the beginning of a significant Irish Catholic presence there. The Irish Dominicans, who were especially to flourish in South Africa in the 20th century — where they made pioneering efforts in multiracial education — opened foundations in Cape Town in 1863 and in Port Elizabeth in 1867. Their first overseas endeavour had actually been in New Orleans, Louisiana, in 1860. At the beginning of the 20th century, too, the Irish Dominican sisters established a successful, still thriving, school for girls near Lisbon in Portugal, known as the Bom Successo. This was pioneering work in women's education in Portugal, since there had previously been no proper schools for girls. Wealthy families had governesses, in the old tradition.

In the 1920s, the high point of Irish missionary activity, the death notices of Irish nuns and priests abroad often sketch out their peripatetic lives. In October 1921, Father Falvey, "a popular Dominican" from Tralee, Co Kerry, died in North Adelaide, Australia: he had studied in Dublin and in Rome and had served in Northern Ireland, England, Scotland, Portugal, and Pompeii, Italy, before proceeding to Australia. Short biographies spell out the lives of Irish religious and émigrés, sometimes sentimentally echoing the wistful feeling for the "auld country" which always lingered:

"Australian exchanges chronicle the death of Sister Mary Ignatius D'Arcy, of St Vincent's Hospital, Sydney, where she laboured in St Patrick's Ward for forty-two years among the sick and suffering poor. The culminating act of sacrifice which brought about her death — in keeping with her beautiful and self-sacrificing life — was the nursing of a poor wharf-labourer, from whom she took the influenza, and died of consequent pneumonia. Born at Killaloe, Co Clare, Sister Ignatius had an intense love for the land of her birth. Her heart, like a bird, was always slipping back to the Island of Saints. It has been beautifully said the 'the souls of the Irish dying in exile revisit the beloved places on their journey after death'."

Some of the lives of these religious émigrés were exciting too. When Mother Angela O'Donnell, from Galbally, Co Limerick, died in 1916, her obituary revealed a life packed with incident. The daughter of John O'Donnell of Ardrahan, Galbally, Mother Angela entered the Order of St Joseph at Cluny (another French foundation settled in Ireland) at Mount Sackville, when she was 18 years old. She was sent to the noviciate in Paris, and thence on to Rome, to be professed as a nun. She remained in Rome for the following 20 years, becoming something of a confidante of Pope Leo XIII, known as "the workers' Pope" for his radical encyclicals. She met and spoke to him every fortnight over these 20 years.

Thereafter she returned to Paris at a time when the anti-religious political programme was at its height. In 1905, a law was passed forbidding all religous teaching in schools, and all religious schools had to be shut down. There were tearful scenes of nuns being sent packing, and angry clashes in Brittany and the Vendée, where villagers tried to defend their Catholic institutions from the coercion of the state. Mother Angela and her sister nuns literally took to the road, like mediaeval pilgrims, walking through France to Spain, begging for their food and taking refuge in barns and stables.

They finally settled in Granollers, a town in Spain just over the border from France, where Mother Angela set up a school, again from scratch. When she died, in 1916, she was accorded full municipal funeral honours by the towns of Granollers and Barcelona. Mother Angela still has relations, incidentally, in Galbally, Co Limerick.

It was not coincidental that the year Angela O'Donnell died, 1916, marked the beginning of the most energetic period of Ireland's missionary endeavour. Although the missionary movement had been building throughout the 19th century, Edmund Hogan — the leading authority on Irish missions — claims that the most remarkable years were between 1916 and 1937.

This period synchronised the idealism of the 1916 period politically, and Edmund Hogan suggests that if so much energy had not gone into the missions, the Irish political troubles might have been a lot worse. Because, as the Troubles of 1919-23 wore on, they became more ferocious and, with the onset of the Civil War, more embittered. But the missionary movement provided an alternative source for this energy, mostly youthful, with its purpose of reshaping the world, diverted to high ideals overseas rather than into the internecine political quarrels which Yeats came to describe as "weasels fighting in a hole".

It is certainly evident that from the formation of the Maynooth Mission to China (St Columban's Foreign Mission Society) in 1916 a ready supply of highly motivated young Irishmen and women became immediately available to, in the words of the *Messenger* magazine, "Convert China".

The Irish Chinese mission was launched by a Canadian priest, John Fraser, who saw the potential among the Irish: he was joined by a lively young Corkman, Father Edward Galvin, and a 27-year-old professor at Maynooth, Dr John Blowick. China held a special fascination for the Irish missionaries: Irish Vincentians had been there in the 19th century, and there had been groups of Irish missionaries massacred by Chinese nationalists in the 1880s and '90s. Nevertheless, the enthusiasm remained, and when the Irish missionary magazine the *Far East* was launched in 1919, it found a public ready to support it spiritually and financially. Subscriptions from women, most particularly, poured in. The emphasis in these missionary magazines was always, firstly, spiritual: in saving the souls of the peoples to be evangelised. Education had previously been part of the package, but now there was also a growing dimension of medical care and health provisions, with emphasis on vaccinations, babycare, women's health, and preventative health care.

The expansion into medical care was probably instrumental in developing the skills of women doctors too. It was observed that in many countries of the East, modesty prevented women patients from seeing male doctors and Catholic women doctors were increasingly working with the missions. There had been an ongoing campaign, from before the First World War, to allow Catholic nuns to administer gynaecological and obstetric care, though the Vatican remained rather stubbornly resistant to this innovation and initially rebuffed such proposals by the Catholic Scottish convert, Dr Agnes McLaren. It was initially thought inappropriate that consecrated virgins should attend women in childbirth: the sisters were to win the right to work in obstetrics and gynaecology in 1936, when the Medical Missionaries of Mary were authorised. But throughout the 1920s they were expanding their general care of mothers and babies.

The fate of Chinese babies was a particular area of human (and feminine) interest in Ireland. There was a remarkable Anglo-Irish nun called Sister Agnes Johnston in Shanghai, who reported frequently to the *Irish Catholic* about the plight of Chinese female babies and young children. Chinese females were subject to being abandoned in hard times: female infanticide and abandonment is, unfortunately, a very old Chinese tradition. A group of Vincentian sisters, the Daughters of Charity, had set up an orphanage to save, and baptise, these abandoned Chinese children, and Sister Agnes would write to Ireland to describe the harrowing circumstances.

"The terrible floods that we have had in China this year have ruined all the crops," she reported in January 1918, "and in the country around us the natives are dying from hunger. Every day more and more little pagan girls are brought in. If we refuse them they will perish by the wayside, as many do, and lose the grace of Baptism. Last Sunday evening, fourteen little girls arrived together from one village, their ages varying from three years to ten years. They told us that three more had started out with them, but died on the way, and they left them by the river. If my good Irish friends could have seen this poor little band of pagans I am sure their hearts would have ached, as mine does every day, for it is my office to receive the poor mites ..."

Sister Agnes was concerned, as is obvious, to baptise these children; she also needed funds to support the orphanage. Quite enterprisingly, she had the idea of giving the poor Chinese babies Irish names: they would be called after sponsors who would name them, making whatever contribution they could afford. The pennies and the sixpences and the shilling coins flowed in: as to this day, the Irish were always ready to be generous to afflicted people overseas. And the names given to the baptised Chinese babies are themselves a snapshot in time of names favoured in Ireland in the years just after 1916: Mary, Mary-Josephine, Brigid, Philomena (very popular indeed by the 1920s, the saint herself was later to be declared mythological by Pope John XXIII), Kathleen, Teresa, Lizzie, Marie, Catherine and Bridget.

There were boy babies too, though less commonly abandoned, and requests were made that they should be named Patrick, Michael, Anthony, Francis, Bernard, Eamon, Alphonsus, Peter-Paul, Philip and Thomas of Canterbury. Sometimes people chose to call the babies after their own children — a Mrs Kavanagh wanted a Chinese child named "Margaret Brigid — for my own little baby girl" (and sent five shillings, more than a dollar at the time, and about a quarter of an average weekly wage). An unknown donor wanted a baby to be named "Annie — after my sister in New York". Thus was a web of Ireland's spirituality woven from Ireland to New York to Shanghai.

Sister Agnes died of typhoid fever in 1919, aged 39. Her work for Chinese children was continued by other sisters, and the interest in caring for abandoned Chinese babies went on. Saving girls from infanticide became something of a preoccupation, as, towards the end of the century, Irish Catholics became concerned about the forced late-abortions of females in China. A special report in the *Far East* of 1925 underlined the problem:

"In more than half the provinces of China, infanticide is still practised, especially by the poor. Girls are the chief victims. Baby boys are rarely destroyed unless they happen to be born with some deformity ... In some provinces, one rarely meets with a family having more than two daughters. The others have been destroyed in infancy ... Near the large cities one sometimes sees a public notice beside a pond stating that it is forbidden to destroy girls."

At the same time, the missionaries tried to show understanding of China's problems, and what caused such occurrences. "The chief cause of this unnatural vice is the appalling poverty of the poor," reported the magazine. The sacredness of human life was not a familiar concept to non-Christians, it was explained, and the parents thought that they were bound to destroy a newborn if they could not support it. Orphanages were being set up as an alternative to child abandonment. (Later in the century, it would become evident that orphanages are far from ideal and often places of institutionalised cruelty, but they were first set up as a remedy against infanticide and abandonment.)

Although they were critical of aspects of Chinese culture (they also deplored the tradition of foot-binding which still flourished: the feet of genteel women would be bound up, as babies, so that they would always be feeble and dependent), the Irish missionaries nonetheless respected the antiquity of Chinese culture, and particularly noted how refined its cuisine could be. Popular features in the missionary magazines would include stories of "Life in a Chinese village", and Chinese proverbs, with their Confucian emphasis on the work ethic, would be reproduced approvingly. "To make a man of yourself, you must toil!" "No good work is done without trouble." "Everything is difficult at first." There was also an attempt to "Irish-ise", as well as Christianise, China, with pictures of little Chinese boys being taught Gaelic games.

Later in the century, when Mao Zedong and the Communists came to power, after 1949, Irish Catholic missionaries would once again be persecuted in China, and the

Church would once again go underground. But during the phase from 1916 to the mid-1930s there seemed to be a tremendous sense of service and achievement in the mission to convert China.

At the end of the 20th century, I wonder if there are still some elderly Chinese Catholics called Eamon and Kathleen, baptised as small babies by those zealous missionary sisters.

While the spiritual empire of Catholic Ireland abroad was genuinely undertaken for reasons of faith, it also brought with it stories of adventure and exciting foreign places which the audience at home enjoyed.

Missionary magazines ran articles on "Apostolic work in Mongolia", "The Ursulines in Alaska", "First Catholic Congress held in Morocco". Life in Lithuania, life among the Syrian Christians, and a nun's account of an earthquake in Puerto Rico were, in their way, adventure stories. Booklets such as "Across Wildest America". An account of an Irish priest's journey from Newfoundland to Alaska, were read rather like descriptions of polar expeditions, which they resembled, with their stories of dark Arctic nights and total isolation.

It was the motto of great newspaperman Lord Beaverbrook that "names make news", and the comings and goings of various religious notables made news for the secular as well as the religious press. "Revd Father Henry Ryan, BA, lately from All Hallows College, Dublin, has been appointed to Towoomba, Queensland." "At Nenagh, Revd H. Spain, who is about to leave for Duluth, USA, was presented with an address and beautiful chalice from his school companions and friends." "The reception took place at Valence, France, of Miss Delia Browne (in religion, Sister M. Paul), daughter of Mr Browne, Fortbrown, Tuam." And visitations which would have caused a scandal in later years were quite innocently reported. "Right Revd Dr Broderick, Bishop of Nigeria, who is a native of Filflynn, North Kerry, has been on a visit to his native county, and has been the guest of Miss McMahon NT [national schoolteacher], Manavally, Tralee." A bishop who lodges with a single lady today might raise eyebrows.

Here, a Limerickman appointed auxiliary Bishop of Sioux City Diocese; there, four Irish Loreto nuns commemorate their golden jubilee in Calcutta — 50 years in India and still "full of deep Irish faith and real Irish wit". It was said by some English historians that in Ireland the clergy became "the native nobility" and certainly some of the social pages of the newspapers treated them as such. Social advancement in church ranks might be charted: "Revd P.J. Geehan, who was appointed Chancellor of the Diocese of San Antonio, Texas, is the son of ex-Sergeant Greehan, Straban, and was educated at Mungret College, Limerick, and the American College, Rome." A cop's son from a small, and poor, Irish town had made it big in Texas! "Revd. W.A. Maher, PP, Indiana, USA, and a native of Thurles, has been elected a member of the Geographical Society of America."

Names make news, indeed, and history and geography too. It was noted that in the Diocese of Danzig in Poland (known, in the 1920s, as the Polish Corridor since it was squeezed between two parts of Germany) was one Monsignor Count O'Rourke, a descendant of the first Christian King of Connacht in the fifth century. Here was Ireland's missionary world and history bound in one: Count O'Rourke's family had been forced to leave Ireland after the Battle of the Boyne in 1690, when life became difficult for Catholics. They migrated to France and thence to Russia, always keeping the faith.

Monsignor Count O'Rourke counted as an Irishman to the Irish still, though he spoke neither Irish nor English. Dr Orla Browne of Dublin — daughter of the celebrated Irish singer Delia Murphy — was confirmed by Monsignor O'Rourke in Rome in the 1930s, and they could communicate only in Italian. Yet the Monsignor's internationalism was a source of pride, not criticism.

The 1920s were bringing new freedoms for women everywhere. The battle for the vote had in effect been won. Irish nationalism had upheld feminism from its inception and, in voting for Constance Markievicz in 1918, had returned the first woman to be elected to the Westminster Parliament. Women had been active in education since St Angela Merici, who founded the Ursulines in the 16th century, but now they were exercising more leadership, as individuals, in the universal church.

The pioneering Dubliner Marie Martin was to found the Medical Missionaries of Mary in 1936 — one of the most significant providers of health in Africa to this day — but she was already at work on her plans during the 1920s, when the Vatican still withheld the appropriate permission. Another Irishwoman who became a celebrated missionary figure was Mother Kevin of Uganda (Teresa Kearney), an energetic woman who had a strong devotional following. She established the Franciscan Missionary Sisters in Africa, and became a passionate propagandist for Africa as well as for the faith. She was a sort of feminist of her time.

There was also Edel Quinn, whose cause has been suggested for beatification: a holy, self-sacrificing and pretty girl who was afflicted with tuberculosis and committed to giving herself to God. She has been compared to Simone Weil, the French mystic. Edel Quinn was a crusading member of the Legion of Mary, an Irish devotional organisisation founded in Dublin by Frank Duff in 1921 (within 25 years it had spread to 55 countries — another "spiritual empire"). Edel, who died in 1944 aged 37, brought a new kind of feminine image to the cult of holiness. She was always beautifully dressed and loved dancing: she even changed the minds of anti-dancing clergy on the issue, convincing them it was about affirming joy, not "base" sexuality. Edel Quinn wanted to become a Poor Clare, but because of her illness was deterred from entering the convent. Instead, she became a missionary in Africa, networking her way across the continent through Irish missionary connections. She was a remarkable and dedicated woman who was regarded as a great source of inspiration in the 1940s and 1950s.

The least plausible accusation against Irish Catholicism is that it was insular. It could be narrow-minded, certainly, in the defence of the faith, but that is not the same as being insular. It was not "island-minded", but universal-minded. It was not nationalist, but internationalist. Its fiercest critics regarded that as an accusation. "Properly speaking," wrote Liam O'Flaherty in 1930, "no parish priest has any conviction on politics. At the back of his mind, he regards the State as an enemy that has usurped the temporal power of the Pope ... The parish priest regards himself as the commander of his parish, which he is holding for His Majesty the Pope." Yet Catholicism's internationalism was a counterpoint to the almost naturally insular tendencies of an island race.

"Ireland's spiritual empire", besides carrying out its spiritual remit of guarding the souls of the diaspora, and bringing more souls to the faith, provided Catholic Ireland with a window on the outside world. The use of Latin in worship emphasised this universality, and the Irish theologians trained at Salamanca and Louvain brought a truly European perspective to Irish culture. In the popular devotional magazine the *Irish Messenger of the Sacred Heart* (selling 300,000 copies per issue in the 1920s), this universality was illustrated by statues of the Sacred Heart throughout the world. Thus the small towns of rural Ireland – Kilbeggan in Co Westmeath, Portumna in Co Galway, Carrickmacross in Co Cork and many others – with their Sacred Heart statues in mid-town are culturally and mystically twinned with Milan, Louvain (Belgium) Valladoid (Spain), Eygelshoven (Holland), Montmartre and Bavaria, far off places with strange-sounding and glamorous names.

Back in 1917, an Irish Sister of Charity wrote enthusiastically to the *Irish Catholic* from Wenchow in China. The experience of being in China was exhilarating, and now the sisters were looking forward to establishing "St Patrick's Church in China". The ground for the Chapel of St Patrick in China had been bought, and the first stones had been laid. It would be a great day for them all when the many Christians and catachumens could invoke St Patrick, apostle to the Irish and, thus, to the world.

Six

Sex, Social Control and Censorship

"Ireland Limited is being run by English syndicates
... We feel poignantly that it is not merely Gaelic
which is being suppressed, but the spiritual life of
our race. We see everywhere a moral leprosy, a
vulgarity of mind creeping over them ... God will
punish Ireland unless she draws back *now* from this
foreign sleaze."

AE (George) Russell, *Ideals in Ireland* (1901)

It takes about ten to fifteen years for the values of an intellectual
elite to flow into mass culture. New notions of sexual liberation
began to express themselves through literature, art, cinema,
fashion, and public behaviour in the 1920s and '30s. The
intellectuals and sexologists of the 1900s — Freud, George
Bernard Shaw, Havelock Ellis — had already preached and
sometimes practised such sexual liberation, and writers such as
James Joyce and D.H. Lawrence were to explore themes of
sexuality with a new candour. Increasing sexual candour was
also exploited by a more globalised commercialism, which
quickly found that you could market a lot more products with
"sex-appeal", as the new word in the 1920s had it.

Picture Ireland in the 1920s: a new and quite frail
democracy, still reeling not only from the Anglo-Irish war but
from the Civil War, which had far-reaching consequences
because the Republicans who had lost that war were suspected
of trying to destabilise the country. Among the diehard

Republicans, there was a bitter hatred of the "Free Staters", the victors who had agreed to a Free State rather than a Republic: there were endless small groups who were believed to be plotting to overthrow the State — the IRA, Saor Eire, Friends of Soviet Russia, the Revolutionary Workers' Group and others.

A small and insecure new state is far more likely to try and safeguard its security with draconian attempts at control and censorship, and the Irish State grew more and more determined to control dissident elements and cultural values. It *was* narrow-minded, and for its own survival it felt that it needed to be. Kevin O'Higgins, the Minister for Home Affairs who was assassinated (by Republicans) in 1927, was a typical embodiment of the new Free State man: high-minded, incorruptible, tough, priggish, ruthless when he judged it necessary to be (he ordered the execution of the Republican Rory O'Connor, who had been the best man at his own wedding), romantic but self-denying (he was in love with the famous beauty who adorned the Irish pound note, Lady Lavery), and upstandingly Catholic.

The Catholic press at the time was full of high-minded thinking and Aristotelian concepts of virtue. A favourite theme was "How to build a nation": in 1926 the *Irish Messenger of the Sacred Heart* gave seven guidelines on "Essentials in Building Up National Character", which boiled down to Religion, Patriotism, Altruism, Moderation, Culture, Good Health and Vocational Training (helping citizens to develop technical and scientific expertise). The aims were progressive and decent, though we would call them paternalistic. The state should be like "a good parent", underlining the sense of respect for authority.

In the realm of "Culture", the goal should be "a distinctive Irish refinement". And this meant an avoidance of the cheap, saucy, sexy and commercial influences which were growing apace, and which Irish nationalists, at the beginning of the century, had frankly described as Anglicisation. It was the English who were peddling all this filth — from penny dreadfuls (crime stories) to saucy music-hall turns. Douglas Hyde, the Protestant pastor's son who was to become the first President of Ireland, had outlined this foul English influence on a tour of America in 1904. "The devouring demon of Anglizisation," he had called it, "with its foul jaws, has devoured, one after another, everything that was hereditary, national, instructive, ancient, intellectual and noble in our race, our language, our music, our songs, our industries, our dances and our pastimes ..." Long before the bishops of Catholic Ireland began to speak seriously about the evil literature of the jazz age, the lofty-minded Irish nationalists had spelled out the agenda for a pure-minded Celtic Ireland in their 1901 manifesto, *Ideals in Ireland*.

This was a most influential book, edited by Lady Gregory (who co-founded the Abbey Theatre), and as a matter of interest most of the contributors, who included Yeats, AE (George Russell), Douglas Hyde and George Moore, were Irish Protestants. This agenda warned that the purity of Irish culture would never survive if it were to be overwhelmed by the new aggressive and "low" spirit of commercial exploitation with which the English media was recolonising Ireland.

So, when the new Irish Free State was born in 1923, a desire to start afresh, to build this pure and unsullied society was born with it. Catholicism eventually flavoured everything that became institutionalised in Ireland, but Catholic Ireland was not the original driving-force to create the pure and unsullied Irish state — nationalism was. But when the pure and unsullied new state was set up, Catholic Ireland gradually came to imprint its indelible mark upon the state's character.

From the end of the 1920s until the late 1960s Eire was to develop an increasingly fierce reputation for censorship, in literature, in films, though seldom, interestingly, in the theatre. Eire was regarded as being exceptionally prudish about what was permitted in the public realm: to scrawl "Banned in Eire" across a book cover in the 1950s was to indicate forbidden, and thus racy, contents. Yet the Irish censorship, though it came to infuriate writers and outrage intellectuals, was largely supported by the general populace. More: it was largely *instigated* by the general populace, who lodged complaints about the books to be censored. Until the 1960s, whenever the subject of censorship arose in public debate, the public at large called for more of it, and even deplored the laxity with which it was carried out.

When the movie *The Barefoot Contessa* with Ava Gardner and Humphrey Bogart, was released in 1954, there was a flurry of letters to the Dublin papers asking "Did the Censor have his eyes shut when viewing this film?" The theme of the movie — although treated with extreme delicacy by later standards — was a man's impotence caused by wounds sustained in the Second World War. Ava Gardner was the "barefoot contessa" who was sexually frustrated because of this event.

In 1957, the popular *Irish Independent* newspaper, which outsold the combined circulations of all its rivals and most accurately reflected mainstream values at the time, vehemently complained that censorship was not doing its job properly and that "the new wave of vicious books" were getting into Ireland at too fast a pace to keep up with confiscation.

At the time that the first Censorship Act was passed in Ireland, in 1929, it was not out of tune with the spirit of the age internationally. At this period many books were still banned in Britain including James Joyce's *Ulysses*, which was never actually banned in Ireland because no ordinary member of the public ever submitted it to the Censorship Board, and the works of D.H. Lawrence — *Lady Chatterley's Lover* was not "unbanned" until the famous trial in 1960. The writings of the French realist Émile Zola were also prohibited — he was regarded as "lowering" in his focus on life in the gutter unredeemed by the upwardly mobile aspirations of a Dickens. Some of the writings of Thomas Hardy which the National Purity League in England regarded as pornographic were also on a prohibited list. Hardy dealt with issues such as rape and family abandonment: he was also known to be an atheist, or an unbeliever, which caused disapproval.

Until the 1950s, customs officers at Dover, the main point of entry to England from the Continent, regularly browsed through the books in a gentleman's suitcase — most especially if he was coming from France, where banned (and blue) books were liable to be published. The historian Paul Johnson recalls this as a regular episode of his youth — His Majesty's Customs officer simply pocketing any book he judged to be unedifying within the realm of England — "I'll have that, thank you." Anything published by the celebrated — or notorious — Olympia Press in Paris, run by Maurice Girodias, which published "hot" writers like Henry Miller, Anais Nin and initially, J.P. Donleavy, was likely to be confiscated, should it be spotted. The idea of the state acting as "a good parent" in the area of moral control was not thought unusual in the early to middle years of the 20th century. That France was lax in these matters was considered to be a proof of its decadence — a point made most vehemently by Alderman Roberts of Grantham, Lincolnshire, Margaret Thatcher's father.

Censorship was an accepted part of life in the United States, too. Prohibition of alcohol and drugs, which started in 1919, was in itself a kind of censorship or state control, and initially it was believed to be working quite well. The *Church of Ireland Gazette*, the Irish Protestant newspaper, praised the outcome of Prohibition, as it catalogued the fall in violent crimes, in domestic violence, in attacks on women and children. America also had quite stern restrictions on sex and on birth control propaganda.

Marie Stopes, the British birth control pioneer, had to tone down her book *Married Love* (which was not improper in its style, even if it was somewhat revolutionary, at the time, for its advocacy of birth control) for publication in the United States. Books blacklisted by the American customs in 1928 included classics from antiquity, including Boccaccio's *Decameron* (Boccaccio died in 1375), Ovid's *Metamorphoses* (Ovid died in A.D. 17), Aristophanes' *Lysistrata* (Aristophanes died around 388 B.C.) — and the unexpurgated English edition of Erich Maria Remarque's anti-war elegy *All Quiet on the Western Front*. The German-born Remarque, who lived until 1970, became a hero of pacifism, which was equated in the United States with an attitude of defeatism.

Prior to enacting its own legislation, the Irish Free State researched the experience of New Zealand, India, Tasmania, Western Australia, New South Wales, and Southern Australia, all of which had passed legislation against "Indecent Publications" in the first quarter of the 20th century.

The Irish also looked at the various methods of control and suppression used in Britain, France, the United States and Canada. France was liberal on published material — as, paradoxically, were most Catholic countries: cultures with a Protestant tradition actually took the written word more seriously. But in 1920 France had enacted an anti-contraception and abortion law which was an interesting model for the Irish. This French law proceeded from a fear of depopulation, after France had lost nearly two million men in the First World War. Contraception was not actually legal in France until 1967, so engrained was French hostility to what was known in the 1920s as "race suicide" (birth control). It was the French model which inspired Eire to ban literature which advocated contraception and abortion — an issue which was to become a central focus of the Irish censorship law.

There was, in general, international concern in the 1920s about the mass increase in what was known as "evil literature". Pornography of one kind or another has always existed, but it has usually been secret and hidden, or kept within certain groups, be they elites or underworld networks. But in the 1920s more frankly stated sexual material was beginning to enter the mass market, and Ireland was far from being alone in its high-minded anxiety about "slush". In 1923, there was an international convention, under the auspices of the League of Nations, which discussed the new problem of pornographic globalisation. There was widespread agreement to take measures to prosecute and punish those engaged in trading in obscene material, and the following states signed the agreement: Albania, Australia, Austria, Belgium, China, Colombia, France, Great Britain, Greece, Guatemala, Haiti, Hungary, India, Italy, Japan, Latvia, Lithuania, Luxembourg, Serbia, Croatia, Slovenia, Siam, Spain, Sweden, Switzerland, USA, Uruguay and Venezuela. The Irish Free State was the last to sign the agreement, on 31 March, 1924, and was to prove the most serious-minded and committed to the notion of combatting what was seen as obscenity.

These international purity campaigns did, unhappily, add to the ambiance of anti-Semitism which existed at the time: some societies blamed the Jews for trading in porn and selling sex

(Girodias in Paris was Jewish, as was Magnus Hirschfield, who founded the Sex Institute in Berlin). Not Ireland. The Irish stuck to their own tradition and continued to blame the English.

Picture the 1920s, then. Jazz. Cocaine — stories in women's magazines speak alarmingly of "dope addicts". Cocktails. Cigarette smoking — openly, and amongst women. Carmine lipstick. Flappers. Bobbed hair. Fast cars. Aeroplanes. Short skirts which obliterated previous notions of modesty. Mixed bathing — which was a constant source of controversy in Britain and America (the London County Council did not permit ladies and gentlemen to share the same bathing area until well into the 1930s), and in America women could be arrested for indecency for wearing swimming costumes at all.

It seemed to those who had come out of the Victorian age that this was a mad, crazy world which needed controls. By 1924, there were two million Americans enlisted in the Ku Klux Klan who claimed that "Catholics, Jews and foreigners with drink, dancing and short skirts" were undermining American values. "Petting" was a crime in some American municipalities. The cinematograph with its "savage" scenes of violence and erotic images had the world gasping: Rudolph Valentino as *The Sheikh* was notorious, and thrilling. The storyline would almost certainly be banned today: it implies that women want to be raped by exotic, dark men. A British parliamentarian — Herbert Samuel, a liberal — described the cinema as "a deadly threat". Charlie Chaplin's films were described as "vulgar and suggestive of evil" in the same debate.

The world was going through a culture shock, similar, in a way, to that of the 1960s. It was all quite deplorable to upholders of tradition. "In that time," wrote the biographer of King George V, who reigned in Britain between 1910 and 1936, "the old standards fell away, were despised and reviled. Religion, marriage, love of country, gentleness in manners and consideration in speech, all these were held up to contempt by those who claimed to be the intellectual leaders of the country.

"Men spoke ill of the dead, and announced that animal lust and self-interest were the only mores of living. It was a confused and troubled time … The people of Britain laid their homage at the feet of the intellectual and the athlete."

It was true about the worship of the athlete. Sportsmen — and sportswomen — were the new monarchs. Celebrities like the tennis champion Suzanne Lenglen made a huge impact, not only in tennis (she won Olympia and Wimbledon championships repeatedly throughout the 1920s), but in costume. Miss Lenglen set a whole new fashion in female tennis dress — shorter skirts and no corsets. Like some later female tennis champions, she was a lesbian, and her masculinised energy and sporting aggression were much admired. But her tennis skirts probably had more influence than any fashion designer; and the designers followed where she had led and made the short tennis skirt a prevailing fashion.

The costume revolution which occurred in the 1920s caused some anxiety, too, in Catholic circles. In Italy, Marchesa Patrizi, the lady president of the Catholic Young Women's Association, expressed the feelings of the time when she said: "We desire that every woman who has the honour to bear the name of Catholic shall realize the duty she has of being chaste, but also of showing in her mode of dress ... repudiating the general moral corruption prevalent in our age."

The subject of modesty in dress begins to be mentioned with some regularity in the Irish Catholic press in the 1920s. Like soap operas today, the *Irish Messenger of the Sacred Heart*, liked to get its message across in story form. A *Messenger* story in 1923, reflecting the worry about unemployment, is about a young woman called Mary, searching for a job. "With hundreds unemployed, what office wants a clerk?" she asks herself. She tries office after office with no success. Mary doesn't smoke and refuses to wear the "extreme fashions" which are in vogue and, in the end, these two virtues help her find a job: she encounters an employer who likes a girl with a sense of decorum. (Being a non-smoker would have helped Mary just as much towards the end of the 20th century as in the 1920s. But in the twenties, to smoke was cool.)

A more punitive story in 1926 tells the sad tale of Betty, a girl obsessed by jazz dancing. Betty's rival acquires a snazzy dress from America, but Betty, alas, is not fortunate enough to have such transatlantic connections. Moreover, so besotted is she with jazz dancing that she has ceased going to daily Mass: the dance craze keeps up her too late into the night.

Her moral character thus failing, Betty steals a silk "jazz" dress. But there is a fire at the dance hall and the chiffon of the scanty frock is set alight. Betty escapes with her life, but she is badly scarred and recognises that her vanity and frivolity caused all the trouble.

The Pope at this time, Pius XI, a good man in other respects (he issued the great encyclical *Mit Brennender Sorge*, which reprimanded Hitler's treatment of the Jews and other minorities), was certainly old-fashioned when it came to chiffon frocks. The sight of flappers in a state of undress upset him, and he inveighed against immodesty in his speeches. Some of the Irish bishops did likewise. In 1920, the Bishop of Meath said that "wearing the Rosary and scapular" should prevent immodest dress. Other bishops were more sanguine and remarked that all fashions pass, as indeed they do. (In America, the Protestant evangelist Billy Graham still felt strongly about this matter in the 1950s: in 1955, he declared that women who wore low-cut frocks were committing "worse than murder".)

Immodesty in dress was usually a charge levelled against women rather than men, but there were times when males, too, were reprimanded. The Southampton municipal authority, in the south of England, decreed throughout the 1920s that male swimmers must not wear trunks, but full swimming suits which covered the top parts of their torsos.

The British Home Secretary between 1924 and 1929 was a crusading evangelical called William Joynson-Hicks (known as "Jix") who sought to close down every night club and jazz den in London as sources of immodesty and immorality. He was also the sworn enemy of saucy songs, the foe of drink and dancing, and plays that mocked religion and patriotism. The London flapper saw her rebellion as being against Jix and his ilk:

Mother's advice and Father's fears
Alike are voted — just a bore.
There's negro music in our ears,
The world is one huge dancing-floor.

We mean to tread the Primrose Path,
In spite of Mr Joynson-Hicks.
We're people of the Aftermath
We're girls of 1926.

The Censorship of Publications Act, which was debated in Dáil Éireann in 1928, took place against this wider international background of anxiety about changing values. The Protestant as well as Catholic press approved of moves to censor and control media. The Protestant paper wrote of the cinema in 1925: "There is no more insidious danger to public and private morals than the cinematograph ... Films should be subjected to a strict censorship." The Protestant press was also concerned that Sunday should not be violated by "savage" cinema shows.

The bill debated was not sectarian: it represented not just Catholic Ireland. It united values in Ireland, which in turn were an echo of wider anxieties.

Moreover, the strongest supporters of censorship were women (as, in the United States, the strongest advocates of Prohibition were women). A moral vigilante movement had been founded in Ireland in 1911, in a copycat version of suffragette vigilantes who operated in Britain. The suffragette movement was a puritanical movement: Christabel Pankhurst (Mrs Evangeline Pankhurst's eldest daughter and chief lieutenant) coined the campaigning slogan — "Votes for Women, and Chastity for Men!"

Vigilantes were politicised women who saw the sex revolution as bringing more women into the way of "vice" and low life. When the Irish Vigilance Association held meetings, it was generally noted that "a great number of ladies" were present. They debated on means of "stopping bad literature from being dumped upon our shores and preventing it from being circulated throughout the country and being read by young people". A priest would often preside (as with the Sinn Féin arbitration courts) but the democratic support came from the womenfolk. They also formed voluntary groups to monitor the cinemas and theatres.

In England, the suffragette vigilante groups — or women's patrols — received semi-official backing. In the 1920s there were over 2,000 such patrols, many paid out of police funds, saving women from moral danger, and sometimes men from drunkenness. Some of the leading lights of these women's groups were characters in themselves: one such was Damer Dawson, a rich philanthropist and "new woman" whose hobbies were alpine mountaineering and fast motors. Miss Dawson's second-in-command was Mary Allen, a window-smashing feminist who had done time in prison for terrorist acts in support of suffragism. (Obliged to sew men's shirts in clink, she wittily embroidered "Votes for Women" on the shirt-tails.) Another prominent activist in the women's patrol movement was Nina Boyle, who had been in the Women's Freedom League — a left-wing offshoot of the Pankhursts' Women's Social and Political Union — among whose comrades was Charlotte Despard, who became an ardent Irish nationalist.

An issue which brought the whole question of sexuality into the open was that of birth control. The suffragettes had not been in the same camp as the sexual radicals such as Havelock Ellis, who from the early 1900s were advocating birth control. There was a divide, then as later, between libertarians and puritans. Most of the politicised feminists were puritans. The sexual revolutionaries were libertarians. Marie Stopes — and her American counterpart Margaret Sanger — were later claimed as feminist pioneers, and Miss Stopes was a feminist in some respects, but the birth control movements were originally as much men's movements as women's movements. Marie Stopes received far more letters from men than from women, seeking to control their fertility, because when men were seen as the family provider, they were financially responsible for every new child born.

The 1920s witnessed more public controversy about the acceptability of birth control, notably with a public fuss about Marie Stopes's book *Married Love,* which was initially considered indecent. There was also more public debate about venereal disease, when, in Britain, the National League Against Venereal Disease was founded in 1924 (as an aftermath to war). As with the AIDS epidemic later in the century, there was a hard-fought debate between those who advocated condoms to combat VD, and those who protested that handing out contraceptives would endorse immorality and reduce the deterrent effect. Veneral disease in France had reached a catastrophic level — VD and syphilis caused 140,000 deaths a year between the wars and 40,000 stillbirths (according to Prost and Vincent). Women were at the forefront of all these debates, which were being aired with more candour than previously. Working-class women, too: in the 1920s, a group of working girls voluntarily formed a Legion of Mary group to clean up Monto, the red-light district of Dublin. Prostitutes disappeared from the Dublin streets more through a kind of feminist democracy than through state (or priestly) intervention.

The increasing publicity, throughout the 1920s and 1930s, attached to the birth control debate was very significant for Ireland: contraception shocked the Irish, though at that time to speak openly about it shocked most people. The Catholic view that God and nature intended sexual intercourse to be fruitful was quite widely held as a correct principle, even if it was not always practised or observed. The London County Council rejected out of hand an application for a birth control clinic to be established in 1920, and the Church of England continued to adhere to its policy that all Christians should "discountenance the use of all artificial means of restriction [of births] as demoralizing to character and hostile to national welfare". The Irish press did not speak openly of birth control but made veiled references to "neo-Malthusianism" and "race suicide". (Malthus predicted — wrongly — in 1798 that food production could not keep pace with population: therefore population had to fall.)

Yet as early as 1912 the poet Padraic Colum noted in his journey around Connaught that the *idea* of birth control was very disparagingly regarded in rural Ireland. In common with most agricultural societies, fertility was equated with success, and any kind of barrenness — whether voluntary or involuntary — with failure. At its most simple, this was the "natural law".

Thus Ireland enacted its Censorship of Publications Act of 1929, and subsequently it included propaganda for contraception (and abortion) among prohibited material. A second act, the Criminal Law Amendment Act in 1935, further forbade the importation of contraceptives to Eire (and raised the age of consent from 16 to 17, where it has stayed).

Significantly, there was no theatre censorship in Ireland as there was in Britain: drama was such a strong part of the national tradition and character that putting the theatre under prohibition seemed somehow Cromwellian. Later, in the 1950s, Dublin's stern Archbishop, John Charles McQuaid, was able to effect the closure of plays which he regarded as subversive, but he had no legal grounds for doing so.

What was astonishing about the Irish censorship was not that it existed — as mentioned, such practices also existed in other countries — but that it was so zealously upheld, and that it lasted quite so long. Abrogation of the censorship only began in 1967. It famously embraced a wide spectrum of books — the good, the bad and the ludicrous: from Casanova's *My Life and Adventures* to the French author Celine's *Voyage au Bout de la Nuit*; from Barbara Cartland's early novel *First-Class, Lady?* (in which the heroine's mother was a prostitute, and which contained the offending word "bastard") to Alexandra Kollontai's *Free Love* (the author was a free-thinker and a Bolshevik) and, more surprisingly, A. J. Cronin's *The Stars Look Down*.

These books were, in the majority, banned because members of the public complained about them to the Censorship of Publications Board. They were not banned by bishops or priests or by orders from Rome (the Vatican did have an Index of morally prohibited books, but it was generally a more intellectually challenging list). Censorship was democratic and people-led. It is very likely that it was women-led, since library committees (which vetted books in provincial Ireland) were very commonly dominated by women, and library committees sometimes fingered offending books. Some priests would have been included among the zealots for book prohibition, or would have encouraged groups which called for bans, but it is avoiding the point — that at least up to the 1950s censorship was widely supported by ordinary Irish people — to try and blame it on clericalism.

With the perspective of time, it is perhaps difficult for us to understand why someone, somewhere, objected to a detective story such as *No Orchids for Miss Blandish* by J.H. Chase, but somebody did, and it was upheld. Murder stories were sometimes regarded as disedifying: when I was 14 years of age, in 1958, my uncle confiscated from me a copy of Agatha Christie's *The Murder of Roger Ackroyd*. He simply thought it unsuitable for a teenage girl to read "grisly" murder stories. (Years later he denied he could ever have done such a thing: with the passage of time, we forget the attitudes we held in the past.)

Who objected to H.E. Bates's *Country Tales*? Was there too much rustic earthiness implied? Who sent in Daphne Du Maurier's *I'll Never Be Young Again*? It is obvious why some modernist writers shocked older people before the Second World War: Marcel Proust and his convoluted themes of homosexuality, or James Hanley's famous pederastic novel *Boy*. More mainstream authors who offended included Aldous Huxley (*Brave New World*, etc.), William Faulkner, Ernest Hemingway (specifically *A Farewell to Arms* and *To Have and Have Not*) and John O'Hara (*Appointment in Samarra, Hope of Heaven and Other Stories*). These writers had new and more robust ways of writing about sex, war, authority, marriage and society, and people were more easily shocked and offended than they are today.

Malcolm Muggeridge's first novel clearly upset the individual who submitted it to the Censorship Board: a courtship scene contained the sentence "His fingers dared to move stealthily towards her breast". A book could indeed be banned for one sentence: Kate O'Brien's *The Land of Spices* fell foul of censorship for the single phrase evoking a homosexual kiss — "She saw Étienne and her father in the embrace of love." Books like Vicki Baum's *Grand Hotel* seemed to someone to be immoral (the characters go bed-swapping) and Somerset Maugham's *Cakes and Ale* got the censor's bullet because it seemed to someone a story of an innocent youth inveigled into sexual experience by an amoral older woman.

The books which were most commonly prohibited by law alone (and were not required to be submitted by members of the public) were those which dealt with birth control. Books about sex and marriage poured off the presses in the 1930s: they were the new thing. Indeed, the very word "marriage" on the cover of a book meant — rather quaintly, in retrospect — a book about sex. It seemed as if Marie Stopes and Margaret Sanger had opened up a most lucrative market in which there was much demand. Obviously, along with the Stopes book on *Married Love*, Margaret Sanger's *Family Limitation* fell within the jurisdiction of censorship, as did *Sane Sex Life and Sane Sex Living* by Walter Long, MD. The full opus of Norman Haire was banned: Haire was a flamboyant homosexual and sexologist (and, as a matter of a fact, an illegal abortionist) who ran the World League for Sex Reform from London's Harley Street. The agenda of this organisation was thought to be far-out, eccentric and quasi-Communist in the 1930s, but all of its goals have now been achieved in most democracies: sex education for schoolchildren, birth control for all, abortion, homosexual rights, liberal divorce, removal of censorship and authoritarian controls.

Even Catholic-based marriage manuals could fall foul of the Irish Censorship Board, as did Dr Halliday Sutherland's *Laws of Life*. This was a book written by a Scottish Catholic doctor (and a great foe of Marie Stopes), which even bore the official *imprimatur* of the English Catholic bishops. It explained in decorous language the theory of the safe period in fertility control (which had only been established, medically, in 1934). Yet despite approval from the English Catholic hierarchy, Dr Halliday's book fell under Irish prohibition in 1941, since it could be read as advocating the limitation of births — the neo-Malthusianism which was contrary to the law.

Up to the Second World War, Irish censorship was seldom a matter for public comment. People had other problems such as health, unemployment and poverty: most people in Ireland were too poor to buy books in great numbers, and were grateful for the modest content of local libraries. The bookworm found his treasures among the second-hand bookstalls of Dublin's quays, which were an enjoyable source of all kinds of bargains and unusual (and unexpurgated) books which turned up there.

It was in the 1940s that critical voices began to be raised. The Second World War would bring about a huge social change all over the western hemisphere. But even at its onset, writers in Ireland were starting to voice more objections to the theory and practice of censorship. (Irish writers felt more strongly about the censorship of the written word than of films, because writing and books were a home-grown product, whereas movies mostly came from Hollywood and were thus a foreign product.)

In 1942, while war raged across Europe, and panzer divisions rolled across the map of the Continent, a Rocambulesque quarrel about censorship occupied the Irish parliament for days on end over a book called *The Tailor and Ansty*, written by an Englishman, Eric Cross. This tale was in the tradition of the rustic bawd, being a series of conversations between an old couple in Gougane Barra, Co Cork, a tailor and his wife, Anastasia or Ansty. It certainly could not have offended the prohibitions on birth control, since it is almost aggressively pro-natal — the couple are forever advocating "more breeding" (the Tailor's comment on the rise of the dictators is that "there wouldn't be half this trouble if more people fell to breeding") and there is much advocacy of "conjugal rights" and the advantages of "making small lads".

There is a bluish poem referring to "a hole in my ass", but most of the text is inconsequential. Like much rustic drollery, it is crude about women. "Women are like cattle," says the Tailor. "There are some of them will breed for you if you only look at them, and some of them go to the 'pusher' time and time again and won't have any calf." "When God made women they straightaway got into mischief. You see, He forgot to give them any sort of brains, and it was too late to do anything about it then. So He had an idea. He invented dust so that they should be all day sweeping it from one end of the house to the other. But it wasn't a great success. They still manage to get into mischief." How a fine writer like Frank O'Connor thought this was great literature is bewildering to me, but banned books become overrated.

So there was a prolonged debate in the Irish Senate when Sir John Keane, a remnant of the old landlord class, proposed a motion to challenge the prohibition of the Eric Cross book, the Kate O'Brien novel banned for its single homosexual nuance, *The Land of Spices,* and the Halliday Sutherland book *Laws of Life.* Some of the senators became exercised about *The Tailor and Ansty* and tried to prevent Sir John from reading excerpts from it in the house, lest it should coarsen the ambiance. Senator Liam O'Buachalla of University College Galway, and Chairman of the Senate, said he was disgusted by *The Tailor and Ansty* and pressed the minister in question to increase the powers of the Censorship Board.

Other senators concurred. There was an element not just of prudery but of outrage that Irish people should be portrayed as foolish, drunken and low. Not only did *The Tailor* appear as obscene to its critics, but it showed the Irishman as an "unvarnished" peasant and an uncouth yokel. A striving Irish bourgeoisie was trying to move away from the "pigs in the parlour" stereotype, and they did not like the notion of an Englishman's comic take on an earthy old Corkonian couple.

It was all very silly, but it reflected the values of the time. The outcome of the controversy, however, was deplorable. The old couple about whom Eric Cross had written the book were subjected to a local boycott, and, according to Frank O'Connor, one afternoon three local priests turned up at the Tailor's home and forced him to burn a copy of the book. The Senate debate had provoked a kind of hysteria. And yet it did have a longer-term effect of gradual, very gradual, reform. In 1945, an Appeal Board was introduced so that authors got the opportunity to have a ban lifted or reviewed. At the same time, the change of climate in the post-war world unleashed a new wave of widespread concern about obscenity and explicit literature. Wars have a loosening effect on public morals, in general, but after they die down there is a strong desire for stability and domesticity. After the war, censorship in Ireland was to wax before it waned, and in the early 1950s the number of books prohibited initially increased.

In the 1939-45 period, an average of 160 books a year were banned (against a total of 16,000 books a year published in the

British Isles). But in the late 1940s, the number of books examined began to grow, and in 1950 the number of books prohibited went from 166 the previous year to 410. In 1952, this reached 539, and the apex was achieved in 1954, when 1,034 books were banned.

Again, most of these books were prohibited because of public submissions. In 1953, for example, the official records show that 838 books were examined by the Censorship Board, and of these 640 were banned. Of these 640 books, 603 had been submitted or complained about by members of the public, through libraries, pressure groups or individual submissions. In some cases, the books were seized by civil servants at the Revenue Commissioners, or by customs officials, and submitted to the Board. Only 37 books were prohibited on the Board's own initiative, judged to fall within the scope of the law, as being likely to corrupt or deprave (11 of the 37 were books about birth control or abortion).

After 1954, the number of books banned began to fall. The Censorship Board banned ever fewer on its own initiative and by 1960 no books were banned on the Board's own judgement. This trend continued thereafter, save in 1965 and 1966 when a single sex manual, whose illustrations were considered too explicit, fell under prohibition. It also breached the law on abortion advice.

From the later 1960s onwards, the tide everywhere was turning against state censorship — the celebrated *Lady Chatterley's Lover* trial in Britain had proved a groundbreaker. And the whole debate began to change in tone. Before the 1960s, even anti-censorship writers generally protested that they would not endorse pornography and were insulted to be bracketed with pornographers. The writer Sean O'Faolain said that what most outraged Irish writers was that they were treated, by censorship, as mere pornographers. After the 1960s, the argument switched to a defence of personal freedom and personal choice. If an individual chose to access pornography, what business was it of the State or the Church?

Little by little, censorship lightened and receded in Ireland. For a long time, Ireland remained more conservative in taste and values than other countries: the magazine *Playboy* was not officially "unbanned" until 1995. By then, all the issues had changed once again. Or perhaps to some extent they had gone back to their roots. In the 1980s and 1990s, feminists took up the theme that explicit sexuality often exploited and debased women and made light of rape. The Ladies Vigilante Committees in the early years of the century would certainly have agreed.

Seven

The Age of the Dictators

"It is only by believing in God that we can ever criticise the Government. Once abolish the God, and the Government becomes the God ...

Wherever the people do not believe in something beyond the world, they will worship the world. But, above all, they will worship the strongest thing in the world."

G.K. Chesterton, *Christendom in Dublin*

Anyone who has read *Angela's Ashes* knows that the 1930s was an era of exceptional poverty in Ireland. There had been a belief that when the British went, and the Irish won the freedom of self-rule, life would get better. In fact, life got worse. Without the financial support of the British Empire, Ireland's economy was a frail sapling, and politicians made matters no better by engaging in economic conflicts with Britain. Social conditions deteriorated during the 1930s – in some cities, the housing crisis grew worse – and TB increased because Irish doctors were slow to accept the BCG vaccination pioneered by French scientists after which it was named (Bacillus Calmette-Guérin). British rule would not have helped here: British doctors did not accept it either until after the Second World War.

In fact, the 1930s were fairly awful everywhere, and the British Empire itself was not spared: the famous Jarrow hunger marches in England bore witness to that. This was to be the age of the dictators in Europe, a dangerous, hungry, volatile and unsettled period. After the great market crash in the United

States in 1929, a wave of disillusion about capitalism swept across the European continent. It was increasingly argued that the cruelties of the free market, which seemed to have delivered millions into poverty and unemployment, must be restrained by the modern state. Fascism, like Communism, arose out of a reaction against free-market capitalism: it was about the State controlling the economy. Some fascisms added racism to the menu; others did not.

Dictatorships also arise when there is a vacuum of power and of values. The Continental dictatorships were born out the ashes of old systems, particularly, in Germany, from the destruction of so many localised aristocracies and regional traditions. Most of the constitutent parts of the Austro-Hungarian empire fell under the control of dictators and strong men. In the Russian empire the destruction of the peasantry, with their attachment to land, private property and the continuity of tradition, had made it possible for Stalin to establish his own unique "new order".

But neither Britain nor Ireland — though both had extremist movements — moved in the direction of the dictatorships. Each, in a way, was saved by its own system of stability. In Britain, the Crown was the focus of continuity and ceremonial, and a hedge against extremism. In Ireland, this role was played by the Catholic Church, a strong family system in agricultural holdings, and the stewardship of Eamon de Valera who was committed to keeping Ireland a modest, but decent democracy.

Eamon de Valera — who critics would say *was* Ireland's dictator — had been born in New York in 1882 of an Irish mother and a Spanish father, whom he never really knew. He was sent back to Ireland to be raised by his Irish grandmother, and grew up in Co Limerick under the tutelage of a scholarly priest, Father Eugene Sheehy (Conor Cruise O'Brien's uncle). He became a brilliant young mathematician and a nationalist revolutionary, winning a parliamentary seat for Sinn Féin in 1917.

In the 1920s, when he was associated with the defeated Republicans vanquished in the Irish Civil War, de Valera was regarded as a dangerous revolutionary by some: the readers of the *Church of Ireland Gazette* were urged to vote to keep "Dev" out of power at all costs, since he was next to being a Bolshevik. But Dev settled down, entered parliamentary politics and grew into leadership. Personally, de Valera was a devout Catholic, but he was not a bigot (he spoke out against Republican attacks on Protestants in the 1920s) or a sectarian. He had good personal relationships with Jewish friends and colleagues.

But de Valera's stewardship did consolidate and endorse the concept of Catholic Ireland. It was during this period that a new partnership between Church and State began, so that politicians who had previously been regarded as dangerous revolutionaries would now defer to Catholic power in almost every sphere.

In the early years of the 1930s, these ex-revolutionaries and ex-gunmen who were now in power were keen to demonstrate that they were *not* any longer the enemies of Mother Church (some of their number had been excommunicated during the Troubles of the 1920s). Sean T. O'Kelly, one of de Valera's ministers who had been in the throes of the Troubles as a Republican, announced proudly in 1932 that the policies of his party were now indistinguishable from those of the Vatican. "The Fianna Fáil policy was the policy of Pope Pius XI." This seemed a shrewd career move at the time since being identified with the Church was a vote-getter for an Irish politician. And thus from 1932 onwards, no factory was opened without a bishop blessing it, accompanied by a political minister or notable in a deferential pose. The historian J.H. Whyte notes that from 1932 the attitude of the Dublin government was increasingly servile towards the Catholic Church, which had become its especial badge of respectability.

This was the year that de Valera assumed the political leadership of Eire; it was also significant because the great Eucharistic Congress was to be held in Dublin in June. The *Irish Messenger of the Sacred Heart* expressed the hope that the Eucharistic Congress would provide an opportunity for national regeneration and voiced the insistent feeling that the new Irish State had not quite matched up to earlier hopes of helping "to rid us of our national inferiority complex".

This Eucharistic Congress — an international gathering, started in Lille, in France, in 1881, honouring the sacramental life of the Church and presided over by a papal delegate — was indeed to be a brilliant success, bringing an international focus on Ireland as a Catholic nation, and enabling de Valera's government to establish itself as the vote-winning great Catholic party for a great little Catholic country.

And it was a wonderful event for the people, most particularly for the Dublin poor. A banner in a downtown Dublin street proclaimed 23 June, 1932 — the day on which the Congress effectively began — as "The Greatest Day in Irish History". An estimated one million people attended the Pontifical High Mass at Phoenix Park on Sunday, 26 June, when Count John McCormack sang 'Panis Angelicus' for the assembled faithful. There was a huge sense of festival, undertaken and carried out with pride and collective self-esteem.

In his book *Christendom in Dublin*, the English Catholic writer G.K. Chesterton reported that for this week in June, Dublin seemed to become the international capital of the Catholic world. "I have been for months in America; but I never saw a real American Indian in America. But I saw one in Dublin. He walked about in the streets with his tremendous tiara of plumes towering up like a grove of palm trees. Under that was the unmistakable high-featured face moulded in copper ... And under that was the dark decorous vesture of an ecclesiastic; for this man was both a Red Indian chief and a Roman Catholic priest." Dublin's role in the universal church was dazzlingly underlined by the colourful costumes and appearances of visitors from all over the world, Chesterton wrote, people whose common link was the Catholicity which they shared with ordinary Dubliners.

The sheer organisation of the event was a tremendous advertisement for Catholic Ireland, Chesterton thought: such huge crowds of people gathered together peaceably, without any fighting, squabbling, drunkenness or crime — at a period when street conflict all over Europe was commonplace. It was also a much-needed advertisement for the new Irish state, which the British had doubted could be run on efficient lines without them. "Anybody who shall say henceforth that the Irish cannot organise, or cannot rule, or are not practical enough for practical politics, will certainly have the laugh against him for ever. There has never been a modern mass meeting, of anything like this size, that passed off so smoothly, or with so few miscalculations or misfortunes."

And this was not done through totalitarian mass control but by the voluntary gentleness and goodwill of the people. This was internationalism *without* politics — the Congress had "brought people together as no politician could." Chesterton was struck by the "democracy" of Irish faith, and the way in which it mixed all types of people together.

Ireland's religion, he wrote memorably, "has always been poetic, popular, and, above all, domestic". Humorous too. A woman sitting next to him on a Dublin tram, wondering if the fine weather will break on the Eucharistic celebration, remarked: "Well, if it rains now, He'll have brought it on Himself." G.K.C. was also much beguiled by a banner hanging between two tenement houses in a slum street which read: "God Bless Christ the King." The Irish faith was poetic, popular, domestic — and proletarian.

The list of religious orders who marched in procession at the Eucharistic Congress was a staggering witness to people power. "Franciscans, De La Salles, Christian Brothers, Marist and Patrician Brothers, Benedictines, Dominicans, Friars Minor, Capuchin and Conventual of the Franciscans, Augustinians, Servites, Carmelites, Barnabites, Jesuits, Oratorians, Vincentians, Passionists, Redemptorists, Oblates, Salesians and countless thousands of designation unknown," reported the *Capuchin Annual*. How could mere politicians go against such a constituency? How could they not see Catholic Ireland as massively supported by the people, who gave their sons in such vast numbers to the church?

The internationalism of the Eurcharistic Congress had underlined the theme of the universal church which had been an element much honoured in Irish Catholicism: and it was from this viewpoint that the *Irish Ecclesiastical Record*, the voice of the Irish hierarchy, mounted a fairly sustained critique throughout the 1930s of the philosophy behind Nazism. (Pius XI, who was Pope until 1939, gave a more outspoken leadership in this respect than his successor, Pius XII.)

What was occurring in Germany after Hitler came to power in 1933, wrote the influential clerical magazine, was a revival of paganism, which "aims frankly at abolishing all Christian belief and worship and substituting for Christianity some reconstructed form of ancient Germanic or Nordic pagan belief and ritual". It was rooted, the magazine explained, both in Nordic paganism and in Prussian militarism. The Nazi movement was giving the Germans a sense of "exultation and self-confidence ... With that exultation has come a tendency to magnify the importance of Germany, and to ascribe to Germanic or Nordic blood a mysterious and almost divine importance." The whole notion of a "national soul" was anti-Catholic, appropriating something spiritual — the soul — for something political — the State.

There were, the Irish clergy were warned, some very peculiar faith movements developing in Germany and seeking to replace Christian rites. "Old centres of Germanic tradition and superstition are being transformed into places of pilgrimage and the calendar has been heathenized." The *Hagenkreuz* or swastika was being promulgated as "a natural connecting-link between neo-paganism and devotion to the Nazi state".

These German faith movements were indeed a sort of new-age religion of the time, drawing on race worship, Germanic tribal rituals, Wagnerian mythologies (and music) and even ecology. Hitler was an early eco-warrior: he was vegetarian, non-smoking, tree-worshipping, animal-loving, at ease in the mountains and in the forest, and loathed city life. Much of this grew out of German Romanticism, though the Nazis added their own values: Hitler regarded city life as decadent and "Jewish".

Nazi ideology despised Christianity as an inferior Mediterranean religion, a faith "devised by Syrians, Africans, Etruscans and other 'inferior' peoples", and built upon the Jewish Old Testament. Influenced by Nietzsche, the ideology gaining ground in Germany during the 1930s rebuffed Christianity for its "effeminate" notions of meekness, humility, acceptance and turning the other cheek. The *Irish Ecclesiastical Record*, which was reasonably highbrow and interested in ideas, understood that Nazism was a threat to Christianity and Catholicism at this point — a threat in a way that other fascist movements, in Spain and Portugal, for example, were not.

The Catholic press also warned Irish tourists not to be overimpressed by how efficient things were in Germany, or to be taken in by the apparent new classlessness in the Reich: some articles had appeared in the secular press alluding to these impressions. If the price of classlessness was worshipping the State — "Statolatry" — it was too high.

The Irish ecclesiastical authorities distinguished, very specifically, between Hitler and Mussolini (described as "barbarous"), and the two other Fascist dictators, Franco in Spain and Salazar in Portugal. They were generally favourable toward Antonio Salazar, the Portuguese Prime Minister from 1932, who was a virtual dictator yet considered benign (he was pro-clerical). He was praised for his, and Portugal's, multi-racialism: Portugal's African and Indian empire had never practiced a colour bar. And then Spain was a special case altogether, especially after the ferocious Spanish Civil War broke out in 1936.

The Cork-born actress Fiona Shaw made what was for her a shocking discovery in the late 1990s. Rooting around among her family's possessions, she found that an uncle of hers had filled in an application form to join Franco in the Spanish Civil War in 1936. As a woman of the theatre who has had her views on Spain formed by the anti-fascist poet Garcia Lorca, she was appalled — and bewildered — that this Irish uncle might have considered joining the Fascist side.

Similarly with the niece of General Eoin O'Duffy, the long-dead leader of a right-wing, pro-fascist (but not very fascist) Irish organisation of the 1930s, the Blueshirts. When it was revealed in 1999 that O'Duffy had had a homosexual love-affair with the actor Micheal MacLiammoir, the General's niece Molly wrote to *The Irish Times* in disgust. She had no objection whatsoever to her uncle having had a gay relationship. But he had really brought shame on the family by going off to fight for Franco.

History is said to be written by the winners; but the Spanish Civil War is one of those unusual episodes in which the losers have imprinted their version of events. After three years of horrible fighting, the Nationalists (Franco and the Fascists) defeated the Republicans (Communists, Socialists and Anarchists), but the Left remains the romantic and even politically correct view of Spain's Civil War. In 1936, however, the majority of the Irish supported Franco, whilst the majority of the British opposed the General. A British Institute of Public Opinion in 1937 found that 86 per cent of British people supported the Spanish Republicans and opposed Franco's Nationalists (and Conservatives). No such poll was taken in Ireland but historians of the period are agreed that Irish feeling at the time was in direct contradiction to British.

It is obvious from the figures of those who fought. Of the 2,000 Britons who fought voluntarily in the Spanish Civil War, only a dozen supported the Nationalists, the historian Fearghal McGarry notes in his study *Irish Politics and the Spanish Civil War*. Of the 900 Irishmen who fought in Spain, three-quarters fought for the Nationalists. (IRA men were to be found on both sides.) Not only, of course, for the Nationalists, but, in their own motivation, for the Catholic Church. General O'Duffy's Irish Brigade who went off to fight for Franco did so in a spirit of defending the Church, and were fêted in Ireland as such. In Spain, each and every night, the Irishmen would make a point of saying the rosary, which mystified the Spanish fighting men, who thought this was something more suited to womenfolk.

And the terrible atrocities carried out against priests and nuns by the Left-wing Republicans, who were so bitterly anti-clerical and aggressively atheistic, were indeed shocking. In her *Daily Telegraph* obituary in 1989, it was noted that the celebrated Spanish Communist orator and fighter known as La Pasionaria (Dolores Ibarruri) took particular pleasure in killing priests by biting their jugular vein. The parish priest of a town called Torrijos was "scourged, crowned with thorns, forced to drink vinegar and had a beam of wood strapped to his back — then shot." Not only were priests routinely put to death and nuns raped *en masse*, and then afterwards pulled apart by being tied to two horses whipped into different directions, but the mothers of priests were routinely executed, just for being priests' mothers. A favourite form of such execution, carried out by the Red troops, was to insert a large crucifix down the elderly woman's throat.

There was alarm and speculation about the sheer numbers of clerics being put to death. Paul Claudel, the French poet, estimated that 16,000 priests had been killed in cold blood by 1938. The English travel writer and Catholic convert Arnold Lunn claimed that the number was nearer 350,000. More reliable reports, received by 1937, claimed that over 20,000 churches had been destroyed or totally plundered. Images of the Blessed Virgin were especially profaned and subjected to obscenities. The Blessed Sacrament was profaned, and Republican gunmen opened fire on tabernacles. "The hatred against Jesus Christ and the Blessed Virgin has reached paroxysm," said a distressed report in the *Irish Ecclesiastical Record* in 1937, sent clandestinely by 48 members of the Spanish hierarchy. "In the hundreds of slashed crucifixes, in the images of the Blessed Virgin bestially profaned, in the lampoons of Bilbao in which the Mother of God is sacrilegiously blasphemed, in the vile literature of the Red trenches, making fun of the Divine mysteries, in the repeated profanation of the Sacred Host, we can glimpse the hatred of hell incarnated in our poor Communists."

One Republican was reported as firing a gun on the tabernacle crying: "I had sworn to be revenged on you! Surrender to the Reds! Surrender to Marxism!" By 1938, the Mass had not been celebrated (at least publicly) in Barcelona for two years and no priests were seen. All in all, 20 per cent of bishops, 12 per cent of priests, and 283 nuns were put to death.

The Catholic press had not unanimously endorsed Franco, especially not at the beginning. "The methods employed by Franco's insurgents do not commend themselves as Christian, much less Catholic," wrote the *Irish Catholic* in August 1935. "Mass executions of defenceless prisoners of war, use of churches and belfrys as arms magazines and fortresses ... are acts which ill become the defenders of Christianity." As time went on, the shift to oppose the Republicans became more evident. The Irish Protestant press was also vehemently opposed to the Left-wing Republicans.

In the circumstances, it is hardly surprising that many Irish Catholics felt moved to support the victimised nuns and priests and to uphold the sacramental life of the Church — which amounted to supporting the Nationalists and Franco. Collections were launched to help Spain: the poor people of Ireland, ever generous in disasters, gave over £30,000 at the church door — the equivalent of more than a million pounds today — for the Nationalist victims of the Civil War in Spain. In fact, poor people on the opposite side were also extremely generous: there are poignant contemporary descriptions in the memoirs of the time of Welsh colliers, their faces etched with hunger, handing over unopened wage packets for the cause of Spain. Spain's Civil War was terrible, but in a strange way it did evoke idealism and altruism in faraway countries.

It was also a characteristic struggle of the time between Left and Right and a rehearsal for World War II. It could have had a destabilising influence in Ireland, where there was already unrest in the streets of Dublin between various factions. There was what some historians have called "an obsessive fear of Communism" or "hysterical anti-communism" in Dublin, but this was not an imagined threat: it was real enough, and gaining ground.

There were, too, many unreconciled Sinn Féin men who had not followed de Valera into parliamentary politics, discontented diehards who would never accept anything but a united Ireland. General O'Duffy, the Blueshirt leader, had himself been an IRA man, then a supporter of Michael Collins, and a former police chief who had grown disillusioned with the weakness of the Irish state.

His Crusade in Spain, however, only lasted six months: it was mainly by way of a gesture, and he returned to Ireland where his support receded and faded. O'Duffy, although vain and blustering, was not a bad man, and his Blueshirt band were not to be compared to Mussolini's bullies or the odious thugs in the service of Hitler.

Eamon de Valera, however, deftly took the Spanish opportunity to lay down a marker of Ireland's neutrality. He believed that to keep Ireland stable, the country must be kept out of foreign imbroglios of any kind. He expressed compassionate sympathy for Spain in general, and then judiciously passed a law forbidding any more Irish citizens to engage in the Civil War in Spain, or elsewhere. In the age of the dictators and the dangerous controversies of Communism and Fascism, Ireland was to be kept under two influences: Irish Catholicism and Dev.

There was some common ground between the dictators and Catholic thinking, however: this was in the sphere of "corporatism", which had influenced the Italian dictator Mussolini. Corporatism, which formed part of the social teaching of the Catholic Church, stresses harmony between different social groups as a Christian answer to the concept of class war. Vocationalism is highlighted, as is subsidiarity (making decisions at the lowest bureaucratic levels). It first appeared in Pope Pius XI's encyclical *Quadragisimo Anno,* issued in 1931, 40 years on from Leo XIII's celebrated workers' encyclical of 1891, *Rerum Novarum.*

Catholic social teaching was an honourable attempt to bring justice, equity and community participation into politics and society, ordering the better off or more fortunate to have a sense of conscience towards their fellow human beings. The origin of the movement can be traced to Baron Von Ketteler (a Bishop of Mainz in Germany) in the 19th century, who mounted a crusade among wealthier Catholics "in the face of misery and material degradation of the labouring population".

In Ireland, the Catholic social movement was taken up with enthusiasm by organisations such as Muintir na Tire, the "Irish Country Development Movement", which was founded by a parish priest, Canon John Hayes at Bansha, Co Tipperary, in the wake of *Quadragisimo Anno.* Muintir na Tire's aim was "to unite in one body the rural workers of the country, not for the purpose of attacking any one section of the community, but to give the agricultural workers in Ireland their due and proper position in the life of the nation". It rebuffed class conflict, or the town versus country argument which was characteristic of Marxism (Marx regarded country folk as "rural idiots"). Muintir na Tire ran "rural weeks" on self-help, based on a French model of *Semaines Rurales.*

It did much to extend electrification, which was only beginning in Ireland in the 1930s; it encouraged local industries, providing free school meals and starting community information services. These organisations were indeed aware of the problems of poverty in Ireland and tried, in their own way, to do something about it. They also built on the work of Sir Horace Plunkett and the writer AE in the early part of the century, when they established the Irish Agricultural Organization Society. And Muintir na Tire encouraged more participation by women in the public realm.

The Catholic press was keenly supportive of all this rural development and self-improvement, and priests were active in promoting electrificiation (some folk were frightened of electricity at the time). In 1938, the *Irish Ecclesiastical Record* listed the "Seven Deadly Sins of Rural Life" thus: "Ignorance, Apathy, Selfishness, Snobbery, Meanness, Distrust and Politics." By "politics", presumably, they meant a certain kind of political scheming which advantaged some and disadvantaged others.

Muintir na Tire was the organisational expression of Catholic social teaching as articulated in the two relevant papal encyclicals. And both of these also provided some background for the 1937 Irish Constitution which remains the basis of the Irish State today, albeit subject to several amendments. De Valera spent 1936 preparing a new Constitution to replace the Free State Constitution of 1922 (one in which he had had no hand).

He consulted papal encyclicals on social teaching and studied French Catholic sources — the *Code Sociale Esquisse d'une Synthèse Sociale Catholique* was an influential document produced by a Catholic social studies organisation in Paris. He was advised, some would say pressured (though Dev was not a man to be leaned on) by John Charles McQuaid, soon to become the authoritarian Archbishop of Dublin. But he also consulted the Church of Ireland (Episcopalian) Archbishop, Dr John Gregg, and the Chief Rabbi. Tim Pat Coogan has called de Valera's 1937 Constitution essentially "a compendium of

Catholic social principles", but it reflected the values of its time and was supported as much by Protestants and Jews as by Irish Catholics. Article 44 of that Constitution (annulled in 1972) recognised "the special position of the Catholic Church", which reflected the prevailing reality principle: over 90 per cent of the people were practising Roman Catholics.

By the end of the century, such attitudes came to be regarded as "theocratic", as in an Islamic state such as Iran, but it was not seen as such by our mothers and fathers, grandparents and aunts.

The 1937 Constitution established "equality before the law" but it went on to distinguish between the two sexes in their social role: Article 41 recognised the role of the mother in the home and the value which she provided for the common good as a home-maker. Again, this later came to be seen as "repressive" to women, but it was not seen in that light in the 1930s. Neither was the preamble to the Constitution, which begins: "In the name of the most Holy Trinity, from whom is all authority derived", viewed as sectarian in 1937. The Holy Trinity — recognised by all major Christian churches, Orthodox, Anglican and Nonconformist — was actually a symbol of ecumenism. Had de Valera chosen to open the Constitutions with an allusion to the Blessed Virgin, that would have been thought unacceptable to Protestants.

Different sections of the community, in any case, underlined different perspectives. Irish Protestants were far more anxious to retain some links with the British Crown than they were about recognising the special position of the Catholic Church, which they were accustomed to seeing as the faith of the majority — not always flatteringly, to be sure. De Valera retained the link with the Crown through the Commonwealth.

In its time, de Valera's Constitution was thought a praiseworthy document. Where it is illiberal, by our standards, and where it certainly reflects the spirit of its age, is in its paternalism, in its assumption that the State is a wise parent which hands out knowledge and bestows grace and favour. The wise parent was Eamon de Valera, and he became the father-figure of his country for the next 40 years. Not a dictator, but a paternalistic helmsman. Not a totalitarian, but an authoritarian, as in the spirit of the age.

The 1930s were pessimistic, on the whole, and a lot worse was to come. Yet this was a decade in which big questions were being asked about big issues. How far should nationalism go? What is the role of the State versus the individual? By 1940, the *Irish Messenger of the Sacred Heart,* which had seen the State as a "wise parent" in 1923, was coming to realise that the State, especially in the cause of "racism and excessive Nationalism", could "suppress individual rights ... and would subordinate all to the preservation of a race or of a State. But the race and the State are for man, not man for the State. The individual has a soul to save but the State has not — and so the individual is of greater importance."

Pius XI's influential encyclical *Mit Brennender Sorge* ("With Burning Sorrow"), in which he anathematises the "blood and soil" ideology of the Third Reich, had a material impact. Catholic Ireland knew that the racist drift under the dictators was wrong and, in the 1930s, often said so. "Racialism stands condemned both by science and religion," Monsignor Cornelius Lucey wrote in 1939. "No scientist of note defends the thesis that one race is by nature superior to another or that any race can lay claim to any appreciable degree of racial purity." (Cornelius Lucey, as Bishop of Cork in the 1950s, was to become a puritanical scourge of the dance-halls. But, politically, he was actively anti-racist and anti-fascist.)

The *Irish Ecclesiastical Record* did retain its opposition to the Nazis and all their works throughout the 1930s and to Mussolini too. They certainly could have been more outspoken about coming to the rescue of the Jews, but that was true about a large section of humanity. It is disappointing, however, that although the Irish media was aware of the persecution of the Jews in the Third Reich, condemnation of this was faint-hearted and evasive.

In the 1920s, there had been strong signs of philo-Semitism in the Catholic press, particularly where there were celebrated instances of Jews converting to Catholicism. (In 1926, a list of Jewish-born priests in America made an honoured appearance in the *Irish Catholic* under the headline: "From Socialism to the

Church." Men who had been Jewish Socialists had converted to Catholicism: Revd Martin Hapner, CSSR, Revd Jacob Hoffsugoth, OP, Fathers Joseph and Augustin Lemann, Fathers Jules and Noster Lewell.) But anti-Semitism was endemic in the 1930s — it appears in many detective stories of the time and in the work of D.H. Lawrence and T.S. Eliot — and, regrettably, Irish Catholicism was no exception. There remained a religious antagonism (that the Jews had rejected Jesus), a prejudice about money and business, and a new belief that Jews were linked to Communism.

Many of the big questions asked in the discourse of Irish Catholicism reflected the uncertainties about economics and politics at this period. Is capitalism right? Does it cheat men and their families of a Just Wage? After the Wall Street crash and the slump of the early 1930s, the question of how much the State should or could cushion citizens from dramatic swings of the trade cycle is explored. John Maynard Keynes, the Left-wing British economist who promulgated deficit budgeting — encouraging the State to spend and borrow — was given a fair wind. Many of the ideas of the time were quite widely discussed.

This continual opposition to "excessive" State power was apparent in the Irish Catholic media up until 1940, when the Second World War added a new tier of censorship in Ireland, and called a halt to all discourse on the meaning of totalitarianism. But right through the 1930s there were constant reminders of the twin evils now bestriding Europe. "Communism and Fascism. Chief Problem of the Church in the Modern World", "Orgy of Nazi Barbarism", "Tirades and Diatribes of Mussolini" were characteristic of headlines appearing in the Catholic press in the latter years of the 1930s.

In 1940, just before the dark curtain of political censorship came down, there was a focus on the whole question, in the *Irish Ecclesiastical Record,* of the Just War. Was there such a thing as a Just War? Yes, war may be lawful, writes Revd John McCarthy, DD, particularly against "state absolutism". The identification of "might with right" — Mussolini is condemned for "glorifying force" — was to be condemned. Citing St Augustine of Hippo and St Thomas Aquinas, it was stated that a nation may indeed have just recourse to war. Thus, in neutral Ireland, where it was forbidden to take sides in the Second World War, this was probably the nearest authoritative endorsement of the fight against fascism.

Eight

The Moral Flavour of Neutrality

"The complete apathy of my countrymen, as the Panzer-divisions steam-rolled liberty out of one country after another, was more than a little exasperating to anyone who felt himself to be, not only an Irishman, but a European."

Arland Ussher, *The Face and Mind of Ireland* (1947)

"There is no kind of oppression visited on any minority in Europe which the Six County nationalists have not also endured."

Editorial in the *Irish Press*, 1 April 1943

The Irish State stood aside from the great conflict of the Second World War and remained neutral. This was judged necessary at the time, but later there would be a social price for this role: from the 1940s until the 1960s Ireland would go into a kind of psychological isolation, not having shared the common experience of Europe and having sealed herself against these experiences more rigidly than any other neutral.

Yet neutrality was wholeheartedly supported by the majority of the people. No historian or observer disputes that. Political censorship about the war — then referred to as "the Emergency" — was ludicrously strict and had a more deforming effect than the literary censorship which was to become so widely criticised. After all, if you really wanted to read a banned book by Aldous Huxley or Kate O'Brien, you were entitled to walk into the National Library in Dublin and read it there (there was always one copy kept in the archive, for the record). And if you were personally motivated to acquire any book, it was not difficult to find ways and means of procuring it.

But wartime political censorship was absolute and all-pervasive; it was also so misleading about actual events as to be effectively mendacious. Outright untruths were told about what was going on or, at the very least, false impressions were made and endorsed. It could also be quite personally spiteful: Frank Aiken, the Fianna Fáil minister who held the job of political censor — and, being an Ulsterman, pursued it with much zeal — would not allow parents who had lost a son in the conflict to add the Latin phrase *Dolce et Decorum Est* to an already austere death notice in *The Irish Times*. Mr Aiken ruled that the famous phrase offended neutrality. (The phrase comes from the Roman poet Horace: *Dolce et decorum est pro patria mori*: Lovely and honourable it is to die for one's country.) It implied that the deceased man's country was, perhaps, not Ireland, or that he was not dying for Ireland by dying in the conflict against Hitler; retrospectively, one could indeed claim that Ireland was saved from invasion by those who died to stop Hitler.

Such petty-mindedness was characteristic of Frank Aiken in his censor's role and contributed to the mean-spiritedness that developed under the isolationism of neutrality.

There was much dissimulation, some of it almost comic. An Irishman who had gone down in a naval battle had to be described as "lost in a shipping accident" — which was considered an hilarious anecdote in Dublin society. Movies such as Charlie Chaplin's *The Great Dictator* were banned lest they offend Germany. Warnings were issued about "anti-German gramophone records" and one of the chief censors, Joseph Connolly, even considered imposing some kind of censorship on toys and dolls, lest they be "toys of war" that could threaten our neutrality.

Count Jan Balinski, a Catholic Polish nobleman who had links with the Polish Government in exile, was appalled by the severity of the political censorship which he found in Eire, and outraged that even Vatican broadcasts about the persecution of the Church in Germany and Poland were disallowed. Jazz, swing and crooning were also not permitted on Radio Éireann (as the Irish national broadcasting station was called at the time), as they were considered to be dangerous foreign influences. Eamon de Valera, Taoiseach at the time and a dominant character, personally regarded jazz as decadent, as there was always an association between it and low life — and drugs. Photographs of snow falling on the Phoenix Park in Dublin — the Irish capital's beautiful enclosed parkland by the river Liffey — were banned from appearing in newspapers on grounds of "military intelligence". For a country that was not at war, the Irish State seemed to verge on the paranoid. But people accepted these conditions readily as the price of staying out of the conflagration.

All wars increase the power of the State and of the political classes. In Britain, many individual and civil liberties were suspended because "there's a war on". Private property could be requisitioned by the National Government quite peremptorily, with no right of appeal. Rationing was imposed by order. Evacuees were billeted on sometimes unwilling recipients. A state at war, on a command economy footing, becomes a kind of totalitarian state — though on a voluntary basis — as citizens willingly suspend their rights for the duration of hostilities. In Britain, the political classes considerably enhanced their own powers during the wartime period: "the man in Whitehall [government offices] knows best" was a phrase commonly used. In Eire — as the Irish state was called at the time — the political classes enhanced their powers not to pursue a war but to protect the country's neutrality. By 1940 Catholic Ireland was sometimes having to play second fiddle to their political masters.

In the 1930s, Irish politicians had seen the advantage of bending the knee to Catholic power; it lent them respectability and enhanced their status with the electorate, which had supreme trust in the Church. But during this wartime period of neutral Ireland, power shifted to favour the politicians, and bishops had to do their bidding. Bishop Morrisoe of Achonry, for example, in his Lenten pastoral of 1941, made a strong moral point about the wickedness of the Continental dictators, who were taking God from His throne and deifying brute force: "We know that the Poles are suffering and we know how the Dictator has treated the Church in Germany. Can we look with indifference on God dethroned from his rightful place in the universe? Can Catholics view with easy minds the possibility of a victory which would give brute force the power to control Europe and decide the fate of small nations?"

The bishop went on to say that for Catholics the faith should have priority over political expediency: principles should come before playing at politics. This note offended the political masters, and the newspapers were forbidden to report this sermon: an appeal from the Church was met with a blank refusal from Mr Aiken's department and Bishop Morrisoe was cautioned to watch his step. No bishop was allowed to offend against neutrality in Eire. De Valera himself refused to allow any freedom of conscience to churchmen on this issue.

Politicians might later complain that they were fearful of the power of bishops and talk disparagingly about getting "a belt of the crozier" — the crozier being the hook-like staff carried by a bishop as a symbol of pastoral authority — but they were well able to defy the power of the crozier when it suited them. It was easy for the political masters now to silence the voices raised against neutrality. The parliamentarian James Dillon, a Fine Gael TD, was virtually the only political figure to oppose the wartime censorship, though Sean McEntee, TD considered that the political censorship was over-zealous. Dillon was opposed to Eire's neutrality, and believed the state should have fought with the Allies against Hitler; for this he was mercilessly lampooned and caricatured as pro-British and a *shoneen* — the uncomplimentary Gaelic word for "lickspittle". James Dillon was a devout Catholic of the old Redmondite school — the Parliamentary Party before 1916 which believed in moderate Home Rule, not revolution — and his anti-Nazi views came from a well-informed and morally developed conscience. But he was virtually turned into a pariah for his non-conformism: he was disowned by his own party, and was obliged to publish his speeches and works privately, distributing them through his own samizdat system. Such was the grip on information and opinion held by the political masters.

The Catholic press did manage to allude to the rape of Poland under the pretext of news stories with a specifically religious angle. They would run a report from an Australian Allied soldier on the grounds that he was a Catholic. They would point out that Mr Churchill had just been piloted back from America in a flying boat by two American Catholic pilots: this also gave the information that Winston Churchill had been in America. They were glad to be able to explain that St Germaine of Toulouse had been made the patron saint of land girls, and thus enlarge upon the work of such land girls — women who replaced male agricultural workers in the Allied countries. Yet it was meagre stuff compared with their earlier scope of reportage and comment and it was clear that their source material was thinning. Before the onset of the war, in 1939, the *Irish Ecclesiastical Record* would list 40 or 50 periodicals received from all over the world; in wartime, this was down to a tiny half dozen or so, mainly from regional American sources. Ireland was being cut off from all outside information and Catholic Ireland was being cut off from its universal hinterland.

The *Irish Catholic* complained about the over-strictness of the Government censorship of news material, and compared it unfavourably to Spain and Portugal, other neutral countries where the flow of information was less rigidly controlled. In neutral Sweden, too, there was virtually no censorship on newsreels and news material. But Frank Aiken, whose Orwellian title was Minister for Co-Ordination of Defensive Measures, believed that Ireland's proximity to Britain, and the shared currency of the English language, made us specially vulnerable to Anglo-American propaganda.

This lack of essential information during the Second World War was to lead some people in Ireland into foolish judgements. Some Irish people were pro-German out of a historic naivety, guided only by the old adage that "England's difficulty is Ireland's opportunity". There was a body of opinion in Ireland which saw Winston Churchill and Adolf Hitler as moral equivalents, and just two sides of the same coin of belligerence. (Churchill had been described as a "warmonger" even by his own people, during the 1930s, a label which stuck.) And Churchill was also very critical of the Irish Free State, which he described as "neutral but skulking". He also greatly regretted the fact that a previous British administration had withdrawn from strategic ports in Eire in 1938. Churchill believed that these naval ports, at Berehaven and Cobh in Co Cork and Lough Swilly in Co Donegal (known as the "Treaty Ports" having been left under Crown command by the 1921 Treaty) could have saved Allied lives. A passage in a bestselling novel, *The Cruel Sea*, actually accuses the Irish State of maliciously and deliberately putting Allied lives at risk by its blind neutrality, and of small-mindedness in not ceding back the naval ports in question.

These political hostilities erupted during a harmless quiz show broadcast from Radio Éireann. The quiz show was light-hearted in tone, and anchored by a popular broadcaster, Joe Linnane. As a special hands-across-the-border exercise, it was being transmitted from Belfast in 1941. The quizmaster asked a contestant: "Who is the world's best-known teller of fairy tales?" The correct answer was "Hans Christian Anderson", but the Irish contestant merrily replied: "Winston Churchill". The audience exploded with cheers and laughter, as they were mostly Belfast nationalists. But formal complaints were made, questions were asked in the House of Commons, and it was a very long time indeed before another Irish radio broadcast was permitted from Belfast. Northern Ireland was at war, and these matters were taken seriously. But among the southern Irish and the Ulster Nationalists, the partition of Ireland was part of the problem.

The Irish felt misunderstood by Britain at this time — well, the Irish have nearly always felt misunderstood by Britain — but it was now particularly strongly felt. It was unfair, wrote one noted contributor to the popular *Capuchin Annual* in 1943, that English newspapers portrayed Irish neutrality so unfavourably. "These articles make no attempt to discover and explain the Irish point of view about Neutrality and Partition and they do not even succeed in giving a recognizable picture of Irish life." English newspapers wanted jazzy stories about bright lights in Eire (Dublin did not have a blackout, unlike the

North and Britain), plentiful food, various entertainments and espionage. The plentiful supply of food in Ireland was of particular fascination to a British society experiencing rationing. When my husband, Richard West, stopped over at Shannon Airport as a child, in 1942, and then flew back to England, his parents met him at the airport with envious eyes. "What did you eat in Ireland?" were their first, food-deprived words. Tales of hearty steaks and endless supplies of eggs — the English were on powdered eggs and a disgusting South African fish called snoek — abounded from Eire.

Popular newspapers are popular newspapers and often prefer tabloid fancy to dull facts: English newspapers have always had a weakness for pixillated "Oirish" stories rather than serious analysis about the country. The *Capuchin Annual* felt it unjust that sexy stories about food and spies were preferred to high-minded political disquisitions on the sound reasons for Eire's neutrality. And the Irish were also aggrieved about the number of stories circulating in England about the good life in "neutral Eire", when in fact there were plenty of privations: there was rationing of imported foods, a shortage of petrol, long and cold train journeys when it was not unknown for the passengers to be obliged to alight from the train and chop down some trees to feed the engine's furnace.

Arland Ussher, an Irish Protestant writer with a keen sense of observation and a deep and patriotic feeling for Ireland, wrote that Ireland's neutrality *was* justified. Nations fight because they are threatened, and Ireland, in this case, was not threatened. Anyone who could stay out of a war, would. What was not so admirable, Ussher went on, was Ireland's indifference. As tanks rolled across Europe, he reflected in 1947, the Irish had looked on with a cold eye. The majority "took no manner of interest in the war — or at most the detached and comfortable interest which one might take in a serial thriller". Ussher blamed the excess of nationalism which had been the emotional diet of the Irish for the previous 25 years. If you mentioned the afflicted victims of war in Continental Europe, all you got by way of response, Ussher notes, was "Kevin

Barry's broken-hearted mother". (Kevin Barry was a very popular song about an 18-year-old IRA volunteer who was executed by the British: a line in the song refers to his broken-hearted mother watching as her son goes to the gallows for Ireland.)

If you alluded to the sufferings of the Poles, or the Jews, or the Czechs, all you got back was a lament about the cruelty of Cromwell. Irish nationalist sentiment promulgated this indifference to the suffering of others: it was as though the Irish had jealously to defend their reputation as "the most distressful nation that ever yet was seen" — a line from another patriotic song — and the sufferings of any other nation were an almost threatening form of competition. In particular, the de Valera newspaper, the *Irish Press*, under the editorship of the ultra-nationalist Frank Gallagher, was keen to underline that no people in Europe had ever suffered as Irish nationalists had. Even in 1945, Sean Lemass, then a Fianna Fáil cabinet minister, was still maintaining that no people in Europe had suffered like the Irish. This, frankly, was self-pity on a national scale.

And where was the Church in all this? There was a great deal of keeping down the collective head. The popes had changed in 1939 from Pius XI — who had issued such a strong condemnation of Nazi Germany in 1937 — to the more prudent Eugenio Pacilli, Pius XII. Pacelli was a trained diplomat, and while not everyone accepts the charges made against him by the author John Cornwell that he was "Hitler's Pope", he certainly preferred to act and speak diplomatically during the war itself than to speak boldly. In the 1930s, the Irish ecclesiastical press material was strongly denunciatory of Rosenberg's theories on race (Alfred Rosenberg was the Nazi ideologist who promulgated the notions of "blood and soil" — that only those belonging to a particular race, rooted in a particular land, could be part of a national community). By the 1940s, these themes were more judiciously ignored, as though, for the duration of the war, controversial ideas were anathema. So there was a different kind of leadership from the top.

In Ireland, the leader of the Irish Church, Cardinal MacRory, hailed from Northern Ireland. Catholics from Northern Ireland were (and are, probably) more likely to be fierce nationalists than the softer southerners. And as they had more experience of being discriminated against as Irish Catholics and Nationalists within the Northern Ireland state, they were likely to be more focused on the ills of the partition of Ireland. Thus it was with Cardinal MacRory. He was not of the ilk that looked outward towards the universal Church, but of those who looked inwards towards Irish traditions. He seemed not to have approved of the Second World War in any case, and called repeatedly for peace (which, by 1940, was being described as appeasement). And he too tended to see the injustice inflicted by the partition of Ireland as worse than anything visited upon the peoples of central Europe. "Partition is not only a grievous injustice against our whole nation — one of the oldest in Europe — but it is a flagrant and intolerable injustice against Catholics doomed to live under the narrow domination of the Belfast Parliament and Executive," he said in 1942, the worst year of the war, and the year when Hitler came closest to victory.

He went on: "When I read day after day in the press that this war is being fought for the rights and liberties of small nations, and then think of my own corner of our country overrun by British and United States soldiers [America had now joined the Allies] against the will of the nation, I confess I sometimes find it extremely hard to be patient." We should not, perhaps, judge people too harshly for the statements they made at a time when political censorship was so very strict that they were necessarily under-informed, to say the least. Nevertheless, it is regrettable that Catholic Ireland was not at this time led by a churchman who could extend his vision to suffering humanity, in the larger sense, rather than be imaginatively limited by the petty bigotries of Fermanagh and Tyrone.

There was, among the Irish Catholic hierarchy, real sympathy for France, since many of the clergy had studied in France or at Louvain, in Belgium. But some of this sympathy was directed towards Pétainist France — General Pétain, the head of the Vichy French, had revoked many of the savage anti-clerical regulations which an earlier French republic had put into place. Elizabeth Bowen, the writer — though also a British spy — claimed that John Charles McQuaid, the ascetic and acidic Archbishop of Dublin, was a Vichyist. Again, we were under-informed at the time as to the weak and collaborationist nature of the Pétain regime, which delivered hundreds of thousands of people, French and Jewish, to the Nazi holocaust.

Yet pro-French feeling was understandable in Catholic Ireland: every second religious order in the country had links with France, and Ireland's missionary status had so often been in association with French religious orders. Pro-German feeling was less usually associated with Catholic Ireland but more usually found among Republican and strongly Nationalist Ireland. John Healy, a noted journalist and commentator from Co Mayo recalled 1939 as the year "when hated England went to war with heroic Germany": that was the way his peers had seen it. Sinn Féin had contacts with the Third Reich, and some Irish Republicans openly expressed the hope that Germany would win the war. There were also some Irish Government servants who were pro-German, notably Charles Bewley, a senior Irish diplomat who had served at the Vatican, and who, by 1937, was Minister at the Irish Embassy in Berlin. He told a newspaper that the Irish Government would do everything it could to promote the "old friendship" between Ireland and Germany — and was heartily reprimanded by the *Irish Catholic* for this attitude. "Our Ministers abroad would appear to have become as prone to saying 'the quare thing' as are all Ministers who do not get a reminder of their duty to the susceptibilities of the people they represent ..." Mr Bewley was well out of order, the Catholic newspaper thundered. And most deplorably, he had said to Germany that "Your Reich and its leader has many admirers among our youth." In Ireland, as elsewhere, commented the *Irish Catholic*, "there may be some ignorant hero-worship of Hitler, but we are safe in stating that so far it is of the character accorded to American gangsters or to criminals ..." (They were thinking of the then notorious Al Capone.) This, of course, was before the wall of wartime censorship came down.

However, if strong Irish nationalists were excited by Germany's power to challenge the old enemy, and if some ecclesiastics sided with Marshal Pétain of collaborationist France, a sizeable number of Irishmen and women took the individual course of joining the Allies and fighting Nazi

Germany just the same. In fact, about 50,000 individuals from neutral Ireland joined the Allies — some soldiers deserting the Irish army to join the Crown forces, which reveals some eagerness for combat. According to Tim Pat Coogan, the "medal rate" for heroism in the Second World War was seven times higher from southern Ireland than from any other Commonwealth country: as the Royal Ulster Rifles marched onto the D-Day landing craft, the men sang the Irish national anthem, being called, appropriately in the circumstances, 'The Soldiers Song'. 40 per cent of them were from the Irish Free State. There were some good jokes emerging from the anomaly of neutral Irishmen fully engaged in battle, notably the one about the Battle of Britain crew engaged in a dog-fight over the Channel with the Luftwaffe: the pilot is from Cork, the co-pilot is from Dublin and the navigator is from Kerry. "Say what you like about de Valera," shouts the Corkman, as the firepower whizzes around him, "but he kept us out of the war!" The joke sums up an ambivalence that was found among the Irish: to volunteer was honourable, and yet, even among these volunteers, there were those who still did not want their country officially involved.

Yet the political censorship office in neutral Eire was effectively bypassed by a most unusual source: the devotional magazines, which transmitted so many messages, sometimes in the form of prayers and sometimes in the form of stories, about those engaged in the theatre of war. The prayers and thanksgivings sent in by the readers of the *Irish Messenger of the Sacred Heart* would certainly have been censored had they appeared in a mainstream publication. But little by little, the *Messenger* became one of the best sources of news from the war.

The editorial policy of the *Messenger,* at the outset, was to support neutrality — and, initially, to blame the onset of war on human greed, vanity and racism. "Men worship money and seek after it instead of seeking after their eternal salvation. Or they worship their own bodies or their 'race' or the State," it intoned in March 1940. There was a prevailing sense of gratitude — which was the general feeling of the country — that Ireland had been spared from involvement in this war. "Amid the almost universal clash of arms, our own country stands apart, free, at least, from the greater and more direful results of war ... Yet while we thank God for His goodness to us, the duty is incumbent on us of doing our best to help the victims of this terrible scourge as much as we can, both spiritually and materially." The *Messenger* had been quite strongly nationalist during the conscription crisis of 1917-18 (when Ireland resisted conscription to the British Army), and as the Second World War loomed it took up this theme again, warning against the dangers of introducing conscription in Northern Ireland: indeed, because of Catholic sensitivities, Northern Ireland was exempted from British conscription practice.

At the outset, therefore, the *Messenger's* position was impeccably supportive of the Irish Government. Yet the magazine was also very responsive to readership feedback — readers wrote in great numbers to request prayers and to give thanks for their blessings — and it became clear that many of the magazine's readers were involved, one way or another, with the war. This caused a subtle but perceptible shift in the *Messenger's* editorial policy: the faith comes first, and takes precedence over Government sensibilities. If Irishmen and women, engaged in the theatre of war, needed the consolation of the faith at this time, it must be given to them.

Initially, the wartime censorship had cast some doubt on the freedom to publish letters from serving soldiers, sailors and airmen (since the cause of their deaths could not be published in *The Irish Times*, it was reasonable to suppose that letters and messages could scarcely be printed in the public realm). Yet the *Messenger* came to the conclusion that Mr Aiken would hardly stoop to censoring religious magazines. Mr Aiken probably thought himself too grand for such endeavours, though the *Messenger* had a large circulation and could be quite influential. And so it began to publish wartime letters with this one in September 1940:

> I doubt whether you can publish this letter, but I should like to offer my thanks to the Sacred Heart for many favours obtained. I am an Air Observer in the RAF and on numerous occasions I have been in tight

corners during this war. However, I have always placed my trust in the Sacred Heart and He has always kept me safe. I often say that little prayer Sacred Heart of Jesus I Place My Trust in Thee, and find it helps a lot. I get and read the *Irish Messenger* regularly.

Extracts from war letters began to reveal the true picture of neutral Ireland for many families; the State might have been zealously neutral, and its position democratically supported, yet many ordinary families were personally involved. "I was a member of the crew of a ship that was so severely bombed that she sank. Only six of the twenty-two in our department were saved and all these chaps were killed, not by drowning, but by bombardment." "I thank the Sacred Heart for the safe return of a young man from the war in France." "My nephew was among the last to leave Dunkirk. His mother was saved from death by fire last week; it was a miracle." "Miscellaneous favours received: Safety during air raids. Safe return from Narvic. Safety of brother prisoner of war." This was all transmitting war news. (Some *Te Deums* continued to be offered for more everyday accomplishments: thanks were also offered for "Prize won at debate.")

Between 1940 and 1942 the story of what was happening in the war-zone continued to be told through the medium of these personal anecdotes, as prayers and thanksgivings were offered for: "Safety of son in Royal Navy ... Husband missing in France ... Prisoner of war in Germany ..." "During the Battle of France and the Battle of Norway, I promised the Sacred Heart I would publish my thanks in the *Messenger* if He would bring my brothers safely through both campaigns. He did."

The active role of Irishmen serving with the Allies emerges through these pages. Thanks are given for: "Father only survivor of vessel sunk in South America and subsequently released from 'Graf Spree'." "Husband saved when ship torpedoed." "Safety of fiancé whose ship was torpedoed." "Safety of friend in Navy." "News of son missing in Greece." "Remarkable escape of my son when with the RAF in France last year. All his squadron but he were wiped out and with some refugees he escaped from Brest in a small boat. After some days they were picked up by a Dutch ship and brought to Plymouth."

> When I joined the RAF fifteen months ago, I prayed hard to the Sacred Heart that I might be a success. I volunteered for Air Crew Duty and was accepted. Then I started praying for my 'Wing' and my 'Stripes' and after weeks of training I was successful in getting my 'Stripes', a month later the 'Wing' came along. I am now a sergeant observer and as I go on my flights at night my last murmured prayer as I fasten my parachute harness is Sacred Heart of Jesus I Place My Trust in Thee.

Thus did faith see an Irishman through. Some of the letters and first-person stories are rather exciting and describe the thrills of danger. In 1941, a "grateful airman" wrote:

> Being on duty I could not leave my post; bombs were falling all around me — one fell only about 120 yards away ... Immediately after that one exploded, another came whistling for me, and I thought I was finished. Having nowhere to take cover, I repeated Sacred Heart of Jesus I Place My Trust in Thee, and then the miracle happened. The bomb fell about fifty yards away and buried itself in the muddy beach to explode ... I find it very good to say the Rosary while raiders are overhead and this is not the first time I have been fortunate enough to escape death narrowly.

Apart from the men on active service, the *Messenger* reflects the experience of those caught in air raids, in Britain and in Northern Ireland. A Dubliner: "I have just come home from England where I had spent the past three months in air-raid shelters. Two weeks ago we were in a very bad raid on Birmingham which lasted eleven and a half hours. I have great devotion to the Sacred Heart and when I received a Sacred Heart Shield from my mother in Ireland I hung it up in the air-raid shelter." From Tipperary: "I return most grateful thanks to the Sacred Heart for the miraculous escape of my brother during a raid on Coventry. Half of the house he was in was bombed, his half intact." From Co Laois: "I beg you to publish this letter of thanksgiving to the Sacred Heart for saving my daughter in an air raid in England. The house she lived in was demolished by a bomb, and when she awoke she found she was the only survivor and escaped with only bruises on her legs."

From Belfast, an all-too-human confession: "I have always led a very bad life, mocking the Church and her priests and I consider myself a brave fellow indeed." But a heavy raid "terrified the life out of me", and "I turned to prayer". Well, one does.

Miscellaneous favours were received: "Safety of relatives in England." "Safety of Brother when ship attacked at sea." "Husband in Air Force granted leave." "I wish to thank the Sacred Heart through the *Messenger* for the safety of my son, who is a sailor, and who was machine-gunned whilst out marching a few weeks ago."

Arland Ussher, the Protestant writer who felt critical about Ireland's indifference to the war, said that there was a national failure to imagine what it was like to be in the centre of a blitzkrieg, but the accounts sent to the *Messenger* often describe such experiences quite well. "Will you please publish this little thanksgiving to the Sacred Heart for saving my daughter during a recent raid in Belfast. The house in which she was staying was completely demolished, but the family got clear..." And:

> A land mine dropped in our road at 3 a.m. on Friday — we were bombed out of our billets, and the house fell in on us in an instant. All the children are safe although there is nothing but death and desolation all round. Will you please have a Mass said in thanksgiving to the Sacred Heart ... Pray, pray, pray for us!

In one sense, this was all to the greater glory of the Sacred Heart — although a cynic might add that this was especially so since only those who survived could write to say so. Yet the mentality of the *Messenger* readers genuinely was an admirable mixture of the trusting and the stoical: if they, or their families, were saved from being bombed, drowned or "machine-gunned", they wished to express their own *Te Deum* of thanks, an urge which has affected kings and commoners. The Sacred Heart badge, or devotion to the Sacred Heart, was not seen as an amulet against bad luck: devout people had also met with tragedy. But it was a consolation, as a Co Clare mother explains in her grief.

> Over a year ago my son was killed in an RAF accident. He was a splendid specimen of manhood, full of innocent fun and deeply religious. One day he was in his workshop when a plane crashed into it and he was killed instantly. They sent me home a Sacred Heart badge that Paddy was wearing and although I did feel deserted by the Sacred Heart, somehow I got the grace of perfect resignation. Two different chaplains who had been with him wrote to me to say that Paddy had been quite unspoiled by mixing with boys of other religions, and in fact said that the boys of his type were sometimes the means of bringing many converts to the Church.

If tragedy struck, people were expected to accept the will of God and to pray for (as they mention) "solace in grief" and "help to bear great sorrow". The grace of perfect resignation, as mentioned by the mother from Co Clare, was much valued. And of course the most important task was to meet death in a state of perfect grace — this was more important than merely saving your life.

"For sixteen days," another mother writes, "[my son] has been in fierce fighting, heavy bombing and shelling in Belgium … He was taken prisoner but made his escape by swimming a canal. He kept repeating Sacred Heart of Jesus I Place my Trust in Thee. When the enemy were only a few hundred yards away he met a priest from Sligo who heard his Confession. He will never forget Dunkirk, being trapped there with no food for four days." She signs herself: "One Who Believes in Prayer." She might also have signed herself "one who breaks the Irish political censorship" as it was totally out of order to refer to the Germans as "the enemy". Ireland was neutral: she had neither allies nor "enemies" in the conflict.

A *Messenger* story set in London in the Blitz, 'The Shelter' by Colman Kavanagh, brings out the theme of "the good death". An Irishman and his wife, living in England, make for an air-raid shelter when a bombing raid is expected. As they make to go inside, the husband notices a girl still outside the shelter who seems very frightened and cannot gain entry. He says to his wife that he thinks he ought to sacrifice his place in the shelter to the young woman; the wife is doubtful and asks if he should risk his own life for a stranger. The Irishman replies, gallantly, "Sure, in a shipwreck, it's always women and children first, so why not the same in an air raid? Aren't our children happy with their granny in Eire, and you know you will be welcome there if anything happens to me. Let me go in the name of God." The wife agrees that he should go outside and allow the girl to come into the shelter; the wife also gives her husband her rosary beads.

The young woman comes into the air-raid shelter, the bombing starts and sure enough, when it is over, the husband is found to be dead outside, his rosary beads still in his hand. His wife says: "He was just starting the last decade when he was struck. I must remember to tell the children that." When the girl who took the man's place is stricken with remorse, the wife — now the widow — responds: "Sure, he died the death of a hero and 'tis a proud woman I am this night." She gives the girl the rosary beads — there is an implication that the girl is also Irish, but has possibly "fallen away" from the practice of the faith — asking her to say a round of the rosary every night for the man's soul. This is regarded as a happy ending, since the husband died in a state of grace and the young woman, it is implied, has been rescued from faithlessness. The life of the body was clearly regarded as of much less worth than the life of the soul.

Another fictional story describes the sense of duty with which a wife faces death in the Blitz over England. In 'Her Decision' by (the probably pseudonymous) A. Grosch, a family in England evacuates the children to Kilbracken in Ireland, again to the home of grandparents. The husband and wife stay together in London. "August passed, and in September the enemy" — again, non-neutral talk — "began his attacks by night." As "the enemy's attacks worsen" the husband suggests that the wife join the children in Ireland, for this is June 1940. But the wife refuses. "If I may, Tom, I'll see it out here, with you, come what may!"

The continual emphasis on the Blitz, and on Irish people being on the receiving end of the Reich's bombs, illustrated how intertwined Irish and British family lives were; by showing the everyday lives of Irish Catholics at risk during the war, the *Messenger* was circumventing the political censor's regulations more artfully than any other publication. A radical literary magazine such as the *Bell* was actually more conformist to political repression than the Sacred Heart's devotional followers. The truth was that the Irish were not — as Tim Pat Coogan again points out in his superb *Ireland Since the Rising,* written in the 1960s — actually morally neutral. They suspected the Nazis were a bad lot, even if they were not informed about the details of the Third Reich. It was just that, as Coogan says, they did not mind seeing England "taking a knock".

In another sense, the period of neutrality also illuminates a certain ambivalence that existed in the Irish mind. In real terms it was only possible for Ireland to be neutral because geographically she was protected by the shield of Britain: had Ireland been on the eastern flank of Britain rather than the western, her neutrality would have been of as little value as Belgium's or Holland's. In Ireland, we are sometimes capable of imagining certain facts about ourselves which are not always literally true: we imagine that Irish is our first language, but in truth it is not. Yet sometimes it is also part of real life to live with ambivalence, the poet Seamus Heaney has said, because sometimes it is the only way to honour a range of conflicting ideals.

As the Second World War wore on, and particularly after the United States entered the fray in December 1941, it began to look increasingly likely that the Allies would win. Accordingly, opinion gradually shifted in Ireland towards more support of the Allies (especially favouring the Americans). But at war's end, Ireland, which had not shared in the conflict, did not share in the triumph of victory. When the notorious camps of Auschwitz and Belsen were first opened, some people in Ireland refused to believe that they were genuine. One Irish newspaper, the *Kilkenny People,* claimed that the concentration camps were staged British propaganda and that the victims portrayed were starving Indians got up to look like European Jews.

There had been benefits for the Irish state of staying out of the Second World War: the avoidance of much grief, upheaval, destruction and sheer cost. Eire did not have such a reckoning to make. Neither would it be faced, a generation or two down the line, with the conscience-stricken anguish of the Germans, or the guilty self-examination of the French, worrying about the extent of collaboration with the occupying power.

But where there are benefits, there are also costs. Eire's neutrality had driven deeper the psychological gulf of partition between Ireland North and South. Northern Ireland felt itself more different from Eire, after the war, than it had beforehand. And the Irish State also saw itself as a more self-contained entity, composed of the 26 counties (rather than the original 32) drawn together with a national sense of coherence under de Valera. Neutrality had consolidated Southern Ireland as a political entity. "Neutrality and the experience of the war years," writes the social historian Terence Brown, "had mobilized Irish public opinion for the first time to consider the twenty-six county state as the primary unit of national loyalty." When Churchill had offered de Valera the option of a re-united Ireland in exchange for Ireland's willing participation in the war on the side of the Allies, Dev had turned him down. The reason that he gave was Partition; and yet paradoxically, in rebuffing this offer, he was effectively copper-fastening Partition all the more. At the time, in 1943, the Irish public was delirious with pleasure at de Valera's rejection of Churchill: the sheer chutzpah of little Ireland standing up to the great British Empire always brought delight to the Irish.

And there were some costs, internationally, too. Ireland was somewhat cold-shouldered by the international community (particularly by the Soviets) for her neutrality, and was not admitted to the United Nations for this very reason until 1956. The neutrals — with the exception of Switzerland, always regarded as a special case — were given a colder reception generally. Sweden was much criticised, and Spain and Portugal — still under their own more benign dictators, Franco and Salazar — were out on a limb until the expansion of the European Community in the 1970s.

Furthermore, missing out on the Second World War, in terms of social change, effectively left Ireland in the 1920s and 1930s for the next quarter-century. The changes which affected women's lives elsewhere would not begin in Ireland for another generation.

The post-war world did not seem immediately better for anyone. Rationing continued in Ireland — and in Britain— due to difficulties of communication and shortage of supplies. Scarcity was a matter of ongoing comment: "With the present scarcity of bed linen," the humorous magazine *Dublin Opinion* quipped, "drunken men should be described as only two sheets in the wind." There was an awareness that things were worse elsewhere. "What Europeans feel most at present is their ribs."

Almost as soon as the European war was over, Catholic Ireland became aware that Stalin was taking half the spoils and that this boded ill for the cause of Christianity. In a celebrated speech in March 1946 at Fulton, Missouri, Sir Winston Churchill proclaime: "An iron curtain has descended across the Continent." The phrase "iron curtain" was immediately taken up with enthusiasm in the Catholic media. The fears of Communism, which had been articulated during the 1930s — and amplified during the Spanish Civil War — now seemed more than fulfilled as Red power spread across half the map of Europe and the Balkans. At one point it looked as though Austria and Finland, too, would be threatened — and Stalin had taken Keralia, a large bite out of Finland. Greece could have gone Communist, especially had Stalin chosen to push the issue. Poland was appropriated by the Soviet bloc, a shameful betrayal of the Polish nation, which never looked on Roosevelt as the wise and kindly statesman presented in western Europe and America. The words "Yalta Conference", where the allies divided up Europe, became to the Poles a badge of shame.

In Britain, a landslide Labour victory seemed to indicate that socialism was everywhere on the march. France and Italy, with huge Communist parties, seemed within an ace of becoming Marxist states. My sister Ursula remembers being stopped from going to France in 1947 because Irish Catholics feared it was teetering on the brink of a Communist takeover (there was Communist participation in Government, and the French Communist Party was very powerful).

It seemed a very frightening world. Catholic Ireland warned that Ireland, too, could be next on the Reds' agenda. "Communism's Three Main Objectives in Ireland," warned the Catholic paper the *Standard* in 1948, were to capture the Dáil, the trade unions and youth. Various left-wingers in Ireland were asked to confirm that they were not members of the Communist Party. This is now ridiculed as "McCarthyism", but Stalin's power did seem unstoppable at the time.

The fear generated by the atom and hydrogen bombs, bringing the post-war generation the terrible knowledge that the entire world could be dashed to smithereens, cast a new sort of gloomy shadow. "The Lady Hope ... definitely gave up the ghost on 6th August 1945," wrote Arland Ussher. The *Irish Ecclesiastical Record* described a nuclear weapon as "a grossly unlawful instrument of war"; its use was "immoral". The humorous magazine *Dublin Opinion* was most preoccupied by the bomb, and declared itself not at all assured by the prediction that man would land on the moon within 30 years. "A famous young European scientist says that he hopes to land on the moon before another thirty years have elapsed. The rest of us are just watching the explosions [of the atom bomb] and just hoping that we won't [perish]." The "famous young European scientist" was Werner von Braun and he did indeed put a man on the moon just 22 years later, in 1969.

Life for the ordinary housewife in Ireland was still hard at the end of the 1940s, even primitive. Much of the country lacked electricity: over 40 per cent of women still cooked on open fires. The dream acquisition for many was a vacuum cleaner. In country parts, water continued to be drawn from the village pump. It was to some extent still a Victorian landscape.

Yet changes were coming, starting with some of the most essential. In 1947, a cousin of mine in Connemara, Co Galway, came home from teacher training college and found that running water had been installed in her home. Until then, water had to be fetched in pails — nearly always by women — from the local pump and laboriously carried home. The first innovation sometimes makes the biggest impact of all. "We were that happy," she recalled, "we wouldn't have called the Queen of England our aunt."

Nine

Marriage, Manners and Morals –
Ireland in the 1950s

"Young man, new to the city, farmer's son, substantial capital, wishes to meet lady of good appearance with own business. View to matrimony."

"Bachelor, 35, steady occupation, some capital, handsome, respectable, wishes to meet respectable, good-looking girl, R.C., 25 to 30, with view to matrimony."

"Business gent, 35, wishes to meet respectable girl."

"Respectable working-class girl, RC, wishes to meet respectable working-class man, strict TT [teetotaller]."

"Working man, 36 years, steady job, good appearance, would like to meet respectable working girl, 30 years, with view to matrimony."

Lonely-hearts advertisements,
Dublin Evening Mail, 2 October 1950

During the Irish divorce referendum of 1995, when voters were asked if they approved the introduction of divorce legislation, a divorced Irishman remarked to me: "It must have been dreadful back in the 1950s when so many Irish people were trapped in unhappy marriages they couldn't get out of."

We too often consider the past through the values of our time and, while there have always been both happy and unhappy marriages, divorce was simply not a priority 50 years ago: the problem was rather trying to get married at all. There were, in Ireland, far more bitterly unhappy single people who had never had the opportunity to marry and were unlikely ever to do so.

Europe and America have always been different in their attitudes to marriage: Americans have a tradition of marrying young and have generally had an optimistic, romantic and sometimes even reckless attitude to marriage. Europeans have been more cautious, more prudent, more concerned about the consequences of making a bad match and its impact on land and dynasty. And among Europeans, the Irish were probably the most reluctant of all to marry.

Loneliness, aged bachelorhood, crabbed spinsterhood — these were the themes which underlined Irish social life in the 1950s. William Trevor's story of a lonely old widower and his lonely ageing spinster daughter, *The Ballroom of Romance*, was all too typical for many individuals. My cousin May Mannion of Clifden in the West of Ireland remembers with poignancy "the number of lonely old bachelors living alone, left behind by the tide of emigration". This, incidentally, was not confined to Catholic Ireland: Irish Protestants also had a low marriage rate and an even lower fertility rate. You would hear of Church of Ireland vicars with a village congregation of five people, three women and two men, all unmarried.

A quarter of the Irish did not marry at all (in comparison to a tenth of the British, which was around the European average). This certainly reduced the potential for unhappy marriages and probably meant that those who did marry were more highly motivated to do so.

It is a repeated human experience that after a great war, the birth rate rises. It has been fancifully said that Nature "knows" that young men have been lost at war and thus seeks to replenish the human resource pool. More rationally, when a war is over, people want to go home, build nests, settle into domestic life and build families. Many of the popular wartime songs would refer yearningly to a peaceful future with wedding bells, a cottage with roses and the patter of tiny feet. Women had indeed experienced independence during the Second World War, had worked in munitions factories and had become motor mechanics. But women too wanted marriage and motherhood after the turbulence of the war. It is sometimes said that when the men came home from war, the women were sent home from work; but popular culture, such as women's magazines of the postwar period, showed women freely choosing marriage and domesticity. In Britain, in America, in all the countries which had been engaged in the Second World War, a baby boom began and the generation born around 1945-46 became known as the Baby Boomers.

But in Ireland, almost uniquely, there was a population crisis caused by a chronic reluctance to marry and to found families. Perhaps not having experienced the Second World War directly, Ireland did not join in with the postwar euphoria which seemed to act as a fertility drug. Marriage-shyness among the Irish was to become a standing joke. A typical 1947 cartoon which appeared in the humorous magazine *Dublin Opinion* showed a dismayed and unsuccessful Cupid with an inadequate bow and arrow, muttering: "Me armament's out o' date. It's a Bren gun I'd want in this part of Ireland."

By the early 1950s, the population was falling at such a rate it was predicted that within a few generations there would be no Irishmen or women left on native soil. "If the past century's rate of decline continues for another century, the Irish will virtually disappear as a nation and will be found only as an enervated remnant in a land occupied by foreigners," wrote Father John O'Brien in a key book of the time, *The Vanishing Irish*. "Today, Ireland is teetering perilously on the brink of near-extinction." Many experts believed that the Irish were already "far along on the path to extinction". These included Dr Clement Mihanovich, director of the Department of Sociology at St Louis University, United States, and an expert on population studies.

The population of Ireland had dwindled from over eight million (8,177,945) in 1841, just before the Great Famine, to not quite four-and-a-half million on the night of 8 April 1951. Decline of the population of the 26 counties (Eire) had gone from six and a half million (6,529,000) to not quite three million (2,960,000) in that period. The Irish State numbered less than three million people at home! It was a haemorrhage that no nation could stand. The Irish, it was predicted, would "vanish like the Mayans, leaving only their monuments behind". Their memory would live among the diaspora, who had quit the old country.

The Church was very much to the fore in raising the alarm about depopulation (and emigration). No one then saw a contradiction in a celibate clergy urging couples to marry and have children, or the paradox in bishops and archbishops, themselves bachelors by definition, scolding the "selfish bachelors and overcautious 'old maids'" who were refusing to marry and beget progeny. When the indefatigable Bishop Cornelius Lucey of Cork coined the phrase "the vanishing Irish" at a confirmation service, rural Ireland could recognise the truth in his references to the "rural depression and decay" which was a threat to the island race. This, he said, was a much more important subject than Partition (which greatly exercised the political classes). "Rural Ireland is stricken and dying," he lamented, "and the will to marry on the land is almost gone."

Much analysis was given to this depopulation topic — "Ireland's supreme problem — the life-blood of the nation that is being drained away", as a Lenten pastoral put it in 1953. Reluctance to marry was a true "social bane". "Many remain unmarried," said the Bishop of Ardagh and Clonmacnois, "who might easily support a family, because for one reason or other they had not the opportunity earlier in life and have now sunk into a lethargic and fatalistic acceptance of permanent bachelorhood.

"In some cases parents are, or have been, at fault, either through unreasonable opposition to the marriage of their children, or through an obstinate refusal to make such domestic arrangements and settlements as would enable them to marry and found a family." This referred to the practice of farmers hanging on to the farm into old age, rather than passing the property over to their sons on reaching adulthood. It was "deplorable", the Bishop said, when parents stood in the way of their sons and daughters marrying. "Rather should parents ...

encourage their children to marriage and to early marriage where possible, instead of practically compelling them to an enforced celibacy until well on in middle age."

The agricultural system which often required a man to wait until he was into his forties or fifties before he was in a position to take a wife was the subject of much popular drama and wry humour. Mary to Johnny, a courting couple both in their late forties: "Johnny, isn't it time we were getting married, *a stoir*?" Johnny to Mary: "Yerra, Mary, aroon, who'd have us now?"

Yet, economics apart, the blame sometimes fell on "selfish men"and, of course, their mothers. There has never been a shortage of experts to affirm that a mother's place is in the wrong. "It is well known that the elderly Irish mother is about the most jealous and unreasoning female on the face of the earth," commented the Irish playwright Paul Vincent Carroll in a contemporary essay on the marriage famine. "Between her and the 'self-seeking hussy' who aims to 'trap' her son — the son being between thirty and forty — there is just no compromise this side of the grave." The Irish mother would be caricatured as the Jewish mother would also come to be — possessed by the idea that no one is good enough for her boy.

The young women of Ireland wanted marriage all right, reported an American priest from Notre Dame University, Edmund J. Murray. But what could these girls do, faced with the marriage-shy Irishman and his dominant mother? "Call it selfishness, lethargy, indifference, love for independence, laziness, the fact of the matter seems to be that Ireland's young and not-so-young men are at fault more than the women or economics or any other cause one might suggest … Ninety-five per cent of Ireland's eligible women would marry tomorrow were the eligible men of the nation to transfer their affections for horses and dogs and football matches and 'pubs' to the nobler activities of courtship and marriage."

These marriage-shy Irishman, Father Murray reported, were driving Irishwomen abroad: they were the cause of the female emigration. He cited the case of a Kerry girl he had met on the Cork to Dublin train, on her way to Liverpool in England. She had been engaged to a local man for ten years, and twice the engagement had been broken off because "his mother didn't think the time was right for him to go off on his own and take a wife". The man was 29, the girl 30. She had just met an Englishman who had proposed to her, and she had accepted.

The Kerry girl's down-to-earth attitude rather shocked the more romantic-minded American: Americans might marry swifter and younger, but the love-match had been an American aspiration for some time. This girl was not particularly in love with the Englishman who proposed to her, but he was pleasant, decent and nice, and he was a husband. The Kerryman might never measure up. "I would have married one of my own," she said,"but what can you do when a man is tied to his mother's apron strings all his life?"

Father Murray was also taken aback by the unvarnished materialism of some of the lonely-hearts advertisements in the Irish papers. Gold-digging was not unknown in America but the business-like listing of assets — or requests for collateral — in the Irish papers still seemed somewhat bald. "Barman, large capital, good family connections, desirous of acquaintance with young lady with her own business, cash or capital: view to marriage." "Protestant gentleman, very respectable, 37, with good means, would be interested in corresponding with young lady with position and means. View to matrimony." In a sense, this was just a more old-fashioned way of arranging marriages. Nine-tenths of the historical data on marriage is about property and assets, and property can be shown to be quite a stable basis for marriage.

But there were also those who blamed the Catholic Church itself for instilling such a cult of chastity and continence into its flock that the Irish had virtually turned away from sexual experience. (Presumably Catholic chastity even rubbed off on Irish Protestants, who seemed equally reticent of carnal knowledge at this time.) The problem, wrote the American Paul Blanshard — a ferocious critic of Catholic Ireland — was that the control of sexuality in Ireland was "priestly".

"In Ireland, everything connected with marriage and sex comes within the scope of the Church's power," he wrote in *The Irish and Catholic Power*, a coruscating attack published in 1953. "Courtship is the business of the Irish priest and petting is the business of the Irish priest and even the etiquette of the marriage bed is the business of the Irish priest — as well as birth control, abortion, mixed marriage, illegitimacy, sodomy, masturbation, divorce, separation, sex education and 'keeping company'. Every Irish Catholic is trained to accept the rule of his Church in all these areas as a matter of course, and in practice he accepts such supervision of personal conduct with far more docility than his fellow Catholics in Latin countries."

Blanshard made much mockery of the mature brides and grooms photographed in the wedding columns of the Irish papers. He also (unfavourably) compared Ireland, which had no brothels, with Italy, where there were 700 licensed brothels "some of them almost in the shadow of St Peter's". Presumably he thought it an acceptable career choice for a teenage girl to become a prostitute.

Blanshard admitted that the fertility level of Irish Protestants was even lower than that of Catholics and that they too were reluctant to marry, but ascribed that to demographics (the Protestants tended to be older, because younger Protestants had been leaving Eire since the foundation of the State). Protestants were also fearful of intermarriage because the *Ne Temere* decree of 1908 meant that the children of mixed marriages had to be raised Catholic.

There was some truth in Blanshard's analysis, but there was a want of historical perspective. Irish reluctance about marriage and the founding of families went back to the Great Famine of the 1840s, more than a century previously. As mentioned, the Great Famine had decimated the population of Ireland — at the beginning of the 19th century, in 1801, the population of Ireland and England had been equal, at about eight million. The Famine was caused by a number of factors, including a lack of accountable democracy in Ireland. But it has also been suggested that overpopulation was a contributory factor. In terms of space, Ireland was not overpopulated with eight million people, but the agricultural system was unequal to the large families depending on it. Peasant tenant farmers with handkerchief-sized smallholdings of potato-beds were marrying early and producing families of eight and ten children; when the single crop that supported them failed, they starved.

After the Famine, it was as though a corrective gripped the collective unconscious: so that the agony of the Famine should never occur again, the Irish altered from the happy-go-lucky, singing, dancing and joking people that Thackeray noted in his journals of the 1840s into a more prudent, cautious, careful and pessimistic people. After the Famine, an obsession developed about not marrying unless you had the land, or the means, to support a family properly. There were to be no more happy, feckless unions and hoping for the best. Victorian respectability endorsed that obsession with prudence, and this had led to a fall in marriage and thus fertility.

There was something else in Irish cultural tradition, too, which might have acted as a brake on love and marriage. Padraic Colum, the poet and observer of Irish country ways, noted that in Irish country life, and in rural literature, love was looked upon as something comical and foolish, inviting raillery and "codding". The Irish thought love was for *amadauns* — idiots — or that it made men and women into idiots. My own mother, who came from the West of Ireland and had deep roots in Irish rural life, was of a romantic cast of mind herself, and yet she retained this Irish country attitude that "means" were a vital underpinning of love itself, and that the making of "a good match" meant land or money.

Deep went the belief that you could not hope to marry and have children unless you were financially secure, and in the 1950s the "vanishing Irish" still took this to heart.

In general, the world of the 1950s was a staid one. The atom bomb was frightening when reflective people started thinking about its implications — never before had it been possible to blow up the whole world in one strike. Stalin held half of Europe, and in 1949 Mao Zedong took over China and claimed it for Communism. In June 1950, North Korean Communists nearly overran the southern half of Korea. France and Italy seemed to be within an ace of becoming Communist. The Catholic press would point out that only Spain had defeated Bolshevism in its apparent onward march to world domination. Indeed, this was the prevailing view of the world in the early Fifties.

Conformity was the spirit of the age. The United States in the 1950s was characterised by the dark-hued 1999 film *Pleasantville* — a sinister suburbia where everyone conformed to the stereotype of suburban dullness, with all true colour and individuality repressed beneath the surface. Conformity in Britain was similarly stifling, with a rigid class system also well reflected in the movies of the time. The London female comic Linda Smith has observed that if there was a Cockney or working-class character in a British war movie, you knew he would be wiped out by the second reel because "the working-class was seen as expendable". Deference to the Royal Family was so extreme that Lord Altrincham (the historian John Grigg) was temporarily disgraced for criticising Queen Elizabeth's speaking-voice, which was then rather high-pitched and girlish. Malcolm Muggeridge received the most dreadful hate-mail for voicing criticism of the House of Windsor, including dogs' excrement in the post and letters saying he had deserved to lose his son (who died in an accident) for criticising the Royals. Muggeridge was also considered to have damaged his career by being so outspoken.

Conformity to the prevailing ethic was the international style of the 1950s, which the Italians, teetering on the brink of Communism, called *gli anni del conformismo* — the conformist years. Each society was conformist in its own way, and in Ireland conformity and deference to authority took the form of strict adherence to the values of Irish Catholicism.

It sometimes strikes me that Catholicism resembles Judaism in its exclusiveness, its comprehensiveness and its legalism. To be a Catholic was, especially in an era which emphasised conformity and authority, to be a member of a universal family in which there were codified rules for every form of conduct. To be outside the tribe — there was a world of people called "non-Catholics" (similar, perhaps, to "goyim") — was to be pitied. And as the Jews fussed about whether you could allow the fridge light to be turned on during the Sabbath or whether you could carry money in your shoe to synagogue (in Jewish law you are not supposed to carry money on your person on the Sabbath), so Irish Catholics similarly fretted about whether using beef lard in cooking constituted a breach of the Friday fast. Or, in order to comply with the regulations that women's heads should be covered in church, they would sometimes wear some incongruous token on their heads rather than enter church bare-headed.

The surrealistic picture of "a woman coming back from the altar balancing a glove on her head, with a most devout face under it" was nothing out of the ordinary, as Pauline Bracken recalls in an entertaining autobiography about growing up in Dublin in the 1950s. I remember this quite well, the glove acting as a token head-covering, and accepted it at the time; now I think of it as something both strange and comical.

Some of the anxious and literal-minded questions asked of the ecclesiastical experts in the *Irish Messenger of the Sacred Heart* really do lean towards the comical, although one must respect the obvious sincerity of the supplicants. (Readers would write in with questions, anxious to follow the church rules and do the right thing.)

Question: "Can a person hear Mass properly without seeing the Altar?" Answer: "Yes."

Question: "May one use powder to fix dentures before going to Holy Communion?" Answer: "Yes."

Question: "Is it forbidden to do tailoring on Sunday if it is done for a pious purpose and no payment is received?"

Answer: "To do tailoring on a Sunday *even* for a pious purpose and without payment is forbidden."

Question: "Is it sinful to knit or to iron clothes on Sunday?" Answer: "We are forbidden to do work on Sunday that is both servile and unnecessary."

Question: "Does a person who says the rosary wearing gloves gain the indulgences granted for the saying of the rosary on blessed beads?" Answer: "Yes."

These questions, though different in substance, are similar in approach to the "Agony Aunt" questions found in British and American women's magazines at this period, which also show anxiety about doing the right thing. ("Should I wear white gloves for a formal garden party?" "May I cross my legs during a job interview, or does that seem unladylike?") Some of the questions to the "Question Box" of the *Irish Messenger* — a very popular feature — were focused on manners as well as morals.

Question: "Should husbands and wives open each other's letters?" Answer: "Certainly not, without permission ... Observance of the ordinary rules of courtesy does much to promote a happy married life."

Question: "Is it a sin to steam other people's letters open and to read them?" Answer: "Unless you are in a position of authority over other people which gives you the right or unless you have their permission, it is a sin to read their private letters." This reflected an interesting social change which was beginning to occur in the 1950s: French sociologists called it "the one new idea in France" — the right to privacy. The notion of personal privacy, for many ordinary people, was an innovation of the Fifties. "For the first half of the twentieth century private life was in most respects subject to communal controls," write Prost and Vincent in *A History of Private Life*. The rise of personal privacy has been linked with the rise of the private bathrooms — in 1954 only ten per cent of French homes had private baths or showers. When so much washing was done in "communal facilities", private life was public. In Normandy, neighbours would know whether a woman was pregnant or not by the state of her washing: menstrual towels were at this time washable and, if a woman was not washing out her menstrual diapers, then she was likely to be expecting a baby. French agricultural life would have been similar to Irish rural life in many of these details.

We can see why Paul Blanshard, who came from the kind of Protestant American background which rebuffed any form of "priestcraft" and emphasised emotional self-reliance, considered the Irish Catholic Church as "infantilising" in the way it handled the anxieties aired by these questions and answers. In a system of authority, there is a correct answer for everything. Seldom, if ever, is the answer to a question: "Use your common sense" or "Figure it out for yourself". The Church was wary of "private judgements" and always acted as though people needed guidance.

On the other hand, in one respect the values propounded were also highly stoical: we, in our time, are much more "infantilised" with our crybaby culture of counselling and claims for compensation for hurt feelings. The 1950s Catholic

Irish were expected to take pain, loss and mishaps on the chin, to "offer it up" and to accept the will of God bravely. And when terrible tragedies occurred, people often did show admirable grace. Typical is the attitude of a mother who wrote to the *Messenger* in 1951 to give thanks that her son had a "happy death". "I wish to return thanks to the Sacred Heart of Jesus and His Holy Mother that my son, who was killed in an accident, had been attended by a priest and received the Last Rites of the Church before he died ... The priest who attended my boy said he died a very happy death." No self-pity, no rage at the injustice of such a loss, but perfect acceptance in grief. All the world's great religions consider this perfect acceptance to be the pinnacle of wisdom and serenity: it is exceptionally difficult to attain.

When wrongdoing occurred there was also much emphasis on *amendment* and *restitution*. For a sin to be pardoned, there had to be "the firm purpose of amendment" and a sincere attempt at restitution. Every effort had to be made to find ways of restitution. Question: "If one has stolen something, and it is impossible to give it back to the owner, what should be done?" Answer: "It should not be too readily assumed that it is impossible to restore stolen property, as it can generally be done anonymously through the post and no one has any objection to that kind of anonymous letter. Practically the only case where restitution is impossible is when the owner is dead, or gone away to an unknown destination, and if dead, has left no heirs. In such a case the obligation can be satisfied by giving the money to Charity." Restitution was characterised as the moral right of the injured party, but it was important too for the moral formation of the offender's own character.

Even in hardship cases, the intention had to be there to make good again. "I stole a large sum of money which I am unable to pay back," a questioner writes to the *Messenger* in 1953. "I would like to go to the Sacraments, but this has held me back. What should I do?" Answer: "You should go to Confession and have the sin forgiven. Provided you have the sincere intention of paying back the money when you can, you can get absolution of your sin."

When bad things have been said against a person's character, the same principle applied. Question: "Some years ago I wrote a nasty letter to a person's employer as a result of which he was dismissed. Am I bound to confess this?" Answer: "Yes, and if the injury to the other person was deliberate, you are bound to make restitution as far as possible to that person."

There is a widespread belief that the Irish Catholic Church concentrated on sexual sins to the exclusion of all others: this is not so. There was a good deal of emphasis on honesty, on fairness in working practices, on crime and morality. One of the best-selling booklets from the Catholic Truth Society in the 1950s was by Revd R.H. Brennan, SJ, *What Belongs to Another*. This outlines the ethics of acting honestly, of not cheating an employer, of not cheating on your taxes, of not cheating your employees of a fair wage. And again, where dishonesty has been engaged in, restitution must be made. "The absolution of the priest does not transfer the ownership of the money or goods stolen to the thief. What has been taken unjustly still belongs to the people who have been wronged, or if they are dead, to their heirs. An essential part of the sorrow for sins against justice is the restitution to repay all that has been unjustly acquired." If it is not possible to restore the cash, goods or other commodities all at once, then it should be done little by little.

These exhortations to honesty must have had their effect — they certainly had an effect on me when reading them and I started to remember dishonest acts of my own I would rather have forgotten. The Irish newspapers of the 1950s had long Lost and Found daily columns in which people advertised the objects they had found on buses, trains, cafeterias and so on. Some of these objects were clearly valuable — purses, jewellery, leather gloves, ball-point pens — a great luxury at the time. (In 1950, a ball-point pen cost 47 shillings and 6 pence — that is, about a week's wage for a city secretary.) To be sure, the finders sometimes hoped for a reward (and reimbursement of the cost of the advertisement) but they went to the trouble to advertise just the same. The religious magazines also noted with gratitude items restored to their owners. Small possessions mean a great deal more when people are poor.

Some of the discourse on honesty borders on the over-scrupulous. There was a long debate in the *Irish Ecclesiastical Record* in this period on the precise meaning of the words "Not transferable" on a railway ticket. Does the person who finds himself in possession of a railway ticket on which the words "not transferable" are printed violate the principles of honesty if he gives away the ticket to another? Is he thereby defrauding the railway company of its due revenue? No, decides the ecclesiastical expert, after due deliberation: there is no grave obligation to observe the rule which forbids the transference of railway tickets because no unjust injury has been done to the railway company. Yet, "We would add, however, that these rules regarding the non-transferability of railway tickets serve a useful purpose. They are designed to prevent fraud and profiteering and are for the public good. Consequently, it would be unethical wantonly and completely to disregard them." It may have seemed pernickety to debate this point, but I did wonder, not long ago, if I could give away an airline ticket which I was not now able to use, although it was clearly marked "Not transferable". The honest answer is that I probably would have done so if I could have got away with it,. which is not very honest conduct, in truth.

In the 1950s, the emphasis on honesty as a religious obligation did have some impact. Outside Dublin the crime rate was miniscule: about ten offences per thousand of the population, and the ten offences included such felonies as riding a bicycle without a light. In 1950, there were 469 men in prison in the Irish Republic and 68 women. By the end of the century, this has increased five-fold.

The mortifying shame of being caught stealing is reinforced by stories in the *Messenger of the Sacred Heart,* as was the extreme care with which a subject such as unemployment benefit is approached.

"I am working without a wage for my parents while unemployed owing to the slackness in my particular work," writes a questioner in 1956. "May I take unemployment benefit?" The answer is yes, but it is significant that the question was asked at all. It demonstrates the scrupulous Catholic young citizen, anxious not to defraud the State, and the taxpayer. And even, in the unlikely event that the question was planted by the editorial team, it is significant that it should have been considered worth underlining. The question, today, simply would not arise at all.

Another case of an honest conscience wrangling with a work predicament arises over a civil servant's "perks". This was discussed in the *Irish Ecclesiastical Record* as a problem that had cropped up in confession. A government employee rides to work on his bicycle, but colleagues at his level of service are now entitled to claim expenses for the running of a motor car. Is the cycling civil servant also entitled to claim similar perquisites, or perks, even though he would rather take his bike rather than a car? Certainly not, is the ecclesiastical answer. It would be quite wrong to take such perquisites from the taxpayer if they are not honestly required.

The Church certainly did regard the whole area of the family as its special constituency, and it was wary of the state moving into spheres which had previously been those of the Church or even of voluntary associations. The Catholic Church was suspicious of the Welfare State, which had been introduced in Britain in 1948. Welfare was suspect for its socialist roots, for the possibly decadent effects it might have on the character (if people were cosseted by the State, they would be less inclined to work) and, above all, for its tendency to spread the power of the state into family and personal life. The power of the State was regarded as anathema. "The power and the spirit behind practically all social legislation at the present time," said Bishop Farren of Derry in 1948, "is taken from the worst principle of both Nazi and Russian materialism."

The Irish bishops preached against what they called "the Octopus State" — reaching into every corner of power — from the end of the Second World War. "Citizens are not mere subjects of the State," said the Bishop of Down and Connor, in 1946, "they are human persons ... They have immortal souls with an eternal destiny and a right to live according to their consciences. As persons, they have a right to own property, to found families, to educate their children and to form voluntary associations ... It is morally wrong for the State to violate these fundamental rights of the individual, the family and society."

Bishops in Northern Ireland were perhaps more aware of the fact that during wartime the State had taken over many areas of civil society; they were also more likely to be critical of the particular state they were in. Nonetheless, the principle of opposition to state power went right through Irish Catholicism at this time.

Thus a major controversy blew up in 1950 over the Mother and Child scheme, in which the Catholic Church in Ireland, effectively led by the draconian Archbishop of Dublin, John Charles McQuaid, halted a proposed government welfare scheme for mothers and children. The Mother and Child controversy came to be seen, later, as a classic power struggle between Church and State in which the Church had overstepped its remit — although the proposed scheme itself was flawed and not workable in the form suggested by the radical young Health Minister, Dr Noel Browne.

Noel Browne, who died in 1996, was a popular, sometimes maverick politician. He was popular because he had energetically pursued a hospital programme to eradicate tuberculosis, in the late 1940s, and this had been visibly successful. TB was a scourge of Irish life and had actually risen during the 1930s. Dr Browne, who had suffered from TB himself as a young man, became so identified with the application of new medical treatment that simple folk came to believe that he had personally "cured the country of TB". Although notoriously difficult to work with and criticised thereby both by his civil servants and other political colleagues, he retained the esteem of the people all his life for the dedication with which he had attacked the affliction of tuberculosis.

In 1950, Dr Browne came up with a new campaign for health and welfare, the Mother and Child Scheme. There was a need for such a scheme, since infant mortality in Ireland was still shockingly high, and the health of multiparous mothers so precarious that overseas medical students would visit Dublin's most famous maternity hospital, The Coombe, just to see the condition of poor mothers giving birth to their 20th child. Dr Browne was right to give his attention to this subject, but the scheme which he produced was rebuffed by the medical profession even before the Church got embroiled. The doctors, too, were worried about the encroachment of State medicine, which might hurt their interests, so their objections were not only on health grounds. Dr Browne's scheme suggested that mothers and children up to 16 years of age should be medicalised by the State, with a view to improving their health; some coercive aspects were also included in the scheme. For example, Dr Browne suggested that a State health visitor should be entitled to gain entry to family homes at any time, in order to monitor the progress of mothers and children.

The Catholic bishops were not opposed to all welfare policies. In 1946, Bishop Dignan of Clonfert had written a pamphlet proposing a national health insurance system. There was always some support for mothers in the home, and Dr Lucey of Cork was an early supporter of family allowances, payable to the mother. But the hierarchy certainly did not care for Dr Browne's bill and used their clout behind the scenes to assist its defeat. What was particularly humiliating for Dr Browne was that he felt obliged to make a grovelling statement in parliament affirming his loyalty to the Catholic Church, lest word get around that his Mother and Child scheme had challenged the Church. "I, as a Catholic, accept unequivocally and unreservedly the views of the hierarchy on this matter," he told the Dáil in April 1951. He went on to say that he would "obey my Church authorities and will continue to do so". Subsequently, in fact, he became a lifelong and bitterly acrimonious critic of the Catholic Church; having had to bend the knee so publicly to Church power must have added fuel to the fire of his subsequent resentment.

Later, a modified and more workable version of the original Mother and Child scheme was introduced by the Fianna Fáil government (Noel Browne had belonged to a minority party that was part of a coalition government) which the Catholic Church approved. In the long run the conflict was damaging, since it was held up as an example of the power of the Church to manipulate political issues. It must be said, however, that whenever the Church exceeded her power, it was because the politicians were themselves unreservedly deferential to the Church and jumped when the bishops said so.

The faithful, as opposed to the politicians, had mixed views about the bishops' warnings against creeping socialism. According to J.H. Whyte in the most authoritative account of this period, *Church and State in Modern Ireland,* the people did not necessarily agree with the bishops on the Mother and Child question at all. Yet some Catholics obviously found it quite acceptable that bishops should be social as well as religious leaders. One of the most successful theatre plays of the early Fifties was Joseph Tomelty's *Is the Priest at Home?* It played to full houses in Cork, Dublin and Belfast and went into at least four editions in printed form. In this comedy, the dominant female character is a Mrs O'Kane, who has much influence in the small town in Northern Ireland where the action takes place. In one set of lines Mrs O'Kane has to deliver — widely applauded at the time, the battleaxe says: "The Bishops are good men. Look at the stand they took in the South about the Health Bill."

The stand the bishops were taking was not just about the health bill but, more widely, about the way in which areas of life previously organised by the Church were gradually being handled by the state. You could, in the very long view, trace this change back to the Middle Ages, when everything from medicine to music had been the province of the Church. Now everything was coming under the aegis of the government.

The adoption of babies and children was another area where government was moving into a sphere previously organised by the churches. There had been informal adoption of babies since biblical times, and since the 19th century church societies had been involved in various adoption arrangements of a more formal kind, although without the weight of the law. Legislation to involve the state only began in the developed countries after the First World War. Britain brought in laws on adoption in 1926, but even then, until well after the Second World War, there remained a church dimension to adoption procedures and it was difficult to obtain a child unless a couple was church-going. By 1950, most countries in Europe had some legislation for adoption in place, but the Netherlands, Portugal and Ireland still had none.

The Adoption Society (Ireland) had been lobbying for the introduction of Irish legislation since the late 1940s. The Adoption Society was a group of kindly and well-intentioned people, some of them childless couples who did not care for the Church-run adoption processes which existed (Catholic and Protestant churches had separate procedures). They proposed that the adoption of a baby should entail a clean break with the birth mother. This, they argued, would mean that the adopting couple could have the baby for their own, and the birth mother could obliterate the "stigma" of bearing an illegitimate child. The birth certificate could erase the mark of illegitimacy by claiming the child as the biological issue of the adopters.

The Catholic Church was not agreeable to the Adoption Society's aims. Most of the public debate was advanced through the letters column of *The Irish Times* (very much a Protestant newspaper at the time) and the Dublin *Evening Mail*, its stablemate, which was hardly a congenial forum for Catholicism — *The Irish Times* was still running job advertisements with "Protestants only" specified.

The Church had several specific objections to the adoption proposals. There was concern that concealment of the identity of the natural parents might cause problems with consanguinity later on — a half-brother and sister could unknowingly marry one another. The Irish Church had always frowned on marriage between cousins, a matter more easily accepted in other cultures. (It was a puzzle to me, as a child, reading the stories of Jane Austen, that characters could marry their cousins.) As the gene pool in Ireland is quite small, the Church's prohibition on consanguinity was probably perfectly sensible.

In 1949, John Charles McQuaid, the Archbishop of Dublin, gave an address in which he emphasised the rights of the natural mother as opposed to the social bonds of an adopter. Dr McQuaid had lost his own mother as a baby and he felt this loss acutely: it is more than likely that this informed his approach. When, subsequently, the Minister for Justice, General MacEoin, and his predecessor, Gerald Boland, consulted the Archbishop on the adoption issue, Dr McQuaid said that he advised against rushing into it because "he did feel that that advocates of legal adoption, in their zeal to safeguard the rights of the adopting parents, tended to overlook the fact that the natural mother and child had rights, too, which must equally be safeguarded in any legislation."

The Church was not particularly supportive, either, in removing the "stigma" against illegitimacy. If it were not there, perhaps, more couples would choose not to marry and marriage was what they were trying to promote.

Again, the power of the Church did halt adoption legislation, for a time. In November 1950, it was announced in the Dáil that the Government would not bring in a bill for the moment. There was also a reluctance to confront the subject, not just because politicians did not like taking on the Catholic Church, but because the Dáil was largely composed of males who did not like to debate subjects they considered embarrassing. Moreover, there was an agricultural prejudice against adoption. Rural Ireland was extremely touchy about anything that interfered with the blood line; farmers disliked the idea that, should an adopted child inherit the farm, the property would go to "a stranger" rather than a kinsman. One member of the Adoption Society was told by a rural parliamentarian that adoption was "like interfering with the stud-book". Certainly, falsifying a birth certificate to claim adopting parents as the natural parents would be akin to that.

Two years on, in 1952, there was to be legislation which made adoption legal in Ireland, though the first act was very basic and carried safeguards ensuring the child's religion was adequately protected. Adoption legislation was further widened in 1964, 1974, 1976 and less again in 1979. By the 1980s adopted children were entitled to trace birth parents, if the parents were willing. Yet adoption remained conservative in Ireland for longer, and there was more resistance to "opening up the books" than in some other European countries. There remains some anxiety about tracing birth parents or tracing adopted children. The church has yielded all control of adoption — it is now a state monopoly in Ireland — and that power, too, will probably be challenged in the fullness of time.

Ireland in the early 1950s is generally seen as being at its most triumphantly Catholic. There seems to have been an increase in devotional fervour after the Holy Year of 1950, when many Irish people went on pilgrimage to Rome by the national airline, Aer Lingus, a source of chest-bursting pride. All the aircraft from Aer Lingus were especially blessed and were christened after Irish saints: the *Capuchin Annual*'s stunning picture of the *St Bridget* hovering over the Eternal City of Rome itself gave a new dimension to Ireland's spiritual empire.

In 1950, the angelus was introduced to the noon and six o'clock time-checks on Irish radio; in the 21st century, it is still there, although there is some minority pressure to have it removed. There were campaigns, in 1950, to have the rosary broadcast on radio too, but professional broadcasters resisted, aware of the competition coming from the BBC Light Programme (now Radio 2), which was producing some sparkling radio comedy at the time. Advertisements for lipstick and cosmetics were permitted on Irish radio for the first time; previously, they had been considered not perhaps quite ladylike. (My grandmother would have considered make-up only fit for actresses and "fast women".)

Marian devotion was on the increase. In 1950, the doctrine of the Assumption was proclaimed (that the Blessed Virgin Mary assumed into heaven), which, interestingly, the Protestant Swiss psychologist Carl Jung said would proclaim a new age of feminine awareness. In Ireland, it was reflected by an increase in the number of family homes given a Marian name. "The house opposite ours is called Tigh Marian [Mary's House, in Irish]," noted the poet Austin Clarke in his autobiography. "Next to us is Villa Marie, and on the other side is what seems to be a variant, Ladywell." Many of the grottoes and Marian statues still seen around Ireland date from the early 1950s and specifically the Marian year of 1954.

Yet, despite the gloom about the "vanishing Irish" and the strict moral tone of the time, Ireland was not without its *joie de vivre*. It never is. In his memoir of bohemian Dublin in the 1950s, *Remembering How We Stood*, the writer and patron of the arts John Ryan paints a lively picture of Dublin life among artists and writers. Halliday Sutherland, the Scottish Catholic doctor — whose book about natural family planning had been banned in Eire in the 1940s — wrote a travel book about Ireland in the mid-1950s, *Irish Journey,* which observes poverty but also plenty of fun. Sport was a particular source of national enjoyment, and Dr Sutherland reports notably on the pleasure of the horse-race (there were still some restrictions on horse-racing in Britain, due to archaic gambling laws). The wonderful sports commentator Micheal O'Hehir brought the joys of hurling, Gaelic football and the national bicycle race into homes all over Ireland via the radio. Sometimes you would pass through a small village where most of the men would be gathered around a single radio. *Dublin Opinion,* the humorous weekly magazine where rugby jokes were a great obsession, was very amusing. The American sociologist priest Dr Murray felt, of course, that the sporting life was making men too selfish to consider the womenfolk ...

There was also a national passion for dancing. Priests — and Protestant pastors — had condemned the dancehall as an occasion of temptation in the past, but this disapproval was beginning to recede. In fact, in an if-you-can't-beat-'em-join-'em spirit, some priests were beginning to organise dances. Monsignor James Horan, who later promoted the building of Knock Airport in Mayo, was an enthusiastic dance promoter, and the Past Pupils Union of various Catholic schools held regular balls. On a Saturday evening in October 1950, the Dubliner and his girl would have a fine choice of dance-halls to patronise: the Four Provinces, Clery's, the Dancing Palace of Variety, the National Ballroom, the Brugh an Arm in Parnell Square, the Olympia, the Crystal, the Arcadia, the Red Island or, if one had tickets, the Garda dances. Judging by the advertisements in the Dublin evening papers, a brisk trade was done in hired tuxedos, white ties and tails.

Drama was another national pastime — amateur drama flourished throughout the provinces and Dublin theatre life was delightful. Noel Coward's diaries reveal how he adored being in Dublin, with its wonderful sociability, and Harold Pinter's slim memoir of life as a touring actor in Ireland in 1950, entitled *Mac,* is a gemlike recollection of a naive, but golden time. "In those halcyon Fifties' days," writes Genevieve Lyons, in a forthcoming memoir, "life really did shimmer. It held such innocence and hope and an abundance of creativity, especially in the theatre. Everyone came there, everyone who was anyone wanted to be there; Grafton Street was the epitome of elegance, and the world met and mingled, sipped coffee, drank "gin and it" in Davy Byrne's and the Bailey, Jameson's and beer in Neary's and they lunched in Jammet's and the Red Bank." Genevieve, now a novelist, was a successful actress at the Gate Theatre and elsewhere, and played opposite Richard Harris in the doomed *Ginger Man* production at the Dublin Theatre Festival of 1959. This was another area of conflict where Church power entered the picture — the Archbishop managed to get the production closed down for indecency, though he had no statutory powers to do so; a spineless management immediately caved in to his objections that it was indecent. The critics' reviews were, incidentally, terrible.

The 1950s in Ireland were not experienced as unrelieved misery, even if for the lonely unmarried or the sad émigrés it was a dreary time. In her memoir of growing up in Dublin, *The Light of Other Days,* Pauline Bracken evokes a calm and comforting child's universe of Maytime processions on the streets, Jimmy O'Dea comedy on the radio, and a sense of innocence, safety and security. "We loved our religion. It was our mainstay and our peace of mind, and it was always comfortingly there." Television had not yet arrived and children in happy families were unaware of the horrors that existed in the world outside, from the atom bomb to the everyday cruelties that always exist behind closed doors.

Ten

The Sixties — The Liberal Dawn

"This revolution of the 1960s has made it clear that the Irish are not a wobbling blancmange of poor, priest-ridden dreamers. That was a popular picture in both the United States and Britain ... Today, however, sex is discussed openly and sensibly in the newspapers and on television, giving the lie to the theory, held for so long, that all Irish babies were found under cabbages."

Alan Bestic, *The Importance of Being Irish*, 1969

The most optimistic period in which to live is when a conservative society is becoming liberal. At this moment, it still retains its moorings and its self-confidence; every window that opens on a formerly stuffy atmosphere proclaims a new dawn; every change seems an improvement.

For a short time, it is possible to imagine that the security and self-assurance of tradition can be maintained alongside the brightest and best of innovation. For a short time, people have the best of both worlds, before the stability of the old dissolves and the anxieties of the new invade.

From the end of the 1950s, the old Ireland began to fade. De Valera, the severe-looking father-figure who had presided over the Irish State at its most isolated — and puritanical — grew elderly and became almost totally blind. In politics, he made way for his successor, Sean Lemass, who became Taoiseach in 1959. Dev himself went on to be President of Ireland — a less-directly political role. Mr Lemass was a modernizer who, in partnership with T.K. (Ken) Whitaker, Secretary of the Department of Finance, began to introduce innovations into the Irish economy. Ireland, though morally conservative, was economically semi-socialist, another phenomenon criticised by Paul Blanshard in *The Irish and Catholic Power*. All major services and utilities were run by the government, and some commodities, such as sugar production, were under the direction of semi-state bodies. In practice Ireland was said to be more socialist than Yugoslavia.

De Valera had been in some ways hostile to materialism (a French academic, Maurice Goldring, compared him to Yeats in this respect — both shared a lofty striving for the ascetic). In one of his most renowned speeches, on St Patrick's Day, 1943, he outlined his vision of Ireland as "the home of a people who valued material wealth only as a basis for right living, ... a people satisfied with frugal comfort and devoted to things of the spirit." Dev's vision was touchingly uplifting, in its own way — he cherished the idea of firesides which "would be forums for the wisdom of serene old age" and villages full of "the laughter of comely maidens". But the truth was, as the historian J.J. Lee has pointed out, that de Valera knew nothing whatsoever about economics (despite being a mathematician). It did not figure in his vision. He certainly would not have understood the modern politician's nostrum: "It's the economy, stupid."

His successor, Lemass, was less the visionary — although he too was a veteran of the 1916 Rising — and more the practical manager. Lemass's nationalism was pragmatic, and he understood that Ireland, under Dev's last administrations, was bleeding to death, economically. In 1958, emigration hit an all-time high — 58,000 left the Republic of Ireland that year from a population of three million. The "vanishing Irish" would vanish unless somebody did something about the economy. Sean Lemass, under the influence of Ken Whitaker, embarked on a programme of investment and expansion, which, almost immediately, stimulated a turnaround effect.

Economic change very often accompanies social change, and we might even say that the first phase of the 1960s, in Ireland, began around 1958.

My recollection of this particular year, as a schoolgirl, is of a peer group obsessed with showbands who toured Ireland playing at dances, and the new awareness of rock 'n roll. Elvis Presley was initially banned on Irish radio as being suggestive — he sure was! — and I heard an aunt of mine describe his gyrations as disgusting. His quiffed appearance was much copied by working-class Dubliners, so that the Elvis look was also characterised as common. A Marxist might say that Elvis was a revolutionary in that he challenged accepted hierarchies, and through him the culture of poor Memphis whites invaded, and finally even toppled, bourgeois norms. Eamonn McCann, in his witty autobiography, *War and an Irish Town,* identified Elvis Presley as the signifier of the coming sexual revolution, for young people in small Irish towns.

For Catholics, 1958 was the year when the distant, bespectacled Pope Pius XII died — he seemed to me as a child to look like Mr de Valera, and they seemed to belong to the same autocratic cast. He was succeeded by Pope John XXIII, the "peasant Pope", from a family of 13, who had gone to school barefoot. John was elected on the 12th ballot, so it was all very dramatic. But from the start, Good Pope John was billed as something new and different — a democrat rather than an autocrat. He would be "the people's Pope".

As schoolgirls, we also thought it was terribly exciting that satellites were being launched into space: the atom bomb age had been superceded by the space age. We found Castro's 1959 Cuban coup even more exciting: Castro looked so cool, so hip, so young. As a style-leader he was something of a forerunner of Che Guevara, his comrade, who, in the Sixties, became an icon adorning student bedroom walls. The Irish always have a soft spot for any kind of a rebel, and in 1959 the rebellious schoolgirl gesture was to scribble "Up Castro" on one's schoolbooks. A scene in an Edna O'Brien novel, set in Dublin in the early 1960s, describes a callow youth, the worse for drink, trying to impress the females by scrawling "Up Castro" on public walls. The alternative culture, in small ways, had begun.

By the early 1960s it was already being noted by observers that life in Ireland was definitely getting better. In 1962, unemployment, emigration and crime were all decreasing. The 58,000 who had emigrated in 1958 were contrasted with the 15,000 who were leaving our shores by 1962. There was every reason to envisage a new dawn, and Alan Bestic, an Irish Protestant married to an Irish Catholic, in his book *The Importance of Being Irish* captured the optimism of the time. Ireland was moving away from the over-controlled, "priest-ridden" climate of the past, he reported. Yet he also found that some of the most energetic agents of change were the priests themselves.

The old priests had given up their former, prudish ways of monitoring courting couples for fear that they were "going too far". Instead, the up-and-coming clergy were progressive and involved with social reform. "The younger clergy are raising their voices in protest about social conditions, identifying themselves with the people on a scale hitherto unknown, and long overdue," he wrote.

Actually, this was not quite as new-fangled as Alan Bestic supposed; there had always been priests involved in social reform, and there had always been priests who identified with the people, from the rebellion of 1798 to the various dockers' priests who crusaded for better conditions for labourers. In the 19th century, the French writer De Toqueville had observed of Ireland: "The feelings expressed (by priests and bishops) were extremely democratic. Distrust and hatred of the great landlords; love of the people and confidence in them." Yet if this democratic spirit of the priests in the 1960s seemed new, it was because they were acting in a new, 1960s style.

Mr Bestic surveyed some of the radical priests on the scene in Ireland's own Swinging Sixties. There was, for example, the saintly Father Michael Sweetman, scion of a patrician Dublin family, who was extremely concerned about housing conditions in the city and was astonishing the natives by sharing forums with Michael O'Riordan, the leader of the miniscule (and slavishly loyal to the Soviet Union) Communist Party in Ireland and a man who had fought for the Reds in Spain.

There was the go-ahead Father Thomas Fehilly — "one of the most progressive minds abroad in Ireland, one of the new frontiersmen" — writing articles with headings such as "Teach Your Children About Sex" in the mass-circulation de Valera newspaper the *Sunday Press*. Father Fehilly was also a champion of "the cause of the itinerants" — Ireland's nomadic people, once called tinkers, then itinerants, and subsequently travellers. Father Fehilly compared the Irish treatment of itinerants with the British treatment of West Indians — there had been serious rioting in London at the end of the 1950s by young West Indians claiming discrimination.

There was the enterprising young Father Peter Canning, one of the "Radharc" group of priests at the national television station, then called Telefís Éireann (which had started up in 1962). "Radharc" ("Vision") was a left-wing Irish-language programme which produced outspoken shows, and media trendsetters. Father Peter, when a curate at Roundwood, in Co Wicklow, would take off his clerical collar, put on an Aran sweater and drop down to the local pub, where he might play the guitar. This was the new brand of Catholic clergy in Ireland now, populist and relaxed.

There was Father Austin Flannery, admirably socially aware — just like Father Sweetman — and involved with problems of the Dublin slums. There was Father Peter Lemass, who would preach in Bray, Co Wicklow, in support of striking garbage workers, and tell the congregation: "We have a moral right to back these men who remove garbage from houses which have Mercedes cars in their garages, and are owned by people who can afford to take holidays on the Continent." The "great landlords" had now been replaced by the privileged Irish swanky enough to have expensive cars and take holidays abroad. Father Lemass, a most popular priest, was subsequently to spend some time in Latin America, where he became involved with Liberation Theology (a radical Catholicism influenced by Marxist tendencies), and, by 1985, was writing in *The Furrow* magazine in praise of Castro's Cuba. He did point out the disadvantages of Cuba as well as the benefits, yet he saw it as a progressive in health and education policies, and perhaps he responded to it, too, as a 1960s rebel might, with the spirit of the age.

There was Father James McDyer, the radical Donegal priest, who had launched a cooperative movement in the north-west of Ireland — a valiant attempt to help Donegal farmers, whose smallholdings were poor.

And there was the marvellous Father Michael Cleary, curate at Marino, north Dublin, who attacked the government for "neglecting the emigrants, among whom he had worked in Britain ... He castigates Irish employment agencies for their irresponsibility, quotes the case of young girls being sent to jobs in cafes which were no more than brothels." Gay Byrne, the TV presenter who was to become perhaps the definitive influence on society in the years between the 1960s and the 1990s, judged Michael Cleary to be a wonderful example of the priesthood. "The new singing rave," Gay Byrne called Father Cleary in 1966, "just returned from London and showing to everybody's amazement that a priest could actually grab a mike and sing while doing a passable imitation of a hip-swinging jive. 'Chattanooga-choo-choo' was a far cry from benediction hymns." The end of Father Michael Cleary's story, which would be revealed later on, was somewhat less hip.

Oh, no, there was no shortage of radical, left-wing and trendy priests who were showing that the Catholic Church in Ireland was shuffling off the old stuffiness and ready to be progressive and forward-looking. There were even some bishops who were on the progressive side — for example, the Bishop of Ossary, Dr Peter Birch, who shared Father Tom Fehilly's concern for the travelling people and preached against the snobbery of settled folk who found it hard to accept tinkers as their brothers and sisters in Christ. "I believe we will have progress here," he told a gathering of young people at Naas, Co Kildare, "when I see an itinerant ordained a priest, or a tinker girl taking her final vows in a convent. You young people have the power and the energy to dissolve the stains in our society, which is riddled with class distinction." (The word "tinker" was considered acceptable at that time, when used in context; it is now as politically incorrect as the South African "kaffir".) A new theme, generally, in sermons was that class distinction was "wounding Christ", a fair enough point in the context of the lilies of the field, though not perhaps always popular with the upwardly mobile section of the faithful.

Some of this new pastoral emphasis on care and concern for the deprived actually reflected the increase in prosperity — among certain groups — occurring in Ireland at this time. An increase in prosperity always brings more class distinction, if class distinction means a gap in income levels. As some people become richer, they become proportionately more rich than others; only societies living at a very basic level can avoid such differences.

Ireland's first steps in prosperity — the first wave of prosperity since the period just before the First World War, and the first wave ever under independence — began to feature, too, in the fictional stories in the *Irish Messenger of the Sacred Heart*.

"At thirty-four, Michael had bought outright his own beautiful bungalow on the edge of Dublin city … His wife had been a well-known mannequin. The bungalow had everything: Venetian blinds, contemporary furniture, fitted carpets, television, washing machine, refrigerator, central heating. It had a beautiful name in script on a rectangle of perspex hanging in the porch. Michael scorned the prosaic number the city council had allotted to the house. Only the bungalow name, the road, the city, stood out on the embossed private notepaper he used."

Michael also has a high level of personal insurance — insurance policies against all losses and damage. But then he finds out he is "not insured against the loss of my soul". He needs *spiritual* insurance, too.

By 1963, Ireland was said to be one of the fastest-growing economies in Europe, but then it was growing from a very low base. In 1961, half of all the homes outside the main urban areas had no lavatory facilities, either indoors or outdoors. In the midland county of Longford, as a typical example, there were only 1,600 indoor bathrooms for a population of 30,000 people. Under the Lemass regime, people without toilet facilities began acquiring — like Michael in the *Messenger* story — washing machines and refrigerators, and, above all, television.

Moreover, for the first time since the Great Famine of the 1840s, the Irish population was increasing.

It especially cheered the national mood that more couples were marrying — always a vote of confidence in the future. Gloomy talk about the vanishing Irish melted away. More Irish exiles were returning home — another vote of confidence in the country's future. Along with these economic changes, the social revolution that progressives had hoped for seemed in sight. In 1965, a gifted historian who became one of the first TV celebrities in Ireland, David Thornley, wrote: "We are for the first time at the threshold of a delayed peaceful social revolution … It seems certain that our island will become affected increasingly by the spread of European social and philosophical ideas, strongly tinged with Catholicism.

"It is reasonably certain that many of the issues of education and social welfare will slowly be transplanted from the field of emotional controversy to that of economic efficiency, and that a great deal more money will be spent on both … Our social habits and our politics will take on a flavour that is ever more urban, and, as a consequence, ever more cosmopolitan. And this in turn will sound the death-knell of the attempt to preserve any kind of indigenous Gaelic folk culture in these islands."

Dr Thornley was both right and wrong. A social revolution would take place in Ireland, and in the early stages it would seem agreeable and rational. But 20 years on, there would be bitter culture wars; and 30 years later the superficial appreciation of trendy priests and progressive Catholic Ireland would end in the collapse of everything the collar had stood for.

President Kennedy paid a joyful visit to Ireland in June 1963, a moment of apotheosis in the new Irish confidence. JFK was the first Irish-American President who was also a Catholic, and his Catholicism had initially been considered a bar to office. His visit to Ireland was, of course, a huge success, and people felt great pride in the good-looking young president — and his beautiful wife — who were such a credit to Irish America and to us all. A few years after that visit, the *Messenger of the Sacred Heart* was to pick out a trio of men, hero figures who "live in the memory of people, inspiring them to continue work which they themselves started, or to put into practice their political and social theories." This unexpected pantheon consisted of President John F. Kennedy, Patrick Pearse, and Karl Marx. It was a measure of how Catholic Ireland had softened towards the Cold War ideology that it would include the founder of Communism among recognised heroes.

In fact, ranting against Communism had begun to dissolve in the first half of the 1950s (although the indefatigable Archbishop of Dublin, John Charles McQuaid, did try to ban Dubliners from attending a football match against Communist Yugoslavia in 1959 — they disobeyed him in droves). Nikita Khruschev, who succeeded Stalin in the Soviet Union, was, in his own way, quite media-friendly. He seemed a cuddly bear of an old peasant who on one occasion took to banging his shoe on the desk at the United Nations; he also visited Hollywood and took childlike pleasure in meeting Shirley MacLaine. Khruschev had denounced Stalin in 1956, which brought a thaw to the Cold War, though he was no friend of Christianity and wantonly destroyed a prodigious number of Russia's most beautiful churches and basilicas. But *détente* was established and that was reflected in a softer approach in the discourses of the Irish hierarchy. "Communism is intrinsically wrong," said Bishop Lucey of Cork, "but Communists are people like ourselves." Concern for social justice and welfare began to replace denunciations of that particularly Irish tautology "Godless atheism". This was a reflection of Pope John's encyclical *Pacem in Terris*.

The decolonialising "wind of change" was blowing through Africa, and the Catholic Church welcomed it. African socialism was seen as something positive in which Irish Catholics had had a shaping hand: as noted earlier, Irish priests had educated Robert Mugabe of Zimbabwe, and Julius Nyere of Tanzania. Had the Irish Catholics who took pride in these gentlemen been able to see the future, they might not have been so quick to consider their achievement a success: Nyere's policies reduced Tanzania to penury, and Mugabe would become just another greedy and corrupt dictator.

The encyclicals coming from Rome set the tone for a more critical approach to the Right, a more conciliatory view of the Left. Pope John's *Mater et Magistra* ("Mother and Teacher", meaning the Church itself), issued in May 1961, called upon the richer nations to assist the poorer ones and questioned some of the rights of property. This theme was continued by Paul VI in his 1967 encyclical *Popularum Progessio,* in which he stated: "Private property does not constitute for anyone an absolute and unconditional right."

The Irish bishops were to take up these themes in their pastorals and magazines such as *Studies, Herder Correspondence, The Furrow,* and *Doctrine and Life,* run by diocesan and religious clergy, increasingly challenged bourgeois capitalism and traditional values. Significantly, the old canon of Irish religious values, the *Irish Ecclesiastical Record,* ceased publication in 1968.

In their own way, liberal and progressive Irish priests of the 1960s were expressing an anti-bourgeois radicalism which would erupt in 1968 among students and intellectuals in Paris, Prague and on the campuses of the United States. It would also animate civil rights marches in Northern Ireland. These priests were able to see, and contrast, the real poverty that still existed in Irish society with the conspicuous consumption of a new class, the so-called Mercedes-and-mohair elite.

But they were also continuing in the tradition of anti-materialism which had been recurrent in Irish Catholicism, a monkishness which has always had an ascetic character. The Irish Christian tradition grew out of the stoical life of the monastery on the windswept rock; it was always hostile to materialism.

Not that the general run of the clergy during the 1960s were necessarily liberal innovators any more than the general run of the people were hippies and radicals. But there was a definite phenomenon of the "Sixties priest", who mirrored the secularist Sixties trendsetters.

By the end of the 1960s, the Sixties priests would be leading protests against the South African Springbok (all-white) rugby tour of Ireland. Some priests were also passionately caught up in the Nigerian civil war of 1967, and this turned out to be a highly politicising experience: Irish priests identified with their

Biafran flock and threw their lot in with the Biafrans, who would be defeated by federal Nigeria. The Irish Government, more concerned about the supply of oil than the self-determination of the Ibo (Biafran) people, backed federal Nigeria, which angered the activist priests. There is still a major study to be done about the effect of this war on these priests, for it was a most distressing war, involving the needless death of many children.

At home, the liberal priests were certainly having an influence. Even Peter Lennon, the *Guardian* writer and coruscating critic of the Catholic Church, conceded in a celebrated series of articles in January 1964 that liberal priests such as Father Peter Connolly, Professor of English at Maynooth, and Father John C. Kelly, a Jesuit with a special interest in the cinema, were significant agents of change in the battle against the Irish censorship of books and movies. John Kelly had been writing about films for some years in *The Furrow*, and his reviews were followed with enthusiasm by those interested in film as art. This was the era, anyhow, when film criticism was a serious form of writing, the genre pioneered in Britain by C.A. Lejeune and Dilys Powell.

The perception of film itself was evolving almost into an art form. It was no longer just "cowboys and injuns" or, as Pauline Kael has so brilliantly summarised it, "kiss kiss, bang bang". Film was now old enough to be art. *Bicycle Thieves*, directed in 1948 by Vittorio De Sica, came to be regarded in the 1950s as a much admired work of Italian neo-realism. François Truffaut's *The Four Hundred Blows*, filmed in 1959, which contained scenes that would formerly have been cut in Ireland (a husband fondling his wife's breasts), was shown in its integrated form because it had artistic merit. Jacques Tati's *Mon Oncle* (1958), Alain Resnais's *Hiroshima Mon Amour* (1959), Michelangelo Antonioni's *La Notte* (1960) were all regarded as serious films with a social commentary and revered by the new generation of movie buffs.

Even Federico Fellini's 1960 film *La Dolce Vita*, which contained controversial scenes at the time, was treated as a thoughtful essay on decadence. Articles and reviews in *The Furrow* were a significant Catholic source of film appreciation.

Indeed, an article by Father Peter Connolly in *The Furrow* was instrumental in bringing an end to the narrowly prohibitive phase of Irish censorship. Father Connolly argued that censorship should distinguish between low-level tripe and good work, and that under Irish censorship regulations far too much good work had fallen under the axe. It was time to review the whole agenda. Brian Lenihan, the Minister for Justice in 1967, is credited with ending censorship in one fell swoop: he introduced legislation which released all past banned books from a limbo of prohibition, and set a time-limit on all current bans. Thus anything banned would have the possibility of appeal and review, which served to soften and modify the approach to censorship.

But the liberalising influence of Fathers Connolly and Kelly had been crucial in preparing the ground for this legislative shift. In 1964 Father John Kelly had called for the "unbanning" of J.D. Salinger's *Catcher in the Rye*, which some member of the public had submitted as subversive — which it was, of course. An American nun championed the book in the Catholic media as a fine work, though a lay teacher described it as vulgar. It was a cult book which my generation regarded as challenging the mores of our parents. (Fashion can be as fickle in literature as in frocks: when I gave it to my own sons to read, in the 1990s, they couldn't see the point of it at all.) More darkly, John Lennon's assassin claimed to have been influenced to murder by it.

Television brought to the fore a number of progressive priests, such as Father Fergal O'Connor, lecturer in politics at University College Dublin, who argued against the British "clean-up-TV" campaigner Mary Whitehouse in a debate. Mrs Whitehouse claimed that TV was responsible for a decline in public morality; Father O'Connor maintained that it was not. In another public debate at the time, Father Patrick Brophy spoke strongly against the Archbishop of Dublin's ban on Catholics attending Trinity College Dublin. The ban was lifted in 1970. (John Charles McQuaid regarded Trinity College, founded by Elizabeth I for the promotion of the Reformed — that is, Anglican — faith, as a danger to faith and morals. Until the end of the 19th century Roman Catholics were not admitted to any of the major British or Irish universities, which were still Anglican foundations.) And TCD had its own tradition of being anti-Catholic and anti-Nationalist.

Among the best loved of these new-style, outgoing, television-friendly clerics was Father Eamonn Casey, later to be the Bishop of Galway and later again to be at the centre of a sex scandal which shocked and scandalised Catholic Ireland in 1992. It was revealed that the Bishop had had a mistress, had fathered a child and had paid off mother and son with diocesan funds. But all that was in the future, in the time of decline and fall. In the sunny morning-time of the 1960s, Father Eamonn was adored as a telegenic and radical priest, who not only cared deeply for the poor and the homeless but was also "great gas" and "great crack".

Eamonn Casey was so identified with the Left that when the scandal about him first broke, there were rumours that it was all got up by the CIA. In true new age, hug-a-tree fashion, he was also patron of an animal-welfare society.

Father Brian D'Arcy, unofficial chaplain to showbands and pop stars, Father Tom Stack, the handsome media priest, and Father Austin Flannery, the Dominican and human rights activist were prominent in 1960s Ireland as good guys who were open-minded and leading the country forward. Traditional Ireland still retained the old-fashioned respect for the priesthood, while progressive young Irish people identified with the younger priests as fellow-progressives. The American observer Donald S. Connery, who came to Ireland in 1963 to research his book *The Irish,* was surprised by how strongly Catholic Dublin still was. He nonetheless noted how pleasant, popular and approachable most of the priests were. A sociological survey of Dubliners in the1960s showed they had only one major complaint about the priests: that the priests themselves were so busy that they did not spend enough time making pastoral calls. A.J. Humphries' *New Dubliners,* regarded still as an authoritative snapshot of spreading urbanisation in Dublin at this time, signalled that the people wanted more of the priests' time. Ordinary people considered themselves the opposite of priest-ridden.

Similarly, in a study carried out by the American Jesuit B.F. Biever in 1962-63, it was found that nearly 90 per cent of his sample agreed with the proposition that "the Church is the greatest force for good in Ireland today". 88 per cent refused to describe the Church as out of date. Respondents said things like, "When you've got the truth, lad, you don't worry about keeping up with the times" and "I wouldn't change a thing the Church is doing; it keeps society here in Ireland a God-fearing one, and in the end there is nothing else worth doing. The Church ... is keeping our people happy and with their feet on the ground." Bruce Biever's studies saw a divergence between Irish Catholics in Ireland and Irish-American Catholics in America.

Catholics in Ireland were trusting of the idea that Church and State should be close: 66 per cent affirmed that they should not be independent of each other, whereas 61 per cent of Irish Americans thought that Church and State should be quite separate. Irish Catholics overwhelmingly thought that the Church was more important than the state.

Father Biever did find that among those Irish with more than 12 years education, more questioning about the Church occurred. Among university-educated people four out of five said they disagreed with the Church's dominance in Irish society. One respondent claimed: "The world is too complex today for a clerical state, and that is what we have in Ireland. What do priests know about politics, except that it leads to socialism?"

Yet the dissenting element seemed more a matter of private grumbling than public action, and such dissenters still went against the grain of the practice of everyday life. Tony Farmar, in his meticulous chronicles of three generations of middle-class Irish lives, noted that in the libraries of University College Dublin, in 1963, the majority of students still stood up for the angelus and recited it at midday and at six o'clock in the evening. V.S. Pritchett observed in 1963 that nearly everyone still made the sign of the cross when passing a Catholic Church in Dublin. On the Feast of St Blaise in February that year, it took 22 priests to bless the throats of the thousands attending a blessing service Mass at Merchants Quay, Dublin.

Bruce Biever himself felt constantly embarrassed, as an American, by the respect accorded to him in Ireland because he wore the collar. He described how he joined a queue to make a telephone call at a public booth when, to his chagrin, a woman in the middle of her own telephone call hung up, came out and ushered him into the phone box. He protested, but was told: "No priest should be standing in line waiting for the likes of me."

Thus, for a harmonious period in the 1960s, the old, devout, Catholic Ireland seemed to coexist happily with the new, changing, more liberal one, with more questioning, less deferential attitudes. The traditional respect for the clergy was still there, and even in the burgeoning urban areas of Dublin the notion that the priest was the community leader remained quite strong.

Yet, from 1962 onwards, traditional Catholicism was beginning to lose ground. Religious vocations began to fall in 1961, perhaps not coincidentally the year that TV came to Ireland.

From the launch of the Second Vatican Council — started by Pope John XXIII in 1962 — the tone in the Irish Catholic press became softer, more conciliatory, less focused on the prohibitions of "Thou shalt not", more open to other faiths. Mixed marriages between Catholics and Protestants began to be described as inter-church marriages. Salvoes against the apostosy of Martin Luther — traditionally held responsible not just for the birth of Protestantism, but for the French Revolution and the rise of Bolshevism by extension — disappeared virtually overnight and were replaced by appreciative articles about Luther's sweeter side (his Marian devotion, for example).

Injustice in South Africa, support for "the American negro", anxiety about old people dying of the cold and such sins as dangerous driving were beginning to replace such old favourites as impure thoughts in the canon of moral offence. It was certainly a turning-point in the annals of Ireland when the Bishop of Cork, the indefatigable Dr Lucey, who had an obsession with the iniquity of dance halls, left off preaching about dancing as an occasion of sin and began instead to inveigh against the wickedness of dangerous driving.

Catholic Ireland appeared to take to the new liturgy —
switching from Latin to English for worship — more serenely
than almost anywhere else. Dublin was the only major city not
to produce a Latin Mass Society in reaction against the changes.
It seemed, on the surface, as though the alterations in church
regulations made no ripple on the surface of faith. The Friday
fast, upheld through the centuries and through real privations,
suddenly did not matter any more. Rules about fasting before
Holy Communion, once rigidly implemented, quite dissolved.
The changes of Vatican II, the second Vatican Council, which
had been held from 1962 to 1965, were profound in terms of
people's everyday lives and yet were made wholly
uncontroversially. You could have said the Irish were passive to
Church authority, and never questioned why an action could be
wrong and forbidden one month and suddenly acceptable and
right the next. In the 1940s the ecclesiastical authorities had
instructed the faithful that it would be breaking the law of the
fast — a serious matter — if they should receive Holy
Communion after having accidentally swallowed seawater in a
swim taken three hours previously; now you could have a
swim, followed by oysters and champagne for breakfast, and
still receive Communion an hour later.

Some of the uncertainty about all these changes could be
perceived in letters from readers to the *Irish Messenger of the
Sacred Heart*. People wrote in to say they were bewildered:
previously they had been told that St Paul had laid it down that
no woman should enter a church without covering her head.
Now they were told this was of no import whatsoever.
Formerly they had mortified themselves by not eating meat on
Fridays; now it was as if that was all in vain. One reader
complained:

> "There's nothing certain about the faith any more ...
> Time was when the Catholic Church stood firm as a
> rock in a sea of change. But now the fasting laws in
> Lent have been relaxed till they are only a shadow of
> what they were ...
> "I remember my mother telling me that if you set
> foot inside a Protestant Church when a service was
> going on, you had taken the first step towards

abandoning your religion. But now we have Protestants and Catholics meeting for public prayer ... When I was at school, the teacher showed us the picture in the paper of Cardinal Mindszenty [the Primate of Hungary, known as a martyr to Communism in 1948 when charged with treason by the Communist government of Budapest] between two Guards. They were Communists, she said, people no Christian would have anything to do with. But now I take up the paper and read about Catholics, with their bishops' approval, meeting communists for an exchange of ideas."

Other readers, once exposed to change, wanted more of it. Questions began to appear such as "Why cannot priests marry, as Protestant clergy do?"

The new openness to Protestants, triggered by the changes of Vatican II and the global ambiance of *détente*, was for the most part very warm and touching. And again, it looked at the start as though it would make a big difference to the way we lived. When Pope John XXIII died, in June 1961, Belfast City Hall flew its flag at half-mast — an astonishing and unprecedented step for an Ulster Unionist city authority. In September 1963 the *Catholic Standard* published the words of the Orange song, 'The Auld Orange Flute', which mocks Catholic religious practices, though with a certain amount of good humour and inverted flattery. The *Irish Independent* newspaper claimed with confidence in the same year that the sting had been taken out of Orangeism now and that the 12th of July, the Orangeman's marching day, was "losing its appeal" in the modern 1960s. Even the advertisements in *The Irish Times* which specified that Protestants were preferred in domestic posts were disappearing.

All around the country, civic receptions were taking place in which Catholic and Protestant showed a new warmth towards one another. A typical example was when the Mayor of Clonmel, Councillor Martin Slater, welcomed Dr Simms, the Anglican Archbishop of Dublin, in May 1965, saying it was fitting that "in this modern age of ecumenism their guest should be a prelate of the Church of Ireland. In these times a new understanding had developed among our people and the old prejudices both religious and political were gratifyingly disappearing."

The welcome for ecumenism was sincere: the rigidity with which Irish Catholics observed the practice of not entering a Protestant church had been risible and sometimes offensive. When an Irish Protestant who had served the country died, such as the first President, Douglas Hyde, in 1949 or Abbey playwright Lennox Robinson in 1958, people would line the route outside the Protestant church at the funeral, but never venture inside.

This change was widely embraced. Indeed, looking back on the period from 1962 to 1965, the religious corespondent of *The Irish Times,* John Horgan (a grandson of the previously cited John Horgan) wrote: "Catholic Irish people were very well disposed towards the whole idea of ecumenism from the end of the Council [1965] onwards." An intrinsic neighbourliness which had been stifled in the past now took advantage of new channels. "Ecumenical meetings at a popular level became almost *de rigueur* for the long winter evenings." The main worry was "the comparative scarcity of Protestants. Would there be enough to go round? In some parts of the West of Ireland, one hadn't been seen for years."

This would surely lead to a *rapprochement* with Northern Ireland and it did. In 1965 the Taoiseach, Sean Lemass, had a much-publicized and well-regarded meeting with the Belfast Prime Minister, Terence O'Neill. This opened the way for a new round of optimism towards Northern Ireland. Soon afterwards it was proposed that the clause in the Irish Constitution which recognised "the special position of the Catholic Church" should be dropped, with a view towards easing relations with the mainly Protestant North. Cardinal Conway, the Cardinal-Archbishop of Ireland at the time, said he "would not shed a tear" to see it go, and by 1972 it was indeed annulled, comfortably carried in a referendum which also reduced the voting age from 21 to 18.

There was not much evidence that this gesture made any difference to Northern Ireland one way or the other.

By the same token, there was also a new sensitivity towards the Jews, again led by Church sources. "No Christian Can Be Anti-Semitic" ran a splash headline in the *Catholic Standard* in January 1964, heading an article on the errors and evils of anti-Semitism at a time when Pope Paul VI was making a pilgrimage to Jerusalem. The following week Monsignor A.H. Ryan stated that "Ireland alone among European nations was free from the reproach of inhumanity towards Jews and said he sincerely hoped the relations of sincere tranquillity which had been enjoyed in the past would remain".

This was meant kindly, but it somewhat naive and occlusive. Ireland had not prohibited the immigration of Jews, like Norway, or massacred them in pogroms, as in the Ukraine, but, as elsewhere, there had been pockets of anti-Semitism — the autobiography of the popular novelist Annie M.P. Smithson deplores the presence of the Jews as moneylenders among the Dublin poor — and de Valera had refused to accept Jewish children as refugees during the Second World War on grounds that they "wouldn't fit in". (Northern Ireland acted more generously towards Jewish youngsters.) Yet de Valera himself was not anti-Semitic and Irish nationalism was for a long time strongly pro-Israel.

In Catholic values the leadership of the Pope can be perceived to percolate right down to the level of popular media. In tackling the stain of anti-Semitism, the leadership was coming from Pope John: he had removed words offensive to Jews from the Good Friday liturgy, which was truly meaningful. I have no recollection of being taught any direct anti-Semitism in my convent education, but I do remember that the words which helped condemn Jesus Christ to death — "His blood be upon us, and upon our people" — were interpreted as an explanation, if not a justification, for the "curse" that lay upon the Jews. Pope John worked to reverse this. He would introduce himself to rabbinical visitors with the words: "I am Joseph, your brother." (His middle name was Giuseppe, Joseph.)

John Horgan's observations about the intrinsic neighbourliness of the Irish, which had been restricted by Catholic-Protestant separation, is borne out by letters to the

"Question Box" feature in the *Irish Messenger of the Sacred Heart* during the 1950s. These show an increasing tendency towards more neighbourly and friendly relations between Catholics and non-Catholics (now called "other Christians"). The question of whether a Protestant friend can be a godfather to a child arises with more frequency, as does the matter of a Catholic being a bridesmaid at a Protestant wedding. This was clear evidence of normal friendships.

In the 1950s the answers had tended to be prohibitive: "It is forbidden to take any part in a non-Catholic ceremony and since a bridesmaid is an official witness it is therefore forbidden." After the Vatican council of 1962-65 such regulations were relaxed. In June 1966 the Irish hierarchy directed that, "For considerations of friendship, Catholics may attend the baptisms of Protestants, the marriages of Protestants at which they may act as bridesmaid or best man, and the funerals of Protestants. Mixed marriages may take place in a Catholic church, before the altar with the usual rites and blessings." A family connection of mine — the sister of an aunt by marriage — remembered ruefully how her wedding to a Protestant had to take place in the sacristy of the church, not before the altar, and at dawn, so as not to "give scandal". People were glad to see the sweeping away of such restrictive practices. Yet a historical institution is at its most vulnerable to weakening, or even collapse, as soon as it begins to change.

The Catholic Church had been the most dominant continuous influence in Irish life over many hundreds of years. But as the 1960s wore on, that position was to be overtaken by a new agency of dominance: television. Television had a dramatic impact everywhere, but perhaps the impact was more dramatic in those societies which had remained essentially unchanged since the Victorian era.

Irish television had come on the airwaves in 1961. Prior to that, it was possible to pick up British television — BBC and the Independent network — but the reception could be unreliable since there were no transmitters broadcasting to the Republic of Ireland. The introduction of a native TV service was duly debated in the Dáil, and it was argued therein that, like radio, it should come under state control. Some parliamentarians showed little enthusiasm for this new-fangled form of information, and at least one TD described it as a passing fancy.

The usual fare of *I Love Lucy* and *The Waltons* was not particularly challenging. It was Gay Byrne's Saturday night TV talk and variety programme, *The Late Late Show*, which evolved into the national forum for less outspoken challenge and debate, eventually becoming more influential than the Church. By the mid-1960s priests noticed that the main topic of conversation after Sunday Mass was what had been on *The Late Late Show* the previous night. By the middle 1970s the priests themselves were taking their text from television, beginning sermons with "As I was watching on TV last night …".

Television likes shock and surprise, and in those early days of still Victorian decorum it was not hard to shock. Early examples came in the fairly simple form of rude words and common abuse. A rebellious Trinity College Dublin student, Brian Trevaskis, called a bishop a moron on *The Late Late Show*, and the country was aghast that a bishop should be so insulted.

But it was in February 1966 that the watershed episode known as "The Bishop and the Nightie" occurred. It was a huge national controversy, in some respects absurd but also highly significant.

It all began harmlessly enough with a light-hearted (not to say pretty mindless) TV quiz. As part of the general entertainment, husbands and wives were questioned separately about various points of domestic life to see whether their answers concurred. One question, to Mrs Eileen Fox of Terenure, Dublin, involved asking the lady what colour nightdress she had worn on her wedding night. Offhand she couldn't recall and then suggested playfully that perhaps she hadn't worn any. This was greeted with laughter and a round of applause. The show proceeded without further incident, but Gay Byrne was astonished to receive a telephone call after the transmission from a reporter on the *Sunday Press* informing him that the Bishop of Clonfert, Rt Revd Dr Thomas Ryan, intended to denounce the "nightie" incident. This occurred in a sermon to be given at Loughrea Cathedral in Co Galway the following morning. There were splash headlines in the Sunday paper,

"The Late Late Under Fire — Bishop Slates TV Act", and subsequently a tremendous hullaballoo.

The Bishop sent a telegram to the TV station saying he was disgusted; in his sermon he called the show objectionable. The Loughrea Town Commissioners backed the Bishop and described *The Late Late Show* as "a dirty programme that should be abolished altogether". The Mayo Gaelic Athletic Association and the Meath Vocational Education Committee passed resolutions condemning the show. The *Irish Catholic* described the programme as "a public discussion of bedroom relations between married couples", and saw in it the impending erosion of all values surrounding the sacrament of marriage and modesty befitting the treatment of sex.

Even the liberal *Irish Times* did not actually defend the transmission, though they felt that the Bishop had overreacted. "His Lordship was killing a fly with a sledgehammer." Saturday night, they pointed out judiciously, was vaudeville night, but they conceded that the episode constituted "a lapse of taste" rather than "an outrage to morals".

Recalling the incident in 1972, Gay Byrne scoffed at what had occurred. It was all quite farcical, he said. He had reason for resentment: Mr and Mrs Fox had been greatly embarrassed by something which had seemed just a joke being turned into a national incident, and their children were being teased at school. There had also been a maladroit effort at an apology from the Bishop which Gay Byrne thought shabbily executed; the Bishop had sent a clerical representative to meet Gay Byrne's brother at a cafeteria in Dublin to convey certain Episcopal "regrets". Why couldn't the Bishop come clean and deal with this straightforwardly, Gay asked, instead of these cloak-and-dagger stratagems?

"The Bishop and the Nightie" story passed into Irish legend as just how absurd some bishops could be in those days, at a time when they were palpably losing their power. It was an overblown incident, and really rather daft; yet at a greater distance of social history, it reveals how, instinctively, the Bishop knew that this new outspoken mode of TV talk would eventually remove all modesty from public discourse. Intuitively, he felt that this was the thin end of the wedge: now it was hints of honeymoon nights in the nude, presently, it would be the full monty, and it was.

Throughout the 1960s, of course, culture was becoming more openly sexualised, as expressed in popular music, images, language and advertisements. Explicitness was gradually increasing in the media. The Profumo scandal in Britain was a major watershed which gave the media permission to discuss sexuality openly. (The Minister of War, John Profumo, had been found to be involved with a prostitute, Christine Keeler, who also had a liaison with a Soviet spy. Mr Profumo, when accused, denied this in the House of Commons but was later obliged to confess.) The Profumo affair was the first time that a political sexual scandal was openly discussed. Previously the media had voluntarily chosen not disclose the private life of politicians — President Kennedy's numerous affairs were kept very firmly under wraps (as was Franklin D. Roosevelt's mistress). The courtroom appearances of the brazen Miss Keeler and her friend Mandy Rice-Davies provided a field day for the newspapers and magazines and became the small talk of everyday life.

In July 1963 a reader of the *Catholic Standard* wrote in to deplore the way in which gossip about Miss Keeler was now regulation fare even by pilgrims on pilgrimage. "On Sunday last I travelled with a large busload of people to a place which one would imagine to have inspired these people to recite the rosary," wrote Mrs J.C., "rather than read and openly discuss the most scandalous details of the recent sad events in England. But practically everyone on that bus was swapping and reading aloud the more lurid Sunday newspapers. The point that Christine Keeler has Co Leitrim connections, that Dr Stephen Ward has so many Irish cousins and Mr John Profumo has Irish relatives only added zest to the scandal search of this Irish busload." Clearly the *News of the World* — the British Sunday newspaper which gave the juiciest titbits — had done its job thoroughly and played up any Irish angle. The reader declared herself most unedified, and there was further correspondence on this issue. Some people thought it was all quite deplorable that the papers should go into such detail — it was the first time that Irish newspapers began to do this, it was maintained — but others thought it reasonably acceptable. "Women are realists and they can discuss sordid and nasty things without being sullied in the least," wrote a lady signing herself Portia.

It was obvious, though, that this was a turning-point for the media to be more frank and also to probe more into salacious details. In Northern Ireland the Protestant newspapers were a mirror-image of conservative Catholic values in this. In the Loyalist *Belfast Newsletter,* the Revd John Young from Belmont Presbyterian Church complained: "Why are the doings of unfortunate degraded individuals being proclaimed on radio, television and even in our own papers? ... It is surely a poor thing that the papers in this province, usually zealous of decency, have seen fit on this occasion to stoop so low. They say that it is news and news must be told. The question is — is it really to help or to hinder, to uplift or debase?" The Belfast papers also objected to the familiarity with which Mandy (Rice-Davies) was being described in the headlines. Readers wrote in to support Revd Young and to deplore "the unutterable filth" which was emerging in the Profumo court cases. Such evidence as necessary should be given *in camera* and not flaunted for all the world to wallow in it. Northern Protestants and Southern Catholics in Ireland may be divided by history and dogma, but they quite often share basic values.

Still, it was a brave new world that was coming into being. The 1960s ushered in social change for all societies and each society changed in its own way: America faced its explosive race problems; Britain began to question the class hierarchies which were part of its fabric; and Catholic Ireland showed a liberal face, and then faced a whole new set of challenges.

Eleven

The Pill, the Church and the New Wave of Irish Feminism

"The more a nation advances in civilization and refinement, the greater is the respect and deference paid to women; the more they are trusted, the greater responsibilities, therefore, are laid on their shoulders. Personally, I am in favour of 'The Rights of Women', properly understood. Women, just like men, if they so desire it may be doctors or lawyers, may be in business, and enter the political arena. Women have succeeded in all these spheres, often beating men."

Revd J.S. Sheehy, 'The Influence of Women in Catholic Ireland', *Irish Catholic*, November 1922

"It can hardly, I think, be questioned that in the great religious convulsions of the 16th century, the feminine type followed Catholicism, while Protestantism inclined more to the masculine type."

W.H. Lecky, *A History of European Morals*

There was a widespread belief that the contraceptive pill was for many years banned in Ireland. Right up until the middle 1990s popular tourist guides confidently, and erroneously, told visitors that the Pill was prohibited in the Irish Republic. ("The contraceptive pill is still banned in Ireland", *Dublin City Guide*, in the Lonely Planet series, 1993.) In fact, the contraceptive was

221

never banned in Ireland. Neither was it particularly difficult to obtain, once it became pharmaceutically available in 1961. "I have at no time had difficulty in obtaining a prescription for the Pill from different doctors," wrote Mrs Dympna McNamara of Sligo in a letter to *The Irish Times* in May 1968. "Neither have any of my friends."

Thus the Pill *itself* was never banned in Ireland. Barrier methods of contraception were prohibited, by legislation passed in 1935. These were contraceptive artifacts, sometimes described then as methods for "race suicide". But the Pill, not having been invented in 1935 and not being an artifact but a pharmaceutical, never came under the prohibition. In fact, I clearly remember anxious feminist discussions in the late 1960s in Dublin when women voiced concern that the Pill was possibly over-prescribed in Ireland because of a shortage of other options.

Yet the Pill has a significance beyond its clinical description: an anovulant medication which prevents conception and implantation. "The Pill" became in itself a metaphor for all of birth control. When a group of young Irish feminists — myself included — staged a defiant stunt in 1971 ostentatiously bringing contraceptives (condoms and spermicides) from Belfast to Dublin and declaring the illegal booty at Connolly Railway Station, the entire incident was dubbed "the Pill Train", although, of course, no Pills were involved. The Pill had to be properly prescribed by a doctor — you did not just enter a pharmacy in Belfast and purchase it. But it was the Pill Train in popular mythology, because the Pill, perhaps appropriately, came to symbolise both the sex revolution and the feminist revolution of the 1960s.

Germaine Greer has frequently pointed out that the sex revolution and the feminist revolution were different, though they were often conflated because of the increasing availability of contraception and legal abortion. The sex revolution meant, in the immortal words of Dr Greer's fellow-Australian Clive James, "More crumpet on the market" (except that in the original, "crumpet" was in a cruder form). The sex revolution came to mean that traditional taboos involving restraints and limitations on sexual conduct dissolved, and eventually, it might be said, virtually disappeared. The Pill was the main gateway to the sex revolution because it rendered fertility control reliable, predictable, aesthetic and invisible. All previous forms of contraception seemed vexatious, intrusive or ugly. Moreover, only the woman herself needed to know she was taking it. The Pill transferred all fertility control, and power, to the woman.

The Pill's impact was sensational; it appeared like a magical potion which seemed to provide mankind with what it had always dreamed about: sex without consequences, sex without cost and sex without strings. Within a short time it would have an impact on every aspect of interactive life between the sexes — from dancing to courtship rituals, from manners to morals. And it would provoke a huge crisis in the Catholic Church.

Feminism was concerned with other issues besides sex, and the traditions of feminism have always been ambivalent about sexual freedom. Modern-day objections by feminists to pornography and prostitution are but a continuation of past form. Christabel Pankhurst's rallying cry "Votes for Women — and Chastity for Men" was to find echoes in late 20th-century feminists' protestations against pornography, against explicit nude pictures in offices, in their touchy characterisation of flirtatious advances as sexual harassment, and of some forms of seduction as "date rape".

Feminism has always had a puritanical dimension, and perhaps logically so: in the sex war, sauce for the goose is not necessarily sauce for the gander. Men and women really are different, sexually — young men have 11 times as much testosterone as young women — and men need be in no rush to commit themselves to fatherhood. A sexual free-for-all between men and women always risked leaving the woman holding the baby; but even with the baby out of the picture, there is a feminist awareness that women may be more vulnerable to losing the battle of the sexes in the long term. A single and childless woman in her forties is at a disadvantage to a single and childless man in his forties. Biology gives men more choice and for longer. Testosterone can prompt males to greater promiscuity, so it is to women's advantage to promote commitment.

Irish feminism had traditionally focused on both emancipation for women — education, entry into the professions, the political franchise — and the nationalist cause. As was seen in the early years of the century, the generation of 1916 was bristling with lively Irishwomen who were committed to women's emancipation, but who, for the most part, saw that as being linked to Ireland's independence. Constance Markievicz, the first woman ever to be elected to the House of Commons on a Sinn Féin ticket, was a classic example of the Irish feminist who fully endorsed the goals of women's emancipation, but the cause of Ireland overtook, embraced and umbrellaed the cause of women.

Sinn Féin and the Gaelic League were both strong on equality between the sexes in the early years of the 20th century when Sinn Féin was formed in 1905 (named, indeed, by a woman, Máire de Bhuitleir). "Women speakers began to be heard at public meetings," notes a contemporary source, "and from now on it may be safely stated that their influence was completely on the side of Irish-Ireland." Jenny Wyse Power, a nationalist woman who subsequently became a Senator in the Free State, went so far as to blame any disadvantages that women suffered from on English rule in Ireland. It was the English influence which created "false sex and class distinctions": when Ireland gained independence, all this would disappear.

Women's emancipation, in terms of the vote, did indeed arrive with the foundation of the Irish State. But class and sex distinctions, strangely enough, did not disappear with the exit of the English! Indeed, the 1920s and 1930s witnessed a Europe-wide increase in both, as disparities between the rich and the poor grew more visible, and with the onset of the Depression of the 1930s every state in Europe sought to reduce the participation of women in the workforce. With millions of men on the dole, it was not thought acceptable at the time that married women should have easy access to jobs. Adolf Hitler's policy that women's domain should be children, church and kitchen — *Kinder, Kuche, Kirche* — was not considered eccentric in the 1930s, even by women. Indeed, women voted overwhelmingly for Hitler's economic policies, which were initially very much focused on getting men back to work. The women of Germany desired that their husbands, as breadwinners, should have employment first. From a modern perspective this may seem unequal but it reflected the way of thinking at this time.

Ireland, being a predominantly agricultural country in the 1930s, was not really comparable to the large industrialised nations. The issue of equality between men and women arises less in farming life, partly because a family farm — where the family relationship is functional — is a kind of cooperative anyway. Men and women work together, and there is a logical division of labour — or at least it seemed logical to people in times gone by. The men do the work in the fields and with the bigger animals; the women have charge of the smaller animals, the vegetable garden and the house. This division of labour within a cooperative at least gave rural women a sense of their own domain, and power within their own domain. In Ireland, for instance, the egg-money — the revenue for selling the eggs the chickens laid — was traditionally the woman's own income on the farm.

The Harvard anthropologists Arensberg and Kimbell, who spent two years in Co. Clare in the late 1930s, painted a charming, perhaps even rosy picture of Irish rural life in their classic text *Family and Community in Ireland*, published in 1940 at Cambridge, Massachusetts. Arensberg and Kimbell portray the Irish country woman at this time as being a person of respect within her community, who, as she grew older, gained more respect and power. Interestingly, they claimed that older women actually commanded more respect than elderly men in Ireland at this time. Of course there were huge variations according to individual circumstances and according to means. But women in the home — especially in rural life — did not see themselves, or were not seen especially as oppressed at this time. People, in general, were poor and women shared that poverty: that was a fact of life.

Yet the anthropologists observed some very pleasing aspects of Irish childhood where the child of the farm grew up close to his mother, learning from an early stage to be part of the economy of the farm. From about the age of three he would be entrusted with small tasks to train him that the family farm is a cooperative in which everyone must make a contribution. Arensberg and Kimbell ascribed the particular attachment that emigrants felt to their Irish mothers to this proximity in the early years of life.

When de Valera came to draw up a new constitution for the 26 counties of the Free State in 1936-37, there was no great outcry from the majority of Irishwomen when he proposed that the State should have a special esteem for the woman in the home. The 1937 constitution — still the basis for today's constitution — was also to indicate that the State could discriminate between individuals having regard to difference of "capacity, physical and moral, and of social function", while maintaining the principle of basic equality before the law. In 1935, moreover, a Conditions of Employment Bill, introduced by Sean Lemass as Minister for Industry and Commerce, gave priority to men in the small industrial sector of the economy. This was indeed opposed by some politicised women, among them Mary Hayden of the National Council of Women and Louie Bennett of the Irish Women Workers' Union, a crusader for workers' rights and a committed Socialist (possibly a Communist). Hanna Sheehy-Skeffington, a crusading radical, left-winger, Republican and atheist — and also Conor Cruise O'Brien's aunt — denounced it as "fascist". The bill was also criticised for not providing enough intervention by the state (which meant that it was insufficiently corporatist) on employment policy.

But the introduction of de Valera's constitutional proposals did elicit a wave of criticism from a group of educated women, and initially it looked as though a new feminist movement might arise in Ireland in the late 1930s. These graduate women, led by Professor Mary Macken of University College Dublin, emerged as the most visible critics of the woman-in-the-home clause. In June 1937 there was a Women's Rights Meeting in Dublin which attracted 1,500 women, and it was announced that a Women's Party would be formed.

Professor Macken was no wild extremist: at that time an individual (like Hanna Sheehy-Skeffington) associated with a range of radical causes, and particularly proclaiming atheism, would be regarded in Ireland as an eccentric and a crank, by Protestants as much as Catholics. (Irish Protestants as a group were extremely hostile to anyone challenging the rights of private property, as radicals were bound to do.) But Mary Macken was obviously clever, nice and, as it happens, very pretty, which is never a disadvantage for a young woman. She acknowledged that some women would want to stay at home.

But she was concerned that the clause establishing their special position in the home would mean that girls would be kept out of jobs and females barred from advancement in the professions. "No woman that I know denies the grandeur of the State's desire to ensure that mothers should not be *forced* to engage in labour outside the home. But many women fear that mothers may be, by legislation directed by a clause under Article 41, prevented from engaging in labour which both she and her husband agree is desirable for the comfort of those constituting the home. It is one thing to guarantee every married man an economic wage; it is quite another to prevent a wife or a mother from taking such. Who is to be the judge in each case?"

Professor Macken emphasised the cooperative aspect of farm work, though she also noted that this aspect of life was now subject to change. "In no country more than in Eire is there more mutual forbearance and cooperation between husband and wife. In few civilized countries do women work harder in farm and business in harmony with their husbands for the advancement of their children. But the economic order has changed vastly in the last thirty years."

The Women's Rights Meeting and the notion of a Women's Party stirred up real interest for a short time, but there were also reactions against it and immediate political differences too. Women who supported De Valera in general supported his constitution. Women who supported family values — there always have been women who liked the idea that the home is a realm where feminine power could be wielded and maintained — welcomed this affirmation of the constitution. "I cannot find anything in reference to women in the Constitution that is worthy of condemnation," wrote Máire de Blacam, who was from a well-known nationalist family. "Every responsible woman who has at heart the interests of Christian society and sees the dangers to the proper equilibrium of the family, must rejoice that the Constitution seeks to protect the father of the family as breadwinner and the mother as home maker."

The Women's Graduates Association, which activated these meetings, were referred to in the daily press as the Graduate Women, which, in an era when most men, let alone most women, were not university graduates, rather set them apart. Accusations were made that some of them were anti-nationalist, again a sensitive topic at the time. Mrs de Blacam claimed that "one of the Professors holding the Women Graduates protest meeting has been consistently opposed to the whole National movement ... thus the meeting seemed to appeal only to the agitating and anti-national elements among the women voters." This was a similar charge to that made against the suffragettes — that they were a Trojan horse for British values in Ireland. The issue soon became entangled with the complex tendrils of Irish politics. Die-hard Republican women who opposed de Valera's constitution had a different critique altogether. For them, the repugnant aspect of the constitution was the continuing link with the British Crown which the 1937 document retained; this was a hundred times worse than anything pertaining to women's role in Irish society.

"Naturally we Republicans do not support the present Government, which is merely a successor to the Cumann na nGaedheal Government [the Free State Government which accepted the hated Anglo-Irish Treaty of 1921] established by England," wrote Kathleen Lynn, a 1916 veteran, speaking for Republican women.

Other Republican women such as Mrs Kathleen Clarke — widow of Tom Clarke, the 1916 signatory — supported the Graduate Women by opposing the 1937 constitution altogether because it "betrayed the spirit of the 1916 proclamation".

Maud Gonne MacBride, the great beauty whom Yeats had adored, and the people venerated when she crusaded against their afflictions of poverty and famine, also denounced de Valera's constitution. "With one of our provinces cut off, and the Republican Army [the IRA] outlawed, and forty-four Republicans [IRA men] in jail ... it seems absurd to talk of a permanent Constitution for Ireland." When Ireland was truly free — that is, when Northern Ireland was recovered from British rule and the Republican ideals met — then "the Article concerning women" could be revised. It is by no means certain, however, that Maud Gonne MacBride would have supported the feminists. A close reading of her life shows that she was at heart a conservative on family issues. She was a true, indeed a fanatical, Republican, but on social issues her concerns were mainly driven by the maternal instinct.

Sean MacEntee, the Minister for Finance, in commenting on the issues raised by the Graduate Women, used the tried and tested male chauvinist tactic of the ungallant put-down and the charge of sexual frustration. "The truth of the matter was that a lot of the women who were talking about women's rights in the Constitution had no men of their own to let off steam against." In his own domestic life he was married to a clever woman, an expert on Balzac; they were the parents of the poet Maire Mhac an tSaoi, also Mrs Conor Cruise O'Brien.

Not much more was heard of the proposed Women's Party; it arose on a wave of enthusiasm and dropped out of sight without trace. Perhaps, after all, its potential leader, the pretty Professor Macken, was too nice for the rough game of political leadership. She would have needed to be a shrieking harridan — as Yeats was inclined to called politically active women — to succeed in launching a Women's Party at this time. Article 41 was endorsed in the Irish Constitution and exists to this day. "The State recognises the Family as the natural primary and fundamental group, and as a moral institution, possessing inalienable and imprescriptible rights ... The State, therefore, guarantees to protect the Family in its constitution and authority as the necessary basis of social order ... In particular, the State recognises that by her life within the home, woman gives to the State a support without which the common good cannot be achieved. That State shall therefore endeavour to ensure that mothers shall not be obliged to engage in labour to the neglect of their duties in the home." There have been proposals to amend it — the phrasing is certainly old-fashioned — but any Irish politician who appears to be attacking the position of the Irish mother in the home comes under public fire. Mothers want their labour in the home to be recognised and valued, after all. Home-making becomes boring and frustrating precisely when it is unappreciated or held in little esteem because it is not financially rewarded directly.

The Second World War was to bring in a raft of new opportunities for women — there is a charming photograph of Queen Elizabeth II, then the Princess Elizabeth, working as a motor car mechanic, changing the tire on an army truck — but this, of course, was not to affect Ireland because of Irish neutrality. It can be said that it was actually during 1939-45 that Irishwomen got left behind in the evolution of women's 20th-century development. During this period the British began to lift barriers against the employment of married women. The "marriage bar", which obliged women in teaching jobs and in government service to resign from their jobs on getting married, was abolished between 1944 and 1946. This impetus came from necessity rather than generosity — the British economy needed the labour of married women.

Meanwhile, Ireland retained the pre-war prohibitions against married women at work.

A new and controversial factor was also entering the picture of women's emancipation which would make Catholicism more hostile to the whole issue, and that was the gradual increase in knowledge about birth control. During the 1920s and 1930s, despite the *Kinder-Kuche-Kirche* agenda elsewhere (or maybe because of it), the Catholic Church had been quite enlightened on the subject of women's advancement. They were not at all against the idea of the education and vocational fulfilment of women — after all, so many energetic nuns, starting with St Angela de Merici who founded the Ursuline Order in the 15th century, had been pioneers of women's education. Catholicism — not unjustifiably — even claimed for itself a tradition of Catholic feminism and pointed to such individuals as Matilda of Tuscany or Blanche of Castile as powerful and educated women of the Middle Ages.

"It was the influence of Protestantism which reduced women's status," claimed the *Irish Ecclesiastical Record* in 1937. This was not untrue, and it is endorsed by the liberal historian Lawrence Stone who has indeed claimed that the Protestant revolution was essentially masculine and, in closing the convents, substantially reduced the opportunities for women's education. Stone argues that men like Martin Luther wanted every woman to be married so as to be under the control of a husband, not off doing their own thing in a community of women. At the same time, by the 19th century Protestant women had begun their own quiet revolution, being involved in the anti-slavery movement, in temperance causes (there were a considerable number of female Baptist preachers against alcoholism in the 1830s) and in areas of social reform, such as prisons and child prostitution.

It is unfair to characterise Catholicism as being historically repressive of women. It was not: it has always been very much a woman's faith. But on sexual matters Catholicism has always been posited firmly in the camp of biological determinism: men and women are different and therefore complementary. Sexuality is about "the transmission of life" (or, as it is more prosaically now known, reproduction), and not, primarily, about pleasure. The Catholic Church would bridle at innovations in sexuality such as birth control, which would throw these very basic principles into question.

Birth control became a controversial issue in the 1920s, when the pioneer birth controller Marie Stopes in Britain (like Margaret Sanger in America) made it so. Stopes wanted birth control to be sensationalised; she understood that publicity would spread the word. But while a gradual acceptance of the subject, and the practice, increased during the 1930s, it was far from being openly spoken about and far from being discussed by doctors. Indeed, the British birth control movement had a 40-year struggle to get family planning recognised as an aspect of public health. This was true elsewhere, and many countries took a long time even to discuss the issue. In France, contraception was not legalised until 1967, and even then, as has been noted, there was a gap of seven years before ratification. The French Left was as puritanical about birth control as French Catholics were; Madame Maurice Thorez, wife of the French Communist Party leader, was one of the sternest opponents of contraception. She believed it would "encourage free love, a decadent bourgeois idea unworthy of Communists".

The National Health Act, which launched the modern British health service in 1946, made no mention of family planning; it was not seen as a health issue. There were family planning clinics after the Second World War, but they were operated on a voluntary basis, sometimes with local authority support. British men, who did compulsory military service until 1958, were accustomed to being given condoms as soldiers; this was mainly (as today, with AIDS) as a prophylactic against venereal disease, which was practical enough, and yet the practice stigmatised the condom as something associated with prostitutes or with promiscuous and diseased women. There is evidence that some men did use condoms with their wives, but this method always suffered from the image problem of disease prevention.

From 1949 some family planning services were available through the British National Health, but the organisation took the view that their purpose in life was not to provide private pleasure; family planning was mainly justified on grounds of women's health and not as a routine part of married life. Women who had given birth by Caesarean section (as Queen Elizabeth the Queen Mother did) were at this time advised not to have more than two children — it was not considered safe to repeat the operation. Such were the worthy grounds on which a married woman might obtain family planning services.

Yet discussions about limiting fertility were in the air. Since the 1930s there was a growing awareness that fertility could be controlled, not just through barrier methods advocated by Marie Stopes but by the Ogino-Kraus method or "safe period". (The safe period — the notion that there are times in the month when a woman is not fertile — was only discovered in the 1930s, by Ogino and Kraus.) The Ogino-Kraus discoveries were discussed in the *Irish Ecclesiastical Record* in 1944.

Articles by Irish nun-doctors, working with the remarkable Medical Missionaries of Mary, also appeared in the 1940s, highlighting the problems of unsafe motherhood in Africa.

Nuns obtained permission to practice midwifery in 1936 (after lobbying the Vatican for well over 20 years), and in their work overseas they became aware of illegal abortions and of the health problems of very young mothers in mission hospitals. Medical complications more often arise when girls under 15 are pregnant, and the Medical Missionaries were concerned about this. Reproductive health care was a focus of attention from the end of the Second World War, and in October 1951 Pope Pius XII made a famous address to the Italian Catholic Union of Midwives in which he alluded to this breakthrough of the safe period. He reiterated the Catholic Church's teaching condemning sterilisation, coitus interruptus and appliance methods of birth control. His reference to the newly discovered safe period, which was not condemned, opened the door to the notion that conception could, in principle, be avoided or minimised by a "natural" method.

There are indications that women in Ireland by the early 1950s were talking between themselves about the possibility of spacing their children. My own mother, who had her last child — me — in 1944, told me that in her generation there was no knowledge of birth control at all, and that it would not have been considered proper to discuss it. But by 1951 this was beginning to change. In April of that year a mother wrote to the expert in the *Irish Messenger of the Sacred Heart*, Father Robert Nash, SJ, on this subject.

After the birth of each child, the lady wrote, she was advised by other Catholic women to "mind herself" and "have no more babies for a year or two". Father Nash noted, in his commentary on this letter, that the same advice was sometimes given by doctors, even Catholic doctors, to their patients. There is a sense, Father Nash comments carefully, in which such advice is sound and in full accord with Catholic standards of morality. "There may be times … when another new baby would entail an expense that the parents sincerely believe they could not face; or the doctor's considered opinion is that the mother's health cannot endure another birth … or the family is badly housed. [But] where a doctor gives this advice, he must make perfectly clear to his patient that he is no way advocating forms of birth control that are condemned by God's law." The fact that Father Nash introduced this topic, aired for the first time in a devotional magazine, shows that he was aware that it was becoming increasingly discussed, though this was six months before the Pope would openly address it.

In 1958 the Church of England took a fresh step in widening the grounds for acceptable birth control. Until this time the Anglicans had accepted birth control as a kind of necessary evil only after long arguments in the Synod, which had begun in 1908. They could have recourse to family planning but they must not avoid their responsibilities to "be fruitful and multiply". Where a mother's health was in jeopardy, or where there were compelling social reasons — as Father Nash recognised — to limit a family, it was acceptable. But in 1958 family planning was described by the Church of England as "a right and important factor in Christian family life".

This was a significant notch up for the birth control movement. Judaism, incidentally, considered birth control to be an acceptable part of family life — but only after the couple had had two children. The same avocation to fulfil the fruitfulness of married life applied, and applies, to orthodox Jewish ethics. (There is almost nothing in Catholic moral thinking which does not have some Jewish roots.) Judaism does not favour certain types of birth control; barrier methods which place a piece of vulcanised rubber between the couple are regarded, in orthodox rabbinical thinking, as breaking the bond of being "two in one flesh". The contraceptive pill was welcomed by Judaism as by far the most acceptable and aesthetic form of birth control.

But from 1958 the subject was increasingly coming into the public realm. A British Cabinet Minister, Sir Ian McLeod, lent his imprimatur to a family planning clinic, when he paid it a formal visit; this was the first time the subject was actually mentioned on the BBC. By 1960, just before the Pill would be made available, BBC TV would be reporting on, and discussing, the introduction of this apparently magical pharmaceutical which would remove evermore the possibility of an unwanted pregnancy. Indeed, I remember when I was 15 years of age turning on BBC television in my aunt and uncle's home — unusually, for Ireland in 1960, they had a television set — for a special edition of *Panorama*. A disembodied hand was shown displaying the Pill, and over the urgent musical introduction a voice asked: "Should the contraceptive pill be available to all women?" I think my aunt may have switched off the TV set or changed channels at this point, but that single moment was quite enough for me to understand that this would be something extraordinary. This would mean that women would be biologically free in a way that had never before occurred in history. This would start a whole new wave of feminism, surely. It did.

For quite a long time, it looked as though the Catholic Church itself would approve of and endorse the contraceptive pill. As in Jewish moral theology, the Pill did not separate husband and wife in the act of congress in the way a condom or even a cervical cap would do. From about 1962 to 1968, when Pope Paul VI went against the recommendations of his own papal commission and prohibited the Pill in his encyclical *Humanae Vitae* (On Human Life), more and more Catholic couples were turning to this form of contraception. When *Humanae Vitae* ruled that Catholics could only use natural (non-pharmacological) methods of fertility control, it caused a furore. There had been high expectations, among priests as well as among married couples, that the Pill would pass the test of supporting responsible parenthood and the holiness of the married state.

Looking back ten years after the encyclical, Peter Butterfield, an academic at University College Dublin, wrote in *The Furrow*:

> I belong to the generation in which most educated and well-instructed Catholics faithfully used natural methods. Before 1968 most Catholics did not (in my experience) discuss the problems of their intimate lives. It was only when tongues were loosened by the encyclical that it became clear how universal was the misery and anxiety caused by these methods, and the extent to which they failed — in some cases rep-eatedly...
>
> Perhaps those whose lives were not personally involved cannot fully understand the impact of the encyclical; truly it seemed to be offering a stone to those who asked for bread, to be laying on men — and women — burdens too great to bear ... It should not be

surprising that large numbers of otherwise faithful Catholics simply think that the encyclical was a dreadful mistake. Even in conservative Ireland what evidence there is suggests that a majority now reject the doctrine, especially among those most concerned — married women under fifty.

In fact, *Humanae Vitae* — a sensitively written, even poetic document reflecting on the beauty of conjugal union and the holiness of the state — showed that the Catholic Church had evolved in its attitudes towards sex and marriage. It acknowledged that there was a case for family limitation, for respecting women's changing role and for population concerns — about which there was growing awareness during the 1960s. *Humanae Vitae* accepted the proposition that there were "new problems" facing the world, in connection with "the rapid growth of births and growing fear that human life may far outstrip the means of its survival", and the fact that "new changes bring new questions in their wake". The big issue was whether procreation was the principal focus of marriage, as Catholicism had always held it to be (and as the Anglican Book of Common Prayer most sternly spells out too: "Marriage was instituted by God, first, for the procreation of children") .

The encyclical acknowledged, too, that the advocates of birth control were making a case for parental responsibility, and not necessarily for free love (in this, the encyclical was too generous to some of the advocates of birth control, who were most decidedly in favour of generalised promiscuity). It commended responsible parenthood and yet insisted that, for Catholics, "every act of marriage must in itself stay destined towards the *chance* of human procreation". Give God a sporting chance: natural family planning was acceptable because there always remains a chance of procreation. The Pill, which in laboratory conditions is 100 per cent effective, most definitely ruled out that chance. The tone of *Humanae Vitae* was softer and less authoritarian than some previous Vatican teachings and the message about marriage itself extremely thoughtful. But towards artificial birth control it remained adamant.

Regrettably, much of the poetic language and lofty ideals about the married state contained in *Humanae Vitae* were lost in the furore over the issue of artificial contraception.

In Ireland the Encyclical had a major impact. Indeed, the Pill issue came to act as the intersection for three separate, though interconnected, matters. One was the way in which it split Irish Catholics into conservatives and liberals, and thus shook the foundations of solidarity that had once made Catholic Ireland a coherent culture. The second was the way in which it stimulated discussion and then opposition to the archaic Irish law which forbade the importation of other contraceptives. And the third was the impetus it gave to the foundation of a Women's Liberation movement in Ireland in 1970, of which I was a founding member. Women in Ireland had hardly ever been anti-clerical; the Church could always rely on them to defend it. But with the Pill generation, Catholic Ireland faced a challenge, for the first time ever, from women.

When I commenced my involvement with contraceptive law reform in Ireland, I was working as woman's editor of the *Irish Press*, a newspaper which still very much had the stamp of de Valera's Ireland. I was of that generation, born at the end of the Second World War, which had a growing sense of individual rights, and I had spent my formative years, from 18 to 25, in Paris and London. I thought it was outrageous that the State should police the bedrooms of private citizens, and the ban on importing contraceptives was contrary to personal rights to privacy. My animus was directed more against the State than against the Church — though of course I was against the Church, in this matter, as well. I was a young woman rebelling at full throttle against most of the established order.

And thus it was that I became part of a group which founded a new feminist movement, calling itself the Irish Women's Liberation Movement. This event was much influenced by what was happening in America at this time — the rise of women's liberation after the publication in 1963 of Betty Friedan's book *The Feminine Mystique*, which was also an influential text in Ireland. It spoke to a generation of suburban Irish wives who, like Mrs Friedan's subjects, felt the isolation, boredom and frustration of suburban life. Other books were streaming off the presses winning converts to what was then called women's liberation: Germaine Greer's exposé of how women had been made into lifeless dolls, *The Female Eunuch*, Kate Millett's *Sexual Politics*, Eva Figes's *Patriarchal Attitudes* and, of course, Simone de Beauvoir's *The Second Sex*, first published in 1949 and, true to form, banned in Ireland.

But if the Irish Women's Liberation Movement was infected by global ideas, it had some very specific applications to Ireland. We produced a pamphlet, *Chains or Change*, which outlined the areas in which women in Ireland were unjustly treated. These were: the legal inequities which still existed (women did not, except in exceptional circumstances, sit on juries); unfair practices in employment (notably the "marriage bar", which barred married women from key jobs); the lack of social support for deserted wives (there being no divorce), for unmarried mothers and in many instances for widows when a husband had had no contributory pension; discrimination in housing where women could not get a mortgage without the endorsement of a man; and the laws against family planning. Interestingly, it did not even occur to us to touch on abortion; it was still a taboo subject, and most Irishwomen would have disapproved of it — many still do. (Of all the social changes that have occurred in Ireland, abortion is the subject in which there has been least slippage of traditional values.)

In fact, the programme outlined by the Irish Women's Liberation Movement in 1969-70 was entirely sensible, eminently reasonable and also eminently winnable. J.K. Galbraith has said that the easiest revolution is the one which entails pushing a door which is already half-open, and most of the demands in the feminist programme were regarded sympathetically. There were opponents — on the Left as well as the Right — to concepts such as equal pay or the employment of married women; some Marxists upheld the primacy of the man's wage, as the family breadwinner, just as strongly as did pro-family traditionalists. Moreover, some trade unionists feared that hiring more women would depress the wages of male workers, since women are less prone to industrial militancy.

Some of the injustices underlined by the Irish Women's Liberation Movement were by no means exclusive to Ireland: women did not sit on juries in Australia and in several other countries women were unable to open a department store account without the counter-signature of a man (since a husband was still legally liable for his wife's debts in many legislatures). More generally, the notion that middle-class married women simply did not take jobs outside the home was widespread. (Of course, working-class women took jobs — and that was precisely why they were drudges.)

However, for all the worthy and acceptable subjects on this "Women's Lib" programme it was the contraceptive issue which proved the most sensational. And when, in May 1971, we wild young feminists took the train from Belfast, carrying contraband contraceptives, ready to declare the items on arrival at Connolly Station, it was a big media story. Like the bra-burning in Atlantic City — which may or may not have taken place — or the flour-throwing episodes at Miss World contests, this piece of street theatre and political agitprop worked brilliantly and paved the way for changes in the law. The customs officers at Connolly Station were mortified with embarrassment when the avalanche of condoms were declared, and we walked through both the barrier and the archaic law. Later that night we displayed the banned items on national television — *The Late Late Show* as ever being the forum of the nation. Privately, I was not without embarrassment myself: I knew that the whole display had been vulgar and crude. Yet I also knew that gesture politics worked. Mary Robinson, who was to go on to be Ireland's first woman President, was among the feminists who had joined the Women's Liberation group and quietly approved of the train episode, yet prudently declined to come on the trip. She was a lawyer, and planned to effect change through the law, rather than joining in with exhibitionist stunts. It took a relatively short time for all the goals in the original manifesto to be achieved. Mrs Robinson finally had the 1935 law against contraceptive devices abrogated — having challenged it as fundamentally unconstit-utional — in 1979.

The Irish Women's Liberation Movement fissured into disparate parts — and quite rightly, since different individuals had different interests. It produced a radical Marxist offshoot, Irishwomen United, a constitutional political organisation, the Women's Political Association, AIM (Action, Information, Motivation) and some other smaller groups. It influenced some women to go into politics — Nuala Fennell quite quickly became a Minister for Women and in 1982 Gemma Hussey became Minister for Education before taking over the Social Welfare portfolio. And Mary Robinson would hardly have become President of Ireland (followed by Mary the Second, Mary McAleese) without its foundation course.

The Irish Women's Liberation Movement raised awareness among men that women needed to be included in public life. Individual Irishwomen who had attained celebrity status during the campaign enhanced the position of women. "Two Irishwomen emerged from the chrysalis of their traditional purdah during the 1960s and wrote their names across the headlines, but in very different ways," we wrote in the *Irish Press* in January 1970. "Bernadette Devlin and Edna O'Brien. Both remarkable women; both bold and sublimely unafraid; both emphatic about what they wanted for themselves and the people that they represented or resembled. Both prototypes of a kind. And yet both so different." Bernadette — who was at that time the youngest Member of Parliament in the British House of Commons — was now the best-known Irish name in the Third World. Whereas Edna "became the first Irishwoman to assert her sexuality boldly and to demand, as a right, the sexual freedom that men have traditionally enjoyed." Edna O'Brien's novels and stories were certainly regarded as breaking new ground for women.

Readers tended to agree with this assessment and the letters praising Bernadette, in particular, were warm. Elizabeth Enright of Ballybunion wrote: "To me Miss Devlin is one of the few people in politics for love of her country; Eamon de Valera did likewise. It is people like those who put Ireland on a pedestal."

The issues of feminism and sexuality were also seeping into religious sensibilities and would become central and often troubling in Irish Catholic culture over the next two decades. As early as 1971 the historian Mary Cullen was writing in *The Furrow*, quoting Mary Bourke-Robinson (President Mary Robinson's maiden name had been Bourke) describing the women's movement as the "one active radical force in the otherwise stagnant pool of Irish political life". Irishwomen have changed, Mary Cullen goes on:

> Childbearing and rearing, which used to occupy the entire adult life of most women, now tends to occupy a part only ... These new women are living in a new environment. Irishwomen are living in a society which has been changing rapidly over the past ten years. The news media, newspapers, radio, television, are confronting more and more people, without possibility of escape, with what is happening in all parts of the world... Over the last few years, Irish newspapers have printed hundreds of letters from women expressing dissatisfaction with their lives. A recurring theme is something like this: 'I love my children, am glad I have them, do not resent devoting time and energy to them, but their sole company does not give me the mental stimulus I need, and the complete twenty-four-hour-a-day responsibility for their physical and emotional well-being gives me no time to be myself, even to think my own thoughts. I feel I am losing the individual person I was before I married.

Some of the letters went further and expressed the frustration of women who felt they had something to contribute to society but were being denied that opportunity. The Catholic Church, says Ms Cullen — who held the position of lecturer at the Department of History at Maynooth — had to take its share of the blame for women being marginalised and ignored.

That the Catholic Church was responsible for marginalising and ignoring women is not a charge which would have been made before 1968: the Lecky view, that Catholicism was essentially a feminised religion, was a much stronger traditional analysis. (The Marquess of Salisbury would scoff at Catholicism as being only suitable for womenfolk.) But what was now altering was society's view of women's place. Women's place was increasingly seen as deserving of equal treatment in the public realm, rather than as the invisible power behind the throne which had once prevailed.

After the 1970s, a new cleavage appeared between the Catholic Church and women of a feminist turn of mind. Previously, the most politicised women in Ireland — the die-hard Republicans and socialists — were nevertheless generally quite religious. In the 1930s, they might organise a seditious jumble sale for Irish-Soviet Friendship, or even throw a stone at a shop-window displaying British goods, but then trot off to recite a decade of the rosary at Wolfe Tone's grave. But the birth control dispute made young women more hostile to the Church. The idea had taken hold that women were entitled to plan their lives and fulfil their hopes without having to submit to endless pregnancies. The Pill did more than control fertility: it sowed sedition; it evangelized for autonomy. It gave women the idea that they could be just as free as men, since never again need the fear of pregnancy hold them back. Life did not turn out to be that simple, but when ideas are new, and their champions are young, it seems that simple.

It would be untrue to regard all Irishwomen as feminists — the majority of women seldom are — or all mothers as discontented with their lot. "I left school at thirteen," wrote a working-class Dublin woman to the *Catholic Standard* in 1968. "I married a working man at twenty and I am now expecting my twelfth child. Through the years my purse has never been empty because my husband and myself placed ourselves in the care of Him who fed the multitude on a few loaves and fishes. My husband is a tower of strength and a pillar of endurance. He has often come home after doing a hard day's work and rolled up his sleeves to do the washing-up and he always helps me to put the children to bed and he gets up as often as myself during the night to soothe a restless little one. It is the opinion of my husband and myself that it is the duty of every good Catholic married couple to have as many children as the Lord sends them. Thanks to the *Catholic Standard* I learned of St Gerard and I have great devotion to him."

That type of heroic Irish Catholic mother (with a highly supportive spouse) would, however, retreat into history, and the generation which followed the 1960s would make other demands on society, on resources and on nature itself.

Twelve

Troubles in the North – Fallout in the South

"It is frightfully hard to explain to Protestants that if you give Roman Catholics a good job and a good house they will live like Protestants, because they will see neighbours with cars and television sets. They will refuse to have eighteen children, but if a Roman Catholic is jobless and lives in the most ghastly hovel, he will rear eighteen children on National Assistance ... If you treat Roman Catholics with due consideration and kindness, they will live like Protestants, in spite of the authoritative [i.e. authoritarian] nature of their Church."

Terence O'Neill, Prime Minister of Northern Ireland, 1969

"God made us Catholics, but the Armalite made us equal."

Belfast graffiti

For decades, Catholic Ireland of the south had felt morally superior to — though economically poorer than — Protestant Ireland in the North. Northern Ireland, we believed, was prejudiced and bigoted against Catholics. In the south of Ireland it was different. We may have been "a Catholic nation", as the *Messenger of the Sacred Heart* put it, and Catholicism was the majority religion, but we did not discriminate against

Protestants in jobs, housing or exclusion. It was true that southern Ireland's legislation often reflected Catholic values — with bans on divorce, homosexuality and birth control, including abortion — but Catholic Ireland believed that most "decent" Protestants supported these values. It would only be the "decadent" remains of the aristocracy, wife-swapping promiscuously, who would object and, sure, they could make their arrangements in England, where they sent their children to school anyhow. This picture was largely true, in fact: Protestants broadly supported the values of Catholic Ireland, although they might dissent on detail, and where they dissented they would make their private arrangements. This was the compromise made by minorities with majorities.

Protestants were sometimes opposed to the laws and customs of Catholic Ireland, but then so were some Catholics. Irish Protestants complained, for example, about the coercive imposition of the Irish language, which many Catholics equally disliked. Irish Protestants also disliked and feared the *Ne Temere* decree, which had been imposed by Pope Pius X in 1908: this insisted that the children of a religiously mixed marriage must be brought up as Catholics. But this was a gripe against the Vatican, not against the Irish state.

There were occasional outbreaks of sectarianism, such as the unattractive episode in Fethard-on-Sea in Wexford in 1957, when there was a boycott of Protestant shops over a mixed-marriage controversy: a Protestant woman had been married to a local Catholic farmer, the marriage had broken up, and the wife had decamped to Belfast and changed her mind about raising the children as Catholics. She would agree to a reunion, she told her husband, if he would agree to the children being raised as Protestants. The row became public, the community weighed in, with the backing of the local priest, and took sides: the Catholic party seemed mean-spirited and the Protestant side cowardly and it escalated into the public realm in a way that a row between a married couple should never have done. It is possible that there was a certain amount of commercial jealousy — towards Protestant shopkeepers in the area — under the surface.

Yet such events were unusual and on the whole Irish Protestants did not visibly claim discrimination in the majority Catholic state. Indeed, they often wrote books overflowing with love and pride for the Irish state: Lionel Fleming's *Head or Harp?* (1965) was a benign memoir of a typical Irish Protestant intellectual who, when asked to choose between allegiance to the Crown or allegiance to Mother Ireland, unhesitatingly opted for the latter. Irish Protestants regarded the Catholic elements of Ireland — such as the police having been dedicated to the Sacred Heart, or the airplanes being blessed with Holy Water — as a charming aspect of Irish traditions: this was the *vin du pays*.

Irish Protestants also did not seem discriminated against because they were often comfortably off. They were generally richer than their Catholic counterparts and, in defence of their class position, it seemed that they sometimes kept hiring practices within their own circles. I have been told that signs could still be seen in the shop windows of Carlow and Kilkenny in the 1950s, "No Catholics need apply". Some job advertisements in the Dublin newspapers were certainly sectarian, and right up to the 1960s some Protestant businesses did not hire Catholics at senior level — the Dublin brewers, Guinness, for example, though excellent employers, simply did not hire Catholics as executives.

Most Irish banks and insurance companies had no Roman Catholics at senior or board level. Irish Protestants were a mercantile class who operated within their own network. The *Irish Times*, Ireland's best-known newspaper, did not engage Catholic reporters until the 1960s: Peter Lennon, in his memoir *Foreign Correspondent*, claims that when he joined the newspaper in 1958 he was only the second Catholic ever to have crossed the editorial threshold (Catholic cleaners were of course permitted, as part of the servant class).

Before the 1960s there was a much stronger concept of separate spheres, as between various groups, just as there was between the sexes. Protestants were not seen as discriminated against in a Catholic state because they had their own circles of power. But Catholics in Northern Ireland were seen as victims of discrimination because they were disempowered.

In the 1970s the Protestant State in Northern Ireland would come under siege and its power structures would be broken. This would lead to repercussions in the Catholic State of Southern Ireland which would also break traditional power structures. What was sauce for the northern goose would be sauce for the southern gander.

Northern Ireland had effectively been created in 1920 as a pragmatic British recognition that the Ulster Unionists would not accept Home Rule. It was always claimed — justifiably — that the border defining the Six Counties which remained under the Crown was rigged so as to ensure a Unionist and Protestant majority in the newly-created province (since the ancient county of Ulster comprised nine counties, three of which were allocated to Eire). But the broad fact remained: by every democratic measure there remained a substantial group of people in the North-East of Ireland who would resist the imposition of rule from Dublin. Short of killing every one of them, or driving them into exile — two options which gunmen like Dan Breen would have been quite content with — there had to be some form of political accommodation. In 1920-21 a united 32-county Ireland under the rule of Sinn Féin just was not on the cards.

And thus was born Northern Ireland, often called Ulster abroad (and by the media for reasons of shorthand), though this name has never been acceptable among the Irish majority: Ulster remains the nine counties of the ancient province, not the six counties of the statelet. It was born with a siege mentality, overshadowed by a long historical fear that the Irish Catholics would one day murder all the Protestant Unionists in their beds. From its inception, it was to be virtually a one-party state — its Parliament at Stormont was aptly described by one of its founders as "a Protestant parliament for a Protestant people". The mindset was that Catholics were in danger of being disloyal, and were not to be trusted. "There are only two classes in Northern Ireland," said the Unionist Member of Parliament Hugh Minford in the 1940s, "the loyal and the disloyal. The loyal people are the Orangemen. The disloyal people are the Socialists, Communists and Roman Catholics." Any Popish link could destroy a man's career at this time: when the former town clerk of Barrow-in-Furness, Lancashire, was appointed as town clerk in Belfast in 1942, an important municipal job at the time, an ugly row broke out when it was discovered that his wife was a Roman Catholic. He was obliged to withdraw from the position.

From the 1920s to the 1960s Unionist politicians in Northern Ireland vied with one another to brag about how *little* they had done for their Catholic constituents (since doing anything for Catholics might encourage them to beget 18 children). Lord Brookeborough, Northern Ireland's best-known and longest-serving (1943-63) Prime Minister, set the tone from his early days as a Cabinet Minister: on becoming Minister of Agriculture in 1933 he immediately dismissed the 125 Catholic workers on his estates so as to set an example to other landowners. He would not have a Roman Catholic about the place, he said. He frequently implored Unionists to employ good Protestant lads and lasses whenever possible. "Roman Catholics were endeavouring to get in everywhere and were out with all their force and might to destroy the power and Constitution of Ulster," he reminded his loyalists. Such prophecies might become self-fulfilling.

In 1944 the Unionist-controlled council of Co Fermanagh was pleased to report that "no cottages have been built under the Labourers' Act [public sector housing] since 1912" — public sector housing being more likely to benefit poorer Catholics. In the 1950s Queen's University in Belfast was found to have virtually no Roman Catholics on its staff, although 20 per cent of the students were Catholics. In 1950 the Unionist MP for West Belfast, T.L. Teevan, warned against the dangers of giving municipal housing to Roman Catholics, for through such a strategy the Unionist majority would be eroded. Geoffrey Bing, in his 1950 pamphlet *John Bull's Other Ireland*, quotes a Unionist writer who warned that there was a deliberate policy of "peaceful penetration" by the Romish hordes into the fabric of Ulster. "Farms by the score and houses by the hundred are passing from under Protestant control and into the possession of Roman Catholics of all brands — Sinn Feiners, IRA, Jesuits and others." Ulster Unionists did have grounds to fear the enemies of their state, but the offensive way in which all

Catholics were regarded with the same suspicion left little room for conciliation or *rapprochement*. In fact, then (as now) there was an extremely respectable Catholic middle class who wanted nothing more threatening than to increase their family's prosperity — an entirely innocent pursuit which tends to diminish subversiveness.

Lord Brookeborough thought all Catholics untrustworthy and said so in an interview with *The Irish Times* in 1968. When asked why he did not permit Catholics to attain higher positions within Northern Ireland, he replied: "How can you give somebody who is your enemy a higher position in order to allow him to come and destroy you?" Even more moderate Unionists, such as the respected historian Tom Wilson, have voiced concern about the problem of Catholics continuously migrating into Belfast — and having a continuously high fertility rate, too.

Brookeborough was unlike Ian Paisley in this respect: Dr Paisley loathes the Catholic Church and considers the Pope the anti-Christ. Yet Paisley has been a dutiful and often highly effective Member of Parliament to his Catholic constituents. He has even battled against Government bureaucracies on behalf of convents of Catholic nuns, whom he regards to be sunk in the deepest error, but he will still do his political duty by them. Brookeborough refused to help Catholics, as voters, in any way and actively stood in the way of their employment. He said that to have a Catholic as a public servant in Stormont Castle would be "like the British Government during the last war having a German in the Admiralty".

Memoirs and autobiographies during the 20th century show Catholics and Protestants in Northern Ireland having minimum contact with one another: David Trimble, leader of the Ulster Unionist Party from 1995, was born in Bangor in 1944 and did not meet a Catholic until his late teens. Protestants and Catholics went to different schools, had different games and different club activities. They were quite often destined for different jobs and professions — to this day, Protestants are more inclined to study engineering and Catholics to major in the arts and humanities. Yet, by the 1960s, they were beginning to meet at university thanks to the British education system, which was opening up a college education to more young people.

Seamus Heaney, writing in *The Furrow* in 1978, captured the intensity of religious sensitivities and the way in which religion marked identity. "As a Northerner my sense of religion and my sense of my race or nationality or politics were inextricably twined together. If you have ever blessed yourself in a city bus (or, more piercingly, not blessed yourself for fear of being noticed) you will know it too." [At this time, Catholics had the custom of blessing themselves when passing a church.] "If you have heard Pioneers referred to as 'the strawberry brigade' [Catholic teetotallers wore a Pioneer Pledge pin, which displayed the strawberry-red Sacred Heart] or seen your Protestant undergraduate friend's eyes dilate as he scanned the Sacred Heart lamp and the view of the Lourdes grotto on the wall of your parents' home, you will know that even the intellectual figure-skating of a Maritain, however exhilarating, is somehow inadequate to illuminate for you the relationship between your imaginative processes and your religious background." Jacques Maritain was an intellectual French Catholic thinker whose social analyses were impressive, but such discourse scarcely related to the crude sectarian divisions of everyday Ulster life.

Yet it was significant that in Seamus Heaney's generation, he was beginning to have Protestant undergraduate friends. This signalled a social change.

Differences were not as pronounced in the countryside as in the town, according to Rosemary Harris's classic study *Prejudice and Tolerance in Ulster*. Sectarianism was least marked amongst hill farmers and, in country life, relations could be amicable, even during the Brookeborough years. Recalling the 1930s and '40s in *A Fermanagh Childhood*, William Parkes writes: "Although we had two schools of different denominations in the village, all the children played together in the evenings and during the school holidays ... Community relations have always been excellent." As Protestants, the Parkeses knew the local Catholic priest quite well — he was their neighbour, and deaf as a consequence of chaplain service during the First World War. Ignoring Brookeborough's admonition not to hire

Catholics, the Parkes family had a maid called Annie, "who was a devout Roman Catholic and really lived up to the Christian faith. Learning catechism is extremely boring for a child no matter what their religion, but Annie managed to bring more meaning and life into the Church of Ireland catechism than I ever experienced before or since."

Such kindly attitudes were not infrequently reciprocated from the other side. The *Capuchin Annual*, a popular Catholic general publication brought out each year, although patriotically Irish and anti-Partitionist nonetheless described Ulster Protestants as "good neighbours, good friends when you make friends with them, and in the casual relations of day-to-day life, agreeable and obliging". The sectarianism of the state did not obliterate the kindness of neighbourly relations, particularly in country areas. "Your Ulster Protestant neighbours were the *kindest* folk you could ever meet," recalls Mrs Rose Kelly of Downpatrick, who grew up on the Antrim coast in the 1940s. "The most honest in trading and business. They would never sell you anything on a Sunday, but if you were short of eggs or anything like that, they would give to you in good heart."

The good neighbour policy could even prevail in the political sphere, so long as the rules of the game were observed, i.e. that the Unionist Protestants were the majority, and it was their state. Maurice Hayes, in his witty and observant memoir of life as a — rare — Catholic public servant at Stormont, wrote that "Politics in local government could be quite accommodating at a personal level, but were generally confrontational on public or symbolic issues. Majorities were winners: they took the spoils and held the field ... One veteran nationalist councillor, finding himself in hospital for a minor ailment, joked to the nurse when she removed the bedpan: 'I've been on the council for twenty years and that's the first motion I've ever had carried.'" Nationalist (Catholic) councils were as obdurate about favouring their own folk as Unionist (Protestant) ones, in the areas which they held. On matters of morality and dogma, a split council would sometimes agree: a Mid-Ulster council, split half and half in the 1970s between Nationalist Catholics and Unionist Protestants, carried unanimously and together a resolution condemning homosexuality and abortion (both having being liberalised by the London government).

The institutional sectarianism of Northern Ireland was, for most of the 20th century, accepted as a fact of life south of the border. At a political level there was a mixture of complacency and resentment: there were "anti-Partitionist" speeches, but at the same time there was a complacent view that one day the Unionists would see the error of their ways. They were not really loyal to the Crown but to the half-crown — that is, their attachment was to the material support provided by union with Britain. Deep down, we did not really respect the sincerity of Ulster Protestants — we thought their Orange marches were all "cod".

We knew that Catholics were disadvantaged in the North, but we also knew they had benefits which made southern Catholics sometimes ambivalent towards their co-religionists up north. The standard of living in Northern Ireland was, until the 1990s, higher than in the South. There was a free health service from 1945, greater access to university education — my mother had family friends in the North whose daughter got to Oxford, an unheard-of privilege — and during my childhood and teenage years Belfast provided much better shopping. My mother thought of Northern Ireland as the place where you got wonderful hats at Robinson and Cleavers for only three guineas. (Hats, like racehorses and consultants' fees, were priced in guineas, being one pound and one shilling.) There were brilliant sweets called Spangles which were not available south of the border. And the North had lots of pictures of the Royal Family — which were not on public display, then, in the Republic — which we thought glamorous. I remember gazing at a magazine photograph of the young Queen Elizabeth, glittering in her crown and jewels, and feeling thrilled by the sheer feminine gorgeousness of the image. Princess Margaret was then a stunning beauty, comparable to Princess Diana in later years. To be able to have such pictures was definitely a plus, and our Catholic friends in Banbridge, Co Down, willingly stocked the magazines in question.

In fact our Catholic friends in Banbridge, whom we would visit, had done very well, as middle-class Catholics within the

Protestant state. The father was a solicitor and the mother was a dentist — the first married women I ever knew who had a profession of her own, which she practised. Possibly the sectarianism of the society even benefited them, since Frank, the father, got the Catholic law business, and Gertie, the mother, pulled and filled the Catholic teeth. They lived in a splendid Victorian house with a picture-book garden in which lupins and red-hot pokers grew with decorous order. Yet many years later the youngest daughter told me she got taunted as a "Fenian bitch" on her way to school, and her brother got beaten up just for being a "Taig", the pejorative name for Catholic. In those days, people — everywhere, not just in Ireland — accepted even unpleasant facts of life as being the way things were. Society in general was more stoical. There were a lot of old peasant proverbs directed your way to encourage you to put up with life as it was. "You have to take the rough with the smooth." "What cannot be cured must be endured."

Not everyone was passively accepting of this situation. My late brother James, a committed, passionate Nationalist, was enraged by the affront of partition and the injustices obtaining in what he persisted in calling "British-occupied Ireland". He was an early supporter of Sinn Féin, and played over and over again on our gramophone the mournful ballad of Sean South of Garryowen. Sean South was an IRA man from Limerick who was killed in a raid on Brookeborough RUC baracks in 1957 during the IRA border campaign of 1956-62 (which was eventually called off for lack of support). South and his companion, Fergal O'Hanlon, were both killed in the raid — South died instantly from the bomb blast and O'Hanlon, who was only 16, bled to death, alone, in an abandoned border cottage. There was a huge funeral in Dublin and ballads composed in their name. The song written in commemoration for Fergal O'Hanlon, 'The Patriot Game', is a genuinely affecting and indeed reflective ("I've learned all my life/Cruel England to blame") composition.

Yet Sean South himself, a religious activist as well as an IRA volunteer, was an advocate of a less Catholic Ireland which would have been a fully theocratic state. He was a member of an organisation called Maria Duce (Mary the Leader) which sought to have the Blessed Virgin as Ireland's spiritual leader, an astonishing concept to any Protestant. His opposition to the state of the Six Counties was that it was British: he obviously did not oppose a sectarian state in principle.

And, as a matter of a fact, the British *were* at fault in not promoting or ensuring their famous fair play in such sectors as the civil service in Northern Ireland. It may be argued that in private business, individuals and families will always be more inclined to hire those they know, but in jobs where employment or advancement is supposed to be through merit and competitive examinations, it is unacceptable not to ensure fairness. No attempt was made by London, until the Troubles started, to remedy the barriers against Catholics in government service. In 1957, for example, there were no Catholics among the 40 most senior officers of the Northern Ireland Civil Service. In 1959 it was found that 94 per cent of the 740 most senior Civil Servants were Protestants; in 1969 just over 92 per cent of people in senior grades were still Protestant. This was nothing to do with ability; Irish Catholics did well in both the English and the Indian Civil Services as soon as these were open to competitive examination.

Some Catholics in Northern Ireland did not care to take the Oath of Allegiance (to the Crown) that Government officials were expected to accept, although this could be more or less sidestepped through a tactful rubber-stamp procedure. But the main disincentive was simply that there was little hope of advancement. In 1958 Patrick Shea, who was considered an outstanding Government servant by those he had worked for, was told by the Permanent Secretary to the Minister of Education in Northern Ireland: "Because you are a Roman Catholic you may never get any further promotion. I'm sorry." Yet in the face of this evidence, London always chose not to get involved with Ireland if it could leave well enough alone. In the mid-1960s, before the balloon went up when Harold Wilson, then British Prime Minister, wanted to intervene in Northern Ireland, he was deterred by his Home Secretary, Roy Jenkins (the biographer of Asquith), crying: "Prime Minister! Prime Minister! Ireland! A graveyard for political reputations!"

But the agenda changed in the 1960s for a number of reasons. There was now a younger generation of Catholics — Bernadette Devlin and Seamus Heaney among them — who had been to university and were more confident, or less apologetic, about demanding civil rights. They were no longer prepared to be "second-class citizens" in a "Protestant state for a Protestant people". And people were influenced by events in America — particularly the civil rights movement and the charismatic leadership of Martin Luther King, who was much admired in the Catholic popular literature of the time. (Admiration for Martin Luther King seemed to help conciliate attitudes to his namesake, Martin Luther, who was thereafter seen less as a hostile Protestant critic of Catholicism and more as a reformer in his own right.) John Hume, too, would always quote Martin Luther King.

The spark which began the Troubles in Northern Ireland was a civil rights march in Derry in October 1968: the Campaign for Social Justice in Northern Ireland had been launched four years previously, in 1964, by two politically moderate Catholics, Conn and Patricia McCluskey. When the McCluskeys started out, the events in Alabama in which Martin Luther King was campaigning for social justice for American blacks were being beamed around the world via television pictures. As early as 1963 a picket outside Dungannon Council Offices in Co Armagh carried the slogan "Racial Discrimination in Alabama hits Dungannon". The protest was against sectarian practices in housing, which was one of the prime issues causing discontent in Northern Ireland.

The eruption of unrest in Derry in October 1968 had been triggered by a public housing scandal: a 19-year-old unmarried woman and a Protestant had been given preferential treatment in the allocation of a municipal house over a homeless Catholic family of six. And so there was a civil rights march led by the Northern Ireland Civil Rights Association, followed by police repression, followed by more protests, followed subsequently by some concessions, followed by more unrest and cries of "too little, too late". It was not the aim of the original activists to destabilise the State of Northern Ireland, but in the wake of the civil rights movement a new militancy towards the State was born.

Yet what happened in 1968 marked a break with past traditions all the same. The civil rights marches were a new kind of protest in that they did not mention the border, or partition, which had previously been the bone of contention. They ostensibly demanded equal rights for Catholics within the Protestant state. And Catholic Ireland would, eventually, be as affected as Protestant Ireland by these developments. The civil rights movement itself, though initially instigated by the McCluskeys who had simply wanted "fair play for Catholics and Nationalists in housing and jobs, and justice in law-and-order issues", went on to be animated by more radical personalities, like Michael Farrell and Eamonn McCann, who seemed to dislike Catholic Ireland almost as much as they opposed Protestant Ireland.

"We were anxious to assert socialist ideas," wrote Eamonn McCann in his sharply observed, and often witty, account of the birth of the Derry civil rights movement. "We used slogans such as 'Class War, not Creed War', 'Orange and Green Tories Out' and 'Working Class Unite and Fight'." He and his fellow civil rights agitators were thrilled when overseas journalists began to pour into the Bogside in Derry, trying to identify a local "Danny the Red" (the French students' revolutionary leader in 1968 was Daniel Cohn-Bendit, known as Dany le Rouge). McCann was asked to supply "articulate, Catholic, unemployed slum-dwellers" for the international media, of which there were a plentiful supply.

The new radical civil rights activists did not look to Dublin for their support unlike earlier Northern Nationalists. They were contemptuous of clericalism, and they rebuffed the socially conservative Catholicism of traditional Nationalists. Eamonn McCann eventually came to criticise Catholicism as much as any Paisleyite, and many of his cohorts of that generation would share this hostility. The Derry civil rights march in October 1968 in a way heralded the end of Catholic Ireland as much as breaking, forever, the Protestant-Unionist hegemony in the North.

Terence O'Neill, the Prime Minister of Northern Ireland, had been trying to modernise, in his own way, the structures in Northern Ireland and to have a more open relationship with the Dublin Taoiseach, Sean Lemass. He believed with reason, that more prosperity would better integrate Catholics into the State, and he pressed on reforms from the mid-1960s: the Electoral Law Amendment Act abolished university and business votes (which had given proportionately more to Protestants); he increased building grants to Catholic schools; Belfast's Unionist Corporation was deterred from naming a new bridge across the river Lagan 'Carson Bridge' (after Edward Carson, Unionist hero); and the B-Specials, an auxiliary police force particularly disliked by Catholics, were disbanded. At every turn O'Neill was barracked and opposed by Unionist colleagues, and always by the fierce, hellfire-preaching Revd Ian Paisley, the fundamentalist cleric and MP.

Protestants were losing privileges now and reacted angrily, particularly at a time of rising unemployment, for the traditional industries of Ulster — ship-building, linen-making — were in decline. The marches and demonstrations of 1968 turned into the street battles and serious civil disorder of 1969. Then came the arrival of British troops (first welcomed by the Catholics) in 1969, the introduction of internment in August 1971, the tragedy of Bloody Sunday in January 1972 when paratroopers shot 13 unarmed Catholics in Derry, and the suspension of Stormont, the Belfast Parliament, in 1972. Most significantly of all, during these years the IRA was revived, partly because the Catholics felt undefended against Loyalist attacks. From 1972 a bitter succession of shootings, bombings, maimings and killings began, which would last until a cease-fire in the middle 1990s.

Catholic Ireland itself reacted cautiously to the onset of the Troubles in the North. It took some weeks for the story to register significantly with the Catholic press. The problems of the North seemed marginal next to the life and death of the stigmatist Padre Pio, who died in 1968, or indeed to the sudden death of the Dublin Education Minister Donogh O'Malley, who had introduced free secondary education. In the week following the Derry marches, the *Catholic Standard*'s front page headline was: "Give Government Land to Peasants, Priest Says", referring not to the Six Counties, but to a priest in Kerala, South India, who was urging land reform. The second story was: "Bishop to Coach Football Team" — an Irish-born bishop in Wagga Wagga, South Australia, was to pitch in with Australian Rules football.

The popular religious literature had never concerned itself greatly with the social problems of the North — and neither had the Dublin politicians for that matter. Fianna Fáil, de Valera's party, had never established a single *cumann* (local party branch) in Northern Ireland. Priests and bishops born in Northern Ireland or in the border area would have generally been more politicised, possibly more apprehensive of Protestants and often more anti-British, but the Church itself had other priorities, certainly up to about 1969. The *Messenger of the Sacred Heart* showed a greater interest in the issue of apartheid in South Africa, which they opposed from the instigation of the law in 1948, than in the problems of Northern Ireland.

Occasionally, employment issues would surface in which Catholics described being discriminated against (in Dublin, let alone in the North) but this prompted anxiety about defending the faith rather than discourse on employment discrimination. For example, in 1954, Question: "Would it be wrong for a man to pretend he was a non-Catholic in order to get more favourable treatment in his place of employment?" Answer: "Yes, it would be wrong. We are forbidden to deny our faith." Nothing was said about the place of employment which apparently denied Catholics favourable treatment. From the mid-Fifties onwards there was also concern about the moral welfare of Irish emigrants going to England, which at that time seemed a more urgent issue than the North. Catholics in the North may have been subject to unfavourable treatment, but at least their faith was not in peril.

In fact, in the late autumn of 1968, the mood in Southern Ireland was optimistic about inter-church developments and therefore about Northern Ireland as well. "Ecumenism" was the buzz-word of the time and this seemed to bode well for the future of North-South relations. The week before the Derry events there had been a jolly report in Dublin: "Royal reception for the Down GAA [Gaelic Athletic Association] team in City Hall, Belfast. Belfast Lord Mayor William Geddis said that 'as an Ulsterman he was proud to welcome any Ulster team whether it played Gaelic, Rugby or Soccer. They are our fellow countrymen and we rejoice in their success.'" This was a generous and open approach by a Unionist mayor to a sporting team associated with Catholic (and sometimes Fenian) Ireland. Other Unionist worthies and aldermen were present, and a prominent Orangeman, Alderman Henderson of the Shankill Road, apparently said: "It's a great occasion and, whether Orange or Green, I'm here to celebrate. Anybody that stayed away is not worth bothering about."

Naturally, there was sympathy for the civil rights movement — practically all the media showed sympathy for the Catholics as underdogs — but the policy of the Church was for more cooperation and cultural exchange, rather than confrontation. In November 1968, when Neil Blaney, a strongly Republican Fianna Fáil member of the Dublin parliament, said that what Ireland needed was "a new approach to partition" — that is, a repeal of partition — the *Catholic Standard* disagreed: practical cooperation with the North would be a better policy than criticism. In fact the new darling of the Catholic press in Dublin was Terence O'Neill (which cannot have done him much good with his hard-line colleagues); despite his sometimes patronising attitude to Catholics, the *Catholic Standard* thought he was a decent man who was bringing in down-to-earth reforms. "Strictly speaking we have no politics on this paper. But we recognize a good thing for the country when we see it and we think that in Terence O'Neill we have seen it."

This attitude was common, now, in Dublin, where O'Neill was seen as a liberal — in the sense of being open-minded and tolerant — from the time he had afternoon tea with Sean Lemass in 1965. But the Catholic Church in Ireland feared and disliked extremism as much as the Ulster Unionist Party did, and for some time there was a careful balancing act between cautious sympathy for the civil rights movement and a marked desire not to harm the fragile bloom of ecumenism and reconciliation which Catholic Ireland was nursing with genuine sincerity.

Thus were Catholic Ireland's responses to the first phase of what turned out to be the Northern Troubles hesitantly caught between an awakening sense of conscience about civil rights for Northern Catholics and an instinctive preference for stability, for not going so far, so fast that the whole boat would be thoroughly rocked. Anyhow, Irish Catholics had just discovered, properly, their own Protestant neighbours and had just started to like Protestants in general: were they now going to have to quarrel with them again? Peace was indeed a thematic note in Catholic Ireland's plan even before anything like war had broken out. By 1971, only three years after the initial Derry marches, the *Irish Catholic* was featuring "rosary walks for peace" in which nuns seemed to play a visible part. Cathal Daly, then Bishop of Down and Connor, was issuing early warnings about the moral dangers of violence.

Indeed, in consequence of the world focus on Northern Ireland as a society divided into Catholic and Protestant camps, the Church — the Churches — became aware of the bad press that this was giving to religion. "This rift in the Christian community," wrote Father J.A. Coulter of Derry in 1969, "ostensibly based on religion, perpetuated by hatreds and injustice, has made us the mockery of the non-believing world; in the name of faith, men have done things that good pagans are ashamed to read of." Father Coulter cited a Presbyterian document which stated "Avowed enemies of Christianity could not have done more damage to the faith than things which have been said and done under the banner of religion", which he heartily endorsed. If religion had played a part in creating this rift, then religion should now play its part in bringing about reconciliation. And this now became the programme for Catholic Ireland for the next two decades: peace and reconciliation as the way forward.

The "men of violence" were distanced wherever and whenever possible, as, in the wake of the civil rights movement, the IRA became reactivated, seeing an opportunity to finish the business begun in the 1920s and to unite Ireland by the gun and the bomb. In September 1971 the Northern Catholic bishops issued a statement warning against those who would use the present troubles to force through a united Ireland without consent. "In the present dangerous situation in Northern Ireland," it said, "it is important that people should see facts clearly … We wish to focus attention on one fact in particular. That is that in Northern Ireland at the present time there is a small group of people who are trying to secure a united Ireland by the use of force.

"One has only to state this fact in all its stark simplicity to see the absurdity of the idea. Who in his sane senses wants to bomb a million Protestants into a united Ireland? At times, the people behind this campaign will talk of 'defence'. But anyone who looks at the facts knows that this is not just defence. They themselves have admitted openly they are engaged in offensive operations. Moreover, their bombs have killed innocent people, including women and girls. Their campaign is bringing shame and disgrace on noble and just causes."

It was, they went on, straining nerves, destroying livelihoods and intensifying sectarian bitterness. The bishops were aware that this was not the sole cause of violence, but they were asking Catholics to understand the genuine fears of Protestants. Violent action was "grievously wrong".

When terrorist bombs began to go off in England as well as in Northern Ireland, Monsignor Arthur Ryan from Belfast wrote: "The Irish people are not at war with Britain. The Nationalist people of the Six Counties are not at war with the Unionists. The Army of the Republic of Ireland is not at war with the Army of Great Britain. The Catholics of Ireland, North and South, are not at war with the Protestants of Ireland, North or South.

"No authority, political or religious, North or South of the Border, has taken any such decisions. The self-appointed 'officials' and 'provisionals' [thus had Sinn Féin split] represent nobody but themselves. But they spit on everybody else. Their war is their own. It is not ours."

The word "authority" had always been a key word in Catholic discourse on the morality of war. It is laid down by Thomas Aquinas that a "just war" must be declared by "a proper authority". From now on the Catholic Church would use its best endeavours to stop the situation deteriorating. It preached peace again and again and again.

At really bad moments, such as Bloody Sunday, the influence of the Church may well have been the only restraining hand which stopped all-out civil war in Ireland. In January 1972, 13 unarmed Catholics were shot dead by the Paratroop Regiment in Derry during a peaceful march. British paratroopers either mistakenly believed that some among the crowd were about to open fire (some paratroopers still claim there were shots from the crowd) or alternatively simply lost control and panicked. Or else, as some Irish Nationalists came to believe, these were just "Brits" who wilfully took the opportunity to kill Irish people. Seamus Heaney considered this the worst moment of this phase of the Troubles — and the most unforgivable. The atmosphere in the week following that event was dreadful. There was a sort of black cloud hanging over the whole of Ireland.

The event itself was replete with stories of human tragedy: the picture of Father Edward Daly (later Bishop of Derry) holding up a white handkerchief as he tried to shield a dying victim is the enduring visual symbol of that day. Bishop Daly recalled a young lad laughing at him as he ran — he was not running very gracefully — and then "the next thing he suddenly gasped and threw his hands up in the air and fell on his face ... He asked me 'Am I going to die?' and I said 'No', but I administered the last rites ... I can remember him holding my hand and squeezing it. We all wept ... We got him to the top of the street. I kneeled beside him and told him, 'Look son, we've got you out.' But he was dead." The boy was 16.

Melancholy, gloom, rage and a brute desire for revenge flooded hearts. The Catholic press conceded that it was a Black Sunday indeed: "Black for the people of Derry, black for the people of Ireland, and if only they would recognize it, black for the people of Britain too." And it was supposed to have been an ecumenical Sunday, when Catholics and Protestants were holding joint services, and "a new fluidity between North and South" was to be observed. That was now all gone. There were angry marches "to purge the nation's grief and anger". At one such march, in Newry, John Hume, Gerry Fitt, Michael

O'Leary, TD (then the *Tánaiste* or deputy Premier in the Dublin government), Ivan Cooper (a veteran civil rights activist and a Protestant), Bernadette Devlin, MP, and the actress Vanessa Redgrave walked hand in hand. The British Embassy in Dublin was burned, which was again described as a way of "purging the nation's grief and anger", although the Catholic press did not approve of such attacks on property. There was also a 60 per cent drop in tourist bookings on car ferries to Ireland for that spring.

Yet, despite the need to express grief and anger, there were calls for calm and a reconciliatory attitude. "It is our task, of all of us as Christians," went the editorial from the *Catholic Standard*, "as human beings, to forgive. Whatever the guilt to be apportioned to the British paratroopers involved, we must bear in our hearts no desires for reprisals nor thoughts of animal revenge, but thoughts of mercy and yes, even of pity ... Our second task is to ensure that there is no repetition of such bloody carnage."

But there was a lot more bloody carnage ahead. The 1970s went on being awful for a long time. Terrorist atrocities took place, like the Abercorn restaurant bombing in Belfast, which happened without warning when it was crowded with Saturday shoppers; two people were killed, and the injuries were horrific. In Claudy, a small town in Co Derry, eight people were killed on a single day by car bombs. Two people were killed and 80 injured by bombs which exploded in Dublin in December 1972, and in May 1974, 22 people were killed in Dublin by car bombs, while five were killed on the same day in Monaghan. Five people were killed and 54 injured when bombs went off without warning in Guildford, Surrey, and 19 people were killed and 182 injured when bombs exploded in two Birmingham pubs. The Guildford and Birmingham bombings later became *causes célèbres* when the wrong people were convicted, and innocent individuals served quite prolonged jail sentences. Yet somebody was guilty of taking those lives and of inflicting lifelong injuries: the fact that they were never caught or charged compounded the injustice.

Twelve people were killed and 23 injured when the La Mon House Hotel in Co Down was destroyed by Provisional IRA fire bombs, said to have been ordered by a senior figure in Sinn Féin. There were plenty of other shootings, sectarian killings (on both sides), maimings, kidnappings, bank raids, payroll raids, destruction of property and assassinations (including the British Ambassador to Dublin and Airey Neave, MP, at Westminster, who was Margaret Thatcher's special mentor).

What especially upset the public — and drove away tourists, depressed business and thus reduced employment — were unannounced explosions in public places, in which the innocent, and often particularly vulnerable — known as soft targets — were the victims. Shame plays a significant role in Irish psychology and history and, although the IRA were by no means the only agents of terrorism and random killing, the atrocities for which they were responsible gradually built up a sensation of shame among Irish Catholics, and protests began to appear in print about the action carried out "in our name". It was shaming that the tag of religion was attached to these things, although studies have shown that most individuals in terrorist organisations are not religious; they cynically manipulate causes which have a religious content for their own ends.

During this period many political solutions for Northern Ireland were attempted, included the Sunningdale agreement proposed by Edward Heath in 1973, which envisaged a power-sharing executive in Belfast but which collapsed the following May in the face of a Loyalist strike. The rise of the peace movement in 1976 had strong Catholic backing from ordinary people as much as from clergy, as peace-walk pictures featured in the Catholic press all through the 1970s show. (The peace movement had been founded by a Catholic and a Protestant woman, Mairead Corrigan and Betty Williams, and an ecumenical Catholic man, Ciaran McKeown. Though problems of personality clashes arose, it had a huge, long-term impact.) By the time the Pope visited Ireland in 1979 and begged the men of violence — "on my knees" — to give up the bomb and the Armalite, Catholic Ireland was firmly committed to some solution through peaceable means.

This seed would finally take root in the late 1980s, but the early 1980s were an intense and emotional time, especially when ten IRA hunger strikers, led by Bobby Sands, starved themselves to death. Bobby Sands' death brought worldwide publicity, and the Christ-like wall portraits of the starved IRA man were chilling iconic evocations of Catholic imagery. Many of these deaths were accompanied too by a grieving mother in a *pietà* composition.

The clergy played an active role in urging the hunger strikers to give up, particularly Father Denis Faul and the Pope's envoy, Monsignor John McGee, and eventually the hunger strikes were indeed called off. Yet the drama they created underlined the necessity to get some kind of agreement under way. They also demonstrated to Republicans that there was a political constituency for Sinn Féin: Bobby Sands had been voted the MP for Fermanagh-South Tyrone just before he died, and the graffiti that went up on the walls acknowledged that fact: "The Rt Hon Bobby Sands, MP". The rise of Sinn Féin as a political movement and the retreat of the Provisional IRA as a paramilitary force can be traced to the support that Bobby Sands attracted. Not for the first time in history the Republican movement had shown that a dramatic gesture, an element of living — and dying — theatre, is a better communicator than words.

And thus the Anglo-Irish Agreement of 1985 was born, which provided a framework for developing political structures. In 1987 Gerry Adams of Sinn Féin and John Hume of the SDLP entered secret negotiations which would eventually lead to the peace process and the cease-fire of 1994. This would by no means be the end of the matter, but the political structures which developed from 1985 and 1987 did change the path of the Troubles and did signal a waning of the violence.

There are those who would accuse the Catholic Church — or at any rate, some of the priests — of being complicit towards terrorism, or towards the IRA. I have heard British people say that the priests of Northern Ireland were soft on the terrorists, or never preached sermons against terrorism. This is not the case. Throughout the 1970s and the 1980s the Catholic Church in Ireland, North and South, relentlessly preached peace. The archives of the religious publications show that. There was a small number of priests — probably under ten in number —

who were either from Republican families themselves (the brother of Raymond McCreesh, one of the ten hunger-strikers who died, was a priest) or were known mavericks. Father Des Wilson was, and is, a left-wing priest in Ballymurphy with some highly unorthodox views, but he has been very much part of the community and is a kindly pastor.

Father Joe McVeigh from Fermanagh is certainly a committed Republican who has published several booklets about injustices consequent on British rule; he comes from a Republican family which experienced, he told me, "a lot of bigotry" in the Brookeborough years. The great Monsignor Denis Faul of Dungannon, was always concerned for prisoners, as was Father Raymond Murray, who often wrote eloquently in *The Furrow*. Denis Faul criticised the British troops when they overstepped the mark: by the end of the century, he was being harassed by Sinn Féin for urging citizens to cooperate with the RUC, the mainly Protestant police force whom Republicans wish to see disbanded.

Cardinal Tomás O Fiaich, who became Archbishop of Armagh and Primate of All Ireland in 1979 (he died in 1990), was indeed inclined to sympathy with the Republican movement. He was born at Cullyhanna, Crossmaglen, the very heart of modern Irish Republicanism, and though he was an enthusiast for the ecumenical movement (and a fine scholar), there were moments when his grass-roots feelings did show. Garret Fitzgerald, twice Taoiseach in the 1980s, told me that he was dismayed to hear the Cardinal refer to Republican prisoners as "the lads". O Fiaich made a couple of strong political comments which put him in bad odour with the British: he described Margaret Thatcher's triumphant visit to the Armagh Ulster Defence Regiment base in 1984 as "disgusting", and he said it was "not wrong to join Provisional Sinn Féin". Gerry Fitt, former SDLP leader and now Lord Fitt, described Tomás O Fiaich as "a disaster" in terms of his political influence.

Yet the Cardinal published very little during the years of the Troubles that was relevant to the situation. The most prolific writer and preacher on the subject of Northern Ireland was Cathal Daly, who would succeed Cardinal O Fiaich. Bishop

Daly wrote prodigiously, notably in the influential magazine *The Furrow,* putting forward an ardent Christian argument against violence and hatred of any kind. He was a most proactive peacemaker. As it turned out, another priest, the self-effacing Father Alec Reid, was one of the main brokers for peace negotiations in the construction of the peace process.

At a popular level, it is noticeable how ecumenically peace-loving the *Irish Messenger of the Sacred Heart* became in the 1970s and '80s. Thinking about peace and non-violence led the Catholic devotional magazine to focus not only on Martin Luther King but also on Gandhi, as a non-Christian exemplar of non-violence. Corrie ten Boon, the Maori Protestant evangelical writer, became a favourite source as well.

The issue of non-violence also entered the abortion debate, a subject of rising concern after the American Supreme Court judgement of 1973 legalised abortion. France passed an abortion law in 1975, which caused some comment in the Irish ecclesiastical journals. (Britain had done so back in 1967, but France, with a strong pro-natalist tradition, was more of a surprise.) It was obvious that legal abortion was going to spread; the link between violence against the person was extended to violence against the unborn. There were some political complications to address here: some of the most sturdy anti-abortionists in Ireland were also strong nationalists and thus inclined to be sympathetic to the IRA. I clearly remember standing in front of a couple of placards in Co Mayo in 1981 which urged: "Stand by Bobby Sands. Save the Unborn Child."

Yet at the same time many of the most ardent peace activists were coherently and consistently pro-life in the other sense of the word too. The abortion agenda helped the peace agenda in the end, as pro-life campaigners understood they would have to make the doctrine of non-violence consistent across the board. Priests like Father Anthony Mulvey of St Pat's in Derry, a co-founder of various community self-help groups and of various housing associations, put the anti-violence and pro-life arguments together in essays published in the religious press at this time. In 1980 Father Kevin Mullen wrote: "Individually our commitment should be to the intrinsic value of every human life throughout its entire trajectory, from the womb to the grave, and our efforts should be towards enhancing in our time respect for the human person who, in the Christian vision, is never beyond redemption." In time, the pro-life movement would also come to include opposition to the death penalty.

The Catholic Church in Ireland was also drifting leftwards, from the mid-1970s. Gandhi and Martin Luther King were joined in the pantheon of heroes by Dom Helder Camera, the Latin American left-wing pacifist, and by Daniel Berrigan, the anti-Vietnam war, Jesuit protester. In 1972 the missionary magazine the *Far East* backed Salvador Allende, the Marxist candidate, to be leader in Chile. His was "a just cause". From 1977 onwards, the concerns of the Irish Catholic Church were much more focused on social issues of poverty and welfare. "Rights" — a word which had once been abhorred as a product of the loathed, atheistic French Revolution — now entered the lexicon of Catholic Ireland. It might be said that Catholic Ireland copied, or followed, in its thinking, what the civil rights movement had started.

The civil rights movement changed Northern Ireland, as a state, forever. The old Ulster of Brookeborough was broken; now it was the turn of the old Ireland of de Valera and John Charles McQuaid to be despatched. Northern Ireland had been chastised, at the bar of history, for its sectarianism and bigotry; Southern Ireland would now stand charged of similar offences. Writing in *The Spectator* in 1994, the political commentator Alan Watkins described the Republic of Ireland as "the most tyrannical theocracy outside of the Middle East". The Orangemen had always said that "Home Rule is Rome Rule" and soon it would be their turn to crow that they had been proved right.

Thirteen

The Eighties –
Rights, Choices and Referendum Wars

"The Catholic Church itself collaborated in every way
it could [with modernisation]. In sympathy with the
switch from abstemiousness to consumerism, it
ended the Friday abstinence, the Lenten fast and the
night-long fast before Communion ... The Church
concerned itself with Third World Causes, and at
home, with those 'social' causes which consumerism
thought proper for churches."

Desmond Fennell, *The State of the Nation*

Events in Northern Ireland were to have a radical, structural
impact on Catholic Ireland, although, as usual, what was
occurring in Ireland was interwoven and intertwined with the
spirit of the age elsewhere.

The Troubles in the North highlighted the grievances of a
sectarian society, and held a mirror up to nature by revealing
Southern Ireland to be, if not sectarian in the same way, at least
a kind of "confessional state". Reformers of all hues in the
Republic of Ireland became anxious to purge the South of the
charge of being a Catholic state for a Catholic people, just as the
North had been described as being a Protestant state for a
Protestant people. Indeed, cleansing the Republic of its Catholic
character became an object of reform in itself, and a prerequisite
for the reunification of Ireland. For surely Northern Ireland

would be more reconciled to the Republic if all traces of "Rome rule" were removed?

Events in Northern Ireland, along with changed thinking elsewhere, helped to alter the mentality of Irish Catholicism. Traditionally this had been rooted in stoicism. There has been a flinty side to Irish Christianity ever since the monks preserved Christian civilisation for the West by hanging on to a bleak rock off the coast of Co Kerry. The stoicism was articulated by the phrase "Offer It Up". If suffering occurred, Offer It Up. If life was unpleasant, difficult, inconvenient or humiliating, Offer It Up. The pains and vexations of life, thus offered up, would be banked as a deposit of grace in Heaven, and in any case Offering It Up gave you backbone, and helped to strengthen your character. An Englishwoman married to an Irishman, who came to live in Ireland, wrote in *The Furrow* monthly magazine in 1966: "I remember being flabbergasted when, after running desperately for a bus which moved off at the crucial moment, I was advised by a lady at the bus stop to 'Offer It Up'." Actually, there was an English version of Offering It Up: it was called the Stiff Upper Lip. This too was an expression of stoicism.

The patient acceptance of suffering and setbacks was to change and be replaced by two influences which the Catholic Church had previously most vehemently repudiated: the concept of rights, derived as it was from the hated French Revolution which had enthroned the Rights of Man in place of man's duty to God; and the unstoppable inflow of psychotherapy and the counselling culture into Catholicism, which for over 50 years had repudiated Freud and all his works. Previously, it was held that Freudian approaches were worthless because they had no moral basis; and psychotherapy was inclined to excuse sin (summed up by the *West Side Story* line "I'm depraved on account that I'm deprived"). But after the cultural changes of the 1970s Irish Catholicism capitulated to both these influences. Suddenly the religious press was full of psychobabble and counselling and talk of rights. The abortion debate was discussed in terms of rights, and the unborn child was said to have a right to life. Previously, Catholicism would not have claimed that anyone has a right to life, born or unborn, since it may be God's will that we might die at any moment.

On the political front there had been, since the end of the 1960s, a softening towards the old enemy of Marxism; by the end of the 1970s it was viewed as a comrade in arms. "Marxists can and do share our indignation at injustice and exploitation," editorialised the *Irish Messenger of the Sacred Heart* in April 1979, though it added that while the diagnosis was similar, the Christian solution was different. "[The Marxist] solution is not seen in terms of reconciliation and the common brotherhood of all in Christ but in progress through a violent class struggle." How strange it was that Irish Catholicism was seeming to embrace — or at least to accept — Marxism just at a point when the system it begat, Communism, was about to crumble; or that it should have moved towards psychotherapy just at a moment when the scientific jury was coming to the view that there was no evidence whatsoever that psychotherapy had ever helped anyone (35 years of analysis did not make Woody Allen any less of a neurotic!).

The civil rights movement in the North certainly helped to shift the focus onto rights, for before that the emphasis had been on acceptance. Rights and justice began to appear more frequently in the lexicon of Catholicism. At another level, of course, these new approaches were arising out of the changes wrought by Vatican II.

A major change in values takes about 15 to 20 years to trickle into the common culture, and so it was that the cultural revolution of the 1960s began to percolate into mass society in the 1980s. The initial reaction to Vatican II — which sought to modernise and renew the Catholic Church — had been euphoric, particularly among the religious, and most notably among nuns. For them it came as a liberation from their seventeenth-century habits — costumes, that is — and authoritarian laws of obedience and subordination. It allowed women trained in repressing the senses to express joy, though in the long run it would empty the convents.

When an expert on Vatican II catechetics, Father Johannes Hofinger, visited Ireland in the mid-1960s, he addressed bigger audiences — mainly of nuns, priests and brothers — than anywhere else in the world. Thousands were turned away from these venues. He delivered 80 dissertations in 20 days. It was like a rock star's tour.

Everything was now subject to shifts and changes, and while the clergy and religious seemed to welcome these revolutions, some of the laity felt threatened and insecure. *Question:* "My parish has a new altar which is very plain, with no decorations or carvings. Why does it have to be so plain?" *Answer:* "It was feared that some of the older altars were so highly decorated that they took away people's attentions from the actual sacrifice of the Mass."

Question: "I have heard that the rosary is 'out of favour' now after the Vatican Council. Is this true? *Answer:* "No, but there is a broader, more Bible-based approach now to the faith." *Question:* "I have heard it said that we Catholics should not talk too much about Our Lady as it embarrasses Protestants and could be an object to unity. What to you think of this viewpoint?" *Answer:* "If anybody talks too much about anything it is embarrassing to everybody."

A picture begins to emerge, four years after the end of Vatican II, of some confusion among the faithful: "I'm still terribly muddled about this 'follow your conscience' business." "Why do they keep on changing the Mass? I wish they would stop and leave it alone." "Why have they changed the name Extreme Unction to the anointing of the sick?" "I'm all mixed up and don't know what's modest and what isn't." There was bewilderment that limbo seemed to have disappeared (where unbaptized souls were said to go, neither heaven, hell nor purgatory being available to them). The word "limbo" came from the Latin word, *limbus*, meaning "fringe". Of the unbaptized infants in limbo it was explained, before Vatican II: "It signifies the place inhabited by infants dying in Original Sin ... it is believed that these unbaptized infants in limbo know and love God by the use of their natural powers and have full natural happiness."

Yet limbo was a source of anxiety to mothers whose babies had died before being baptised, and in the 1990s there were some poignant reburials of unbaptised babies, long deceased, in church graveyards, previously the unbaptised had not been interred in consecrated grounds. After Vatican II, no more was heard of limbo.

Vatican II brought about many improvements in the practice of the Catholic faith. The old Latin Mass had been holy and mystical, but most people just did not understand it. The new Mass in the vernacular made sense and encouraged participation. The laity were involved at a more equal level in worship, rather than being a passive audience to the celebrant, the priest. Petty rules and regulations about fasting and women covering their heads were swept aside. And yet no sooner had the changes from Vatican II bedded in than came reports that younger people were falling away from their faith. *Question:* "Why do so many young persons ... fail to practice their religion?" *Question:* "I find my grown son, aged twenty-one, holds very different view than I do on religious matters, like Sunday Mass, and he is constantly criticizing the Pope and the Church. I have told him that I hold what I hold and don't wish to argue with him ... But I worry should I do more than pray for him, which I do. Should I take him up on his statements and argue with him?" Such concerned mothers are advised to leave their growing offspring alone and set a good example. Previously, they would have been told to exercise their authority.

Where once the family rosary was central to Irish life, by the early 1980s a dramatic decline was evident. By 1982, wrote a Catholic mother in *The Furrow*, it had become virtually impossible to get her children to join in any family prayers at all. They had tried everything to make family prayers work, but even in families where there was cooperation, the endeavour now generally ended in failure. "The advent of the teenage years depressed us both," wrote Mrs Nuala Bourke. "We tried all sorts of things, reading Scripture, spontaneous prayer, and back again to the one lonely decade of the rosary, at times even being satisfied with one Our Father in an almost desperate attempt at Family prayer. Although they obediently joined us, their obvious embarrassment forced us to abandon each effort in turn."

There had been a good press for trendy clerics in the 1960s, but in the 1970s ordinary Catholics expressed their discomfort with some of the more progressive approaches. "I get very upset by the strange ideas I sometimes hear nowadays even from priests." "I am worried about priests' casual attitude to the Sacred Heart." "A priest who works in our parish wants us to address him as 'Tom', not 'Father Tom'. I find this off-putting and older people don't like it one bit. I'm very confused." "My niece who is a nun told me I should not be fussing around with devotions — not indeed that I have many. I have great belief in the Green Scapular and always try to get to Mass and Holy Communion on the First Friday. Are these things no longer approved of by the Church?"

The more relaxed attitude of some priests in confession was criticised too by Mary Ingoldsby writing in *The Furrow*. She felt dismissively treated in a Dublin City Confessional when the priest snapped, "You don't have to tell these things. Say three Hail Marys." Another priest in a religious community told her she certainly did not need to come to confession more than once a month. "All the Church requires of you is that you confess your mortal sins once a year at Easter time." The lady wanted more spiritual help than was apparently available through the confessional.

It is possible that she seemed over-scruplous to her confessors, but she was not alone in remarking that post-Vatican II priests seemed to want to reject everything from the past. "A young priest said to me the other day that the Church should never have made things tough for its people," wrote a trade unionist in 1969. "He said evening Mass was better than getting up early on Sunday morning and that the old parish sodalities were well gone and that religion should be made handy for everyone." Some lay Catholics obviously regarded this as a rejection of their past devotions, as though the Offering It Up they had done had counted for naught.

Nuns and priests already in religious life found the changes brought about by Vatican II liberating; clearly they had felt repressed by the rigid regimes of the past. They had served their time under tough regimes. But human beings are strange creatures: sometimes they respond well when asked to give of themselves in a self-sacrificing way, and sometimes they respond tepidly to the call of an easier life. The fall in vocations to the clerical life actually began in the aftermath of Vatican II and were signalled by a new uncertainty in the popular devotional press. Pictures of young men entering the seminary were now captioned with the question "Will He Stay?" Between 1965 and the end of the 1980s vocations in Ireland fell by 75 per cent — Mass-going dropped by a third over approximately the same period.

And with the new emphasis on the role of the laity, men who might otherwise have become priests were having second thoughts: "Father, I was thinking of becoming a priest, but now that the Vatican Council has pointed out the immense scope of the lay apostolate, I am hesitating." The new bone of contention was the possibility of allowing priests to marry. "Why cannot priests marry, as Protestant clergy do?" Throughout the 1970s and 1980s celibacy was the main problem theme in *The Furrow*, which at this time was probably the most influential voice of Irish Catholicism. The liberalisation of society — indeed, the sexualisation of society — was making it increasingly difficult to observe celibacy. And it very probably had never been easy.

Recalling his time as a young seminarian in the 1950s in a personal anthology, Father Joe Dunn wrote that he and his fellow students used to be briefed each day by the Dean on the manner of their conduct. "*Averte domine oculos meos*," the Dean would say as the young clerical students set off on their bicycles, to which the juniors responded, "*Ne videant vanitatem*." ("Cast down my eyes, O Lord, lest they see this world's vanities.") Clerical students were not permitted to speak to girls — even their sisters had to keep at some distance. A young seminary student would be scolded if found to have been out walking without a hat. Any aberrant behaviour had to be reported — all were enjoined to report on the misdemeanours of others — and for a young man to be caught in the bedroom of another young man at seminary college meant instant dismissal.

Yet tough and repressive and rigid as the regulations were for Father Joe Dunn as a student priest, not a single member of his class of 22 left the priesthood to marry. Ten years later, when the situation had become more liberal, nearly half of those ordained in a similar group quit in order to marry.

"Normal young people, rightly or wrongly," concluded Father Dunn, "are not nowadays prepared to accept that level of restrictions on their freedom." He wrote that while he had "no wish to get into arguments about the morality or otherwise of sexual explicitness on television", he would nonetheless "point out that the changed environment brought about by television makes lifelong abstention from sex very much more difficult."

Joe Dunn, a liberal and a successful film-maker for Irish television, composed some of this retrospective essay on a beach in Greece, where he observed a woman — he presumed that she must be Swedish! — swimming topless. Afterwards she lay down on the beach where her boyfriend caressed her breasts with sun-oil. Joe Dunn noted laconically that this was an experience he had never had, and never would have now; he had kept to his vow of celibacy, and he believed that most of the men he knew in seminary college had done likewise. But he thought it must be much more difficult for young men now — he was writing in the 1990s — when sexuality had become so much more visible, so much more unavoidable. He could not see that the celibacy issue would go away. Father Dunn died of cancer in 1996.

The notion that celibacy is difficult is not new and it has been held by some Protestant (and Jewish) thinkers that it may have a distorting effect on the character. In his classic text *The History of European Morals,* written in 1869, W.E.H. Lecky contrasts the sane and balanced outlook — for him — of the married Protestant clergy with the punitive asceticism and zealotry of the Roman priesthood. (Lecky's appreciation of domesticity and the comforts of a home life were highly chauvinistic: the Protestant clergyman, for him, was serviced by a submissive wife who did all the household management!)

Celibacy, Lecky proclaimed, was akin to "proclaiming war on human nature". It perverted the imagination of Catholic priests. "Separated from most of the ties and affections of earth, viewing life chiefly through the distorted medium of the casuist or the Confessional, and deprived of those relationships which more than any others soften and expand the character, the Catholic priests have been but too often conspicuous for their fierce and sanguinary fanaticism, and for their indifference to all interests except those of their Church; while the narrow range of their sympathies, and the intellectual servitude they have accepted, render them peculiarly unfitted for the office of educating the young, which they so persistently claim and which, to the great misfortune of the world, they were long permitted to monopolise." Lecky, an Irish Protestant, was anti-Catholic, yet it is bizarre how his opinions would, 140 years later, be taken up by Irish Catholic critics of their own Church, who would make exactly these claims. In the sexualised era of post-1968, celibacy would appear even more of a distortion.

Even by the 1930s, anti-clerical Irish writers like Liam O'Flaherty were attacking the celibacy of the Irish priesthood. O'Flaherty was a Republican and a sometime Communist, and he opposed clerical power on a political principle — no priest, he said, had any loyalty to a secular state: the priest's only patriotism was for "His Majesty, the Pope". But he poured contempt on the priest's celibate, and childless, state. "Their corrupted and unscattered seed grows within them like a foul weed, poisoning the growth and flowering of all healthy passions. Their gift of life is brought by them to the grave and they refuse to hand it on to some lovely child that would grow about their withering thighs and charm their old eyes with an image of their youth." A celibate priest, wrote O'Flaherty, is a "savage" because of his condition.

Some of these anti-clerical writers failed to understand the context of Irish clan society. In past times, many Irish priests were part of a large constellation of kinship networks — priests often came from large families, which meant many siblings and a wider extended family too. Though a priest in the family certainly had a special kind of status and would be respected, he would also have to run the gauntlet of everyday family rough-and-tumble, including teasing. Kate O'Brien's saga *Without My Cloak* depicts the manner in which the family priest, Father Tom, has to put up with a certain amount of sarcasm and mockery from siblings, who rolled their eyes at his flowery sermons.

The brother-sister relationship is strong in Irish anthropology and many an Irish priest was as close, or closer, to his sister's children than their biological father. (The maternal uncle is a key figure in many kinship cultures: for Arabs and Albanians, the mother's brother is more important in a boy's life than the father. Interestingly, modern genetic science has established that biological characteristics in men can be inherited from the maternal uncle — the gene for baldness, for example.)

Maire McEntee, daughter of Sean McEntee (one of de Valera's closest colleagues) had three distinguished uncles in the priesthood: her highly cultivated mother spent as much time with her favourite priestly brother as she did with her politician husband, and the children actually saw more of their priestly uncles than their busy politician dad. So the charge that Irish Catholic priests were severed from family links did not usually hold true. A high proportion of Irish priests were farmers' sons, a class most particularly rooted in dynastic values. Irish priests had surrogate families and, as it was to be revealed, some of them had biological issue too.

From about 1973 onwards, notes J.H. Whyte, the standard authority on Church and State in Ireland, the Catholic Church in Ireland was moving away from its traditional position of power and towards the more "Protestant" concept of being the conscience of society. There was, says Whyte, "a graceful withdrawal" from the corridors of power, and only a few old-timers, such as Bishop Jeremiah Newman of Limerick, resisted this. Church and State had always been separated in the Irish Constitution — unlike in Britain, or Northern Ireland, clergymen of any kind could not stand for parliament or hold political office — but the "special position" of the Catholic Church had been recognised since 1937. This special position had been removed by referendum in 1972, with the broad support of the Church itself. Nuns and priests were beginning to withdraw from education — partly because their numbers were falling anyhow — although, interestingly, Catholic schools remained in demand among parents. (In Britain, by the 1980s, Catholic schools were so oversubscribed that it became a battle to get one's child's name down for a good Catholic school at all.)

From the early 1970s, too, the Irish Catholic Church began to shift towards a left-wing analysis of society. "The hierarchy," states Whyte, "could now be classified as a left-of-centre critic of Irish society. In March 1970, Cardinal Conway [then Cardinal-Archbishop of Ireland] called for a narrowing of income gaps. In 1971, the Bishops' Council for Social Welfare helped to pioneer the study of poverty — a growth area of Irish social study in the 1970s — by holding a conference on the subject at Kilkenny." In 1973 the Catholic charity Trócaire ("Mercy") was launched. In 1976 the hierarchy — at the height of the oil crisis recession — called for an economic reformation in which the better-off would bear a greater burden and make sacrifices for the sake of the poor. Taxation, as it happened, was already rising rather alarmingly for wage-earners: Christian "justice" might as easily have argued the unfairness of overtaxing a working father trying to raise his children and having the government confiscate up to 40 per cent of his paypacket, but the prevailing economic thinking of the time was that the wage-earners must be increasingly highly taxed to make sacrifices for the poor. In 1978 the Bishop of Galway, Eamonn Casey, attacked the Irish Government for not providing enough aid for developing countries.

In 1979 Bishop Peter Birch, a compassionate man, said that the competitive economic system was essentially unchristian. In the same year a joint statement by the Irish bishops called attention to the social tensions in Irish society, and to the lack of concern for "weaker groups" — all perfectly within the tradition of Christian support for the underdog.

A key turning-point in this reorientation was the joint pastoral letter issued by the Irish bishops in 1977, 'The Work of Justice'. Unemployment and poverty were targeted as the two social evils besetting Catholic Ireland: 20 per cent of the people could be classified as poor, it was estimated. Jesus Christ seemed undisturbed by the fact that "the poor you always have with you", but the Irish bishops begged to differ, suggesting there should be a "national programme to eliminate poverty". This was to be done by the tried and tested, and repeatedly failed, system of relieving the poor by penalising the better-off. Juan Perón and his wife Eva had pursued just such a system in Argentina, which they called *justicialismo*: it reduced Argentina from being one of the seven wealthiest nations in the world to a Third World economy.

The Irish bishops' pastorals, from 1978 onwards, also emphasised justice as the primary virtue, although it is most infrequently invoked in the New Testament. The Trócaire agency, widely supported by the clergy and the hierarchy, was set up to aid the poor in Third World countries, displaying a distinctly Marxist flavour in its crusades. Gone was the time when "Ireland's Spiritual Empire" emphasised the saving of souls and the need to bring Christ to the pagan world. Now the objective, according to Trócaire's advertising hoardings, was the defeat of white South Africa's expansionist designs on Mozambique, and the moral wickedness of trading with Johannesburg at all. There is a celebrated photograph of Bishop Eamonn Casey of Galway, Chairman of Trócaire — who was to shock Catholic Ireland in 1992 with the revelations of his affair with the American Annie Murphy — standing in front of a Trócaire poster which proclaims: "Apartheid is too high a price to pay for South African goods."

As a matter of a fact, the Catholic Church had opposed racism in South Africa as early as 1898, but this opposition had previously been based on the Christian call to treat all people as equal in the eyes of God. In the left-wing, politicised Irish Catholic approach of the 1980s, spirituality did not seem to come into it any more. The agenda was to oppose "the Right".

When President Reagan visited Ireland in June 1984, it was to a somewhat dusty reception: he was greeted by a subdued mood in Dáil Éireann and with howls of protest in the streets for his "aggressive" nuclear policies and alleged bullying of Central America. Concern about the onset of a nuclear war, in the Catholic periodicals of this time, always assumed that such a war would be started by the Americans.

Bishop Casey was the most prominent of the anti-Reagan protestors. He criticised and corrected Reagan for remarks about left-wing Nicaragua which he considered quite distorted; but worse, according to Dr Casey, Ronald Reagan had ignored the human rights abuse in Guatemala — an American "client state" — and El Salvador.

A Dominican nun, Sister Caoimhnin Ní Uallachain, led a public fast "which gave her the opportunity of linking with the suffering peoples of El Salvador and the Philippines". Several nuns and priests joined her in a rotating fast in the Garden of Remembrance at Parnell Square in Dublin, in solidarity with El Salvadoreans, black South Africans and the people of the Philippines. The letters columns of the newspapers were so full of denunciations from priests and nuns of the wickedness of President Reagan that one Jesuit wrote wondering why no one seemed to suggest saying prayers for this poor, misguided President's soul.

There is nothing wrong with priests, nuns and other clergy having political opinions — and indeed a social conscience — and it is part of their job to identify with the poor. All the same, it was a surprising turnaround to see so much heavy denunciation of American policies among Irish Catholic voices, and an almost amnesiac forgetfulness of a previous enemy — Communism. It is a paradox that the despised Ronald Reagan stood out as a major world leader who was willing to oppose abortion, one of the Catholic Church's most passionately held causes. It could also be argued that "Reaganomics" did more to relieve poverty by stimulating employment than any number of socialist-inspired National Plans might have done.

Had Ronald Reagan appeared in Ireland 30 years previously, he would have been applauded as an Irish-American hero for his firm stand against Communism and his unyielding defence of the unborn child. But by the 1980s he was the baddie. In 1984 Father Peter Lemass, a well-liked Dublin priest who had links with Latin America, wrote that Reagan's Star Wars defence policy was the greatest threat to the human race that had ever existed. Father Lemass wondered if he, personally, would live to see the year 2000 — that is, if the Americans and their accursed Star Wars strategy would allow any of us to reach that year. When that time arrived, in fact, historians would be claiming that the defence policy initiated by President Reagan would be what finally broke the Soviet Union, whose crumbling economy could not outspend the United States.

Peter Lemass — who did not survive to see the Millennium — was more drawn to Fidel Castro than to Ronald Reagan. He quoted with approval Castro's words: "We should make an alliance between religion and the Revolution. Where do the contradictions between Christian teachings and socialist teachings lie? We both wish to struggle on behalf of men, for the welfare of men, for the happiness of men." Fidel's Jesuit education had clearly not been wasted: he knew how to argue a fine point. And before the end of the century, he would welcome John Paul II to Cuba, making common cause with the fiercely anti-Communist Pope. God works in mysterious ways. Yet there is an essential contradiction between Christian and socialist teaching: Marxism and socialism traditionally dismiss altogether the dimension of the soul, whereas Christian teaching depends upon our acceptance of man's spiritual life.

If Christianity itself forgets or omits the spiritual dimension, then it parts with, and fatally weakens, its own Unique Selling Proposition.

The authority of the Catholic Church in Ireland began to fail for a constellation of reasons, in the 1980s, although the full extent of that decline would not be evident for virtually another decade. Camille Paglia claims that romanticism always declines into decadence; what is at first happy and free, descends into anarchy and perversion. Men find freedom intolerable, and they seek new ways to enslave themselves, through drugs and depression. Sexual liberty turns to licence and depravities. A case could be made for the romantic dawn of the 1960s turning to the pornographic free-for-all — paedophilia a globalised industry, for example — by the end of the century. And some of the most scandalous signs of decadence were to emerge from the Catholic Church itself.

In the 1980s, before any of the scandals which were to have such a destructive impact broke, the Catholic Church's territory was already being colonised by the spirit of the age. Instead of confession, there would be counselling; instead of stoicism, the culture of rights and litigation; instead of fasting, eating disorders; instead of the rosary and the drama of the Stations of the Cross, soap operas and heroin needles. Dublin working-class women, once the Mothers of Courage of the slums, were, by the middle 1980s, drifting into a culture of drugs and opiates, and the most devoutly religious parts of old Dublin, which had so entranced G.K. Chesterton when he reported the Eucharistic Congress of 1932, would soon be the very heartland of the drug epidemic.

Social and cultural theories launched in the 1960s were now becoming facts of everyday life. One of the developing ideas in Western society was the spread of private choice and personal autonomy. A prosaic case of the rental of a country cottage illustrates this development rather well.

In 1981 Miss Kelly, a civil servant in one of the main towns of Co Mayo, rented out a cottage which her father had bequeathed to her in his will. The tenants who took the cottage were a couple from outside the area, who, it became obvious, were cohabiting without benefit of marriage. The local priest made a critical remark to Miss Kelly about the arrangement suggesting that the unmarried couple could be "an occasion of scandal" and were giving a bad example. Miss Kelly, a young woman and a practising, but modernised, Catholic, replied quite courteously that she felt that the private morality of her tenants was none of her business. They were good tenants, they paid their rent on time and they kept the property well; she did not care to make moral judgements about other people. The priest, who was an elderly man, was not happy about this, but he said no more. Presently he died.

The following year Miss Kelly acquired some new tenants — the cohabiting couple having moved elsewhere — and this time the individuals showed all the signs of being an even more scandalous *ménage à trois*, being composed of a man and two women, with a newborn baby: it was supposed that the man was cohabiting with both the women, and it was never clear which was the mother of the baby.

But neither then, nor later, was anything further said to Miss Kelly, as the property-owner, whether by priest or layman, concerning the effect on public morals of this trio. The successor priest kept his own counsel. And within the space of three or four years it was generally accepted within the locality that whatever lifestyle a person embraced — providing it did not unduly interfere with the community — was a matter of personal choice.

Within the next decade, many Irish priests would have taken what would previously have been called a "Protestant" view of some moral choices. In 1994 a woman I know in Dublin mentioned to her priest in confession that she had a lover with whom she was cohabiting, on and off since he lived part of the time abroad. She was past childbearing years and her lover was a widower, but there were financial disincentives to their marrying. "I'll leave it to your own conscience," the priest told her.

These incidents illustrate a major transition from the mores of a previous generation, when virginity in a woman was prized and sins against chastity deplored, when priests — and the laity, too — regarded themselves as guardians of community morals, and when bishops might still be consulted by the civic authorities as the appropriate time for the ending of public dances.

At one level, the changes in Irish life grew organically out of the changing world culture and in particular the view, which took hold everywhere from the 1970s onwards, that individuals had the right to choose their own way of life independently of outside authorities. Many of the slogans popularised by the feminist movement — notably in the campaigns for legalized abortion — summed up the new philosophy of private life and private choices. "Not the Church and not the State — women shall decide their fate." "The woman's right to choose" was a brilliant catchphrase, since it drew, even unconsciously, on a Christian philosophy which had been particularly dear to Western thinking and Catholic doctrine: free will. The "right to choose" began to apply to a far wider agenda, both personal and commercial. "Choice" became the buzz-word of the 1990s, invoking free market competition as well as personal ethics.

And throughout the 1980s there was a growing view among the more influential clergy that prohibitions — notably sexual ones — had been overemphasised in the past and that we should be less exercised by the peccadilloes of the flesh. Immorality should focus more on injustice, discrimination and prejudice and less on mere sex. We should worry more about inequalities before the law, wrote one distinguished theologian in 1979, or the punishment of young offenders, and less about contraception, prostitution or pornography.

Catholic clergy of this vintage had come of age during the iron rule of John Charles McQuaid, who had died in 1973 and who had preached and practised for 40 years an ascetic, 17th-century war against the flesh. Now the population was reacting against all this. So it seemed that out would go Thomas Aquinas and Jansenism — the French 17th-century thinking that had emphasised the distinction between the higher nature of the soul and the lower nature of the flesh — and in would come thinkers such as Freud, Erikson, Adorno (a Marxist literary critic who attacked "the authoritarian personality"), D.H. Lawrence and Carl Rogers, some of the writers now esteemed by Catholic theologians.

By the 1980s repression was the new evil; sexuality was part of our "personhood", to be accepted, not repressed and kept forever under control. A hundred and twenty years after Lecky had denounced this "war against nature", Catholic thinkers were coming around to his point of view; eighty years after sexologists like Havelock Ellis had appalled the Church, some in the Church had decided, after all, that if you can't beat 'em, join 'em. "Sexuality is the cup of passion, humour, constancy and love ... Human sexuality is a dimension of persons and personal fulfilment transcends many limitations," wrote Father Maurice Reidy.

Just as D.H. Lawrence was going out of fashion in the academic world (loathed by feminists for his phallocentric views, and regarded as a proto-fascist for his preoccupation with "blood and soil"), he was coming into fashion with certain of the Irish Redemptorists; by 1981 Father Ralph Gallagher was writing in praise of the author of *Lady Chatterley's Lover*. We must not see morality, narrowly, in terms of sex, wrote Father Gallagher. "Justice is an integral part of morality, and not an optional extra ... It is heartening to see public concern about El Salvador, South Africa and the Philippines."

There was also a noticeable new questioning of traditional attitudes to homosexuality, which had previously been pronounced to be against nature — Christianity, Judaism and

Islam having historically held this view in common. A characteristic example of this new liberal tone among the clergy was a strong article in *The Furrow* in 1979 about the pastoral care of homosexuals, written by Father Gallagher. Formerly, Redemptorist priests had had a reputation for being rather fierce and for delivering sermons melodramatically conjuring up hellfire — often regarded as an entertaining diversion in rural Ireland. The writer Patrick Kavanagh recalled how gnarled old countrymen would be quite flattered by the visiting Redemptorist castigating them as sinning Don Juans. But the Redemptorists had radically changed: they were now more interested in counselling than hellfire.

Father Gallagher questioned, in this ground-breaking article, the traditional Christian view of homosexuality as being *contra naturam*: the theory, he said was undergoing serious scientific review. "Many debates on homosexuality reveal prejudice, fear and unsupported statements rather than the elements of reason and freedom which, theoretically, are the basis of ethical analysis ... Homosexuals should not be judged to be immoral any more than a blind person if prenatally the visual tracts are not complete." Seventeen years before geneticists would claim to have identified a "gay gene", an Irish Redemptorist priest was suggesting that homosexuality could begin in the womb.

Moreover, some of the unhappiness experienced by homosexuals was the *fault* of the Church. "The alienation and loneliness of many homosexuals have been contributed to in no small way by the attitude of society and of the Churches." We should, he counselled, be cautious in using scriptural texts about homosexuality (the Old Testament and St Paul in the New Testament condemn homosexuality — the "Sin of Sodom"); rather we must challenge the notion that homosexual acts are intrinsically evil or "imperfect". Homosexuality must be seen as part of a proper understanding of sexuality "in its wider sense". And this wider sense was arising because sex was no longer simply about procreation.

Conservatives had warned that contraception would lead, eventually, to the acceptance of homosexuality as an equal kind of sexuality; once it was accepted that "the transmission of life" was not the essential point of sexual congress, then all forms of sexuality would become equal. Ralph Gallagher was arguing this point affirmatively. "We must take cognizance of the changed emphasis on procreation in a theological understanding of sex. It can no longer be regarded as the single dominant norm by which all sexual behaviour is judged. The reality of personal sexual encounters is too wide to be compromised into the univocal notion of procreation." Father Gallagher had found himself deeply impressed by a letter from a homosexual man who had struggled with his orientation, and who had written thus: "The most important thing that happened to me was the realization that homosexuality was natural for me, and from God." This was indeed a development from the 1960s: "if it feels good — do it!" What *feels* natural, *is* natural. Feeling was replacing cold reasoning as the measure of attitudes and actions.

The Church's teaching on homosexuality remained "confused", according to another Irish theologian, Joseph S. O'Leary, writing in 1987. "All I can recommend is that we continue to practise uncensored dialogue and disinterested research, and refrain from too-confident promulgation of negative opinions of the kind which have had such damaging effects in the past and have so often subsequently proved to be incorrect." Yet, for Father O'Leary, "the self-accepting homosexual person is generally sufficiently at ease with his or her own sexuality to be able to consider various theories about homosexuality, even negative ones, quite serenely."

By the late 1980s homosexuality was accepted in the theological journals as a subject for just such uncensored dialogue (by the late 1990s it was common to claim that a disproportionate number of priests were gay anyhow). Although homosexuality had not been the subject of overt Catholic discourse before, it is worth remembering that in the late 19th century Roman Catholicism was considered to be especially attractive to homosexuals and decadents: Oscar Wilde, Aubrey Beardsley and J.K. Huysmans (author of the cult novel of the 1890s *À Rebours*) were drawn to the odour of Roman incense and the acknowledged effeminacy of Catholicism. Catholicism, not being so orientated towards the

Old Testament, was less overtly hostile to homosexuality than biblically-based Protestantism.

Still, this new thinking on homosexuality was linked with new moral theology, with the focus on the *person* not the *sexual object*. Homosexuals were, first of all, persons. In a paradoxical way, this new Catholic thinking was rather in contradiction to the gay rights campaigns which tended to define persons by their sexuality — homosexuality.

Much of the theological writing on homosexual themes which appeared in the 1980s was intelligent and humane, and showed a generous and sincere sensibility towards holy men who happened to be homosexuals. Lesbians, at this stage, were not mentioned; since lesbianism does not involve "the sin of Sodom" it has had less biblical significance. And it did not involve the law either; the Victorians had banned male homosexuality for Britain and Ireland, but had not mentioned lesbianism. This is sometimes ascribed to the difficulty of explaining female homosexuality to Queen Victoria, but it is more likely to have been because male homosexuality has historically involved more public acts. There was a brisk trade in rent boys and flourishing homosexual brothels for men in Victorian London; whereas female homosexuality has generally been more private and discreet.

Alongside this new sensibility towards homosexuality, there was a growing endorsement of feminism within Catholic thinking. Feminist theologians such as Rosemary Radford Reuther began to emerge. Patriarchy within the Church was targeted as an evil, and the idealised image of the Blessed Virgin as a role-model was inextricably linked with the asceticism, not to say misogyny, of the Church fathers, the perpetrators of patriarchy.

"The Virgin Mary was held up as an appropriate model for Catholic girls," wrote Helen Sheehy in 1965, deploring this tendency in Catholicism. "Mary was presented as docile, submissive and celibate — even within marriage." Ms Sheehy describes "churching" as "a ritual purification to cleanse [the woman] from the effects of her original sin of sexual intercourse" after childbirth. This was not, actually, the case: since the 1940s the *Irish Messenger of the Sacred Heart* had been at pains to explain, repeatedly, that the churching ceremony, held six weeks after childbirth, was "an act of thanksgiving for the safe delivery and the gift of motherhood." Churching was also practised in the Anglican faith — there is an elaborate ritual for it in the *Book of Common Prayer*. It also performed a practical role: women were not expected to have sexual intercourse again until after the churching ceremony. This probably helped restrain husbands from resuming sexual relations immediately after childbirth, which many men would otherwise have been keen to do, and which few mothers feel inclined to do. Not coincidentally, mothers now usually have a medical check-up six weeks after the birth of a baby which has to some degree taken the place of the churching service.

Yet theological feminists thought all these rituals patriarchal and anti-woman. We needed a complete revolution, wrote Ms Sheehy, in a male-dominated Church. "Today's sexual ethic promoted by a male celibate Church finds no answering chord in the hearts of many women ... Feminist theology seeks to re-image God." Rosemary Radford Ruether followed Freud in seeing God the Father as a form of infantilism, and replacing this with God the Mother would be equally infantile. The feminist theologians were also following in the footsteps of Sartre, for whom autonomy and choice were the distinguishing traits of human experience. There were many more articles on these lines which showed how the cookie was crumbling.

Autonomy and choice were now sweeping away traditional prohibitions on abortion in other countries. Aware of this international wave, and that a more liberal attitude to contraception elsewhere had weakened opposition to abortion, pro-life activists in Ireland successfully struck pre-emptively: two Taoisigh — Irish Prime Ministers — Charles Haughey and Garret Fitzgerald, agreed to the proposal to add a pro-life amendment to the Irish Constitution defending the entitlement to life of the unborn child. The wording of the amendment was: "The State acknowledges the right to life of the unborn child, and with due regard to the equal right to life of the mother, guarantees in its laws to respect, and as far as is practicable, by its law to defend and vindicate that right."

The referendum called to endorse or reject this amendment, in September 1983, was to be a bitter cultural and moral conflict; rightly did the author Tom Hesketh call it, in his book on the subject *The Second Partitioning of Ireland*. The partition now was not between North and South, but between rural and urban Ireland, between Catholic and secularising Ireland, and also between liberal Catholics and conservatives (or those conservative on this issue). Many harsh words were exchanged on both sides: abortion brings out a lot of emotional pain, which makes it a distressing argument at the best of times. It was an argument dominated by the laity; with some exceptions, the hierarchy and clergy were not prominent in the conflict. Their overall attitude was that they would not have chosen to engage in this debate, but once it was joined, they had to be supportive of the anti-abortion movement.

I followed the course of this referendum closely: it was a miserable time and I loathed the tenor of some of the arguments. Abortion arguments drive people to such extremes, on both sides, and yet it is also an argument where each of us is called to stand up for our consciences. It is an argument where you have to speak up for what you believe is right. That does not make it easy.

It was a melancholy time for my family, too, because my brother James was slowly dying from cancer and I remember, on referendum day, crying all the way in a bumpy bus from Galway to Clifden, in Connemara, thinking of his thin shoulders underneath his jacket as he turned to pour tea. He was an Irish Nationalist who did not care for either side in the abortion referendum. He disliked Holy Joes, or anyone he thought was parading virtue; he also disliked the secularising liberals and smart alecks who he thought were out to destroy Ireland's Gaelic and Catholic heritage. When I awoke in Clifden the next morning and heard the result, I knew that James would be gratified: the referendum had been carried by two to one, though the turnout had not been spectacular. It would please James that the secularising liberals had been defeated and that Gaelic-Catholic Ireland had spoken; and yet he would also be glad that it had not been too decisive a turnout and that the Holy Joes would have scant cause for triumphalism.

Many gloomy predictions were made by the liberals about the outcome of the pro-life amendment. It was said that nothing would stop women travelling to Britain for abortions if they chose to, and it was predicted that childbirth in the Republic of Ireland would become more dangerous because life-threatening pregnancies could not be terminated in any circumstances. It is true that Irishwomen travel abroad for abortions, though overall the rate of abortion among them remains considerably lower than the European average (about eight per cent of pregnancies) so the law has some discouraging effect all the same. It was not true, though, that pregnancy in Ireland was to become more dangerous. Quite the contrary. Ireland became one of the safest countries in the world, according to World Health figures, in which to have a baby. By 1993 the Republic of Ireland had the lowest rate of maternal mortality and one of the lowest rates of perinatal (new-born) mortality. An American rabbi specialising in medical ethics has told me that when you do not have easy access to abortion "it makes the doctors try harder" to bring a woman safely through pregnancy.

So the ban on abortion did not prove hazardous for the health of mothers. But pro-life advocates were to be mortified by an event which did indeed cast the abortion laws of the Republic in a ghastly light. In February 1992, a 14-year-old Irish girl became pregnant after having been subjected to sexual molestation and statutory rape by a neighbour, a friend of her father. When she went to London to have the pregnancy terminated, her father informed the Garda in Dublin, as a consequence of which the Garda requested, at the instigation of the Attorney-General, that the girl be brought back to Ireland, since the abortion was "unconstitutional". A controversy which attracted worldwide attention followed.

Within Ireland there was widespread sympathy for the teenager, and there were many recriminations too about the effect of the abortion ban, which seemed virtually to imprison a rape victim. The *Irish Times,* in a celebrated editorial, compared Ireland to the Ayatollah Khomeini's Iran. Commentators overseas described the Republic as "a theocratic state" whose laws were mediaeval. Eventually, an entitlement to seek an abortion was conceded through the courts, although the grounds for the exception — that the girl was suicidal — were hardly satisfactory. The girl might well have been suicidal, but the threat of suicide is a weak reason for case law. (In the end, the young girl miscarried anyhow.) Pro-life activists believed that the *de facto* right to abortion had now been established — if the mother's life was endangered by suicidal feelings — and much of what they had established by referendum had been effectively overturned. Indeed, some pro-life people suspected a ruse in the way the X case, as it was called, had been managed.

The 1983 referendum was divisive and rendered somewhat inconclusive because of subsequent events. But it laid down a marker which established that Irish society was essentially hostile to abortion, and antipathy to casual abortion has broadly held. Pro-natalism has deep roots in Irish culture; there is some well-observed Victorian sociology about the diaspora Irish at their very poorest, in English slums of the 19th century, remaining remarkably resistant to the child-abandonment or abortion strategies which were found all around them.

Yet we are not just talking about Catholic Ireland here: anti-abortion values are shared by the majority of Ulster Protestants, and most strongly endorsed among the most emphatically Protestant and Loyalist groups. Among those who supported the 1983 amendment to protect the unborn child in the Republic of Ireland were the Revd Ian Paisley, MP, and the Revd Martin Smyth, Grand Master of the Orange Order. Uncomfortably for liberals, the pro-life movement is probably the most strangely ecumenical in the whole of the island.

The abortion question is not over in Ireland, or elsewhere, for that matter, since there will never be agreement on the ethics involved. The question of terminating a pregnancy where the child would be born severely handicapped will be increasingly contested. Medical advances will continue to alter the picture too: fetal donation may not be that far off, meaning that abortion need no longer involve destroying the unborn, but donating it elsewhere.

But aside from abortion, the "liberal agenda", as it was called, was now moving on apace. By 1993 the law forbidding homosexual relations between men was rescinded, and the age of consent set at 17 for both sexes, in both heterosexual and homosexual relations. Because this was not a constitutional question, it did not require a referendum, but was passed with all-party support in the Dáil, although surveys showed that the public at large was not sympathetic to the change.

There had been a divorce referendum in the Republic in 1986, which was defeated, partly because Catholic sensibilities were still hostile to divorce, but probably more essentially because women were not sufficiently protected in the case of a division of property and assets. But there was no doubt that there would be another attempt to introduce legislation for the dissolution of marriage, and this was duly done, with a second referendum on divorce in 1995.

Divorce had been prohibited in 1925; there had been some minority dissent, most notably from the poet W.B. Yeats, who was then a senator. In retrospect, the Irish Free State's ban on divorce was considered to be an insult to Irish Protestants, who would not have shared the absolute ban imposed by the Roman Catholic Church. Yet at the time a wide number of Protestants shared Catholic values on this issue, and the letters columns of the *Church of Ireland Gazette* even showed some admiration for the Free State's defence of marriage. The Anglican Archbishop of Dublin, Dr Gregg, also supported the ban on divorce at the time, on the grounds that the prohibition of divorce would be a lesser evil than its endorsement.

Yet modernisation was altering this, and by the 1990s the Church of Ireland was recommending an abrogation of the prohibition. So were liberal Catholics, including some noted Catholic clerics, who felt that Church and State should be separate and that it was not the Church's job to regulate the laws of the State. The Catholic Church made its views clear — that it regarded marriage as indissoluble — but it also stood aside from the political fray. The arguments on both sides came almost wholly from the laity. Again, to some extent, the battle-lines were drawn between liberal, secular Ireland and traditional, Catholic Ireland; between the cities and urban areas, on the one hand, and rural, agricultural areas on the other. Some on the liberal side saw in this 1995 vote a crucial termination of what they called "the Confessional state".

And indeed, all the big guns were supporting the introduction of civil divorce. All the political parties were behind the pro-divorce vote, as were all the national media. President Mary Robinson, though technically neutral (the Irish Presidency is a ceremonial office), had fought for divorce rights as a lawyer, and advocated divorce freedom as a political activist. The Government itself spent half a million Irish pounds on publicity in favour of a "yes" vote — and half a million buys quite a lot of commercials in Ireland. And there were many individuals who had experience of marriage breakdown, personally or in their families, who campaigned vigorously and effectively for the change.

And yet, in spite of a concerted propaganda campaign — some of it perfectly sincere — to get divorce accepted in modern Ireland, the referendum itself was a cliffhanger. The proposal to introduce divorce in Ireland was carried, in the end, by half of one per cent. The final vote was "Yes" to divorce: 818,842, being 50.3 per cent of the turnout, and "No", 809,728, being 49.7 per cent of the turnout. It had been a rainy and inclement day in the West of Ireland, where the No votes were stronger; had the sun shone for a couple of hours, the result might have been tilted the other way.

Yet the liberals and secularisers had won their first significant political victory against the traditional values of Catholic Ireland, and the champagne bottles were opened to celebrate a new dawn of personal freedom and private choice. But such political changes were not the body-blow which brought about decline and fall: that would come from the Jacobean tragedy of clerical scandals which rolled out unceasingly in the last decade of the 20th century.

Fourteen

Decline and Fall

"Evil as we believe the influence of Roman Catholicism to be, and evil, as too often, are the teachings of the Roman priesthood in Ireland, yet ... suppose it were gone tomorrow, by what would it be replaced? Without doubt, by an atheism, a materialism and most probably an anarchy which would sink Ireland lower in the scale of human progress than she had ever sunk before."

The Church of Ireland Gazette, February 1903

"These are the Nineties. And the new Ireland is here to stay. And Lent doesn't matter. Religion doesn't matter. Irish Catholicism is now seen as something you grow out of."

The Church in a New Ireland, Sean MacReamoinn (ed), 1996

When the scandal of Bishop Casey of Galway broke over Ireland in May 1992, it seemed unprecedented in the history of Irish Catholicism. Bishop Eamonn Casey had had a love-affair in 1974 with an American divorcee, Annie Murphy, had fathered a child by her, deserted her and suggested that the child should be placed for adoption; and then in a desperate attempt to hide the truth he had used diocesan funds to pay off the mother's claims.

People were flabbergasted, breathless, appalled and disbelieving. Catholic commentators went back over 200 years to look for a parallel. Some even expressed the view that this was such an aberration, such a one-off, that it was the unique exception which proved the rule that Irish Catholic clergy were generally people of high probity, decency and honour.

As a journalist, I too initially judged it to be just one of those things: a single scandal. My editor at the *Irish Independent*, Jim Farrelly, suggested that I write a piece on "The Irreversible Damage to Catholic Ireland" on the back of the breaking news story. "Oh, come on," I replied airily, "one bishop hardly makes a decline and fall. Think of the Borgias, anyway." (Roderigo Borgia, who died in 1503, was Pope Alexander VI and led a life of unrelenting licentiousness. He was also one of the most splendid patrons of the arts that the Vatican has ever had.)

In any case, I did not particularly share the view, then widespread in Ireland, that Eamonn Casey was a wicked seducer of a helpless young woman. I knew perfectly well from my own experience that a sexually knowing woman — Miss Murphy was 27 at the time of her involvement with Eamonn Casey — can often exercise compelling emotional power over a less experienced, even if older, man. Men can be seducers: they can also be easy game. It was just as likely that Annie Murphy had targeted Eamonn Casey; priests and, even more, bishops are exciting forbidden fruit to predatory women, and she later admitted that she did want a child.

But the personal agenda behind the story was not really the point, at this stage of the game. The point was that this had never knowingly or openly occurred before, in the lifetime of Irish Catholics. Bishops, whom they revered as holy men who laid down the law on morals and doctrine, men to whom respect was due *because* their celibacy was a personal sacrifice, were stained. The higher you climb, the harder you fall. There was a bitterness in the common reaction. "These are the fellows who were telling *us* how to behave," a middle-aged woman in West Cork said to me. "These are the guys who were quizzing us, in Confession, as to whether we had entertained bad thoughts. No, no, no."

Comment on the Casey affair unleashed a kind of public ire against the clergy that had not been openly expressed in Ireland since the beginning of the 20th century, when there had been some fierce, even savage, criticism of the Catholic clergy by such authors as Michael MacCarthy (*Priests and People in Ireland*), W.P. Ryan (*The Pope's Green Island*) and P.D. Kenny (*Economics for Irishmen*). This wave of anti-clericalism in the 1900s was exclusively male and generally radical, proceeding from the socialism and nationalism of the period which saw clericalism as backward. The focus of the complaints concerned money and politics. Even the most excoriating anti-clerical critic of that time had not accused the priests of betraying the vow of chastity which they took, and the high standards of chastity they encouraged in others. The storm of scandal that broke over the head of Eamonn Casey was something else. Moreover, women were now just as fierce as radical young men in their criticism.

In a powerful piece in the *Sunday Independent* Anne Harris arraigned an Irish bishop in public in a way that an Irish bishop had never before been called to account in an Irish newspaper. Eamonn Casey, Anne Harris wrote, was "a cad and a scoundrel". Annie Murphy, the Bishop's former paramour, had told her story (a lurid version was to appear in a book she co-authored, *Forbidden Fruit*). "With every word of Annie Murphy's story, the iron entered the Irish soul about Eamonn Casey," Anne Harris wrote.

> It purged the soul with pity and with terror. The pity was not for the man ... It was for a woman abandoned and a baby denied. The terror was not of an avenging woman. It was of the corruption of the Church, so clearly illuminated through her account of her lover's behaviour when confronted with the consequences of his affair; the attempts to brainwash her into believe she needed cleansing and should give up her child; the refusal to jeopardize his own career by acknowledging his son ... If he were anything other than a bishop, he would be called a cad and a scoundrel. But precisely because he *is* a bishop, and an arbiter of moral

standards, he *is* a cad and a scoundrel. And now a coward for running away.

Once the scandal had broken, Eamonn Casey left Ireland for Central America.
"For 17 years," Anne Harris went on,

… Eamonn Casey denied his own deep nature and was thus corrupted as a man and suborned as a bishop. Surely, as a man the first instinct in life is the response to nature. How could he deny his fatherhood? Does the priesthood obviate the duties of fatherhood? If it does, it's merely another measure of the unnatural constraints the Church forces on its people to coerce them into denying their own flesh and blood." The moral constructs of Catholic values were thus thrown into hypocritical contrast. "Their other measures — denying their followers condoms and divorce — are sewn into the political fabric of Irish life.

The tone of this essay seemed to me to capture the mood of Ireland at the time. There were a few who defended Bishop Casey and saw in his story an all too human weakness; most individuals have made mistakes, and have sought to hide their mistakes too. Yet the anger was undeniable. When Gay Byrne, the celebrated Irish TV presenter, made a passing remark in defence of Eamonn Casey at the end of an interview with Annie Murphy, the letters columns of the newspapers overflowed with protests that Mr Byrne should have seen fit to defend the renegade and at his apparently less than sympathetic attitude towards Ms Murphy.

There was also private criticism from within the clergy. Eamonn Casey had never been a safe pair of hands; he was always a bit of a hell-raiser, famous for reckless, fast driving, and fond of a drink. He had been a popular priest; with his left-wing profile for work among the homeless, campaigns against the South African regime and association with Central American movements that were highly critical of US policy. All in all, it was the conservatives in the Catholic Church who muttered that he should never have been appointed a bishop in the first place. In a more traditional Ireland, his partying and drinking would have been an obstacle.

The Casey scandal was unprecedented and breathtaking. But even when it began to blow over, it was not the end of the larger issue. It was not even the beginning of the end, nor yet the end of the beginning. From 1992 onwards, a veritable avalanche of clerical sexual scandals would pour into the Irish public arena, giving any passing observer the impression that the Irish priesthood, once held in such faultless regard, was steeped in the morals characteristic of Imperial Rome in its declining years.

Within three years of the Casey story, Catholic Ireland would grow accustomed to opening its newspapers daily to be regaled with report after report of horrific and pitiful cases of sex charges against Catholic priests. But these were not run-of-the-mill revelations of love stories, but distressing cases of sexual abuse, or of priests being uncovered in *louche* surroundings. August 1993: "Two Catholic priests have been jailed this year after being found guilty of child sexual abuse. A third priest, who has admitted charges involving thirty incidents of indecent assault on an eleven-year-old boy is currently awaiting trial." November 1994: "A priest has been given a fifteen-month suspended sentence by Dublin Circuit Criminal Court for sexually assaulting a male hitchhiker." The priest had claimed that the teenage boy had consented to what had taken place, but the claim was rejected by the court. November 1994: "Dublin priest dies in gay sauna. Liam Cosgrave, a native of Co Cork, who was in his sixties, collapsed and died in the Incognito Sauna Club in Bowe Lane, off Dublin's Aungier Street, shortly after 6 p.m. The club owner, Mr Liam Ledwidge, said two other priests gave him the last rites. He said that priests made up a significant number of the club's membership, after barristers and solicitors." Father Cosgrave had been a regular visitor to the gay club for several years.

November 1994: "Father Daniel Curran jailed for seven years for abusing children. RUC says it wants to interview thirty Catholic priests and brothers in relation to child abuse. Nearly a dozen are in jail or under investigation." November

1994: "Church silent on alleged assault by priest. The Archdiocese of Dublin has refused to say whether it gave Gardaí information on the past activities of a priest who had been the subject of a Garda investigation into an alleged sexual assault against a boy earlier this year. Gardaí have prepared a file for the Director of Public Prosecutions on the assault against the thirteen-year-old boy, which is alleged to have occurred in a hotel toilet following a funeral."

December 1994: "Sex abuse victims sue Archbishop Connell. The Archbishop of Dublin, Desmond Connell, and a priest who was convicted of indecently assaulting young children in the North Dublin parish of Ayrfield, are being sued by two of the priest's victims ... [who] claim that the Church has a responsibility to face."

April 1995: "Church's new sex scandal. £27,000 paid to man abused by priest. Former altar boy tells of ordeal." June 1995: "Fifteen sex charges against priest. A priest appeared in court yesterday on fifteen charges of indecently assaulting a youth." The forty-year-old curate was making a remand appearance at Tuam Court. Initially he had been charged with one count of attempted buggery of a youth, more than six years previously.

July 1995: "A de la Salle brother, Florence Scally, was charged in Co Down with sex offences against young boys (a charge he vehemently denies) ... a Dublin priest, Tony Walsh, received a twelve-month sentence for sexually assaulting a twelve-year-old boy ... Cardinal Cahal Daly said that several Northern bishops were cooperating with the RUC in connection with its inquiries into 'a small number of individual priests'." And it emerged that "the Director of Public Prosecutions is considering whether the paedophile priest, Brendan Smyth, should be charged with alleged offences in the Republic". The Brendan Smyth case was to be quite appalling, and was to bring down the Dublin government.

November 1995: "Alan O'Sullivan, now a 33-year-old architectural draughtsman, told [reporters] that Father Patrick Hughes had raped, buggered and taken pornographic photographs of him between the ages of nine and eleven. Patrick Hughes, aged 68, made an out-of-court settlement of £50,000 to his former pupil. The abuse had come to the attention of the Archdiocese and Hughes had been sent to a psychiatrist. He was allowed to continue in his ministry." November 1995: "Dublin Court to Try Sex Charge Priest. A Catholic priest charged in Kilkenny Circuit Court yesterday on five counts of sexually assaulting young men had his case transferred to the Dublin Circuit Criminal Court ... The 49-year-old former parish priest had been relieved of his duties by his bishop ... He is charged with buggery, attempted buggery, sexual assault and two charges of indecent assault on young men on dates between January 1, 1988 and December 1, 1993."

This is but a taster. There were many more reports such as these. When I asked to see the cuttings file at the Independent Newspapers in Dublin on "clerical abuse", I could scarcely credit the sheer volume of the indictments. The files bulged with newspaper material.

During these events of the mid-1990s I would hear people in Ireland say: "It *can't* get any worse." And then it did. On one Monday in November 1994, the three leading stories on RTE, the national television network, were the political repercussions following the Brendan Smyth case, the collapse and death of the Dublin priest in a homosexual sauna club, and the conviction of a Galway priest for a sexual assault on a young man, all in one news bulletin. I made no more jokes about Renaissance Popes. The wave upon wave of charges and convictions — nearly all were convicted as charged — was relentless, squalid and depressing.

The Brendan Smyth case was not only squalid and depressing, it brought down the Government of Albert Reynolds. It was also particularly shocking not just because the offender was an apparently unrepentant paedophile, but because there was evidence that the religious authorities had covered up for him over a number of years. In 1968 he had been given psychiatric counselling for his compulsion, but without any apparent amelioration. (The paedophile condition is notoriously resistant to treatment: it is a highly persistent perversion.) In its efforts not to "give scandal", it appeared that the Church authorities had virtually facilitated a paedophile to continue in his weakness. We must, as Leslie Stephens once said, distinguish between a vice and a weakness: the first is a conscious and deliberate choice, the second may be a personality problem over which there is less control.

Smyth was a priest with the Norbertine order. He was arrested by the RUC in March 1991 on suspicion of offences against children while in Northern Ireland, and released on bail of £100; he returned to his monastery at Holy Trinity Abbey, Ballyjamesduff, which is across the border in the Republic. He subsequently refused to return to the jurisdiction of Northern Ireland in order to have enquiry papers served on him, and declined to answer or return calls from the police in the North.

"Instead, he used the abbey to shelter from the law, and throughout his more than two years on the run played a game of cat and mouse with the detectives by continuing to make secret trips back to Belfast to visit family and friends," wrote Chris Moore, who investigated the Smyth case for Ulster TV and wrote a coruscating book about it. The Irish Attorney-General's office — which had been so extraordinarily speedy in acting on the notorious X case, when a 14-year-old rape victim went to London for an abortion — dawdled like an Ottoman bureaucracy when it came to Brendan Smyth. There was no urgency in extraditing him. It emerged, in October 1994, that warrants issued by the RUC in April 1993 had never been acted upon, and the papers lay mouldering in the Attorney-General's Dublin office.

Questions were raised in the Dáil. The Taoiseach's deputy, the Tánaiste, was not happy with the way the Coalition administration of Albert Reynolds was handling this; the Labour Party refused to support the Government and the Government fell, to be replaced by a three party coalition, led by John Bruton. The Peace Process in Northern Ireland had commenced in August 1994, when the IRA had declared a cease-fire, and Albert Reynolds had been a key figure in supporting this procedure. Mr Bruton's party, traditionally more hostile to the IRA and extreme nationalists, would now assume the reins. Some observers predicted that the Peace Process would falter without the stewardship of Albert Reynolds — all because of a paedophile priest. The Peace Process did in fact go forward, but when there was a setback, in February 1996, with an IRA bomb in the London docklands, some in Dublin claimed that the breakdown might never have occurred if Albert Reynolds had still been Taoiseach.

But the Brendan Smyth affair made international headlines because of its political significance. The priest was finally charged in Belfast, convicted and imprisoned for a long spell. His victims had been a series of young children, though a curiously Victorian aspect of the affair was that reports refused to clarify what acts Brendan Smyth had actually carried out. After some difficulty, I finally ascertained that his offence had been to interfere with young boys and girls by fingering their genitals. (Some of Smyth's former victims initially failed to report his behaviour not just because they were inhibited by the power of the Church, but because in the words of one of them "there are good priests at the abbey, very good priests, and I would not want to hurt them".)

The episode seemed yet another onslaught in the ongoing decline and fall of the Irish Catholic Church. Another shocker hit the country in 1995 with revelations about the life of Father Michael Cleary.

Michael Cleary had died of cancer in 1993. He had been one of Dublin's best-known and most popular priests. Back in the 1960s he had been hailed as the best type of modernising young priest, hip and cool, accessible to the young, quick to play a guitar and sing a pop song, and yet at the same time possessing firm moral convictions and a strong social conscience. Michael Cleary spoke with a working-class Dublin accent, and did not seem to seek the refinements of bourgeois trappings.

In more recent years, he had felt himself marginalised because he had been so affirmative on the pro-life issue. He had made himself visible on two issues that the "liberal establishment" disliked: radicalism on property — he campaigned for the homeless — and a firm stand against abortion. He had an aversion to abortion which ran from some deeper emotional vein than logical argument alone.

There is often a personal reason at the back of logical arguments anyhow, and in Michael Cleary's case it emerged that the personal reason was that he had secretly fathered two children himself. People who beget children in clandestine circumstances know how much easier it would have been to choose abortion, for abortion removes the evidence and no one need ever know. Bishop Casey, for all his left-wing views on other issues, remained passionately anti-abortion.

But when it emerged, in 1995, more than a year after Michael Cleary's death, that he had had a hidden private life with Phyllis Hamilton, who was his wife in everything but name, and that he had had two children, one of whom was placed for adoption, it seemed to Catholic Ireland yet another shocking case of priestly hypocrisy. "My Secret Life as Priest's Wife for Twenty-Seven Years" was a splash front-page headline for the Dublin tabloid, the *Sunday World*. Ireland was again agog with astonishment, bewilderment, disappointment and prurience. What was further dismaying about the Cleary case was that his companion, Ms Hamilton, had originally been a homeless girl he had taken in for protection. It seemed to be breaking a trust to offer a young woman the protection of a home, and then to cohabit with her.

In a sense, Michael Cleary's case was harder to understand than Bishop Casey's, or even the cases of the paedophile priests, who were subject to a perversion they may have found uncontrollable. Eamonn Casey had had an affair, which anyone can understand and identify with; after it was all over, he had put it to the back of his mind and hoped it would recede into the past. That too is perfectly understandable: most people hope their sins will not be found out. (Casey's tactical error was to continue as a high-profile member of the hierarchy after the event.) But with Michael Cleary, his domestic arrangements were a continuing, ongoing situation, even while he was apparently living the life of a celibate and crusading priest. Catholics are taught that they must affirm even what they cannot practise. Perhaps Cleary believed that he was striking the best compromise he could: who are we to judge his motives? But most people who knew him — and I knew him slightly — were struck dumb by the post-mortem revelations of his circumstances. I was also surprised to note, at his funeral, that his sisters arrived dripping in furs and gold jewellery. This was the "working-class Dublin priest"? His folks were publicans and publicans are traditionally rich.

Both Michael Cleary and Eamonn Casey had been most visibly involved with the Pope's historic visit to Ireland in 1979.

In response to all these horrors, Bishop Brendan Comiskey, the Bishop of Ferns in south-east Ireland, had said that the church must learn to be humbler in accepting its errors. Now he too was in the frame: he disappeared to the United States in 1995 to seek treatment for alcoholism at a time when he was being publicly accused of complacency over a paedophile priest in his diocese. The Health Board authority in the area had concluded in report that Father Jim Grennan, by now deceased, had sexually abused seven children. Despite this, Grennan had appeared at the altar for a major confirmation service, under the protection, it seemed, of Bishop Comiskey. Parents of the abused children walked out of the church, and there remained throughout the area a feeling of shattered betrayal.

In March 1999 another priestly scandal broke in Bishop Comiskey's diocese in the Wexford town on Fethard-on-Sea, which had gained some notoriety in 1957 when a sectarian spat broke out and some Protestant shops were boycotted. Father John Fortune, a flamboyant priest with a knack of raising money, committed suicide; he too was wanted in connection with a child-abuse sexual charge and misappropriation of funds. He was said to have created his own little empire at Fethard, undisturbed by Episcopal supervision. "The priest was disporting himself like the mediaeval Cardinal Wolsey," wrote John Drennan in the *Sunday Independent*. "A chancellor was even appointed to cycle around the parish collecting his 'levies'." He bid fair to take over the town's community life: it was said that only the GAA could stand up to him.

The last years of the 1990s and the turn of the century into the new millennium were marked by a continuing stream of priestly and religious scandals. Television programmes were broadcast and books were published revealing horrible cruelty and physical abuse suffered by orphans and children in care under the supervision of nuns and priests (notably Bernadette Fahy's story of surviving Goldenbridge Orphanage, *Freedom of Angels* and Mary Raftery's and Eoin O'Sullivan's *Suffer the Little Children*). Goldenbridge Orphanage in Dublin, run by flinty-hearted nuns, had also been the subject of a harrowing television documentary. Equally distressing were the accounts which emerged about the treatment of unmarried mothers and "fallen women" in the Magdalen Laundries, which had been run by religious orders in the earlier part of the century. The Magdalen homes were an idea copied from Scottish Calvinism — examined by Linda Mahood in her study *The Magdalenes*. In the 1920s and '30s, the Catholic press had been proud of the reputation of the Magdalen homes in their care for "poor fallen women". It had been regarded as an act of charity to house such unfortunates and to allow them to work out their redemption in laundry work. Now it emerged as a thoroughly brutal idea.

The press coverage of the Irish Catholic Church in the last years of the century was ferocious: it would have been difficult to have found anyone in the secular press with a good word to say. Many of the fiercest critics now were women. "To hell with prayers," wrote Mary-Ellen Synon in the *Sunday Independent*. If the Church had been more proactive in cleaning up its act, instead of passively calling for prayer and understanding, some of the victims of their cruelty might have been spared their experiences. It was true that the responses of the Church itself always seemed weak; it would try not to let such abuses happen again; there would be guidelines and workshops and counselling and helplines. A million pounds was immediately spent on a helpline and counselling for abuse victims of the industrial schools mentioned in *Suffer the Little Children*. It was ironic that the Catholic Church was using the very psychotherapeutic techniques which, 50 years previously, it had so condemned in the works of Freud.

Mary McAleese, a prominent academic and Belfast Catholic, soon to become President of Ireland, described the Catholic Church in Ireland in 1995 as "a shabby, bleak procession of Pontius Pilate lookalikes, abusing priests, disinterested [sic] abbots, impotent cardinals and unempowered parents". Nell McCafferty, a Derry radical and nationally known feminist, wrote that Catholic priests had lost all credibility on sexual issues and should never be trusted alone with children again. They had lost all entitlement to discourse upon sexual morality. "Next time they open their mouths on love, sex, contraception, abortion, homosexuality, pleasure — on anything that goes on between consenting healthy adults — their words should be publicly quoted back to them. They did not know; did not appreciate; did not understand ... Now let them shut up while people put themselves and their families back together again and knock some delicious, loving sexual pleasure out of life. In the meantime, beware the local priest. He is a danger to your mental, physical and sexual health. Never leave one alone with a child. Not ever."

There were stories and bad-taste jokes about priests and paedophilia ("What do curates have after dinner?" "Under Eights."). On a BBC Radio 4 quiz game there was a category called "Priests, Ireland and Debauchery". In November 1995 the Cardinal-Archbishop of Ireland, Cathal Daly, who had preached so hard and so long against violence in the North and striven so much to show a true Christian spirit to all, was put through a public humiliation on the national TV network's *The Late Late Show*. The audience jeered at him so that he could hardly finish a sentence. Other priests in the studio adopted the tone of the audience; there was a distinct mood of the medieval stocks.

Father Brian D'Arcy, the influential media priest with a significant following, said that the problem was that the Church had shown its hardness towards people — by not accepting divorce, for example, and those in second relationships — and it was all coming back on them now. The Cardinal was charged with not supporting the ordination of women and a variety of other liberal measures. This did not have a lot to do with the question of erring priests — the acceptance of married priests might have been nearer the mark — but those who had found the Church's laws exacting gained a certain satisfaction from seeing the institution brought low.

In January 1996 the Catholic hierarchy launched its report *Child Sex Abuse — Framework for a Church Response* after "virtual persecution in the media over publicized cases of sexual abuse by priests and religion", as the publication *Response* noted. This document pledged that where clerics were accused of abuse and there were reasonable grounds for suspicion, cases would be handed over to the Garda. "The days of shifting a priest accused of sexual abuse from parish to parish, diocese to diocese, or country to country, are over," reported *Response*. The *Irish Times* called it "Beginning the Healing," but noted: "It will take a long time for the scars left by these scandals to heal. New wounds are still being opened in the courts almost every week." There continued to be more cases in the pipeline.

There are 17,000 religious in Ireland: we might, I believe, suppose that 16,900 of them are not committing and never have committed, any form of abuse of minors. And that most of them are not breaking their vows. I have never knowingly met a priest or a nun who has behaved improperly, and those I have met who have kicked against the system, such as Pat Buckley (he set up his own church and made himself a bishop in it), struck me as oddballs, or screwballs. Most priests I have known have been good people: one has to judge as one finds. Most nuns I have known have been dedicated to their cause, be it the education of girls or the relief of the poor. A minor, and altogether feminine, streak of snobbery is the worst charge I would make against nuns. A lot of Irish people of my vintage would feel the same way: priests, in any case, are their brothers, their uncles, their cousins, as are religious sisters family members.

And yet the scandals left the people with the feeling that the clerical way of life was in itself an error, and that Catholicism as a system had been seen to fail to practise the virtues it so ardently preached. It seemed perhaps that the priests who had been anathematised — such as the liberal Father James Good, who had been "silenced" in the 1960s for his opposition to *Humanae Vitae*'s ban on artificial birth control, were the decent ones, whereas priests such as Father Ivan Payne, jailed for appalling child-abuse offences, had been an acceptable part of the system. It was as though everything the Catholic establishment stood for had turned out to be wrong, and everything it had opposed turned out to be right. Even those values which the Catholic Church advanced, and which the people agreed with, such as opposition to abortion, seemed cheapened and discredited by the treatment which had been meted out to helpless children. If the child in the womb was to be valued, why was the child in the orphanage, the industrial school, or in care to be beaten and terrorised?

The very concept of "Catholic Ireland" was, by the end of the century, gone. It was mercilessly caricatured in television farce such as in the popular, well-over-the-top comedy *Father Ted*, in which priests appeared as jokers, fools or debauched old drunks crying "Drink! Feck! Women!" The very phrase "Catholic Ireland" was deemed repulsive, and offensively sectarian too: it was, moreover, hurtful ("hurtful" being the vogue Millennium word) to Protestants, Jews, Muslims and non-believers. Ireland, whose economy had suddenly taken off in the 1990s, would look forward to a pluralist, multi-ethnic future in which the phrase "Catholic Ireland" had no place. Modern-minded younger Irish people were now keen to remove the last vestiges of "the confessional state", as they disparagingly called it, from culture and society. There is a movement to remove the angelus bell which marks midday, six o'clock and midnight on radio and television, and to annul the aspects of the Irish Constitution which refer to God. Ireland did not *need* Catholicism any more to bolster its identity, or to distinguish it from the British: it was now a confident, rich country with its own identity, in which Catholicism played no necessary part.

"Political vision and world-class talent have transformed Ireland from a priest-ridden backwater to a confident nation on the cutting edge of a new Europe," wrote John Naughton in the *Observer*. Ireland, wrote *Time* magazine, had finally come of age, having thrown off its ancient hatred of Britain and its traditional deference to the Church. "Ould Ireland's gone forever," Fintan O'Toole wrote triumphantly in the *Guardian*: the hold of the Catholic Church was broken. Ireland was, thankfully, moving towards liberal secularism, and being Irish was becoming *cool*. This was only possible because being Irish had lost the label of also being Catholic. "Thank goodness for the demise of Catholic Ireland, both as a meaningless slogan and a meretricious reality," wrote Sean O'Conaill in the *Catholic Herald*. By common agreement, it was indeed "Goodbye to Catholic Ireland".

Fifteen

What Heritage for Catholic Ireland?

"I have always wondered how the Catholic Church
got such a stranglehold on the Irish. They are such a
pagan race."

John Boorman, British film-maker, *The New Statesman*,
22 May 1998

"While still a fledgling state off the coast of Britain,
Ireland had clung to anything that helped to define it
as something other than British. Now, as it matures in
the company of other Europeans, the country can be
whatever it wants. And what it wants to be is secular.
Up to a point."

Marian Keyes, *Sunday Times* survey on Irish 30-year-olds,
February 2000

In the wake of the clerical scandals, all surveys showed a
decline in the Catholic Church's credibility and a growing
hostility towards the institutions of Catholicism. And among a
younger generation, it appeared that many aspects of Catholic
teaching seemed vague and unfamiliar. Teachers of religion,
such as Anne Looney, writing in the mid-nineties in *The Church
in a New Ireland* (edited by Sean MacReamoinn), noted that the
average class of high school children in Dublin had scarcely
heard of Lent, and the concept of a penitential season —
unvaryingly observed as part of the national way of life 30

years previously — was greeted with a puzzled silence. Traditionally, the significance of St Patrick's Day in Ireland, on March 17, was that it was a welcome break in Lent. Lent was a time not only for fast and abstinence, but a season when marriages did not take place, and dances and parties were off the menu. In what we knew of Catholic Ireland, that was the way of life, just as the season of Ramadan is part of any Islamic community or state.

Surveys in the mid-nineties, comparing attitudes in Britain, the United States and the Republic of Ireland, indicated that the young Irish were actually more materialistic than their neighbours across the Irish Sea or across the Atlantic. By 2000 a special *Sunday Times* survey of Irish 30-year-olds was claiming that, for the young Irish today, "Money is the new religion and they're queuing to pay homage to the folding stuff. God plays second fiddle to Bill Gates, hell is a two-mile tailback on the Stillorgan dual carriageway, while sin is forgetting to nail down decent equity options. This generation is more likely to worship at a stock exchange than at a cathedral, to seek a pension advisor than a confessor." Both politics and religion were less significant (and less esteemed) than the "dash for cash".

Ireland had undergone a radical culture change from the early 1990s, with the rise of a boom economy dubbed the Celtic Tiger (in imitation of the so-called Asian tiger economies of the Far East). This was, in effect, a capitalist revolution the impact of which has been sensational. In 1986 the Irish economy had been on the verge of bankruptcy. Successive governments had over-borrowed, over-taxed and over-spent: it was a pauper economy, condemned by such illuminati as the *Economist* magazine, under the headline: "How the government spent the people into a slump." Ireland had the second highest rate of unemployment in the European Community, after Spain.

Ten years later, after introducing fiscal disciplines, liberalising the economic structures and curbing government spending, Ireland was being praised as the fastest-growing economy in Europe. European structural funds helped to improve conditions and thereby attract investment, but the change went beyond mere subsidy. People began to believe that by their own enterprise, they could prosper. The fall of the

Berlin Wall in 1989 had a psychological effect, too: people stopped believing in socialism or socialistic nostrums, notwithstanding the fact that the UK, France and Germany all returned left-of-centre governments in the mid-1990s. (The example of Sweden, where too much welfarism and government spending had radically slowed down the growth of the economy, was also no end of a lesson.)

By the beginning of the Millennium, the Irish economy's performance was astonishing; unemployment was down to about four per cent, which technically is full employment. The Tánaiste, Mary Harney, announced in spring 2000 that Ireland would have to attract 200,000 new skilled workers by immigration.

Not since the Norman invasion of 1169 had Ireland been a country of worker immigration.

For as long as anyone can remember, Ireland has been a poor country. Its poetry and songs, its patriotic pride and its exiles' yearnings, have all been posited on this poverty, or lack of materialism. Its leaders, like de Valera, have praised an ideal of wholesome simplicity and the high-mindedness of "frugal comforts": Dev wanted the Irish people to be devoted "to the things of the spirit". Its religion too has underlined the holiness of poverty and the shallowness of money and possessions. The beauty of prayers was illuminated by the mendicant poverty — and humility — of the supplicant, and the material world itself was an "exile" from our true home in Heaven. Now, a whole culture, a whole heritage, had to be reconstructed, it seemed. There are some poor people in Ireland (and there is deprivation linked to social problems such as family breakdown and dysfunction, drugs and alcohol abuse), but Ireland is no longer a poor country, and will almost certainly become an exceptionally rich country.

Market capitalism, which is essential to the Celtic tiger boom, depends on individual lifestyle choices, initiative and tolerance of diversity. It also depends on people valuing, not rebuffing, material gain. The authoritarianism of the Catholic Church, with its traditional stress on orthodoxy, is anathema to the market. Individualism is essential. Those who have studied their Max Weber (*The Protestant Work Ethic and the Rise of*

Capitalism) would say that it was not coincidental that Catholicism receded as capitalism triumphed; they would say it was necessary for Catholicism to recede in order for capitalism to triumph. The Protestant mindset, that you make your own choices for salvation, bypassing any form of "priestcraft", is a cultural precondition for free market capitalism. Were there any conspiracy-theory Trotskyists left under the age of 60, they might almost suspect a capitalist plot to discredit the priests, to free Ireland for market capitalism.

The clerical scandals of the 1990s were certainly appalling: lowering, depressing and unedifying. They shamed a system which had been so high-minded in upholding chastity and continence. They hugely undermined the Church's authority to teach and preach. They made people angry and distrustful, both at the evidence of sexual abuse and at the apparent covering-up of such occurrences. They put every priest and nun in the dock and, when a cleric was accused of a crime, the benefit of the doubt seemed to be withheld. A dreadful case was heard before Dublin's Central Criminal Court in June 1999, when it was reported that a nun had "held a young girl by the ankles while a man raped her in her bed in a childcare centre".

The victim, it was reported, was 10 at the time, and the 50-year-old Mercy nun, Nora Wall, was charged with rape and unlawful carnal knowledge, along with the alleged male perpetrator. The case was subsequently withdrawn, on the instructions of the Director of Public Prosecutions: it was ill-constructed and should not have been brought. Nora Wall was freed but no apology was issued to her. The tenor of the reporting made sensational claims about the nun charged with rape, and it almost seemed that the public, sated on sex abuse cases involving the clergy, were prepared to believe the worst. "No priest or nun — as poor Nora Wall has discovered — is given the benefit of the doubt any more," wrote Kevin Myers in *The Irish Times.* "The accusation serves as a conviction, the allegation as a proof: the hallmark of the true witch-hunt."

Almost as distressing as the clerical sex scandals were the revelations of cruelty perpetrated by religious towards Irish children in state care, as most particularly highlighted by Mary Raftery and Eoin O'Sullivan in a television series and a book,

Suffer the Little Children. This was a detailed study of industrial schools — in fact, reformatories — and so-called orphanages run by religious, on behalf of the Irish state, from the 1920s up to the 1970s. What emerged was an unremitting catalogue of cruelty, neglect and abuse, with witness after witness recalling the most dreadful beatings and unwarranted punishments inflicted on helpless children. These children and young people were often put into the institutions for trifling offences — playing truant from school, for example — or were placed in state care because their parents were too poor to cope. It was suggested that in some cases the religious sought to maximise their "clientele" — to have a continuing flow of children placed in their care — so as to obtain the state fee for each child.

The scale of the cruelty seemed so systematic that it was as though it was inherent to the structure of our history. Not only were the religious who ran these institutions accused before the bar of history: so was the Irish state, which utterly failed to take responsibility for those in its care. So, indeed, were the complacent middle classes, who used these reformatories as a source for servants, and so was the media, which remained indifferent to the punitive regimes around them.

Reviewing the television broadcast of the series in the *Sunday Independent*, Brendan O'Connor wrote in May 1999: "Our dark past has become an original sin that blackens the soul of every man, woman and child in this country." Facing the cruelty meted out to children in the care of the Catholic Church and the Irish state has become, for the Irish, a similar exercise to the French facing the fact that the majority of the nation probably collaborated with the Nazi occupation. Indeed, more than once the victims of the Catholic Church have been compared, in the Irish media, to the victims of Nazism. This is patently wrong, since millions did not die in gas chambers, but it is a measure of how strong the reaction has been to the revelations of past injustices.

And these revelations, aggregated by the sexual scandals, add up to a wholesale discrediting of the heritage of Catholic Ireland. If everything in the past was so wrong, does it not change the way that we view our past? For along with Catholic Ireland, Mary Raftery and Eoin O'Sullivan seem to indict independent Ireland itself. They imply that had Ireland remained within the United Kingdom, these terrible things would never have happened, since Catholic Ireland was so lamentably hand-in-hand with the Irish State. Home Rule was Rome Rule. Meanwhile, in Britain, by the 1930s, social policy was evolving and a kinder approach to child-care was developing.

The cumulative effect of clerical crimes and convent cruelty seemed to alter Irish perspectives on our collective heritage. So the *Angela's Ashes* movie was correct, after all: Catholic Ireland had been a horrible society, in which horrible people prevailed. It had been a society in which harshness made for inhumanity.

In 1957 a Dublin Jesuit, Father Kevin Smyth, said that he thought that the chastity of the Irish priest was inextricably linked with the chastity of the Irish people, a fact often remarked upon by visitors. "Priestly purity would not endure if the people were not chaste: we depend more than perhaps we realise on the goodness of our people." Forty years later, this was seen not as an encomium but as a problem. The cult of chastity had had too high a price. It had driven men into perverted conduct and made women cruel and hard. "Too long a sacrifice," wrote Yeats, "can make a stone of the heart." The wholesale emphasis in Irish Catholic culture on "the things of the spirit" had turned into a dreadful tormenting of the creatures of flesh and blood. The famous old Irish stoicism — Offer It Up — had made a stone of the heart. What emerges in the Raftery/O'Sullivan study was that those who raised children seemed to care *only* for their spirits, to the detriment of the children's starved and beaten little bodies, and their own humanity.

As a matter of a fact, even if these scandals had never happened or been revealed so sensationally, Ireland would have grown more secular, along with the rest of Europe, anyhow. Indeed, the Protestant churches in Ireland, which were not publicly involved in such sex scandals, were subjected to the same decline as the Catholic Church. Younger Protestants were not going to church, and it was not linked, now, with the spectre of intermarriage (Protestant-Catholic intermarriage is not significantly high). The Church of Ireland won great praise from the Irish media for ordaining women, in the 1990s, but it in no measure added to its congregations. The media likes the notion of ordained women as a progressive idea, but the media seldom adds to the numbers at worship.

Before 1992, the benchmark year that began the avalanche of these scandals, secularism was gaining ground and indeed had been doing so since the 1970s, when the Irish Church, under the stewardship of Cardinal Conway, consciously began to "withdraw gracefully" from the political sphere of influence. From the 1980s the Catholic Church, which had fought long and hard to retain control of education, initially against British secularising ideas, began to perceive that lay teachers would eventually take over the bulk of the schools, and that the schools would become largely laicised.

Indeed, the Catholic Church bequeathed to the Irish state, and to the Irish people, an education system in mint condition, an education system which has been crucial to the success of the Celtic Tiger economy. The stunning performance of the Irish economy was facilitated by two facts. One is that Ireland is an English-speaking country, despite countless millions of pounds, not to mention blood, sweat and tears, having been spent on the revival of the Irish language, and using English fluently and articulately has made Ireland a European centre for teleservices and computer-based investment (since English is the world business language). The second is that because large Catholic families were still in production back in the 1960s and 1970s, a disproportionately high percentage of the Irish population is young. This is the population which has adapted to the new information technologies, and been well educated in schools founded by the Catholic Church. (The much-criticised Christian Brothers schools have produced a particularly high rate of successful, and rich, young achievers, as the number of old CBS boys listed in Maureen Cairnduff's *Who's Who in Ireland* indicates.)

The religious withdrawal from education reflected the recession of Catholic power over the last 30 years of the 20th century. It also reflected the fall in vocations to the religious life which began to decline after 1965, the end of Vatican II. Religious practice among the young was reducing by the 1970s, and with the death of the de Valera generation — Dev died in 1975 — a certain idea of Ireland as an Irish Catholic nation was fading too. The 1980s marked the beginning of the drug affliction in Dublin and, soon, elsewhere in the country. Religious practice declined most dramatically in poorer parts of Dublin, just as drug use rose: by the end of the 1980s Tallaght, in west Dublin, had one of the lowest church-going figures in the country — about eight per cent of the population were regular church-goers. It seemed that the poor swapped their devotions for the valium pill and the heroin needle. Events in Northern Ireland were hardly an edifying signifier for religion. As the world media characterised the conflict as being between Catholics and Protestants, the tabloid view gained ground that all wars are caused by religion — never mind claims of land, tribe, flag, ethnicity, resources or the impact of colonising invasions.

When it was reported that the Blessed Virgin was said to be appearing at Ballinspittle, West Cork, in 1985, the intellectuals' interpretation of this phenomenon was that it was "the last cry" of a dying order. (The Church, ever conservative to recognise apparitions, did not give its imprimatur.) It was old Ireland's fanciful fantasy.

The bitter culture wars over abortion and divorce in the 1980s deepened the consciousness of a liberal versus a conservative Ireland. And sad incidents occurred, which people often took to be the fault of Catholic Ireland, such as the Kerry Babies scandal in April 1984, when a newborn baby's body was found on a Kerry beach, stabbed several times. A young unmarried mother who had indeed given birth to a child who had died — although a different baby — was arrested for the crime. But the Gardaí had clearly erred, and a tribunal of inquiry was held. The case was never really resolved satisfactorily, but the world media descended on Ireland and the Kerry Babies scandal was reported as a "typical" tale of cruel scapegoating of single mothers in an over-moralistic climate.

The Ann Lovett case in January 1984 was even more pitiful: she was a 15-year-old girl from Granard, Co Longford, who died giving birth to a child in a Church grotto. She had gone there, apparently, in the hope that the Blessed Virgin would assist her. The local people closed ranks and refused to assist an invading media, in a stubborn collective act of solidarity. There were calls for another inquiry, but local feeling was too uncooperative to any inquisition. The Minister for Education at the time, Gemma Hussey, felt that the only remedy was a wider application of sex education, and this has been implemented in the school curriculum, despite objections that the drift of such sex-education is too "value-free".

The phenomenon of young girls giving birth to clandestine infants was widely ascribed to Ireland's Catholicity and backwardness. It was suggested that if condoms were more widely available (there were still some restrictions on the display of contraceptives until the mid-nineties), these things would not happen. In fact, clandestine birth has been a growing problem in many countries — young girls can go into a particular kind of denial about a pregnancy. In March 2000 the city of Hamburg in Germany took drastic action by establishing a safe "baby dump", in an effort to cope with the problem of dead and abandoned babies. Despite access to contraception and a liberal abortion law, the number of clandestine births and abandoned infants in Britain steadily increased throughout the 1990s. Yet when it occurs in Ireland, the Catholic Church is somehow held to blame.

Indeed, by the 1980s, the Catholic Church in Ireland was already being held to blame for much that was going wrong in Irish society. The decline of the Catholic Church in Ireland curiously mirrored the problems occurring with the Royal Family in Britain; it had become the constant object of media speculation and criticism, the ridiculed "outdated" symbol of an unacceptable past ill-attuned to the modern age. Books about Ireland, which had been lavish in their praise of the charm and sweetness of Irish Catholicity in the 1930s and '40s, were, by the 1980s, critical and sour. As soon as the drug problem arose in Dublin in the mid-1980s, the Catholic Church was blamed for this affliction too (rather than the criminals who had introduced opiates). It was, it was claimed, the Catholic Church's repression which had led to drug abuse.

The secularisation of contemporary society is an accepted fact, just as it is a fact that science and technology play an ever greater role in our lives today. Mores have changed. Young Irish people today have no problem with divorce or cohabitation. (The Taoiseach, Bertie Ahern, is separated from his wife and goes about the world with a companion, which is coolly accepted as his choice.) 30 per cent of children in the Republic are now born out of wedlock — until 1979 it was always below five per cent, and during many earlier decades it was around two per cent. Homosexuality is regarded tolerantly, though less approved of by older people — but that would be a similar profile in Britain, France or the United States. Abortion is the secular value which has made least inroads among the Irish: some may practise it, but few approve of it. Politics and politicians, the subjects of a series of scandals in the late 1990s, are not esteemed by the young. Individualism, and libertarianism, have grown apace. Censorship of any kind is regarded as unacceptable.

These trends are broadly similar everywhere. But in post-Catholic Ireland there is added to the generalised secularisation apparent elsewhere a sense of "the payback agenda". The opinion-formers in Irish society seem uniformly to believe that Catholic Ireland was a mistake, from beginning to end. Power corrupts: absolute power corrupts absolutely. The Church had too much power and actually created an environment where bad men and spiteful women could prevail. The clergy, and traditional Catholics in Ireland, have grown accustomed to the idea that the Church gets a terrible press. When Pope John Paul II issued his celebrated apology for the Church's sins in the past, it was predictable that Vincent Browne in *The Irish Times* should see fit to comment that the Pontiff had not gone half far enough. Many more apologies are to be demanded.

As a journalist dividing my time between working in London and Dublin, my experience is that it is much less of a disadvantage being identified as a Catholic in London than in Dublin. In the London media, it can be helpful to be a Catholic: you are expected to know about a range of moral issues which are continuously up for discussion. In the Dublin media, it is a distinct disadvantage if you are known to be an observant

Catholic; it is even considered risible and absurd. As political correctness in Britain and America has come to mean rigid conformity to a set of liberal orthodoxies, so, in Ireland, it has come to mean opposition to the Catholic Church, and the concept known as "Catholic Ireland". The decline of socialism has made a quirky contribution too: rich Irish liberals, in possession of a house worth half a million pounds and a range of glittering share options, feel it would be a little incongruous to write "Up Cuba" on their metaphorical copybooks. But they feel they must have one last remaining gasp of radicalism to stay cool in their own self-esteem, and that is where anti-Catholicism comes in, dead handy.

And yet, in spite of all the indicators which show the decline of Catholic Ireland, I personally believe that there will be a resurrection of the values it represented, and a continuity of the faith itself. It will, in the future, be a different kind of "Catholic Ireland" from the one we once knew, not least because the Ireland of the future will become a more diverse society, with more immigrants − certainly more Muslims, for example − and more people of colour, who may have different religions or none. Or these may, too, be Catholics, since the one charge that cannot be made against Catholicism is that it was racist. I also believe there will be some kind of a "united Ireland" in the near future, but not the united Ireland of song and story, as dreamed of by Wolfe Tone or Robert Emmet. There will be some kind of a "reconstituted Ireland", possibly based on a federal system, which will knit together North and South in economic cooperation. Economic cooperation and working together as a single market would be favourable for prosperity.

A unified or reconstituted Ireland, of whatever kind, will enhance the Catholic Church: Catholicism does better when it is part of the nation, rather than part of the state; it does better when it is not a monopoly, or part of a political system, but holds the hearts of the people.

In the melting-pot of values, tolerance will be essential, but so will continuity. Yet the more secular society becomes, the more people need moral values, and indeed a spiritual life, as a counterpoint to the cold legality and neutral materialisation of globalised culture. Parents, as we know, call for a secular society and then desire that their daughters be sent to a convent school, so as to be formed in an ambiance of moral values.

Irish parents, who might favour a more secularised state in general, still seem to wish their children to attend schools with a religious ethos: schools which provide a religious background constantly pass the market test of attracting more pupils. As the novelist Marian Keyes has observed in the *Sunday Times* Irish youth survey, parenthood has a peculiar effect on sophisticated 30-somethings. "One couple I know lived together for years, got married in a civil ceremony on a boat in the Caribbean, and never put foot in a church except on Christmas Day. But now their eldest child is approaching school-going age and they've started going to Mass *en famille.*" In Maytime, the streets of Dublin are beflowered by sweet little girls in their First Holy Communion frocks: the rites of passage of First Communion and confirmation have remained important.

And contradictorily too, despite the recent discovery of the joys of money, the Irish remain a spiritual people. Indeed, in a 1999 Eurobarometer survey, young Irish people still emerged as the most spiritual in Euroland. Over 48 per cent of the Irish aged between 15 and 24 still believe in God and practise their faith. (This contrasts with just 8 per cent in France.) A 1998 study carried out by the Irish Bishops Council for Research and Development found that although Irish Catholics felt the Church had been seriously damaged by scandals, nevertheless their own personal beliefs and practices continued. This was what George Bernard Shaw always said: in Ireland, the church is the people.

In grassroots Ireland, pilgrimages and novenas remain popular. Local saints are honoured and the dead are prayed for. An Irish funeral is still something which the Church handles with beauty, sensitivity and delicacy. It is surprising, in the end, how many apparent agnostics, or even anti-Catholic Catholics, are accompanied on their final journey with bell, book and candle. The terrifying increase in suicide, particularly among young males, which is too dramatic and too recent to be ascribed to mere under-reporting in the past, may be linked to the decline in religion: yet it is also an area where pastoral care is often most urgently needed, and where certain priests exercise a gift for counselling families bereaved by suicide.

The Church has been rocked; society is more secularised; prosperity is altering culture; Catholic power has receded. But the faith goes on.

History changes perspectives, and will continue to change perspectives. What we think now will not be what people think in 30 years' time. Events in history are continually reassessed, and new developments put past occurences in a constantly changing light. In the fullness of time, much that is now disparaged about Catholic Ireland will be seen in a more mellow context. People always have done bad things, and always will do bad things: that is not the fault of any institution but part of human nature. That is the meaning of original sin. Even paedophile scandals take on a different perspective as time passes and data grows: Raftery and O'Sullivan may claim that Britain evolved a more humane system to treat children in care, but that has not stopped ghastly child abuse crimes occurring in British care homes either. In February 2000, the Waterhouse report in Britain uncovered an extensive system of child abuse in Welsh children's homes during the 1980s: hundreds, perhaps thousands, of children were subjected to paedophile cruelty and abuse. Expert opinion is now tending to the view that anywhere there are children, paedophiles are drawn. This excuses nothing, but it explains something.

What must be understood, above all, about the history of Catholic Ireland is that the Church never did "get a stranglehold on the Irish", as John Boorman puts it. At all times in history, the Catholic Church in Ireland came from the heart, soul and will of the Irish people. It was not an invading or occupying force: it grew organically out of the soil, the land, the sea, the climate, the sky. At all times it reflected the values of Irish society, as well as reacting to values and trends in universal culture.

Catholic Ireland represented the heart of the historical nation, but it did not ask for a Catholic State. The Church was against the Rising of 1916, and against the establishment of a wholly independent State. Catholic Ireland was presented with the Irish Free State in 1921, and launched its mission statement calling for a classless society dedicated to justice, culture, voluntarism and mental and physical health. It did not live up to its ideals, but neither do most of us.

Mrs Catherine Broadberry, who was born in Co Meath in 1930, wrote to me in the mid-1990s and described the Catholic values of her childhood. The faith, she says, was "very precious really, something very wonderful, still ongoing and deeply imbedded with us: part of us. We learned so much from our parents, within our own homes, and saw also the results of our labours, which to me were 'labours of love'." I have with me still my mother's well-thumbed prayer book, with its devotions and prayers so ardently offered up: thus the faith was transmitted, as a pearl beyond price, which should raise our hearts and fill our souls with rapture.

Sixteen

Remembrance of Times Past:

Distinguished Irish Voices on
Catholic Ireland

As the 20th century turned into the 21st, and we entered the third Christian millennium, the Ireland which my generation had known, when young, was fading. There have been many critical, and some savage, accounts of Catholic Ireland in the years of the mid-20th century, when the Irish State reflected, almost monopolistically, Catholic values. But there are also many benign recollections of Ireland as it was then. As a coda to my own researches, I have collected here the memories and impressions of some distinctive Irish voices ...

Maeve Binchy

is probably the most successful Irish author in the world, constantly at the top of the Irish, British and American best-seller lists in popular fiction. She is also one of the best-loved of Irish authors, as well as a journalist of distinction and wit. She was raised a Catholic, but is not now a believer. She is married to writer Gordon Snell and lives in Dalkey, Co Dublin.

Like every other Irish child born around 1940, I thought that the Pope had been a guest at my parents' wedding. The papal blessing was there on the wall saying that William and Maureen had prostrated themselves at his feet, and I knew they had never been in Rome. I wasn't sure how he had been let out for the day, but guessed he must have worked something.

I thought the angelus rang at 12 noon and 6 p.m. in every country — how else would people know it was lunch time or tea time?

I was always ambitious and when I was young I wanted to be a saint. There would be a Saint Maeve's Day and children would have a holiday from school and have processions with statues of me all around the country. God was Irish and Our Lady was Irish and St Patrick was the Managing Director up there keeping our places ready for us.

And because I felt so strong, I also felt guilty about being bored by interminable sermons in a church full of coughing parishioners. Instead, I would talk to God in my head and tell Him about the world down here. Interpreting things for Him, and making endless requests. Like could He take my baby sister back. I knew I had prayed for one, but she was taking up too much time and too much attention away from me and I would have preferred a rabbit. Like that I assumed that the only reason I was fat was because God loved me so much, because I remembered that bit about whom the Lord loveth he persecutith. And being fat at school was a fair amount of persecution all right.

We had parents who loved us, a happy home, wonderful hard-working nuns who taught us well at the Holy Child Convent school, pleasant priests in the parish, so obviously our

Irish childhood passed very well indeed. I used to read school stories and wonder where the nuns *were* in them, thinking that all children *had* to be taught by nuns, otherwise it didn't take.

I never met a nun who slapped my fingers with a ruler, or was cruel. I never met a priest who threatened hell fire or excommunication. If there were Church scandals back then, and of course there must have been, we never heard of them.

We did have a distant relative, a priest who was rumoured to drink a little too much whiskey, but the main thrust of that was to ensure that he kept well away from driving a car.

It was a very enclosed society in that we didn't travel much then, there just wasn't the money, we feared foreign influences, our books and films were censored for us. I knew I believed back then that it was very hard to get to Heaven unless you were a member of the one, true, holy Catholic and apostolic church, and used to heave a sigh of relief that I had been lucky enough to have been born within that particular tribe.

I know I thought a lot of things that might not be sound in terms of Canon Law and for this I don't blame parents, teachers or parish priests. I had and have a vivid imagination, and may have taken a lot of things on board myself. I knew a couple, a harmless middle-aged pair who had married in a registry office, not a church, and yet still attended Sunday Mass. It was an enigma that obsessed me for years. Imagine them trying to talk to God and pretend to Him that they had got married in a Church, as if He didn't know already. As if I hadn't told Him regularly, as well.

But as the years went on, everything changed. The teachings of the Second Vatican Council crept slowly in, the economy improved, the people could travel and come back rather than travel away for ever as emigrants. The wind of change that was the Sixties finally blew into Ireland, television opened up worlds far beyond our own. No longer was this comfortable safe little world, where everyone was Irish and Catholic and good, anything we could believe in.

Possibly because I was dealt a good hand with a very secure happy family life, I had no angst, resentment or rage when losing my own place in the Irish Heavenly Scene. I would *love* to believe it all again, the same way I would like a Tooth Fairy and Santa Claus. And maybe some day I will. But at the moment, if I were to try it would be like inventing a religion for myself, fooling myself and others into thinking I had a belief that is not there. I have nothing but envy for those who are still linked in. They think they will see their parents again, they think we might all be happy ever after, while I think it's a big sleep. Who would not envy the sureness and certainty of that wonderful Irish Catholic youth?

I think Catholicism in Ireland today is actually stronger and better than it was when we were young. All right, so the numbers are way down, but still, only those who really believe are part of the Church now. The attendance at Mass is not inflated by those who were only there for fear of what others might think if they did not turn up.

I don't doubt those who say they were frightened and repressed by the Church. I can only add that I never was. So obviously I don't think that the legacy of my Irish Catholic education was at all destructive or oppressive. I think it was over-colourful — filled with saints and martyrs and traditions and feast days and hymns and bells and miracles and incense — and, looking back, it was all like a huge happy pageant.

I keep hoping that somewhere along the road of the rest of my life I might meet that happy band of characters and join up with them once again.

John Banville

is an Irish novelist of international reputation and a noted literary critic for *The Irish Times* and the *New York Review of Books*. He was born in Wexford in 1945 and attended the Christian Brothers school and, later, St Peter's College. He has won many literary awards, including the Guardian Fiction Prize, the AIB Literary Award and the Italian Premio Ennio Flaiano. He is a member of Aosdána, the Irish literary academy, is married to Janet Dunham and has two sons.

I grew up in the Fifties. I am appalled when people look back at the Fifties nostalgically. Wexford was a safe town. Our horizons were very near.

I wasn't beaten very much at the Christian Brothers. There were a few who were absolute savages – I remember one saying, after Wexford had won a hurling match, that we needn't feel any pride. It was a Wexford man who brought in the British. That was Dermot McMorrough (who was responsible for bringing in the Norman English). Yet I also remember wonderful Christian Brothers, when I was small.

At the end of every day there was one who used to read us *The Wind in the Willows*. There was another who used to bring his gramophone in and play us music – a wonderful man. I remember a large good-looking man who taught us, too. He was reading a poem – a love poem – and he went blank for a moment and said, "You boys don't know what love is, but you will …". There was so much loss in that look, so much loss in his life. There were fine men amongst them.

The diocesan priests beat us far more. They were very confident of their power. I was lucky because I was clever and did my exams, so I didn't get beaten much. Once, I remember it happening. It would be three whacks on either hand as hard as he could. That was a Father Sheridan. He was a brute. There was another priest, a Father Larkin, who was absolutely wonderful. He was the English teacher who pushed me to write. I met him once, afterwards, at the airport: he was coming back from Peru where he would spend time on the missions, with poor people.

There was a dark sexuality behind the beatings. There was an awful lot of homosexuality, between the boys and between the boys and the priests. I suppose there was a deep fear of women in the Irish Church. The most wounded, the most injured of the boys would become priests themselves, I think.

Yet I'm grateful for my background in Catholic Ireland. It brings a splendid baggage of grief for any writer. And I hate to see the way the country has become so materialistic now. We had a conference at *The Irish Times* where we were discussing who we would put on Nelson's Pillar if it were to be re-erected. I suggested Bishop Casey. He caused the whole collapse. The calmness with which the country took it, really, was amazing. The whole system just collapsed, and so quickly. I heard a Dublin woman saying to a child recently: "If you don't fuckin' behave yourself, I'll send you to them paedophiles."

I think one never loses the faith, at some deep level. I think it is true that, once a Catholic, always a Catholic. I have a sister who is quite devout and she tells me that the spirituality is always there, and I'll come back to it, and maybe she is right.

Pierce Brosnan

was born in Navan, Co Meath, in 1953. His father deserted the family when Pierce was a young boy, and subsequently he and his mother went to live in the London area where she worked as a nurse. Pierce did some repertory, TV and film work in Britain before moving to America, where he became established with the TV thriller series *Remington Steele* in 1984. He appeared with Robin Williams in *Mrs Doubtfire* in 1993, and made his first James Bond movie, *Goldeneye*, in 1997. Since then he has become established as the new '007'. His first wife, Cassandra, died of cancer in 1991, and his present partner is Keely Shaye-Smith. He has two children and two step-children.

My mother and I went through a lot. She left Ireland as a deserted wife in the 1950s, and it took great courage — to go out there and try to seek a better fortune for yourself and your son. If she'd stayed in Navan, she'd have been the poor relation. She thought, bullshit, this is terrible.

It was a place ruled by religion, a place where the Church had you right there, under the thumb. Yes, the Church was supported by the people, but it was stifling, really.

I only met Tom [Pierce's father] the once. I was 33 years old, and you want to say, "Why? Why did you do it?" By that time Tom was an old man. I got along with him — good. But he was a stranger. I hadn't seen him for 33 years. Then, there's a knock on the door, your father's going to come in that door and have a cup of tea. He seemed like a nice man. But a stranger. He came with a busload of first cousins, whom I'd never seen before and have never seen since. I think they were all shocked by the media attention, after I'd been Bond.

In growing up, in becoming an actor, no one showed me the way. No one told me what to do. No one has really prepared me for anything. I found out first-hand. I just had some gut instinct or feeling about how to be an actor, exploring that part of myself, at 17 or 18. There was no one there for me. It was all in my own head.

There was no one at school. The Christian Brothers tried to mangle me — the most despicable men, cruel, cruel. If I had been to another school would I have been beaten just as hard? Maybe, but not with the word "Christian" in front of it. Those men were terrible. At last, Ireland seems to be facing its nasty little secrets.

They went way off-course from their original aims and just mangled young men. There was nothing Christian about the men who taught me in Navan. They were repressed, mean, cruel and not loving, not sharing. There was not one — not one that I saw — who was decent, who was encouraging. I saw the boys being kicked, beaten — straps, lovely little leather straps concealed beneath their habits. I get so goddam angry when I think about it. I saw what they did. I saw the consequences in other young men's lives.

That aside, the love that was there from my extended family was bountiful.

I enjoy being a family man today. I enjoy being an actor and I enjoy being a movie star. But it took me a long time to be happy and to be confident about what I'm doing. America liberated me.

Andrea Corr

> is a singer/songwriter, born in Dundalk in 1974, and the lead vocalist of the extraordinarily successful group The Corrs — a family of three sisters and a brother. Along with U2 and Riverdance, The Corrs have been named as Ireland's leading exports.

The legacy of Catholic Ireland certainly does mean a lot to me. It is engraved in our society, although as a woman there are a lot of arguments I might have with the Church. The essentials are right. The Ten Commandments are right. But it's a man-made institution and mistakes are made. In the past, it sometimes left people with the sense of sin about sex and this affected young people in their married lives. Yet the moral standards in Ireland are good. We are very lucky and I feel a sense of pride in the Ireland of my background. Irish values kept the family together, and of all the countries I have been to, I think of Ireland as one of the happiest.

Our father is very much a practising Catholic. Our mother — she was a very natural, earthy woman [Jean Corr sadly died in November 1999], and I think she would have had her criticisms of the Church. She wouldn't have thought that men in collars should tell her how to live her life ... Yet the fundamentals of the Catholic Church remain right, and I cherish the legacy. I had a very nice time at school [with the St Louis nuns]. A lot of our faith, though, is down to our parents.

For the future, the Church will have to loosen up. The hypocrisy will have to go. It should definitely embrace all people. The Church should not be judgemental — we will all have to meet our own judgement. The Church should be comforting. It should be a helping thing. Life isn't easy for a lot of people, and the Church should be an anchor. We've all got the same sins, and the same sins as the people before us had, too. We should be honest about that.

A mass of people praying in a room together is just so bonding. It is so good for people to be able to do that. My father told us stories about sectarianism in the past, about how you couldn't go to a Protestant funeral. But I didn't experience anything like that in my generation. I would bless myself passing a Protestant church just as much as I would bless myself passing a Catholic church. I consider every church holy.

Religion makes life more interesting. You have to figure a lot of things out for yourself. People fall down. They cut themselves. They have to get up again, and religion should help to heal and re-make their lives when that happens. And I think, mostly, that it does.

Father Austin Flannery

Dominican friar, editor, teacher, human rights activist and among the most revered of the progressive Irish Catholic clergy, Father Flannery was born in 1925. He studied at St Flannan's College, Ennis, Dominican College, Newbridge, and Blackfriars College, Oxford. A leading specialist on the Second Vatican Council, he also gave long-standing service to causes such as the Irish Anti-Apartheid Movement. He is still involved in writing, editing and active priestly duties.

I lived in North Tipperary. My parents were very kind. It would have been a small farm, and a kind of all-purpose shop. Until cars became frequent, a small shop in the country had to stock everything. My father was wonderful, my mother too. I was the oldest of the family and I think we were very happy. We were seven. We were sent to school in Ennis, and then to Newbridge.

Like many diocesan colleges, St Flannan's would be rough. We were not well fed, which was common. Newbridge was the Dominican college, and as a kid of 12, I was amazed to find a priest who would try to make life happy for us. I was happy enough and I went straight to the Dominican order.

I think my parents were fairly well-to-do for the time, except that my father was terribly kind-hearted, and would always give "tick" — credit — and the poor people weren't always able to pay. The bus came twice a week, to Limerick. There were no trains. We were mountainy people.

The people were generally poor, but there was no violence. The police barracks was next door to us and they had very little to do. Very kind-hearted men. The school was close to us as was the church. The parish priest was a bit remote — he lived elsewhere, and the curate was a bit odd — eccentric, but not in an evil way. Nobody minded that. If he was any way behind with Confession, he would say, "Kneel down there now and I'll give you all Absolution". A general confession kind of thing.

I knew the kind of extreme poverty that was portrayed in *Angela's Ashes* existed. Not so much the nastiness. It wouldn't have seemed a repressive society to me because my family were kind. And we were probably the best off family in the parish.

My parents were very devout. And they lived their faith. Religion was just the natural environment.

With regard to the Church in the last decades of the 20th century — Margaret McCurtain, a very fine historian, was interviewed on television recently and she described the Catholic Church system as "collapsed" in Ireland. I think I would avoid the word collapsed, but I would certainly say decreased, in a major way.

A young girl I was speaking to the other day was telling me that she was going to America with her boyfriend. Fifteen or twenty years ago, this would never have been said openly or, if mentioned, with an apology. All that is gone. This is a huge change. The Church, which preached so strongly against sins against chastity, is suddenly simply ignored in this area.

I would see the future as the authority of the Church disintegrating. Unless there is a huge change coming which we haven't seen signs of, I'd say Catholicism and Christianity would be smaller religions. There is going to be a vacuum.

At the same time, my sister's children, they all go to church. Then with other members of my family, the younger people don't go to church. There are all shades.

I first felt this decline in the late 1970s, certainly the early 1980s. I have been in Dublin since 1957. In '57, every Sunday Mass was crowded, and every weekday Mass, there'd be large crowds. All that changed quite quickly. There was of course a fair amount of getting rid of tenements here in central Dublin, so people moved out that way. Yet even here, around Dominic Street, few enough people go to church now. However, Irish people in everyday life are still quite courteous to a priest, though they might not have much regard for the clerical church. They're usually kind-hearted.

Up to the 1980s, they would salute you, and say "Bless you, Father". Now they don't. That is not replaced by a sneer or anything. It's good for us not to meet with such deferential attitudes. I would have known a lot of people who would have been politically anti-clerical, Left-wingers and that. But I didn't experience any personal animus.

I think it's a good thing that the laws on divorce and the like have been changed — it's not the State's job to enforce Church teaching. Though it's not the State's job to aggravate social or marital problems either.

Perhaps the Church overemphasised sexual sins in the past. And it didn't do enough to emphasise the holiness of marriage. In the past, people would ask you to "say a prayer for me, Father". Maybe the priests needed the prayers too.

Frank Longford
The seventh Earl of Longford was born in 1905, and has had a long and distinguished career as writer, academic, politician, historian and prison reformer. Husband of historian Elizabeth Longford, he is also the father of a dynasty of remarkable writers and historians, including Antonia Fraser, Thomas Pakenham and Rachel Billington. He is also the father-in-law of the playwright Harold Pinter. The family seat, Tullynally Castle, is in Co Westmeath.

I was influenced most in my life by Eamon de Valera, who was my hero. He's the greatest man I've ever met. He was "Catholic Ireland" to me. A combination of being a very religious, spiritual man and a very astute politician. He was sentenced to death after 1916 and I often wondered if that affected his whole life. I never saw de Valera as an extremist or narrow-minded. He was incredibly morally upright.

Ireland certainly was a very poor country when I was young. Starving, even. We would have school treats in front of the house, in front of Tullynally Castle, when I was about seven or eight. There'd be a Protestant school treat — quite a small number, wearing shoes and stockings. The Catholic school treat — they were in rags. I'm not joking — rags and barefoot. These would be Catholic children on the estate.

Then I remember in the 1950s, the standard of living in Ireland was half that of England: now it is level. The gentry were much richer than the ordinary Catholic people, who were generally poor. Ireland has raised herself up from the bottom. Irish people are clever and they have had the opportunities now ... I never thought that the poverty in Ireland was the fault of the Catholic Church. I thought the problem was a lack of resources, principally. It was a country without rich resources. I remember an admiration for the Catholic schools, though. A Protestant seminarian told me that he thought the Catholic education was excellent.

There were divisions between Catholics and Protestants in Ireland in the 1930s. I remember that a Catholic couldn't get into the Kildare Street club. Even when my brother [Edward, the preceding Earl] died in 1961 — my brother was a famous man in Dublin and a Senator — the Catholics in Ireland didn't go into the [Anglican] cathedral for the service. We were not offended. It was obvious there was so much respect for him. I stayed in Co Wicklow with Robert Barton, a landowner and a signatory of 1916. Erskine Childers was a Protestant and became President of Ireland. There was a division between religions, but it was never vicious.

I never really talked about religion to de Valera. If I prayed with him, it would have been in his house. He used to visit the Blessed Sacrament five times a day. He had a little oratory, something like that, in his home. I never went to church with him.

I met John Charles McQuaid briefly. He didn't make a special impact on me. I rather deplored his stern attitudes, keeping Catholics out of Trinity and that. But I didn't feel that the Church was too dominant in people's lives — I didn't get that impression. If it is weaker now, I would be sorry. I like a country to have religious faith. The stronger, the better.

It's up to intellectuals to stand up against the Church where they disagree. I'm against the Pope on women priests, for example.

I do think that being Irish has affected my whole life.

Edna O'Brien

is one of the most significant of living Irish writers. Her early novels in the 1960s — notably *The Country Girls* and *The Lonely Girl* — introduced a new genre of women's writing in Ireland. Her work has been acclaimed internationally, particularly in the United States where she publishes regularly in the *New Yorker*. Some of her early work attracted criticism from the clergy for what seemed, then, a permissive morality, and she herself has been critical of the ethos of Catholic Ireland. Edna O'Brien is an iconic figure in Ireland, honoured as a literary and poetic beauty and a kind of pioneer for modern women. She was married to the late Ernest Gebler, and is the mother of two sons.

The legacy of Catholic Ireland, like all legacies, is mixed. There is a good part and a debilitating part. The good part is conscience. Consciences are so important they should be donated. The bad part is the ever-abiding sense of guilt.

It is hard to adjudicate, for the long-term. With the Celtic tiger now, Ireland is a very secular country. Young people have an amnesia about the kind of world we knew. The Catholic Ireland of my childhood had a profound effect, an everlasting effect, on me.

A lot of the people I knew — I am thinking of my own mother — their obedience and deference to the Church was very much founded on fear. Yet my own experience of faith was most intense. The Stations of the Cross, the Body and Blood of Christ ... it was, for me, so deeply felt. It made me fearful and it is with me for all time. Yet it gave me more *feeling*. And feeling is the most important thing in the world.

There was cruelty. But the people raising us believed in chastisement, in punishment. Today, I don't think there is the same intensity of appreciation — of feeling — for literature and poetry. I don't see the hunger for literature and poetry that I had.

The world — not just Ireland — is more raucous now. But there is still a lurking spirituality amongst the Irish. Hopefully.

Peter Sutherland
is chairman and managing director of the renowned merchant bankers Goldmann Sachs International, former Attorney-General of Ireland and European Union Commissioner for Competition. He has received many European prizes and honours and is one of Europe's richest Irishmen. Peter Sutherland was educated at Gonzaga College in Dublin, and then University College Dublin. His wife is Spanish and they have three children.

It is fashionable to criticise the legacy of Catholic Ireland. Even the use of the word "legacy" suggests something that is past. I believe that the ethos in which my generation was raised, insofar as it was related to the Church, was overwhelmingly positive. If there are criticisms of the way we are today then they are not the responsibility of religion. To my mind the values instilled have had enormously beneficial results. Take the activities of our missionaries and aid workers in the developing world: our contribution as a people on any measurement is outstanding and surely reflects a sense of purpose inculcated through our schools.

It may be said that the Catholic Church has been at times rigid and authoritarian and there is no doubt that this is true, but it is easy to be critical of historic events and I believe the legacy today is not a bad one. Certainly in my schooling I saw no evidence of a hard-line, illiberal approach — quite the contrary — but I appreciate that the Jesuits had a particular and distinctive position which was much more liberal than the average. Today I am very proud of my children who are products of Catholic education in modern times. It seems to me that young people today have an attachment to values that is significantly greater than in older generations. I am glad that my wife and I stuck to our decision to educate our children in Ireland even though this was difficult at times because of foreign assignments.

If I had a criticism it would be related to an anti-intellectualism which characterised parts of the Catholic Church. Only recently has questioning been welcomed, but elsewhere the same phenomenon was evident and we should not be excessively self-critical.

Pauline McLynn

is now Ireland's leading comedienne. She helped to make the wacky television series, *Father Ted*, one of the most successful comedies in Britain and Ireland during the 1990s. She is also a serious straight actress — she appeared as Frankie's aunt in the film of *Angela's Ashes* — and has written a successful novel, *Something for The Weekend*.

I'd be of the generation — I was born in 1962 — which would associate the Catholic Church with Ireland being held back a bit. I went to a Mercy Convent, and I had a lovely time at school, but then I went to Trinity — the big "Protestant University"! — and since that time I've grown away from organised religion. I wouldn't identify at all with the notion of "Catholic Ireland" — it's just not the way most people of my generation perceive this country. I am very glad that Church and State are now separated.

But if the Catholic Church is sincere in its apologies for the abuses of the past, and it can convince people of its sincerity, then I would say its future could be quite progressive. It could be a very attractive proposition for anyone who is interested in organised religion. I'm not. I would have a certain spirituality: I try to be kind to other people and animals and I worry about the world in an ecological sense, but I'm fine without organised religion. But then I don't have any children. If I did, maybe I'd be taking a leap into faith — who knows?

If the Catholic Church weathers this storm [of sexual abuse], yes, I think it'll be fine in the future. It will be there for those who want it, in Ireland, even if it's not part of the Irish identity.

Dr A.J.F. O'Reilly (Tony O'Reilly)

Tony O'Reilly, who was born in 1936, is an Irish newspaper magnate, the retiring Chairman of H.J. Heinz in the US and a former outstanding international rugby star for Ireland (capped 29 times). He is probably the richest man in Ireland, and certainly one of the most influential. A patron of many cultural and educational endeavours, he has helped to generate much indigenous investment through the Ireland Fund. He is the father of six children and the grandfather of many more. He is now married to Chryss Goulandris.

The formal church as we know it has fallen into a degree of desuetude. People do not seek the advice of the Church as once they would have. At the same time, the Church preaches so much that is right. If Jesus Christ came back among us he would be proud of what has been achieved. He'd be critical too, of course!

The Catholic Church's legacy in Ireland is both positive and negative. It generally taught good things. It made you very disciplined. It measured the rhythm of life, the liturgy of life. When you're young the rhythm of life is very important. The sense-laden smells coming out of the thurible at benediction time. There was this wonderful wafting odour which I remember with our football matches. The *Tantum Ergo. Credo in Unam Deum*. The music of the Catholic Church — the great Gregorian chants. I am very comfortable with all of these things. I still remember being an altar boy and the beauty of the Latin rhythms.

On the negative side, it inhibited a lot of people, particularly people with artistic temperaments, from expressing themselves. Yet I don't look on the Ireland in which I grew up — in the 1940s and '50s — as a nasty place. Not at all. It was an intensely exciting place. The only place in the world to be is the place you are in now. In a sense we are all prisoners of our childhood. The laws then were so clear. The choices so simple. In that way we all remember back to our childhood and the world that was with affection and, to an extent, with rose-tinted glasses.

Could I have received a better education anywhere in the world? I would say no. I went out into the world better-equipped with a Jesuit education and the influence of my parents — I had a liberal, Christian, tolerant and mercantile outlook. I was at Belvedere College in Dublin for 12 years — they took me when I was six, though in fact my parents were not actually married at the time — showing, particularly in light of that era, the inherent flexibility of the Order.

I have a very happy memory of the Church in "Catholic Ireland". I would give it seven or eight out of ten. The legacy — it's a better Ireland today than it was 50 years ago, and it will be a better Ireland in 50 years time than it is today.

Acknowledgements

A list of acknowledgements which appeared in the first edition of this book is a little too lengthy to repeat here, but I would take this opportunity to thank all those who helped and advised me. For this edition, I would like to add my special thanks to Father Fergus O'Donoghue, SJ, and to Ciara Considine, of New Island Books, who has been so helpful, reliable, observant and clever.

A Note on Sources

Books mentioned or drawn on in the text are listed in the bibliography.

Newspapers and magazines are also listed here.

A full annotation of the historical sources, with footnotes, appears in the first edition of *Goodbye to Catholic Ireland*, published by Sinclair-Stevenson, London, in 1997.

Newspapers and Magazines
Capuchin Annual
The Catholic Standard
The Church of Ireland Gazette
The Dublin Evening Mail
Dublin Opinion Books
The Far East
The Furrow
The Irish Catholic
Irish Digest
The Irish Ecclesiastical Quarterley
The Irish Ecclesiastical Record
The Irish Independent
The Irish Messenger of the Sacred Heart
The Irish Press
The Irish Times
Irishwoman's Journal
Studies
Woman and *Woman's Own* (U.K.)

Adams, Michael *Censorship: The Irish Experience*. Dublin, Scepter Books, 1968
Adamson, Ian *The Ulster People: Ancient, Mediaeval and Modern*. Belfast, Pretani Press, 1991

Alcock, Antony *Understanding Ulster*. Belfast, Ulster Society Publications Ltd, 1994

Andrews, C.S. *Dublin Made Me*. Cork, Mercier Press, 1979

Ardagh, John *Ireland and the Irish*. Harmondsworth, Penguin, 1994

Arensberg, Conrad and Kimball, S.T., *Family and Community in Ireland*. Cambridge, Harvard University Press, 1940

Arnold, Mavis, and Laskey, Heather *Children of the Poor Clares: The Story of an Irish Orphanage*. Belfast, Appletree Press, 1985

Augusteijn, Joost (ed) *Ireland in the 1930s*. Dublin, Four Courts Press, 1999

Avery, Gillian *Victorian People*. London, Collins, 1970

Bardon, Jonathan *A History of Ulster*. Belfast, Blackstaff Press, 1972

Barry, Tom *Guerrilla Days in Ireland*. Dublin, Irish Press, 1949. Reprint, Anvil Books, Dublin, 1995

Beale, Jenny *Women in Ireland: Voices of Change*. London, Macmillan, 1986

Beattie, Geoffrey, *We Are the People*. London, Heinemann, 1992

Bence-Jones, Mark *Twilight of the Ascendency*. London, Constable, 1987

Bestic, Alan *The Importance of Being Irish*. London, Cassell, 1969

Bew, Paul *Ideology and the Irish Question: Ulster Unionism and Irish Nationalism 1912-1916*. Oxford, Clarendon Press, 1994

Binder, Pearl *The Peacock's Tail: A study of fashion change*. London, Harrap, 1958

Bing, Geoffrey *John Bull's Other Ireland*. London, Tribune Pamphlet, 1950

Birmingham, George A. *An Irishman Looks At His World*. London, Hodder, 1919

Bishop, Patrick, and Mallie, Eamonn *The Provisional IRA*. London, Heinemann, 1987

Blanchard, Jean *The Church in Contemporary Ireland*. Dublin, Clonmore and Reynolds, 1963

Blanshard, Paul *The Irish and Catholic Power*. Boston, Beacon Press, 1953

Blythe, Ronald *The Age of Illusion: Glimpses of Britain Between the Wars 1919-1940*. Oxford University Press, 1983

Boland, Bridget *At My Mother's Knee: An Autobiography*. London, Bodley Head, 1978

Bourke, Joanna *Husbandry to Housewifery: Women and Economic Change and Housework in Ireland 1890-1914*. Oxford, Clarendon Press, 1993

— — — *Working-Class Cultures in Britain 1890-1960*. London, Routledge, 1993

Bowen, Kurt *Protestants in a Catholic State*. Dublin, Gill and Macmillan, 1983

Bowman, John *De Valera and the Ulster Question*. Oxford University Press, 1989

Boyce, D.G. *Nationalism in Ireland*. London, Croom Helm, 1987
— — — *The Revolution in Ireland 1879-1923*. London, Macmillan Education, 1988
Boyd, Andrew *Holy War in Belfast*. Dublin, Anvil Books, 1969
Boylan, Henry *Dictionary of Irish Biography*, Gill and Macmillan, 1978, 1998
Boyne, Don *I Remember Maynooth*. London, Longman, 1937
Bracken, Pauline *Light of Other Days: A Dublin Childhood*. Cork, Mercier Press, 1992
Brady, Joseph *The Big Sycamore*. Dublin, M.H. Gill, 1958
Breen, Dan *My Fight for Irish Freedom*. Dublin, Talbot Press, 1924
Broderick, Joe *Fall from Grace*. Dingle, Ireland, Brandon Books, 1992
Brodrick, William St John (Viscount Midleton) *Records and Reactions, 1856-1939*. London, John Murray, 1939
Brown, Terence *Ireland's Literature*. Dublin, Lilliput Press, 1988
— — — *A Social and Cultural History of Ireland: 1922-1985*. London, Fontana, 1985
Browne, Noel *Against the Tide*. Dublin, Gill and Macmillan, 1986
Bryant, Arthur *George V*. London, Peter Davies, 1936
Buckley, Vincent *Memory Ireland*. Harmondsworth, Penguin, 1985
Burton, Katharine *According to the Pattern: The Story of Agnes McLaren and the Society of Catholic Medical Missionaries*. New York, Longman, Green and Co, 1946
Butler, Hubert *Escape from the Anthill*. Dublin, Lilliput Press, 1986
— — — *The Sub-Prefect Should Have Held His Tongue*. London, Allen Lane, The Penguin Press, 1990
Byrne, Donn *Hangman's House*. Dublin, Allen Figgis edition, 1970
Byrne, Gay *To Whom It Concerns*. Dublin, Torc Books, 1972
Cahill, Edward SJ *The Catholic Social Movement*. Dublin, Irish Messenger, 1931
— — — *The Framework of a Christian State* Dublin, Irish Messenger, 1932
Cahill, Thomas *How the Irish Saved Civilisisation: The Untold Story of Ireland's Heroic Role from the Fall of Rome to the Rise of Mediaeval Europe*. New York, Doubleday, 1995
Canning, Father Peter *Bishops of Ireland 1870-1987*. Donegal Democrat, Co Donegal, 1987
Carbery, Mary *The Farm by Lough Gur*. Cork. Mercier Press, 1982.
Carlson, Julia *Banned in Ireland*. London, Routledge, 1990
Carroll, Joseph *Ireland in the War Years 1939-1945*. Newton Abbot, David and Charles, 1975
Carty, Xavier *Irish Missionaries*. Dublin, Catholic Communications, Veritas 1970
Central Statistics Office *That Was Then, This Is Now*. Dublin, Government of Ireland Publications, February 2000

Chesterton, G.K. *Christendom in Dublin*. London, Sheed & Ward, 1932

Chubb, Basil *The Government and Politics of Ireland*. London, Longman, 1992

Clark, Kenneth *Civilisation*. Harmondsworth, Penguin Books, 1987

Clarke, Austin *A Penny in the Clouds*. Dublin, RKP, 1968

— — — *Twice Round the Black Church: Early Memories of Ireland and England*. London, Routledge, 1962

Clarke, Kathleen *Revolutionary Woman: An Autobiography 1878-1972*. Dublin, The O'Brien Press

Cleeve, Brian *A View of the Irish*. London, Buchan and Enright, 1983

Coffey, Diarmid *Douglas Hyde: President of Ireland*. Dublin and Cork, Talbot Press, 1938

Coldrey, Barry *Faith and Fatherland: The Christian Brothers and the Development of Irish Nationalism 1838-1921*. Dublin, Gill and Macmillan, 1988

Collis, Joyce *The Sparrow Hath Found Herself a Nest*. Dublin, Browne & Nolan, 1943

Colum, Mary *Life and the Dream*. London, Macmillan, 1947

Colum, Padraic *My Irish Year*. London, Mills and Boon, 1912

Comerford, R.V., et al *Religion, Conflict and Co-Existence in Ireland*. Dublin, Gill and Macmillan, 1990

Concannon, Helena *The Queen of Ireland: an Historical Account of Ireland's Devotion to the Blessed Virgin*. Dublin, M.H. Gill and Son, 1938

Connell, K.H. *Irish Peasant Society: Four Historical Essays*. Oxford, Clarendon Press, 1968

Connery, Donald S. *The Irish*. London, Eyre and Spottiswoode, 1968

Considine, Bob *It's the Irish*. Doubleday, New York, 1961

Coogan, Tim Pat *De Valera: Long Fellow, Long Shadow*. London, Hutchinson, 1993

— — — *The IRA*. London, Pall Mall Press, 1970

— — — *Ireland since the Rising*. London, Pall Mall Press, 1966

— — — *The Troubles: Ireland's Ordeal 1966-1995 and the Search for Peace*. London, Hutchinson, 1995

Cooney, John *The Crozier and the Dáil*. Cork, Mercier Press, 1986

— — — *John Charles McQuaid: Ruler of Catholic Ireland*. The O'Brien Press, Dublin, 1999

Corish, Patrick J. *The Irish Catholic Experience: A Historical Survey*. Dublin, Gill and Macmillan, 1985

Corkery, Daniel *The Hidden Ireland*. Dublin, M.H. Gill, 1925

— — — *Nightfall and Other Stories*. Belfast, Blackstaff Press edition, 1988

Costello, Peter *The Heart's Grown Brutal*. Dublin, Gill and Macmillan, 1977

Coxhead, Elizabeth *Daughters of Erin*. London, Colin Smythe, 1965

Craig, Alex *The Banned Books of England*. London, Allen and Unwin, 1937

Craig, Patricia (ed) *Rattle of the North: An Anthology of Ulster Prose*. Belfast, Blackwater Press, 1992

Cross, Eric *The Tailor and Ansty*. Cork, Mercier Press edition, 1992

Cruise O'Brien, Conor *Ancestral Voices*. Dublin, Poolbeg Press, 1994

— — — *Parnell and his Party*. Oxford, Clarendon Press, 1957

— — — *Passion and Cunning*. London, Paladin, 1990

— — — *The Shaping of Modern Ireland*. Dublin, RKP, 1960

— — — *States of Ireland*. London, Hutchinson, 1972

— — — *Writers and Politics*. Harmondsworth, Penguin, 1976

Danaher, Kevin *In Ireland Long Ago*. Cork, Mercier Press, 1962

Daniel-Rops, Henri *A Fight for God: 1870-1939*. London, Dent, 1966

Den Riencourt, Amaury *Woman and Power in History*. Bath, Honeyglen, 1974

De Vere White, Terence *A Fretful Midge*. Dublin, RKP, 1947

— — — *Kevin O'Higgins*. Dublin, Anvil Books, 1969

Devoy, John *Recollections of an Irish Rebel*. Dublin, Shannon University Press, 1929

Doherty, J.E., and Hickey, D.J., *A Chronology of Irish History Since 1500*. Dublin, Gill and Macmillan, 1989

Dominian, Leon *The Frontiers of Language and Nationality in Europe*. New York, American Geographical Society, 1917

Donoghue, Denis *Warrenpoint*. London, Jonathan Cape, 1990

Doyle, Lynn C. *The Spirit of Ireland*. London, Batsford, 1935

Doyle, Paddy *The God Squad*. Dublin, Raven Arts, 1988

Drudy, P.J. (ed) *The Irish in America: Emigration, Assimilation and Impact*. Cambridge University Press, 1985

Dudley Edwards, Owen *The Sins of Our Fathers: Roots of Conflict in Northern Ireland*. Dublin, Gill and Macmillan, 1970

Dudley Edwards, Ruth *James Connolly*. Dublin, Gill and Macmillan, 1981

— — — *Patrick Pearse: The Triumph of Failure*. London, Faber & Faber, 1979

Duff, Frank (ed Charles T. Moss) *A Living Autobiography*. Dublin, Maria Legiones, 1983

Dunn, Joe *No Lions in the Hierarchy*. Dublin, The Colomba Press, 1994

Dwyer, Barry, and English, Graham *Faith of Our Fathers and Mothers: A Catholic Story*. Pymble, Australia, HarperCollins, 1990

Eagleton, Terry *Heathcliff and the Great Hunger: Studies in Irish Culture*. London, Verso, 1995

Eire: Department of Justice *Annual Reports of Censorship of Publications Board* and *Annual Reports of Censorship of Publications Appeal Board*.

Eksteins, Modris *Rites of Spring: The Great War and the Birth of the Modern.* London, Bantam, 1989

Elliott, Marianne *Wolfe Tone.* New Haven, Yale University Press, 1989

Ellmann, Richard *Yeats: The Man and the Masks.* Harmondsworth, Penguin, 1987

Engels, Frederick *The Making of the English Working Class.* Oxford, Blackwell, 1948

Ervine, St John Greer *Mixed Marriage.* London, Maunsell, 1920

Fahy, Bernadette *Freedom of Angels: Surviving Goldenbridge Orphanage.* O'Brien Press, Dublin, 1999

Fallon, Brian *An Age of Innocence: Irish Culture 1930-1960.* Gill and Macmillan, Dublin, 1998

Farmar, Tony *Ordinary Lives: Three Generations of Irish Middle-Class Experience.* Dublin, Gill and Macmillan, 1991

Farrell, Michael (ed) *Twenty Years On.* Dingle, Brandon Books, 1988

Fay, Gerard *The Abbey Theatre.* Dublin, Clonmore and Reynolds, 1958

Feeney, John *John Charles McQuaid: The Man and the Masks.* Cork, Mercier Press, 1974

Fennell, Desmond *Heresy: The Battle of Ideas in Modern Ireland.* Belfast, Blackstaff Press, 1993

— — — *The State of the Nation: Ireland Since the Sixties.* Dublin, Ward River Press, 1983

Ferris, Paul *Sex and the British: A Twentieth Century History.* London, Michael Joseph, 1993

Figgis, Darrell *AE (George Russell): A Study of a Man and a Nation.* Dublin and London, Maunsell and Co, 1916

Fingall, Elizabeth *Seventy Years Young.* London, Collins, 1937

Fisher, Trevor *Scandal: The Sexual Politics of Late Victorian Britain.* Stroud, Alan Sutton, 1995

Fisk, Robert *In Time of War.* London, Deutsch, 1983

Fitzgerald, Garret *All in a Life.* Dublin, Gill and Macmillan, 1991

Flackes, W.D. (with Sydney Elliott) *Northern Ireland: a Political Directory 1968-88.* Belfast, Blackstaff Press, 1980

Fleming, Lionel *Head or Harp?* London, Blackstaff Press, 1980

Foale, Marie Therese RSJ *The Josephite Story.* Sydney, St Joseph's Generalate, 1989

Fogarty, Michael, et al *Irish Values and Attitudes: The Irish Report of the European Value Systems Study.* Dublin, Dominican Publications, 1994

Forristal, Desmond *Edel Quinn.* Dublin, Dominical Publications

— — — *The Second Burial of Bishop Shanahan.* Dublin, Veritas, 1990

Foster, R.F. *Modern Ireland 1600-1972.* London, Allen Lane, The Penguin Press, 1988

— — — *Paddy and Mr Punch.* London, Allen Lane, The Penguin Press, 1993

Fox, R.M. *Louie Bennett: Her Life and Times*. Dublin, Talbot Press, 1958
— — — *Rebel Irishwomen*. Dublin, Progress House, 1937
Freud, Sigmund *Civilizations and its Discontents*. Vol 21 of Collected
   Works, London, reprinted by Dover Thrift Editions, 1994
Gallagher, Tom, and O'Connell, James (eds) *Contemporary Irish Studies*.
   Manchester University Press, 1983
Garvin, Tom *Nationalist Revolutionaries in Ireland: 1858-1928*. Oxford
   University Press, 1987
Gaughan, J. Anthony *Olivia Mary Taaffe (11832-1918): Foundress of St
   Joseph's Young Priests' Society*. Ireland, Kingdom Books, 1995
Goldring, Maurice *Pleasant the Scholar's Life*. London, Serif, 1993
— — — *Forty Years of Irish Broadcasting*. Dublin, Talbot Press (published
   for RTE), 1967
Gray, Tony *Ireland This Century*. London, Little Brown & Co, 1994
— — — *The Irish Answer*. London, Heinemann, 1966
— — — *Mr Smyllie, Sir*. Dublin, Gill and Macmillan, 1991
Greene, David *The Irish Language*. Dublin, Three Candles, 1966
Gregory, Lady (ed) *Ideals in Ireland*. London, Unicorn, 1901
Grote, Georg *Torn Between Politics and Culture*. Germany, Waxmann,
   1994
Grousset, Paschal *Ireland's Disease: The English in Ireland*. Belfast,
   Blackstaff Press, 1986
Hamilton, Phyllis, with Williams, Paul *Secret Love: My Life with Father
   Michael Cleary*. Dublin, Mainstream Press, 1995
Harris, Rosemary *Prejudice and Tolerance in Ulster: A Study of Neighbours
   and Strangers in a Border Community*. Manchester University Press,
   1972
Harriss, John (ed) *The Family: A Social History of the Twentieth Century*.
   London, Harrap, 1992
Hart, Peter *The Irish Republican Army and Its Enemies: Violence and
   Community in County Cork 1916-1923*. Oxford University Press, 1999
Hartley, Olga *Women in the Catholic Church: Yesterday and Today*.
   London, Burns, Oates, 1935
Haste, Cate *Rules of Desire: Sex in Britain – World War I to the Present*.
   London, Chatto and Windus, 1992
Hastings, Max *Ulster 1969: The Fight for Civil Rights in Northern Ireland*.
   London, Gollancz, 1970
Haverty, Anne *Constance Markievicz, Irish Revolutionary*. London,
   Pandora, 1988
Hayes, Maurice *Minority Report*. Belfast, Blackstaff Press, 1995
Hayes, Paul *Fascism*. London, Allen and Unwin, 1973
Headlam, Maurice *Irish Reminiscences*. London, Robert Hale, 1947
Healy, John *No One Shouted Stop!* Achill, House of Healy, 1968
— — — *Nineteen Acres*. Galway, Kenny Books, 1988

Healy, T.M. *Letters and Leaders of My Day*. London, Butterworth, 1919

Hepburn, A.C. *The Conflict of Nationality in Modern Ireland*. London, Edward Arnold, 1980

Hesketh, Tom *The Second Partitioning of Ireland: The Abortion Referendum of 1983*. Dingle, Brandon Books, 1990

Hickey, D.J. and Doherty, J.E. *A Dictionary of Irish History 1800-1980*. Dublin, Gill and Macmillan, 1987

Himmelfarb, Gertrude *The De-Moralisation of Society: From Victorian Virtues to Modern Values*. London, Institute of Economic Affairs, 1995

Hindley, Reg *The Death of the Irish Language*. London, Routledge, 1990

Hocking, Joseph *Is Home Rule Rome Rule?* London, Ward Lock, 1912

Hogan, Edmund M. *The Irish Missionary Movement: A Historical Survey 1830-1980*. Dublin, Gill and Macmillan, 1990

Holden, Wendy *Unlawful Carnal Knowledge: The Story of the X Case*. London, HarperCollins, 1994

Holloway, Joseph (eds Robert Hogan and Michael J O'Neill) *Abbey Diaries*. Champaign, Southern Illinois University Press, 1967

Hone, Joseph *W.B. Yeats 1865-1939*. Harmondsworth, Pelican Books edition, 1971

Hopkin, Alannah *The Living Legend of St Patrick*. London, Grafton Books, 1989

Horan, Monsignor James *Memoirs 1911-1986*. Dingle, Brandon Books 1992

Horgan, J.J. *From Parnell to Pearse*. Dublin, Browne and Nolan, Richview Press, 1948

Humphries, A.J. *New Dubliners 1966: Urbanisation and the Family*. London, RKP, 1966

Hutchinson, John *The Dynamics of Cultural Nationalism*. London, Allen and Unwin, 1987

Inglis, Brian *Downstart: Autobiography*. London, Chatto, 1990

– – – *West Briton*. London, Faber and Faber, 1962

Inglis, Tom *Moral Monopoly: The Catholic Church in Modern Irish Society*. Dublin, Gill and Macmillan, 1987

Innes, C.L. *Woman and Nation in Irish Literature and Society 1880.-1936*. London, Harvester Wheatsheaf, 1993

Iwan-Muller, E.B. *Ireland: Today and Tomorrow*. London, Chapman and Hall, 1907

Jensen, Sue Curry *Censorship: The Knot that Binds Power and Knowledge*. Oxford University Press, 1988

Johnson, Paul *A History of the Modern World from the 1920s to the 1990s*. London, Weidenfeld and Nicolson, 1991

Johnston, Denis *Orders and Desecrations*. Dublin, Lilliput Press, 1992

Joll, James *Euroe Since 1870*. Harmondsworth, Penguin 1990

Kavanagh, Patrick *The Green Fool* London, Michael Joseph, 1938

— — — *Tarry Flynn*. London, Pilot Press, 1948

Keane, Molly *Good Behaviour*. London, Abacus edition, 1992

Kearney, Richard (ed) *The Irish Mind: Exploring Intellectual Traditions*. Dublin, Wolfhound Press, 1985

Kearney, Richard *Myth and Motherland*. Derry, Field Day, 1984

Kearns, Kevin C. *Dublin Tenement Life: An Oral History*. Dublin, Gill and Macmillan, 1994

Kedourie, Elie *Nationalism*. London, Hutchinson, 1960

Kee, Robert *The Green Flag* London, Quartet, 1976

— — — *Ireland: A History*. London, Weidenfeld and Nicolson,1980

— — — *The Laurel and the Ivy*. London, Hamish Hamilton, 1993

Kennedy, Dennis *The Widening Gulf*. Belfast, Blackstaff Press, 1988

Kenny, Herbert A. *Literary Dublin*. Dublin, Gill and Macmillan,1974

Kenny, Ivor *In Good Company: Conversations with Irish Leaders*. Dublin, Gill and Macmillan, 1987

Kenny, Mary *Abortion: The Whole Story*. London, Quartet, 1986

— — — *Death by Heroin: Recovery by Hope*. Dublin, New Island Books, 1999

Kenny, P.D. ("PAT") *Economics for Irishmen*. Dublin, Maunsell, 1906

— — — *The Sorrows of Ireland*. London, Maunsell, 1907

Keogh, Dermot *Ireland and Europe 1919-1948*. Dublin, Gill and Macmillan, 1988

— — — *The Vatican, the Bishops and Irish Politics:* Cork University Press, 1995

Kerrigan, Gene *Another Country:Growing Up in '50s Ireland*. Dublin, Gill and Macmillan, 1998

Kerrigan, Gene, and Brennan, Pat *This Great Little Nation: The A-Z of Irish Scandals and Controversies*. Dublin, Gill and Macmillan, 1999

Kevles, Daniel *In the Name of Eugenics*. Harmondsworth, Pelican, 1985

Kiely, Benedict *Drink to the Bird: A Memoir*. London, Methuen, 1991

Kollontai, Aleksandra *Free Love*. London, J.M. Dent and Sons, 1932

Krause, David *Sean O'Casey and His World*. London, Thames and Hudson, 1976

Langan-Egan, Maureen *Women in Mayo 1821-1851: A Historical Perspective*. University College Galway Press, 1986

Larkin, Emmet *The Roman Catholic Church and the Fall of Parnell 1888-1891*. Liverpool University Press, 1995

Larkin, Maurice *Religion, Politics and Preferment in France*. Cambridge University Press, 1995

Laverty, Maura *Never No More*. London, Virago edition, 1985

Leathard, Audrey *The Fight for Family Planning: The Development of Family Planning Services in Britain 1921-1974*. London, Macmillan, 1980

Lee, J.J. *Ireland 1912-1985: Politics and Society*. Cambridge University Press, 1989

Lee, J.J. (ed) *Ireland 1945-70*. Dublin, Gill and Macmillan, 1979

Leslie, Sir Shane *The Irish Tangle for English Readers*. London, Macdonald, 1945

Levine, Edward M. *The Irish and Irish Politicians*. University of Notre Dame Press, Chicago, 1966

Lewis, Peter *The Fifties*. London, Heinmann, 1978

Lockingon, W.J. *The Soul of Ireland*. London, Harding and More, 1919

Longley, Edna *The Living Stream: Literature and Revisionism in Ireland*. Newcastle-upon-Tyne, Bloodaxe Books, 1994

Loscher, Clement *The X Case: How Abortion Was Brought to Ireland*. Cork, Human Life International, 1992

Louis, Sister M. *Mother Kevin: The Unconventional Nun*. Dublin, Catholic Truth Society (undated pamphlet)

Luddy, Maria, and Murphy, Cliona *Women Surviving: Studies in Irish Women's History in the Nineteenth and Twentieth Centuries*. Dublin, Poolbeg Press, 1990

Lynch-Robinson, Sir Christopher *The Last of the Irish R.M.s*. London, Cassell, 1951

Lynd, Robert *Essays on Life and Literature*. London, Dent, 1951

– – – *Home Life in Ireland*. London, Mills and Boon, 1912

Lyons, F.S.L. *Culture and Anarchy in Ireland 1890-1939*. Oxford University Press, 1979

– – – *Ireland Since the Famine*. London, Weidenfeld and Nicolson, 1971

– – – *Parnell*. Biographical essay published for the Dublin Historical Association, Dundalk, 1963

MacAonghusa, Prionsias (with Liam O Reagain)*The Best of Tone*. Cork, Mercier Press, 1972

Macardle, Dorothy *The Irish Republic*. London, Gollancz, 1937

McCann, Eamonn *War and an Irish Town*. Harmondsworth, Penguin, 1974

McCarthy, Michael *Priests and People in Ireland*. Dublin, Hodges Figgis, 1902

McCartney, Donal *The World of Daniel O'Connell*. Cork, Mercier Press, 1980

McCurtain, Margaret, and O Corrain, Donncha (eds) *Women in Irish Society*. Dublin, Arlen House, The Women's Press, 1978

MacDonagh, Michael *The Irish at the Front*. London, Hodder and Stoughton, 1916

– – – *The Irish at the Somme*. London, Hodder and Stoughton, 1917

MacDonagh, Oliver *O'Connell*. London, Weidenfeld and Nicolson, 1991

— — — *States of Mind: A Study of the Anglo-Irish Conflict.* London, Allen and Unwin, 1983

MacDonagh, Oliver, et al *Irish Culture and Nationalism.* Canberra, Australian National University, 1985

McDonald, Walter *Some Ethical Questions of Peace and War.* London, Jonathan Cape, 1919

— — — *Reminiscences of a Maynooth Professor.* London, Jonathan Cape, 1925

McElroy, Gerald *The Catholic Church and the Northern Ireland Crisis.* Dublin, Gill and Macmillan, 1991

McGarry, Fearghal *Irish Politics and the Spanish Civil War.* Cork University Press, 1999

MacGill, Patrick *Children of the Dead End.* Dublin, Cahban Books edition, 1985. First published 1912

Mac Greil, Micheal *Prejudice in Ireland Revisited.* Survey and Research Unit, St Patrick's College, Maynooth, 1996

MacLochlainn, Piaras F. *Last Words* Dublin, Kilmainham Jail Restoration Society, 1971

MacLysaght, Edward *Changing Times: Ireland Since 1898.* Gerrards Cross, Colin Smythe, 1978

MacMahon, Bryan *The Master.* Dublin, Poolbeg Press, 1992

MacNamara, Brinsley *The Valley of the Squinting Windows.* Dublin, Anvil Books edition, 1976.

MacReamoinn, Sean (ed) *The Church in a New Ireland.* Navan, Co Meath, Colomba Press, 1996.

MacReamoinn, Sean. *Pobal: The Laity in Ireland.* Navan, Co Meath, Colomba Press, 1986

MacSharry, Ray and White, Padraic. *The Celtic Tiger.* Cork, Mercier Press, 2000

MacSwiney, Terence J. *Principles of Freedom.* Fourth edition, Dublin, Irish Book Bureau, 1964

— — — *The Revolutionist.* Dublin and London, Maunsell, 1914

MacThormaid, Brendan Mary *Deathless Glory: Commemorative Pamphlet for 1916.* Dublin, Massey Brothers, March 1966

Mahood, Linda *The Magdalenes: Prostitution in the Nineteenth Century.* London, Routledge, 1990

Manning, Maurice *The Blueshirts.* Dublin, Gill and Macmillan, 1970

Mansergh, Nicholas *The Irish Free State: Its Government and Politics.* London, Allen and Unwin, 1934

— — — *The Irish Question 1840-1923.* London, Unwin University Books, 1965

Marreco, Anne *The Rebel Countess: The Life and Times of Constance Markievicz.* London, Weidenfeld and Nicolson, 1967

Marwick, Arthur *The Deluge.* London, Macmillan, 1965

Maume, Patrick *D.P. Moran.* Queen's University Belfast, Institute of Irish Studies, 1993

— — — *Life that is Exile: Daniel Corkery and the Search for Irish Ireland.* Queen's University Belfast, Institute of Irish Studies, 1993

Miller, David W. *Church, State and Nation in Ireland 1898-1921.* Dublin, Gill and Macmillan, 1973

Montgomery Hyde, H. *The Lady Chatterley's Lover Trial.* London, Bodley Head, 1990

Moore, Chris *Betrayal of Trust,* Dublin, Marino Books, 1995

Moore, George *Hail and Farewell.* London, Heinemann, 1911-14

Morton, H.V. *In Search of Ireland.* London, Methuen, 1930

Morton, J.B. *The New Ireland.* London, Paladin Press, 1938

Mulvihill, Margaret *Charlotte Despard: A Biography.* London, Pandora, 1989

Murphy, John *Ireland in the Twentieth Century.* Dublin, Gill and Macmillan, 1973

Myers, Kevin Programme notes to *Observe the Sons of Ulster Marching Towards the Somme.* Dublin, Abbey Theatre, 1994

Newman, Jeremiah *Ireland Must Choose.* Dublin, Four Courts, 1983

— — — *Return to the Sacred: A Socio-Religious Analysis.* Dublin, Four Courts, 1986

Ni Dhonncadha and Dorgan (eds). *Revising the Rising.* Derry, Field Day, 1991

Noel, Gerard, and Stanford, Peter *The Anatomy of the Catholic Church.* London, Michael Russell, 1994

Norman, Edward *A History of Modern Ireland.* London, Allen Lane, The Penguin Press, 1971

O'Brien, Jack *British Brutality in Ireland.* Cork, Mercier Press, 1989

O'Brien, John (ed) *The Vanishing Irish: The Enigma of the Modern World.* London, W.H. Allen, 1954

O Broin, Leon *Frank Duff: A Biography.* Dublin, Gill and Macmillan, 1982

— — — *Protestant Nationalists in Revolutionary Ireland.* Dublin, Gill and Macmillan, 1985

O Ceallaigh, Daltun (ed) *Reconsiderations of Irish History and Culture.* Dublin, Leirmheas, for the Desmond Greaves Summer School, 1994

O Ceallaigh, Sean *Ireland's Spiritual Empire.* Dublin, M.H. Gill, 1952

O Cierin, Kit and Cyril *Women of Ireland: A Biographical Dictionary.* Kinvara, Co Galway, TirEolas, 1996

O Conaire, Padraic *The Finest Stories of Padraic O Conaire.* Dublin, Poolbeg Press, 1982

O'Connell, John *Dr John: Crusading Doctor and Politician.* Dublin, Poolbeg Press, 1989

O'Connor, Fionnuala *In Search of a State: Catholics in Northern Ireland.* Belfast, Blackstaff Press, 1993

O'Connor, Frank *The Collar: Stories of Irish Priests.* Belfast, Blackstaff Press, 1993

— — — *My Father's Son.* London, Macmillan, 1968

O'Connor, Ulick *Celtic Dawn: A Portrait of the Irish Literary Renaissance.* London, Hamish Hamilton, 1984

— — — *A Terrible Beauty is Born.* London, Granada, 1981

O'Connor Lysaght, D.R. *The Communists and the Irish Revolution.* Dublin, Literaire, 1973

O'Donovan, Donal *Kevin Barry and His Time.* Co Kildare, Glendale, 1989

O'Drisceoil, Donal *Censorship in Ireland 1939-1945: Neutrality, Politics and Society.* Cork University Press, 1996

O'Duffy, Eoin *Crusade in Spain.* Dublin, Browne and Nolan, 1941

O'Dwyer, Peter *Mary: A History of Devotion in Ireland.* Dublin, Four Courts Press, 1992

O'Faoilain, Sean *The Irish.* Harmondsworth, Penguin, 1947

O'Faoilain, Sean *Vive Moi! An Autobiography.* London, Rupert Hart-Davis, 1967

O'Flaherty, Liam *Shame the Devil: An Autobiography.* Dublin, Wolfhound Press, 1981

— — — *A Tourist's Guide to Ireland.* London, Mandrake Press, 1929

— — — *The Martyr.* London, Victor Gollancz, 1933

O'Gorman, Paddy *Queuing for a Living.* Dublin, Poolbeg Press, 1995

O'Hegarty, P.S. *The Victory of Sinn Féin (How it won it, and how it used it).* Dublin, Talbot Press, 1924

O'Leary, Peter (An t-Athair Peader O Laoghaire) *My Own Story.* (translated from the Irish by Sheila O'Sullivan) Dublin, Gill and Macmillan, 1973

O' Mahony, T.P. *Jack Lynch.* Dublin, Anvil Books, 1979

O'Neill, Maire *From Parnell to De Valera: a Biography of Jennie Wyse Power 1858-1941.* Dublin, Blackwater, 1991

O'Reilly, Emily *Masterminds of the Right.* Dublin, Attic Press, 1988

O'Reilly, Luke *The Laughter and the Weeping: An Old China Hand Remembers.* Navan, Co Meath, Colomba Press, 1991

O'Riordan, John D. *Irish Catholics: Traditions and Transitions.* Dublin, Veritas, 1980

O'Riordan, Monsignor Michael *Catholicity and Progress in Ireland.* London, Kegan Paul and Co, 1905

O'Ryan, William Patrick *The Plough and the Cross: A Story of New Ireland.* Dublin, Irish Nation, 1910

O'Sullivan, Donal *The Irish Free State and its Senate.* London, Faber and Faber, 1940

O'Sullivan, Michael *Mary Robinson: The Life and Times of an Irish Liberal*. Dublin, Blackwater, 1993

O'Toole, Fintan *Black Hole, Green Card: The Disappearance of Ireland*. Dublin, New Island, 1994

Pakenham, Thomas *The Year of Liberty*. London, Faber an Faber, 1988

Parks, William *A Fermanagh Childhood*. Belfast, Friar's Bush Press, 1988

Paul-Dubois, Louis *Contemporary Ireland*. Dublin, Maunsell, 1908

Pinter, Harold *Mac*. London, Pendragon Press, 1968

Plunkett, Horace *Ireland in the New Century*. London, John Murray, 1904

Plunkett, James *The Boy on the Back Wall and Other Essays*. Dublin, Poolbeg Press, 1987

Pritchett, V.S. *Dublin: A Portrait*. London, Bodley Head, 1967

Prost, Antoine and Vincent, Gerard (eds) *A History of Modern Times, Volume 5: Riddles of Identity in Modern Times*. Cambridge, Harvard University Press, Belknap Press, 1991

Purcell, Mary *Matt Talbot and His Times*. Dublin, G. Goodliffe Neal, 1976

Purcell, Mary *To Africa with Love: The Life of Mother Mary Martin, Foundress of the Medical Missionaries*. Dublin, Gill and Macmillan, 1987

Quinn, Bernadette *Out of that Childhood Country*. Book Guild, Lewes, Sussex, 1995

Quinn, Richard with Caroll, Robert *The Missionary Factor in Irish Aid Overseas*. Dublin, Dominican Publications, 1980

Redmond, Lar *Show Us the Moon: The Dublin Days of Lar Redmond*. Dingle, Brandon Books, 1988

Robertson, Olivia *Dublin Phoenix*. London, Cape, 1957

Robinson, Lennox *Curtain Up: Autobiography*. London, Michael Joseph, 1942

Robinson, Lennox *Ireland's Abbey Theatre*. London, Sidgwick and Jackson, 1951

– – – *The White-Headed Boy*. London, Putnam, 1925

Rose, June *Marie Stopes and the Sexual Revolution*. London, Faber and Faber, 1992

Ryan, John *Remembering How We Stood*. Dublin, Lilliput Press, 1987

Ryan, W.P. *The Pope's Green Island*. London, James Nisbet, 1912

Sandulescu, C. George (ed) *Irishness in a Changing Society*. London, Colin Smythe, 1933

Sanger, Margaret *My Fight for Birth Control*. London, Faber and Faber, 1912

Sawyer, Roger *We Are But Women: Women in Ireland's History*. London, Routledge, 1993

Scheper-Hughes, Nancy *Saints, Scholars and Schizophrenics: Mental Illness in Rural Ireland*. Berkeley, University of California Press, 1979

Seymour, John *Blessed Isle: One Man's Ireland*. London, Collins and Brown, 1992

Shannon, William *The American Irish*. Macmillan, 1963

Sharkey, Olive *Old Days, Old Ways*. Dublin, O'Brien Press, 1987

Shaw, Francis *The Canon of Irish History* (essay). Studies, Dublin, summer 1972

Shaw, George Bernard *John Bull's Other Island*. Harmondsworth, Penguin edition, 1984

– – – *The Matter with Ireland* (edited and introduced by David H. Green and Dan H. Lawrence). London, Rupert Hart-Davies, 1962

Shearman, Hugh *Anglo-Irish Relations*. London, Faber & Faber,1948

– – – *Not an Inch*. London, Faber and Faber, 1942

Sheehan, Canon *My New Curate*. Cork, Mercier Press edition, 1989

Sheehy, Michael *Is Ireland Dying?* London, Hollis and Carter, 1968

– – – *Divided We Stand*. London, Faber and Faber, 1965

Sheridan, John D. *The Rest is Silence*. London, J.M. Dent, 1957

Smithson, Annie M.P. *Her Irish Heritage*. Cork, Mercier Press edition, 1988

Smithson, Annie M.P. *Myself and Others: An Autobiography*. Dublin, Talbot Press, 1944

– – – *The Walk of a Queen*. Cork, Mercier Press edition, 1988

Smyth, Ailbhe *The Abortion Papers, Ireland* Dublin, Attic Press, 1992

Smyth, Ailbhe (ed) *Irish Women's Studies Reader*. Dublin, Attic Press, 1993

Speakman, Harold *Here's Ireland*. London, Arrowsmith, 1926

Spenser, Edmund *A View of the Present State of Ireland*. Oxford University Press edition, 1970

Stone, Lawrence *The Family, Sex and Marriage in England 1500-1800*. Penguin Books, London, 1980

Stone, Norman *Europe Transformed: 1879-1919*. London, Fontana, 1983

Sutherland, Dr Halliday *Irish Journey*. London, Geoffrey Bles, 1956

Sweeney, Paul *The Celtic Tiger: Ireland's Economic Miracle Explained*. Dublin, Oak Tree Press, 1998

Sweetman, Rosita *On Our Knees: Ireland 1972*. London, Pandora Books, 1973

Taillon, Ruth *The Women of 1916*. Beyond the Pale Publications, Belfast, 1996

Taylor, A.J.P. *The First World War*. Harmondsworth, Penguin, 1966

Taylor, Alice *Quench the Lamp*. Dingle, Brandon, 1990

– – – *To School Through the Fields*. Dingle, Brandon, 1992

Taylor, Lawrence J. *Occasions of Faith: An Anthropology of Irish Catholicism*. Dublin, Lilliput Press, 1995

Terraine, John *The First World War*. London, Macmillan, 1965

Thackeray, William Makepeace *The Irish Sketch Book 1842*. Belfast, Blackstaff Press edition, 1825

Thomas Ellis, Alice *Serpent on the Rock: A Personal View of Christianity*. London, Sceptre, 1994

Thompson, William Irwin *The Imagination of an Insurrection: Dublin Easter 1916*. Oxford University Press, 1967

Tierney, Mark OSB *Modern Ireland 1850-1950*. Dublin, Gill and Macmillan, 1972

Tóibín, Colm (ed) *Seeing is Believing: Moving Statues in Ireland*. Mountrath, Ireland Pilgrim, 1985

Tobin, Fergal *The Best of Decades: Ireland in the 1960s*. Dublin, Gill and Macmillan, 1984

Tomelty, Joseph *Is the Priest at Home?* Dublin, Duffy, 1954

Tone, Wolfe *The Autobiography: 1763-1798*. Dublin, Maunsell edition, 1910

Toner, Jerome *Rural Ireland*. Dublin, Clonmore and Reynolds, 1955

Toucher, Patrick *Fear of the Collar: My Extraordinary Childhood*. Dublin, O'Brien Press, 1991

Townshend, Charles *The British Campaign in Ireland 1919-1921*. Oxford University Press, 1975

Tracy, Honor *Mind You, I've Said Nothing*. London, Metheun, 1953

Tuchman, Barbara *The Proud Tower: A Portrait of the World before the War 1890-1914*. London, Macmillan, 1966

Tynan, Katharine *The Wandering Years*. London, Constable, 1922

Ussher, Arland *Postscript on Existentialism and Other Essays*. Dublin, Sandymount Press, 1946

− − − *The Twilight of the Ideas and Other Essays*. Dublin, Sandymount Press, 1948.

− − − *The Face and Mind of Ireland*. London, Victor Gollancz, 1949

Walsh, John *Growing Up Catholic*. London, Papermac, 1989

Ward, Margaret *Maud Gonne: A Life*. London, Pandora, 1990

− − − *Unmanageable Revolutionaries: Women and Irish Nationalism*. London, Pluto Press, 1983

Waters, John *Jiving at the Crossroads*. Belfast, Blackstaff Press, 1991

Weber, Max *The Protestant Ethic and the Spirit of Capitalism*. London, Routledge edition, 1991

Whyte, J.H. *Church and State in Modern Ireland 1923-1979*. Dublin, Gill and Macmillan, 1980

Williams, Desmond (ed) *The Irish Struggle: 1916-1926*. London, RKP, 1966

Wilson, Tom *Ulster: Conflict and Consent*. Belfast, Blackstaff Press, 1989

Wohl, Robert *The Generation of 1914*. London, Weidenfeld and Nicolson, 1980

Yeats, W.B. *Autobiographies.* London, Macmillan, 1956

Young, Filson *Ireland at the Cross Roads.* London, E. Grant Richards, 1907

Zuckmeyer, Carl *A Portrait of Myself.* London, Secker & Warburg, 1970

Zweig, Stefan *The World of Yesterday: An Autobiography.* London, Cassell 1943